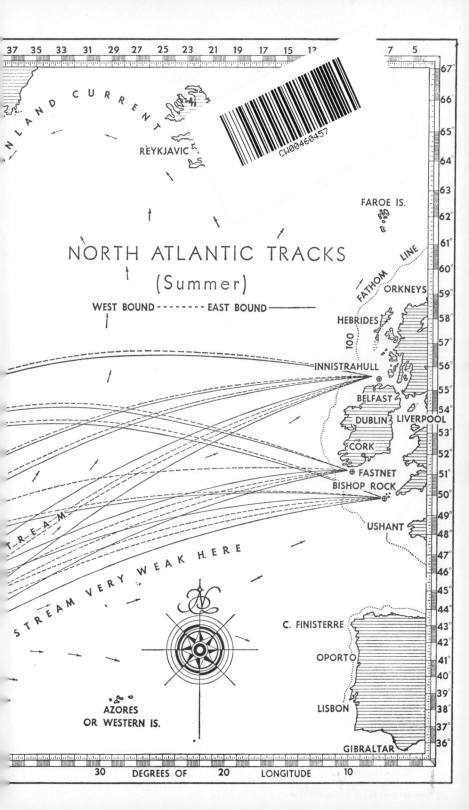

PSL LIBRARY OF OCEAN TRAVEL

TRAMPS AND LADIES

MY EARLY YEARS WITH STEAMERS

by

SIR JAMES BISSET

WITH A NEW FOREWORD BY

WALTER LORD

PATRICK STEPHENS

TRAMPS AND LADIES

THIS book continues the memoirs of Sir James Bisset, which began in *Sail Ho!* Here he tells of his seafaring life in the early days of steamships: on dirty little tramps carrying unromantic Swansea coal, or frozen Canadian lumber; on cargo-vessels loaded with farm animals for the Argentine, or potent Jamaica rum; on migrant ships taking Greeks, Hungarians, and Italians from Europe to the United States; and, finally, on the Ocean Greyhounds of the Cunard Line, competing with Norddeutscher Lloyd, White Star, Hamburg-Amerika, and other famous shipping companies, for the coveted Atlantic Blue Riband. A powerful climax of the book is the author's personal recounting of the tragic circumstances surrounding the sinking of the *Titanic* in mid-Atlantic in 1912 after she had struck an iceberg. James Bisset, then an officer in S.S. *Carpathia*, first vessel to arrive on the scene, brings to vivid life his recollections of the rescue of the survivors from the icy waters, and of the amazing events that followed.

The Champion Cunard Liner, S.S. *Mauretania*, (built 1906), passing a tramp steamer in mid-Atlantic

*(From the oil painting by
John Allcott
in the possession of
P. R. Stephensen)*

Tramps and Ladies

My Early Years in Steamers

by

SIR JAMES BISSET

K.B., C.B.E., R.D., R.N.R., LL.D. (Cantab.)

Commander of the Legion of Merit (U.S.A.)
Commodore (retd) of the Cunard White Star Line
Wartime Captain of *Queen Mary* and *Queen Elizabeth*

[*Written in collaboration with P. R. Stephensen*]

PATRICK STEPHENS

First published in the United Kingdom by
Angus & Robertson (UK) Ltd, 1959

British Library Cataloguing in Publication Data

Bisset, James, *1883-1967*
Tramps and ladies: my early years in
steamers.
1. Shipping
I. Title
387'.0092'4

ISBN 1-85260-140-X

*Patrick Stephens Limited is part of the Thorsons Publishing Group,
Wellingborough, Northamptonshire, NN8 2RQ England*

Printed in Great Britain by The Bath Press, Bath, Avon

1 3 5 7 9 10 8 6 4 2

Here's to the luck of the Second Mate,
　　Bright as a morning breeze
On the Ocean Blue, with his yarns (all true)
　　Of sailing the Seven Seas;
And here's to his dream of his "little lass",
　　And the gift of that golden day
When, waiting past, he shall stand at last
　　At home with his English May.

Lines written by an American lady passenger
in R.M.S. *Carpathia*, at sea, July, 1912.

PSL LIBRARY OF OCEAN TRAVEL

Also available

Mauretania
by Humfrey Jordan

Other titles in preparation

Romance of a Modern Liner
by Capt E. G. Diggle

A Million Ocean Miles
by Sir Edgar T. Britten

The Ocean Tramp
by Frank C. Hendry

Atlantic Ferry
by Arthur J. Maginnis

PUBLISHER'S PREFACE

The *PSL Library of Ocean Travel* is a collection of significant books on ships and the sea, long out-of-print but now re-issued in facsimile editions.

All the books to be included in the Library — each of which has been selected by members of a 'panel' of distinguished maritime authors and collectors — have been chosen for the rarity of their original editions, for the authoritativeness of the writer, and above all, for their readability. Autobiographies, biographies, histories of famous ships of the past and the reminiscences of eminent mariners and sea travellers are all included, and will have a wide appeal to the thousands of present-day ship enthusiasts who have a deep interest in the maritime history of the past hundred years. For the majority of such readers, these books may be unknown and would otherwise be entirely unobtainable.

Many of the original volumes used in the production of these new editions have been supplied by Mainmast Books, of Saxmundham, Suffolk, IP17 1HZ, England, from whom all volumes in the *PSL Library of Ocean Travel* may be obtained.

Tramps and Ladies by Sir James Bisset, originally published in 1960 by Angus & Robertson, is the second volume in the *PSL Library of Ocean Travel*, and the publishers would like to thank Walter Lord for providing a foreword for this facsimile edition.

FOREWORD
to this new edition
by Walter Lord

They all had a book in them. The old Atlantic liner captains were such enthusiastic writers, it often seems that when not on the bridge, they must have been in their cabins organizing their memoirs. These reminiscences have much in common: great emphasis on the quirky millionaires who graced First Class, and mighty little on anything unpleasant. One White Star commodore, captain of the *Adriatic* in 1912, managed to leave out the *Titanic* completely. It's as though the disaster had never occurred.

A happy exception to this reticence is Sir James Bisset, Commodore of the Cunard Line and captain of the *Queen Elizabeth* when he retired in 1947. At the time of the *Titanic*, Bisset was Second Officer of the *Carpathia*, the gallant little Cunarder that picked up the lost liner's survivors. His account of the rescue is one of the best, and he adds some very knowledgeable observations. To Sir James, the *Titanic* and her sister ship *Olympic* were both clumsy vessels, and hard to handle.

Bisset's memoirs are studded with this sort of candour. Nothing is sacred. One of the most memorable vignettes is the picture of himself as a young officer on a tramp steamer, serving under a skipper who was usually drunk, or sleeping in his bunk, or both.

Sir James boasts another virtue not often found among these old sea captains who have put it all down on paper: he writes with commendable clarity. He realizes that most readers are unfamiliar with the intricacies of running an ocean liner, and he goes to great lengths to explain the various duties of the crew, the system of watches, and the whole mass of practices, customs and usages that evolved over the years. With the ocean liner rapidly becoming extinct, this information is becoming ever more difficult to find.

And what changes have occurred! Today, when Atlantic travellers are shot across the sky sealed in a metal tube, it is hard to realize that only 80 years ago, when young Bisset was just breaking in with Cunard, it took 324 men shovelling 1,000 tons of coal a day to power the *Mauretania* across the ocean in less than a week.

Sir James Bisset describes this vanished era with candour, clarity and, it might be added, with warm affection. His memoirs take up three volumes, but each stands on its own, and this volume, recounting his climb from second mate on a winderjammer to the command of a Cunarder, seems the perfect way to help launch this exciting new series of facsimile reprints, the *PSL Library of Ocean Travel*.

WALTER LORD
New York, USA

PREFACE

The liner, she's a lady.

—Kipling

THIS is the second of an intended set of three volumes, describing nautical life as I enjoyed it in fifty years of seagoing service, from 1898 to 1947. The story tells of the development of seamanship as I observed it during that period. The first half of the twentieth century was, in technical progress, at sea, as on land and in the air, the most dazzling in the history of mankind. Seamen of my generation have witnessed the extinction of sailing vessels on the regular transocean routes, and a tremendous improvement of mechanical propulsion, using at first coal and then oil fuel, until mammoth vessels of 80,000 tons were attained, which, in wartime emergency, could and did carry as many as 15,000 souls within one hull.

My recollections, though restricted in their scope to personal experiences, include documentary descriptions of that transition from sail to steam, and onwards to the competitive development of the gigantic transatlantic liners. My gradual promotion from the half-deck of a Cape Horn barque to the bridge of a cargo-steamer, and then to bigger steamers, was, especially in its earlier stages, similar to the experience of thousands of other officers in sail and steam, in the mercantile marine. The lore of steamers, as of sail, would require many books, by many writers; but only a few men with that knowledge to impart have been able to have it preserved in print. My memoirs may supplement those of others, as a contribution to the records of the basic changes in seafaring technics from wind-driven to mechanically propelled navigation.

Books on steam navigation may occupy a special shelf in libraries, alongside the shelf of sailing-ship books. The *mystique* of sail presents a romantic rather than realistic view of life in windjammers; but the thousands of men who have served, and are still serving, in steamers, are aware that the routines and exceptional incidents of life at sea in screw-driven vessels are worthy also of a definition in literature, which has not yet been finally achieved.

A time may come when there will be a *mystique* of the coal-burning steamers, which in their heyday had a lore of their own that is now becoming almost as obsolete as the lore of sail. The old four-funnelled *Mauretania*, for example, burnt 1,000 tons of coal a day. To tend the 192 furnaces that heated her twenty-five boilers, she had a "Black Squad" of 324 firemen and trimmers. That hard labour down below was dispensed with when she was converted to an oil-burner in 1921. The *Titanic* carried 250 firemen and trimmers, most of whom went down with her. That era has gone. It had its zenith in the period preceding the 1914-18 war.

Having kept diaries and other records throughout my seagoing career, I am now enabled, with the encouragement and assistance of my friend P. R. Stephensen, to tell my story systematically, in chronological sequence. This includes descriptions of the day-by-day routines in coal-burning steamers, and the ordinary happenings of a young officer's life, which are so much more typical of seafaring than the occasional moments of excitement or tension that constitute dramatic action. The normal and the exceptional together make the full picture of any man's experiences, at sea as elsewhere.

It is not easy to describe the technics of a profession in non-technical language, but, after having been "quizzed" for many years on nautical details, by passengers in liners and troop transports, I have had some practice at these elucidations. I have therefore attempted here to explain nautical procedures in terms which may help to make them clear to land folk who only occasionally, or never, go to sea, or to young people who read a book to learn something from it.

The first volume in this series, *Sail Ho! My Early Years at Sea,* described my adventures as an apprentice and Second Mate in Cape Horn sailing vessels from 1898 to 1904.

The present volume, dealing with my service in steamers from 1905 to 1913, includes my recollections of knocking around in tramps for two years before I joined the Cunard Line in 1907, and then proceeds to the "ladies" (as Kipling termed the Ocean Greyhounds of that period).

While I have certainly no desire to emphasize the "sensational" or exceptional aspects of seafaring, it is necessary, for the completeness of this record, that I should include in this volume my observations on the disaster of the *Titanic* in 1912. My notes, made on and near the scene of the tragedy, have not hitherto been published. The lessons derived from that terrible mishap were immediately applied in safety precautions, which have made voyaging in passenger-liners, in peace-time, the safest of all methods of travel. In this sense those who perished in the wreck of the *Titanic* bequeathed a benefit to posterity. My analysis of that disaster is made from a seaman's point of view.

In the third volume of these memoirs, now in preparation, covering the period from 1913 to 1947, I hope to be able to put on record some naval incidents of the 1914-18 war, and my service in bigger liners, such as the *Mauretania* and the *Berengaria;* to tell of the *Usworth* rescue in 1934; and then of my voyages in command of the *Franconia,* the *Queen Mary,* and the *Queen Elizabeth* as troop transports during the 1939-45 war and its immediate aftermaths. This concluding part of my story, with its unusual responsibilities and hazards, came as a sequel to the long years of sea-experience and disciplines of which the foundations were laid in my early years in sail and steam. I was appointed Captain in the Cunard service in 1931, when I was forty-eight years of age, after having been at sea for thirty-three years. I was given command of the *Queen Mary* in 1942, when I was nearly fifty-nine years of age, after having been at sea for forty-four years. The third volume of these memoirs will be entitled *Commodore's Farewell.*

I acknowledge with gratitude the kind co-operation of Mr Felix Riesenberg, Jnr, of New York, and Mr Harold Woodward of Sydney, for suggestions made by them on their reading of the typescript; of Mr John Allcot, of Sydney, for his cover designs; of Mr Ron Parsons, of Sydney, and Mr Alfred Hine, of Ditton Park, Buckinghamshire, England, for assistance in checking details of nautical history; of the Directors of the Cunard White Star Line, the Curator of the Imperial War Museum, London, Miss Millicent Vincent, and the Nautical Photo Agency, Beccles, Suffolk, for supplying photographs used as illustrations; of Mrs J. W. Lockyer for typing, and of my publishers in Sydney, London, and New York, for their care in the details of book-launching.

JAMES BISSET

Manly, Sydney
Australia

CONTENTS

ILLUSTRATIONS

CHAPTER ONE

*From Sail to Steam—Farewell to the "Wind-
bags"—The Ambitions of a Young Salt—Out
of Work and Looking for a Job—Trudging
the Liverpool Docks—The Ocean Greyhounds—Some Famous Cunarders of My
Youthful Days—The Golden Lion Too Grand
for Me—Many Rebuffs—The Early Bird Gets
the Worm—I Make a "Faux Pas" and Recover
—The S.S. "Rembrandt"—My First Impressions of Her—My Uniform Suit—A Third
Mate's Hopes.*

IN February, 1905, at the age of twenty-one years and seven
months, I passed the Board of Trade examination for First Mate
at Liverpool, England, and decided to look for a job in a
steamer. As old shellbacks used to put it, I had made up my mind
to "knock off going to sea and go into steamboats".

I had served my time as an apprentice and Second Mate in sail,
on four voyages around the world, via Cape Horn, in the preceding six years, and had thereby gained a knowledge of handling
sail, which would obviously be of no use to me in a steamer. Yet
I believed, like all other men trained in sail, that the practical
knowledge of seamanship, laboriously acquired under canvas,
would have at least some application in the working of a steam-
driven vessel.

This was a belief to buoy my confidence, which needed some

1

support, as the truth of the matter was that I had never been on the bridge of a steamer, and had no practical knowledge of the work and routine that would be required of me. Though I held a First Mate's Certificate, I had no chance of obtaining a position as First Mate in a steamer until I had gained practical experience as a junior officer on some steamship voyages, without too much responsibility while I was "learning the ropes"—not that there were many ropes in a steamer!

It was my intention and ambition to study for the examination for Master Mariner, which would enable me, if I were lucky enough, eventually to attain command of a vessel; but that summit of ambition could be hoped for only after many years of service as an officer in subordinate capacities. In the meantime, it was required that I should serve not less than eighteen months as First Mate or Second Mate in seagoing vessels, after passing my First Mate's examination, before I would be allowed to sit for the examination for a Master's Certificate. My immediate aim, then, was to "get my time in", if possible, by signing on as a Second Mate.

My youthfulness and inexperience in steam were a handicap; but it happened also that, at that time, the supply of ship's officers looking for work in steamers at Liverpool exceeded the demand for their services. Day after day I tramped the dockside district, from end to end, seeking a job, without success. Liverpool was my home town, and the place of my birth. I was living at home with my parents, after being paid off from the sailing ship *County of Cardigan* three months previously, and my savings were nearly exhausted. My funds were so low, and my prospects of getting a job in steam seemingly so remote, that I walked miles rather than incur the expense of a few coppers to travel on the Overhead Railway.

I was tempted to apply for jobs that were offering in sailing vessels, but I resisted the impulse. It was a wrench to leave sail and go into steam. Life in sailing vessels was hard, as I knew only too well, but it held many joys to appeal to the temperament of the ocean roamer—"wild, wide and free". My common sense told me that windjammers were doomed to extinction by the competition of steam; yet, in 1905, there were still many hundreds of sailing vessels under the British flag, and hundreds more under the American, French, German, Scandinavian and other national flags. They were owned and manned by diehards, of an ageing generation, and were kept going, with increasing financial difficulties, by the force of habit inherited from centuries of tradition.

Ambitious young officers of my generation, looking to their own future, could see clearly enough that steamers offered better wages and conditions, shorter voyages, and—above all—better chances of eventual promotion than the poor old, beloved and beautiful, but impoverished "windbags" could ever offer. Having for this practical reason made up my mind to go into steam, I persisted in that intention despite the setbacks I received.

As I trudged the dockside, I looked wistfully at the Atlantic Mail steamers berthed there. Then, and in the three months that I had been ashore, while studying for my First Mate's Certificate, I had viewed them with envy as something far beyond my modest ambitions at that time. I was only a Cape Horn sailor, trained in a little barque of 1,098 tons and a little full-rigged ship of 1,323 tons that carried dirty or smelly cargoes, such as coal and guano, safely through the world's fiercest storms and wildest waters. We shellbacks had a pride of our own, but we knew that we were ignorant of the methods of working these leviathan liners owned by the Cunard, White Star, Inman and other Western Ocean steamship companies.

In their stylishness, size, speed, power and glory, the Western Ocean liners were in a class far superior to the modest scope of my immediate ambition. Some of them were twenty times bigger in tonnage than the handy little vessels in which I had learnt to be a seaman. I did not have the nerve to apply for a job in such grand and regal looking vessels. I knew my limitations. I would have to learn how to handle steamers, as I had learnt seamanship in sail, the hard way, from the bottom rung of the ladder; but, at twenty-one years of age, with a First Mate's Certificate to show, I would be off to a flying start—if I could get a start!—and time was on my side.

Among the Cunard liners voyaging to and from Liverpool in those days were the old *Umbria* (8,128 tons) and *Etruria* (8,120 tons). They were sister ships, launched at Glasgow in 1884 and 1885, and had been on the transatlantic run for twenty years. They were the last Cunarders with auxiliary sails. In forty-four years after Samuel Cunard, with Robert Napier, George Burns and David McIver, had founded the Cunard Line in 1840, until the launching of the *Umbria* and *Etruria*, there had been a total of eighty vessels in the Cunard service, all of them steamers with auxiliary sails. Of these, fifteen were wooden-built paddle

3

steamers, two were iron-hulled paddle steamers, fifty-nine were iron-hulled screw steamers, and four (including *Umbria* and *Etruria*) were steel-hulled screw steamers; but every vessel had masts and yards with sails, for extra propulsion, and as a precaution in case of engine breakdown.

Liverpool was the terminal port in Britain for the Cunard services to Halifax, New York and Boston. We Merseysiders were reared with a special pride in the Cunarders. I was only a babe in arms when the *Umbria* and the *Etruria* were launched, but many a time in my boyhood I had wistfully peered through the barriers at the busy scene when they sailed from Liverpool landing stage on Saturday afternoons with the mails and passengers, bound across the Western Ocean for that Land of Opportunity, Enchantment and Adventure—the Land of Buffalo Bill and Pawnee Joe—the New World—America!

The Blue Peter whipping at the masthead, and the Cunard house-flag—a golden lion rampant on a red ground, with a golden ball (the terrestrial globe) in his forepaws—fluttering in the breeze at the maintruck, high above the scene of bustle and excitement on board the ship and on the quay, as the time of departure neared, were the pennons of romance and grand adventure, which, to my schoolboy imagination, had seemed entirely beyond my reach. Now, as a weatherbeaten and unemployed young salt, I thought, one day, as I moodily watched the *Umbria* cast off her moorings and move into the stream, that that Golden Lion was still far too grand for me. Then I continued trudging the docks, in quest of a job that would be more in my style.

The *Umbria* and the *Etruria,* and their two immediate predecessors, the *Servia* (7,392 tons, launched 1881) and the *Aurania* (7,269 tons, launched 1883), were the forerunners of the "Ocean Greyhound" design of transatlantic liners—long and sleek, or "streamlined". Their proportions of length to beam were approximately nine to one. They were the first steel-built screw steamers of the Cunard Line.

The *Umbria* and the *Etruria* each had a length overall of 519 feet and a beam of 57 feet. Their length "between the perpendiculars" (excluding the fore rake and the stern overhang) was 501 feet. They had two stumpy funnels (or smokestacks) amidships, and three masts, which originally carried square sails, but were later schooner-rigged. In their earlier years of service they were, with the exception of the freak *Great Eastern* (12,000

4

tons, length 695 feet overall, beam 83 feet, launched 1858) the biggest merchant ships in the world. They were also the fastest, with a speed on their trials of 19½ knots.

In the year she was launched, 1885, the *Etruria* took the Blue Riband of the Atlantic—for the highest average speed of the year on a measured crossing—with a passage of 6 days 5 hours 31 minutes, from Queenstown to Sandy Hook, at an average speed of 18.93 knots. In 1887 she made the eastbound passage at 19.90 knots. The two sisters held the Blue Riband for five years, the *Umbria's* best passage being on a westbound crossing at 18.89 knots.

These two remained for many years the biggest single-screw steamers in the world; but mechanical confidence went too far when, after several years of service, the auxiliary sails were discarded. Soon after this decision was put into effect, the *Etruria* lost her propeller in mid-Atlantic. Having no wireless, she drifted helplessly. Intense anxiety prevailed among the relatives and friends of the passengers and crew, and among shipping people generally, on both sides of the Atlantic, when the world's most famous passenger-liner was posted overdue and missing. But, after ten or twelve days, she was sighted and joyfully towed for a thousand miles to Liverpool by a small steamer, the S.S. *William Cliff*.

Bigger and faster steel vessels, with twin screws and no auxiliary sails, had been built for the Cunard Line in the 1890s. The sister ships *Campania* and *Lucania* (12,950 tons, length overall 622 feet, beam 65 feet), launched in 1893, each held the Blue Riband, with speeds of 21.33 and 22 knots respectively. They were the first twin-screw Cunarders.

Other "big" Cunarders, which were in service in 1905, regularly putting in to Liverpool, were the *Ultonia* (10,402 tons, launched 1898); the sister ships *Ivernia* (14,057 tons) and *Saxonia* (14,280 tons), both launched in 1900; the *Carpathia* (13,603 tons), launched in 1903; and the sister ships *Caronia* (19,593 tons) and *Carmania* (19,524 tons), both launched in 1904, the latter being the first and only triple-screw Cunarder. Her wing screws were driven by reciprocating engines and the centre screw by turbines —ahead only.

The size, speed and luxurious appointments of these Western Ocean Greyhounds made them appear as visions of overwhelming magnificence and splendour to the mind of a very young sailing-ship officer trudging the docks out of work. I wondered

5

how long it would take me to gain enough experience in steamers to be able to apply with some confidence to the Cunard Marine Superintendent for a job in one of those floating palaces. That prospect receded as I began each day with hope and ended it in despair—cold, weary and "broke"—after walking miles and meeting with nothing but rebuffs in that wet February of 1905, dismally aware now that hundreds of other officers, older and more experienced than I, had a similar idea to mine; namely, to "get into steam", by hook or by crook.

Then I got a lucky break, or a reward for sheer desperate persistence. On 1st March, 1905, I tumbled out of bed as usual at 5 a.m., in the cold and dark, and, after a hurried breakfast, walked three miles from our home to the docks, in the belief— which I was beginning to doubt—that the early bird gets the worm.

I went first to the Shipping Federation office (an employment agency), and walked in as its doors were being opened. A clerk, who was probably sick of the sight of me, sang out from the back of the office as I stood at the inquiry counter, "Lamport & Holt want a Third Mate for the S.S. *Rembrandt*. Get down to the Huskisson Dock as quickly as you can, before someone else grabs it!"

As he pronounced the name *Rembrandt* with a stress on the first syllable, I did not quite catch the name, and was a little puzzled by what I fancied I heard. But I wasted no time, and, hastening to the nearest station of the Overhead Railway, I spent a precious twopence for a ride to the Huskisson Dock.

I found the Marine Superintendent in his office at the end of the dock. He was a big, bluff, bearded man. As soon as he saw me, he knew what I was after. "Looking for a job?" he growled.

"Yes," I replied. "I hear you want a Third Mate for the S.S. *Remnant!*"

"*Remnant!*" he roared. "*REMNANT?* What the hell do you think Lamport & Holt own—a fleet of ragbags? Her name is *Rembrandt*, the name of a famous artist, and don't forget it! She's a twin-screw steamer, on the run from Buenos Aires with cargo and passengers. A very fine vessel, too, one of the best in the Western Ocean. *Remnant* indeed! Ho! Ho! So you want to be Third Mate in a *Remnant*, do ye? Ever been in steam before?"

I admitted my inexperience, and said I was sorry I had not

6

caught the ship's name properly. Luckily for me, the M.S. had a sense of humour. "You'll learn," he said. "What are your qualifications?"

He wrote down particulars of my name, age and sea experience, and looked at my certificates and testimonials. "All right, Mister," he said. "You can have the job. Six pounds a month and provide your own uniform. See my clerk about that, and report on board tomorrow morning at seven o'clock for duty. The *Rembrandt*—now, don't forget, *REMBRANDT!*— will be sailing for the Plate in six days. Best o' luck, m'lad!"

The clerk was a weedy, middle-aged, miserable-looking man, with a drooping moustache and a frugal outlook on life. "Good gracious!" he grumbled. " 'Aven't you got a uniform suit? 'Ow can you go to sea without a uniform suit?"

"I've been in sail all my time," I told him. "Came home round the Horn with a cargo of guano, and we didn't need a uniform suit for that kind of work."

"Good 'eavens, I s'pose you didn't! Well, this is what I advise you to do. Go to Lewis's, and get a blue serge double-breasted suit for thirty bob. Tell them you want a set of brass buttons and clips, and also a set of black buttons and clips. The buttons make all the difference to a uniform suit, see? You wear the brass buttons when you're on board, and the black buttons when you go ashore, see? So you'll 'ave two suits for the price of one, see? And 'ave you a uniform cap?"

"Well, yes," I said. "A badge cap I wore when I was Second Mate in the ship *County of Cardigan*. It has the badge of William Thomas & Co. Ltd."

" 'Eavens above, that won't do! Better get a new uniform cap with Lamport & Holt's badge on it—L. & H.—see? Then you'll be all set!"

I thanked him for his good advice, then hurried outside, elated, and strode along the dock to the berth where the S.S. *Rembrandt* lay. She was partly obscured by the wharf sheds when I first sighted her, but I could plainly see her name and port of registry painted under her high stern with its white taffrail, and the mooring lines with their rat-shields in position.

For some minutes I stood in silent and deep contemplation, trying to take in her details, so unfamiliar to me. A wisp of smoke and a plume of steam rose from her funnel amidships, and there was a rattle of winches as slings of cargo were hoisted inboard, with the voices of the stevedores or one of the mates occasionally singing out an order.

Athwartships, forrard of the funnel, was the Bridge, a high island deckhouse, the holy of holies with its mysteries which were now so soon to be revealed to me. My spirits sank as I realized how differently everything was arranged in comparison with the layout of a sailing ship. She was a flush-deck steamer, with two steel masts, but no yards were crossed on them. They had stays, but very little rigging. The foremast had a crow's nest for the lookout men, and the masts carried flag halyards for signals, but were otherwise bare of all the intricate top hamper of sail.

The twelve cargo derricks, angled on the masts, spanned, when they were hoisted, four hatches opening down to capacious 'tween-decks and lower holds. The derricks, at my first glance, seemed out of place and unbalanced. An outstanding impression was of the height of her sides and bulwarks amidships, as compared with sailing vessels, in which the main deck was usually below the level of the wharf planking when they lay at a berth; but in this, as in other steamers, the bulwarks amidships stood eight or ten feet above the wharf level. It seemed to me that it would be almost impossible for her to ship water abeam, or to roll the lee rail under. No more flooded decks for me!

Not wishing to announce my presence prematurely, I surveyed my ship—yes, My Ship now!—from a cautious distance, with mingled feelings and a confusion of first impressions which on the whole were distinctly exhilarating. The S.S. *Rembrandt* was certainly no "remnant", but a well found vessel of her class. She was not a leviathan nor an ocean greyhound; nor was she a rusty old tramp. Her paintwork was smart enough to be a credit to the owners of a passenger-carrying cargo-vessel of moderate size on the South American run. I took in enough of her details at my first meditative, bemused survey of her, to turn away, after a little while, elated at the prospect of getting such a good start in my career in steam.

Then I hurried home, on the Overhead Railway, to get some money, and to tell my mother that I was a steamship officer—at last! She well knew what it meant to me to achieve such an ambition, after years of hard work and study, and weeks of disappointment which had seemed like years. This was the turning point in my nautical career, and mother knew it, as mothers always know.

"Your father will be proud of you," she smiled. "And so will your brothers and sisters—and so will I, when we see you in your uniform, brass buttons and all!"

Hastening to the outfitter's shop, I found myself, a few minutes after I had entered, standing in front of a long mirror, admiring myself in my first real uniform suit and my new cap. An officer in a Western Ocean passenger-steamer! It seemed too good to be true. No more for me the dungarees of an officer in sail, supervising the loading or discharge of coal or guano in torrid remote ports, or manning braces and tending halyards, up to the armpits in swirling water on decks flooded with icy seas, rounding the Horn—I hoped!

No more hounding men aloft, at risk of life and limb, to take in or make sail in a howling hurricane; no more tedious pully-hauly, sweltering in the doldrums; no more starvation on the bare whack of putrid pork and hard biscuits! But, on the other hand, it suddenly occurred to me, there would be no more of the peace and quiet of a sailing ship, snoring along in the trades with all sail set and everything drawing; no more of the exhilaration of running the easting down; no more thrills of gazing aloft at graceful curving sails and the intricate maze of the rigging outlined against a blue or starry sky. . . .

For the rest of my nautical life, maybe, I would be going to sea in oblong steel boxes with smoking funnels, thumping engines, vibrating propellers, rattling derricks and clattering winches; I would be dolled up like a gilded popinjay in my brassbound uniform, to impress the passengers; and perhaps there would be very little real sailorizing to be done. Ah, well, the decision was taken!

The smart young officer looking at me out of the long mirror appeared well satisfied with his uniform suit.

"Fits you perfectly, sir," remarked the salesman, reassuringly.

"I'll take it," I said.

"Will you be wearing it now, or will you take it wrapped?"

"I'll wear it now, and you can wrap my other suit," I told him.

"Will you wear it with the brass or the black buttons, sir?"

"The brass," I said.

Going home, resplendent, I fancied that the Liverpool lasses were eyeing me with more than the usual amount of appreciation conferred on eligible prey. My parents, brothers and sisters were outspoken in their admiration of my uniform; but my father, a dour Scot, said, "Dinna forget to polish the buttons, or they'll go green!"

That evening, with the efficient and fussy help of my dear mother and sisters, I packed my sea-chest and sea-bag for the new adventure. My sea-chest had a vivid picture of the barque *County of Pembroke* on the inside of the lid—painted by myself in my apprenticeship days, in lavish and garish colours. I arranged with a cabman who lived in our street to call for me at six o'clock in the morning, to drive me to the docks.

He was there on time, with his old horse-drawn four-wheeled growler. We rattled over the cobbles, and arrived at the Huskisson Dock at a quarter to seven.

My brass buttons shining and my badge cap smartly askew, I mounted the gangway of the S.S. *Rembrandt,* and, with my best imitation of a lordly air, handed threepence to a dockside down-and-out who carried my dunnage up the gangway and dumped it on the deck.

The Third Mate had arrived.

CHAPTER TWO

*Joining My First Steamer—Everything
Strange to Me—Contrasts in Luxury—Load-
ing Cargo—Noah's Ark in the Shelter Deck—
The Ship's Complement—The Excitement of
Sailing Day—Our Passengers—"Extra Cargo!"
—Clearing Out—"Lampy" and the Lights—
The Pilot Comes Aboard—Casting Off—My
First Watch on the Bridge—Pitfalls for the
Unwary—Experience Teaches.*

CAPTAIN JULIAN ROYCE of the S.S. *Rembrandt* was a fine
seaman of the old style, who had been trained in sail. He was
not wearing his uniform. It was his custom in this home port
to spend most of his time ashore, coming on board for a short
time each day to look around and attend to the ship's business.
He knew from the Marine Superintendent the details of my experience in sail. "You'll find things very different in steam,"
he warned me, "but, if you keep your wits, you'll soon learn your
way about."

He introduced me to the Mate, John Carey, and the Second
Mate, James Birse. They were both wearing their rather shabby
brassbound uniforms and badge caps, and I was glad that I had
mine on, to make a suitable show. They greeted me briefly but
cordially.

The Mate, a red-headed Irishman with a brogue, said brusque-
ly, "We're taking in cargo today. Get your things into your

cabin, and go down below in Number Two hold as quickly as you can, to keep an eye on the stevedores, and see they don't smoke, or pilfer cargo. Mr Birse will show you your cabin." He hurried away, like a man who has a thousand important matters to attend to. His burly figure was the personification of efficiency. He had served his time in sail, and ten years as an officer in steam. He held a Master's Certificate, and stood every chance of soon being given a command in Lamport & Holt's service.

The Second Mate had also served his time in sail. He was five years older than I, and had been three years in steam. He showed me my cabin, which was next to his, in the midship-house (under the bridge), with a door opening on to the deck. Each of the officers had a cabin to himself. Mine was small but clean and comfortable, with white painted iron bulkheads and deckhead, planked deck, a glassed port, a neat bunk—with mattress and bedding, including sheets, supplied. There were lockers, a washstand and shaving mirror, a water tap at the washbowl, and—marvellous!—electric light!

"Better than living under the poop in a windbag, eh?" grinned Birse. "Are you sorry you're going into steam?"

"Not yet," I said, and added, "This looks grand to me."

"You'll find your way around. You'd better hurry down below. They've started loading already in all the four holds. Number Two is forrard of the bridge. Anything you want to know?"

"Yes," I said. "Do I change into dungarees to go down below and work in the cargo?"

Birse laughed scornfully. "Dungarees? We don't wear dungarees in a passenger-steamer! You'll never need 'em again unless you go back into sail, or into a tramp steamer!"

"How many passengers do we carry?" I asked.

"Ten or a dozen. They're not aboard yet, but we have to wear our Number One brassbound suits to impress them when they do come on, and we wear uniforms also when loading, to let the stevedores know who's who. If you're ready, come with me now, and I'll show you what's what. I'm in charge on deck forrard, while loading is going on, and the Mate's supervising the after hatches."

As we stepped out on deck, I glanced around, and had a feeling of dismay. Everything was unfamiliar to me. Abaft the bridge was the engineroom, or stokehold, protected by its "fiddley" (iron grating), through which I could glimpse a sudden glow of flame, as a stoker shovelled coal into the donkey-boiler furnace, to keep a head of steam on for working the winches and to drive the dynamo for the electric light.

On the after-deck were two gaping holds, into which cargo was being slung, from derricks rigged on the mainmast, with a rattle and clatter of steam winches. We walked forrard, and a similar scene of mechanized pandemonium prevailed there. The deck on which we trod was of steel. I glanced aloft at the bare fore-mast, and my instincts were shocked by the lack of graceful rigging and yards. *So this is Steam*, I thought, dejectedly.

"That's Number Two hold," said Birse, pointing to it. "Keep an eye on the slings when you're going down."

He hurried away, to grapple with his other duties. As action is the best cure for melancholy, and youth doesn't spend much time on regrets, as a rule, I quickly lost my feeling of depression, and, waiting until the next sling of cargo was clear, I went down the vertical iron ladder into the hold, and stood to one side, watching the four gangs of stevedores—one in each corner of the hold—stowing the bales, boxes, crates and packages of a cargo of general merchandise.

In the half darkness, it was difficult to watch one gang—let alone four. These were not sailors, and I had no right to interfere with the way in which they were doing their work, unless they made some gross mistake which might waste space, or cause the cargo to shift, and endanger the stability of the ship at sea. Each gang had its own foreman, and they had much more experience in stowing cargo than I had. My brass buttons may have had some moral effect on them, and would probably deter them from broaching cargo, and certainly would prevent them from smoking, if their foreman could not control them; but I immediately realized, after sauntering around among the packages, and peering here and there, that, if I said nothing, I would not reveal my ignorance. If I kept my eyes peeled, I would pick up some hints on stowing cargo which might be useful to me on future occasions.

After awhile, it was borne in on me, that, as no officer was down below in the other three holds, mine was only a put up job to keep the Third Mate occupied and out of the way on deck for the time being; so I didn't worry much more about it, and spent the rest of the forenoon in the enjoyment of being a Steam-boat Officer—at last!—with nothing to do except stand around observantly, with a knowing look.

13

Work knocked off at noon for lunch. I went up on deck, and the Second Mate said, "Have you brought sandwiches with you? There's no food supplied while the ship is in port, but we can make tea for ourselves in the 'steam vase' in the pantry."

As I had not brought lunch with me, Birse shared his with me that day, and the problem was solved. The "steam vase" was a step up in the world from the conditions I had known in sailing ships, which had no facilities for making tea on board while we were loading in home ports, so that we had to go ashore for our lunch in the dockside eating-houses or cocoa-rooms which were known as "British Workmen's Public Houses".

The Mate showed me the passenger-accommodation, and introduced me to the Engineer Officers—Chief, Second, Third and Fourth—all Scots and dour men. The dining-saloon had two long tables, each with twelve chairs, which were screwed to the carpeted deck. The officers and passengers dined together at sea. There was a "smoking-room", fitted with lounge chairs and a writing table; and a "sitting-room", with settees, easy chairs and a piano! All these rooms were carpeted and panelled. What luxury!

The S.S. *Rembrandt*, a single-screw steamer, 4,279 tons gross with steel hull and steel decks, had been built at Glasgow by D. & W. Henderson Ltd, and launched in 1899. She was 380 feet long, 45 feet beam, and had an average speed of twelve knots. She could carry 4,000 tons of cargo and twelve passengers. She was on the regular run from Liverpool to ports in Argentina, Uruguay, Brazil and the Canary Islands, making on an average four voyages a year.

Home every three months! It seemed astonishing to me, after my service in sailing vessels, when I had made four voyages around the world in *six years*. All my thinking had to be recast.

The *Rembrandt* carried a crew of eight seamen, plus a boatswain, lamp trimmer and storekeeper, six firemen and six coal trimmers, who were quartered under the foc's'le head. There was a cook, and a galley boy to help him; a chief steward, second steward and a stewardess. They and the carpenter—there was no sailmaker!—were quartered under the poop, where there was also some steerage passenger-accommodation, used by stockmen when she carried cattle.

The navigating officers therefore had at their disposal only eight seamen—four in each watch, working four hours on and four off. Of these, when the ship was at sea, one seaman was at the wheel on the bridge, and another on lookout in the crow's nest. The other two were handy on deck, relieving the wheel and lookout after two hours in each watch. In port, all eight seamen were available for cleaning and painting ship and overhauling gear. Any splicing of mooring ropes or wires was done by two of the seamen who had the positions of boatswain and lamp trimmer; but the mechanical gear and all machinery were the concern of the engineers, not of the seamen. The loading and unloading of cargo was done by stevedores from on shore, though under control of the Mates.

It therefore appeared to me, as I took all this in, that seaman-ship, as I had learnt it under sail, was practically non-existent in a steamer. With no sail to handle, and scarcely any rigging to keep in repair, there appeared to be little work for seamen in a steamer, except cleaning and painting ship, steering and keeping lookout, mooring and unmooring. There were no planked decks to holystone except round about the bridge; no teak rails, and very few brass fittings to polish. The only men who had hard work were the stokers and trimmers, and I had nothing to do with them.

It seemed to me that the life of a steamship officer was going to be dead easy, compared with that of an officer in sail. As I pondered the possibilities, I came to the conclusion that my new job required more brains than brawn; whereas, in sail, both were needed in equal measure.

After further consideration, and the experience of years, I became aware that seamanship in a steamer requires close at-tention to routine detail, and constant alertness for unpredic-table emergencies, in which instinct based on experience and special knowledge controls reactions which mean the difference between safety and disaster for the ship, and perhaps for the lives of all in her; but on this, my first acquaintance with life and work in a steamer, some time was required before I could over-come what I thought was a real sailorman's dislike of going to sea in an oblong iron box with a smoky stack and thudding engines, and no true sailorizing to be done. . . .

The Mate kept me at my duty of nominally supervising the stowing of the cargo in Number Two hold, until, after three days, the hold was full and the hatch covers put on. He then sent me down below in Number Four hold aft, which was the last to finish loading. In the meantime, great activity was occurring on the shelter deck, where a gang of carpenters and shipwrights were building wooden stalls and pens for some pedigreed livestock we were to take to Buenos Aires. I now learnt that one of our passengers would be an Argentinian millionaire, the owner of a ranch (*estancia*) up the country from Buenos Aires. He had been on a visit to England, Scotland and Ireland, buying prize-winning stallions, mares, bulls, cows, pigs, poultry and dogs to take back home with him.

"We'll be a Noah's Ark," said the Mate, irritably. The millionaire, a powerfully built man, with a broad-brim hat, curled moustaches, and smoking a large cigar, came on board with his head stockman and groom, to inspect the shelter deck and stalls, and appeared to be satisfied with the accommodation to be provided for his valuable animals.

We were due to "sail"—such was the inaccurate term applied then, and still applied, to the departure from port of vessels not carrying one stitch of sail—at midnight on 7th March, 1905, the tide being full soon after that hour.

The loading of the cargo had been completed on the preceding day, and the hatchways covered with their hatches and tarpaulins, and battened down. This was the carpenter's work, and the Mate had left it to me to supervise. That day, too, the bunkers (surrounding the stokehold) had been filled with 1,000 tons of coal, from railway wagons run alongside and hoisted bodily from the bogies with a crane. The ship's tanks had been filled with many thousands of gallons of fresh water for the boilers, and for the personal needs of the passengers and crew—and the animals—on the outward voyage to our first port of call, Buenos Aires, some 6,000 miles, which we were scheduled to cover in three weeks. The water was piped in, under supervision of the carpenter, who had to sound the tanks to make sure that they were full, and that the ship did not get out of trim, or develop a list as the water was used.

On "sailing" day, all hands joined up at 8 a.m., ready to assist to load the animals, which were coming at that time, and also to receive the passengers later in the day.

Conditions of manning steamers were entirely different from those in sailing vessels. As a rule, a steamer seldom remained in port for more than a few days, or in her terminal port for longer than a week. She could arrive and depart on a fixed schedule, for she was not at the mercy of wind and weather, and could not be becalmed, or "headed off" by adverse winds.

16

Sailing vessels made port when they could, and remained in ports for weeks, sometimes for months, awaiting cargoes or charters. Their crews were paid off when they arrived at their home ports at the end of a voyage; and new crews were not signed on until sailing eve.

The old traditions of sail were continued in steamers, to a certain extent, in that crews signed on and signed off in their home ports, for each voyage; but, as the stay in port was so short, the ship's complement very often signed off and signed on again immediately, on arriving home; and were given instructions at the Board of Trade office to rejoin on a certain date— that would be at 8 a.m. on the day of sailing.

While the ship was in her home port, a shore gang of seamen in her owners' employ did whatever was required in cleaning and painting the ship and overhauling her gear. They were like the riggers who bent sail in sailing vessels at the dockside, but had given up going to sea.

Under this system, most of the A.B. seamen, firemen and trimmers in the S.S. *Rembrandt* had had continuity of seagoing employment in her for many voyages previously. The firemen and trimmers were all "Liverpool Irish". They were tough-looking characters, who worked in the stokehold in dungaree trousers, hobnailed boots, and flannel shirts, with a "sweat rag" round their necks, and came up on deck, clambering out of the fiddley like demons out of hell, grimy and sweaty, for an occasional breath of fresh air, or to go forrard off watch. They worked four hours on and eight off.

The A.B. seamen were old salts, who knew their work. Some of them, and some of the firemen and trimmers, came on board at midnight on sailing eve, slightly merry, to keep up traditions; but they turned to next morning, none the worse for wear and tear.

Loading the livestock was a novelty to me. It took most of the forenoon. A special gangway and staging were used, with planked sides and slatted gangplanks, along which the grooms and stockmen led and coaxed the timid and excited animals, and brought them to their stalls and pens, on the shelter deck. Two grooms and two stockmen were to travel with them, quartered under the poop. The millionaire rancher was on deck early, to see that the precious living cargo was stowed without mishap.

There were a dozen racehorses, and a dozen stud beef-cattle, some of them worth thousands of pounds. After they were safely stowed in their stalls, several crates of prize pigs and poultry were swung inboard with a derrick and tackle, and six beautiful muzzled greyhounds were led in on the leash, and kennelled. The stalls and pens had planked decking, covered in straw. Bales of hay, and bags of chaff and corn, were slung in and stowed in a compartment among the animals.

The shelter deck, which we called "the Zoo", "the Menagerie", "the Farmyard" or "Noah's Ark", was enlivened by squeals, grunts, snorts, neighs and bellows from the horses, cattle and pigs; barks and howls from the hounds; and clucks, crows, quacks and gobbles from the prize poultry, at intervals throughout the day and night. It soon gave off a strong aroma of animal smells and stinks which are usually unfamiliar in a ship.

During the afternoon, the passengers and their baggage came on board. The Blue Peter (the "P" signal-flag, a square of blue with a white square centred on it) was flying at the fore yardarm, meaning, as old-time codebooks explained, "All persons are to repair on board, as the ship is about to sail." It might mean, also, in some cases, that all persons who had a claim for debt against the ship, or her master, should come and get it settled, before they were left lamenting.

At our maintruck fluttered the house-flag of Lamport & Holt, and at the foretruck the flag of Argentina, our country of destination. Fluttering from the flagstaff on the poop was the "Red Duster"—the ensign of the British Mercantile Marine.

Lamport & Holt's ships had their hulls painted black, with a white line along the boot-topping, and white painted masts, derricks, ventilators, and superstructure. The funnel was painted in three broad bands of black, white, and blue. The Company was an old established one, which had operated sailing vessels since 1845 and steamers since 1865. Its house flag was a design of three horizontal stripes—two red and one white between.

Our passengers included the millionaire, his wife and three children, with a maidservant and manservant; two businessmen of Buenos Aires; and three English commercial travellers. The Chief Steward (who acted also as Purser) took charge of them, and installed them in their cabins. The Second Mate gave me his idea of good advice: "Take no notice of the passengers, except at meal times, when you have to be polite to them. Otherwise, treat them as extra cargo!"

The Captain had a busy afternoon, conferring and signing

papers with the owners, agents, shippers, consignees' agents, steve dores, chandlers, towage agents, health officials, and port officials, to get his clearance papers. The First Mate and the Second Mate were here, there and everywhere, inspecting the moorings, the fenders, the hatch covers, the lashings of any movable gear, the lifeboats, and everything else that might affect the safety of the passengers, cargo and livestock and the seaworthiness of the ship. The Engineers were oiling and greasing their engines and the winches, and raising a full head of steam down below.

I appeared to be the only person on board with nothing special to do—the odd man out. I rushed around with the Mate or the Second Mate, trying to make myself handy, and wondering what was the use of a Third Mate in a ship, anyway?

Some of the male passengers, having finished stowing their luggage, strolled out on deck for a smoke, and leaned, as passengers will, idly against the rail, looking overboard in meditation. This gave me a series of minor shocks, as the first rule at sea in sailing ships is that no man must be idle on deck. Satan finds mischief, and Mates find work, for idle hands to do. I checked myself just in time from bawling at the idlers to get a move on.

Night fell, and the lights were switched on. A gong sounded for dinner. The Mate said to me, "You and the Fourth Engineer stand watch on deck while we're at dinner, and you can have yours afterwards. Check the navigation lights and the spare oil-lights with Lampy."

I knew from my examination textbooks the lights required under the International Rules for Preventing Collisions at Sea. A sailing vessel under way, between sunset and sunrise, carries only red and green sidelights (red on the port side and green on the starboard) and a white sternlight—these being all oil-lamps —but a steam vessel carries also a white light on the foremast and another on the mainmast (fifteen feet higher than the one on the foremast), and various other lights for use in special cases, such as "anchor lights" and two red "not under command" lights, beside a Morse signalling lamp, and pyrotechnic flares.

In the S.S. *Rembrandt* the lights were electric, including those on the mastheads; but the Board of Trade Regulations required every steamer to carry a spare set of oil-lamps, filled, trimmed and ready for instant use in case of any breakdown in the electric lighting system.

The A.B. in charge of the oil-lamps was known as the Lamp

Trimmer, or "Lampy". He was an old Cape Horn sailor, who, in addition to looking after the lamps, did any sailorizing work that might be required, such as splicing ropes or wires. I went to the lamp locker, and found Lampy already there, testing each of his lamps in turn, by lighting and trimming their wicks. He knew his work better than I did, but, as a matter of routine, I stayed with him until all the lamps were tested.

"These 'lectric lights ain't reliable," he growled. "Can't beat the old oil-lamps and the old salts, sir! What do they do when their lights go out? 'Lampy, Lampy,' they sing out, and I get the spare oil-lamps hoisted up in a jiffy—or where'd they be? Sunk, that's where they'd be!"

As the Fourth Engineer and I had our delayed dinner, final preparations were made for putting to sea. Two tugs came in through the river lock to the dock, and took their stations ahead and astern. At 11 p.m., a Mersey Pilot came aboard, and the gangway was hauled up. The Mate went forrard with three seamen, and the Second Mate aft with three more, to cast off the moorings, and make the towlines fast.

I was ordered to go up on the bridge, to stand by with the Captain, the Pilot and the A.B. at the wheel. This was one of the great moments of my life.

My job was to work the engineroom telegraph. "It's foolproof," the Captain said. That was a very doubtful compliment to my intellect. I examined the instrument carefully, to be sure that I would make no fool's error. The dial was clearly marked. With the handle vertical, the pointer indicated STOP. The dial showed three speeds, AHEAD—SLOW, HALF and FULL—and likewise ASTERN, three speeds.

Concentrating my attention, I waited, eager to work the fascinating gadget, which would set the propeller revolving at the Pilot's orders.

The Pilot looked out gloomily from the wing of the bridge. "A dirty night," he remarked. "Rain and sleet and wind, and as black as the inside of a cow!"

The Captain sang out through his megaphone, fore and aft, "Make fast the tugs and stand by to cast off moorings." When this was done, he sang out, "Let go fore and aft!"

"*Slow ahead,*" the Pilot ordered.

I moved the handle of the telegraph cautiously, and precisely. There was a clang of the bell in the stokehold down below, and, with a gentle shudder and vibration, the screw began to revolve, and we were under way.

Within a few minutes, as we neared the lock, the Pilot said, "*Stop!*"

Clang! and the vibration ceased as we glided into the dimlit lock, nosed by the tugs, with much singing out of orders from the Marine Superintendent on the wharf, and answers from the Mates and the tugmasters.

The Captain and the Pilot conferred. "Better not go through until high water," said the Pilot. "That will be in an hour from now."

"Make fast there forrard!" the Captain sang out. Then he said to me, "Go forrard and tell the Mate we'll lay in the lock for an hour until high water."

I sprang down the companionway from the bridge, and hurried forrard in the darkness. When I reached the fo'c'sle head, being unfamiliar with the hazards there, I had not sufficiently noticed that there were two holes in the iron deck—one on the port side and one on the starboard side—the hawsepipes where the anchor cables were hove through to the windlass. Hastening along the port side, I trod in the hawsepipe and fell flat, feeling a sharp pain as my shin made contact with the iron edge of the hole.

Instantly I scrambled to my feet. "What's wrong with you?" asked the Mate. "Drunk?"

"Nothing much," I said, as calmly as possible, though I was wondering if I had broken my leg. "The Captain says we're to lay in the lock for an hour until high water."

"All right, then," the Mate grunted. "'Hurry back, and watch your step."

He gave orders to make the ship fast, and I hurried to the bridge, along the starboard side, giving a wide berth to the hole which had caused my downfall. The result was that I fell into the hole on the other side, in precisely the same manner, and nearly broke my other leg!

The pain was severe, and I could feel blood trickling down both shins; but, at such an important moment in my nautical career, I had too much pride to tell the Captain that I was injured in such a lubberly way.

Arrived on the bridge, I stood by the telegraph again, trying not to wince or show any pain. I was afraid the Captain might send me below. I couldn't bear to be ordered off the bridge the first time I was ever on duty on it. The blood was trickling into my boots. I looked down anxiously to see if it was staining the deck.

The Captain remained on the bridge, yarning to the Pilot. I was suffering from pain and chagrin, but determined to give no sign of either. After what seemed to me a very long hour, we got under way again, with much megaphoning, and clanging of telegraphs, and passed through the river-lock gates into the Mersey stream.

The tugs towed us to midstream, and then cast off. We proceeded downriver, seven miles, at first dead slow, then at half speed.

The lights of Liverpool receded astern. We crossed the Bar, and the *Rembrandt* rose to the surge of the seas in a brisk north-westerly gale. The pilot steamer, with her all-round red light eight feet below her white masthead light, came in sight, and sent off a small boat as we hove to, and the Pilot climbed down the Jacob's ladder, and shoved off.

"Full speed ahead!" the Captain ordered. I moved the telegraph, exulting in its clang. Next came the order, "Off stations and set watches"—and sea-routine had begun.

It was 2 a.m. The Second Mate came on the bridge and took over. The Captain wrote out his night orders and went below.

"You can turn in," the Second Mate said to me. "It's been a long day, and you'll be on again at 4 a.m. with the Mate."

I limped from the bridge. My shins were bruised and bleeding, but no bones were broken. I had learnt, in the school of experience, that, even in steamers, a man has to be ready to take some hard knocks, and to watch his step.

CHAPTER THREE

Learning the New Routine—Sailorizing Made Easy—The Bridge—The Patent Log—Traffic in the Irish Sea—Scilly Light Abeam—The Chops of the Channel—Open Water—I Take Over a Watch—An Ambition Achieved—We Arrive at Buenos Aires—A Glimpse of the Gay Life—Montevideo—The Famous Haven of Rio de Janeiro—"Seeing the World"—Colourful Bahia—The Ease of Navigation in Steam —Canary Wine—Las Palmas—Home and Time to Leave Her—"On the Beach" Again.

AT 6.30 a.m., the second steward brought tea and toast to the bridge. I went into the wheelhouse and showed him my bruised shins. "I'll put a dressing on it, sir," he said. "When did you do it? How did it happen? Why didn't you call me before? I'm the assistant doctor in this ship!"

"It happened last night," I told him. "I fell into the hawespipe forrard in the dark. I'm green in a steamer, and I didn't want to disturb the Captain when the pilot was aboard."

The steward was an old sailing-ship man. "Things are different in steam, sir," he said sympathetically. "The Cap'n doesn't attend to injuries in a steamer, unless they're very serious. He leaves 'em to me or my boss."

With ointment and bandages on my shins. I limped into the saloon for breakfast, when I went off duty with the Mate at

8 a.m. We were steaming southwards in the Irish Sea, doing twelve knots in a quartering northwesterly breeze, with clear skies. In these narrow waters, the First Mate and Second Mate stood alternate watches on the bridge, four hours on and four hours off, as in sailing vessels.

I stood watch with the First Mate, to be initiated into the routine. It took me quite a while to get used to walking to and fro on the bridge, with little to do except to keep a lookout, watch the steering, take bearings on occasional landmarks, and check the compass error. No sails to trim, no pully-hauly, and little need to take heed of the force or direction of the wind!

This was sailorizing made easy! The engine telegraph stood at FULL AHEAD, and there would be no need to touch it again, perhaps for weeks, until we neared port, unless an emergency arose. The helmsman—so-called from sailing-ship tradition—was a grizzled A.B. He handled the wheel, keeping the ship on the set compass course. The steering gear was steam driven, and moved the rudder at the slightest touch of the wheel, requiring scarcely any manual effort.

The Captain came occasionally onto the bridge to look around for a few minutes, and to receive the reports of the officer of the watch, but spent most of his time below, in his cabin or the chart room, working out navigational sights, setting courses, making official log-book entries, attending to the ship's papers and to other routine matters, and to complaints or whatever emergencies might arise. His was the final responsibility, and he was on duty twenty-four hours a day, as Captains always must be, to be called or informed instantly if anything unusual developed, and on the prowl around the ship whenever he felt inclined.

In these narrow waters, we navigated by bearings of landmarks, and by dead reckoning, and took routine sights of the sun, moon, or stars, as required. Dead reckoning was computed from readings of the "patent log", which was a novelty to me, though I knew in theory how it worked.

In sailing vessels we had used the "hand log"—a drogue towed astern, indicating the speed in knots by a line running out from a reel over the stern rail, marked with knotted yarn, checked with a half-minute sandglass. To "heave the log" was a manual operation, usually performed by one of the Mates and two or three of the apprentices. It gave only an approximation of the speed at the moment when the log was heaved. This result was reliable for dead reckoning only when the force and direction of the wind remained constant, which rarely happened.

The patent log was in every way a superior instrument. It could be used as well in a sailing vessel as in a steamer, but most owners of sailing vessels begrudged the expense. Its operation was simple and accurate, almost "foolproof". The device consists of a metal fan, towed astern for the whole voyage after clearing port. The vanes of the fan revolve as it is towed through the water at the end of a woven line 100 fathoms long. The revolutions of the fan are conveyed by the line to a dial secured to the rail aft. This shows the number of nautical miles the ship has run since the dial was set. It is usually set at noon, and thereafter read every hour by a junior officer or one of the Able Seamen. In a steamer the dial is usually carried at the end of an outrigger, to keep the fan clear of the wash from the propeller, which would cause it to give a false reading.

The Mate sent me to read the log, which was an activity of some use, compared with my standby efforts on the bridge.

The poop—with its centuries of tradition as the quarter-deck, the Citadel of Authority, in sailing vessels—was bare and desolate in this flush-deck steamer. There was nothing on it except an auxiliary steering wheel, the sounding machine, and mooring bitts and winches. There was no skylight of the Captain's cabin, no polished brass and teakwood fittings, no binnacle, no harness cask with putrid pork smelling to high heaven. It was just the after end, or as a lady passenger called it, "the blunt end" of the ship, with no sentiment attached to it; yet, beneath its overhang, the propeller throbbed, churning the water with the power that drove us on; and the rudder, though operated by remote control, kept us on course.

From force of habit, I glanced forrard and aloft; but the midship deckhouse blocked the view of the bow, and there was no swelling canvas aloft: the mainmast was bare, and there was no whistle of the wind in the rigging. I read the dial of the patent log, and as I did so, softly sang to myself the words of the old favourite:

> Once more he heaves the reeling log,
> Which marks the leeway and the course:
> *Larboard watch, ahoy!*

Passengers were lounging around on the deck, smoking and

talking—idle. Not a seaman among them! My heart sank as I realized that men in steamers do not sing at their work. Never again, perhaps, would I hear and join in a chanty chorus as a crowd of toughened men tailed on to the main topsail halyards or to heave up the anchor, "Rolling Home", working in unison and rhythm with songs on their lips—the songs of seafarers for centuries, doomed to disuse in a mechanized world.

Only the thudding of the engines, driving the ship on, regardless of wind and weather: and men the servants of the machines! Ah, well, it was no use regretting the passing of "the good old days". Progress was inevitable, and I, like everyone else, would have less work to do when machines replaced muscle power and wind power. There was a new lore to learn, and I was young enough, and keen enough, to learn it.

Returned to the bridge, I reported the log reading to the Mate, and resumed pacing on the port wing, eyeing the weather and the interesting variety of traffic in the Irish Sea. We were now in St George's Channel, off Cardigan Bay in Wales, and there were many fishing trawlers at work, flying signals to indicate what sort of gear they were using, such as lines, trawls or seines. It was necessary to alter our course slightly to give them a wide berth.

As a matter of routine, we scanned every vessel that came in sight for signals of identification. In these narrow waters—so-called, though St George's Channel is from 60 to 80 miles wide —vessels often hoisted their code-numbers of identification; but some shipmasters economically avoided wear and tear of their flags which might become tattered in the breeze.

We were seldom out of sight of vessels under sail or steam, proceeding up-channel, down-channel or across-channel. Among them we sighted several full-rigged ships and barques standing to the northward on tacks, nearing their home ports after months at sea. They had the right-o'-way when they were standing across our bows, or at any other time. The Mate and I scanned these dear old windbags with sentimental affection, discussing their rig, and imagining—though without too much envy—the scene on their decks and aloft as they worked up-channel in the choppy seas whipped by the nor'westerly breeze.

The S.S. *Rembrandt* did not carry wireless—which, in 1905 was still a novelty—and in consequence all our signalling was visual. We met a warship, and dutifully dipped our ensign to her. The lookout man in our crow's nest did not have a telephone—this instrument was rare in ships in those days. When he sighted anything unusual, he sounded a bell to attract the attention of the officer of the watch, then sang out, "Sail on the port bow", or whatever else he sighted, and if necessary we altered course accordingly. As a rule the lookout man sounded his bell once for an object to starboard, twice for an object to port, and three times for an object right ahead.

Early in the watch he reported a sailing ship dead ahead. The Mate and I soon sighted her royals and topgallants on the horizon, but, though we were doing all of twelve knots, she kept her distance ahead of us, and we never sighted her topsails. Evidently she was a flyer, outward bound from Liverpool or Glasgow, carrying a full press of sail in the fair wind. We discussed her with admiration.

At 12 noon, we took sights of the sun for latitude, and the Second Mate took over on the bridge. I went below for four hours, and from force of habit turned in to my bunk; but not to sleep, as my efforts on watch had certainly not exhausted me. At 1 p.m. the gong sounded for lunch, and I went to the saloon, fully brassbound, to enjoy a well-cooked, well-served meal and the company of the passengers. This was the life!

From 4 p.m. to 8 p.m., I was again on the bridge with the Mate. The strangeness was wearing off, and I had grasped the essentials of a routine that was to govern my way of life for more years ahead than I could imagine at that time. At midnight, when I came on watch again, we had the Scilly Islands Light abeam, the last landmark of England, and we were rolling in the Chops of the Channel in a stiff westerly gale.

No pully-hauly, no flooded decks, nothing to do but navigate! The bridge was sheltered from wind and rain. I had a woollen overcoat and scarf, but there was no need for oilskins and "soul-and-body lashings". It was a soft life, in comparison with what I had been used to, but not mentally so. There was need for continual alertness and keen lookout for lights ahead and athwart our course in this track of the Atlantic shipping bound to and from Southampton and Portsmouth, the Straits of Dover and the French ports.

The night was as black as the Earl of Hell's riding boots, with heavy rain, so an extra lookout man was posted on the bow. In thick weather, the visibility is often better from the lower position on the bow than from the crow's nest or the bridge.

The Mate paced the weather side and I the lee side of the

bridge, on the lookout for lights ahead of us or on the bows, especially of sailing vessels, whose sidelights and sternlights, of oil-lamps, as we well knew, often burnt dimly. We glanced frequently at our own sidelights, to make sure that they were "burning brightly".

But the ocean is wide, and there is sea room for all. We sighted three sailing vessels, standing up-channel with the fair wind at a cracking pace, and one laboriously beating to windward, besides several steamers standing across our bows, but we gave them all a wide berth.

When the Second Mate took over at 4 a.m. the gale was easing. I turned in to my bunk and slept soundly, after listening for awhile, with some dislike, to the thumping and thudding of the engines, and the metallic clang, as the stokers down below rattled their shovels impatiently on the furnace doors as a signal to the trimmers to hurry along with more coal.

In two days more, making an average of approximately 280 miles a day, we were far from the land, and beyond the track of westbound and eastbound shipping, except for that to and from Northern Spain, Portugal and the Strait of Gibraltar.

Then came another of the occasions in my life which were memorable for me, as the Captain decided that I had gained enough experience to stand a watch unaided on the bridge. I took over the watches from 8 a.m. to noon, and from 8 p.m. to midnight. As far as the Mates were concerned, the day was now divided into three watches—four hours on and eight hours off for each of us—a luxury!

It was a clear day and fine weather when I stood my first watch on the bridge, with no company except that of the helmsman, and occasional visits from the Old Man, who satisfied himself that I had "learnt the ropes" as a steamboat officer, at least in the open ocean! Time would make that routine very familiar to me, but would never dim the memory of the thrill of satisfaction I felt when I first paced the bridge of a steamer, responsible for her navigation and safety for the time being, even though there were no difficulties in sight!

Time dims many memories, and long usage creates habits which become almost automatic; but the first experience gives the keenest enjoyment, when every faculty must be alert, to anticipate and ward off mishaps of any kind adversely affecting efficiency, economy or safety. On that clear and sunny morning, in the wide ocean, I had nothing to worry about; but I was more worried then, by the weight of my responsibilities, than many a time later in far tighter corners. Nothing abnormal occurred in my first watch on the bridge, except the tumult of my inner feelings, which I carefully concealed. At the change of the watch at noon, when I handed over to the Second Mate, after we had both taken sights, and compared calculations, the Old Man said to me, "Well, you did nothing wrong!"

And that was high praise. . . .

The voyage out to Buenos Aires, of a little over three weeks, was "uneventful", which means only that no major mishaps occurred, and we arrived on schedule; but it was eventful and momentous for me, as in that time I learnt routines and acquired habits which would remain with me for the rest of my seafaring life.

I was lucky to learn the ways of steam in a well-found steamer, with the tutoring of seniors who knew their work completely. The S.S. *Rembrandt* was not "shipshape and Bristol fashion" in the sense of the sailing vessels, in which crews of twenty or more seamen and apprentices had to be kept constantly at work on deck and aloft, furbishing ship, when not handling sail. But the steel blocks and wires for working the derricks had to be kept in good fettle, and there was a constant battle to counteract rust, by washing and painting in all parts of the deck.

The trade winds, so important in sail, made no practical difference to us, as we churned along in the fine weather latitudes, almost indifferent to wind and weather.

Occasionally we sighted other vessels, in sail or steam, and exchanged signals, if they were within visual signalling range; but for the greater part of the route we were alone within our horizon. As we passed through the "doldrums", we saw some windbags becalmed—poor unfortunates! How vividly I could imagine the feelings of the men in them when they sighted us steaming along at twelve knots in comfort while they lay at a standstill, with limp sails, waiting and whistling for a breeze!

That settled any doubts that might have lingered in my mind on the wisdom of my decision to go into steam.

After what seemed to me an amazingly quick passage, we were in Lat. 35 deg. S., and standing in westwards into the wide mouth of the Rio de la Plata, keeping a lookout for the Light Vessel off Montevideo, which marks the approach to Buenos Aires. Soon we sighted some steamers leaving port and exchanged signals. We reduced speed, and timed our arrival at the Light Vessel at dawn. There we embarked an Argentinian pilot, and by 5 p.m. we were safely berthed at Buenos Aires. The river throughout the passage from the Light Vessel to the city is shallow and muddy, with strong currents. Many steamers and sailing vessels have been grounded there on the mudbanks, sometimes remaining for weeks, until a flood in the river enabled them to be floated or towed off.

Our passengers were quickly ashore, and then began the unloading of the livestock, which had all arrived in good condition. Next day the hatches were opened, and we began discharging cargo, with the steam winches and derricks, and the labour of stevedores. My job was to stand by Number Two hold, with the foreman stevedore and the consignees' agents, to exercise a general supervision, while the Mate and the Second Mate watched the other holds; but our presence was mainly a matter of formality, and we were more ornamental than useful. Our seamen were given some painting to do, on deck and overside, but there was none of the complicated overhauling of gear necessary in sailing vessels in port.

We lay at Buenos Aires for a fortnight, discharging and taking in cargo. The Second Mate and I went ashore in the evenings, to stroll the boulevards of this beautiful city, with its many open-air cafes and bright night life offering attractions limited only by our restricted financial resources.

Compared with the ports I had been in on the West Coast of South America, Buenos Aires was a large and thriving city, with beautiful public buildings and modern shops, and everything up to date. At this time it had a population of nearly a million, and reminded me somewhat of Melbourne, Australia, in its wide streets, mild climate, and carefree atmosphere.

The time came all too soon when we cast off our moorings, and, with a Plate Pilot on board, dropped downriver, 125 miles, to Montevideo in Uruguay, where we were to load hides, and take on some passengers. Here we remained four days, with some explorations ashore in the evenings—the attractions being similar to those of Buenos Aires, though less stylish.

Montevideo was a favourite sailing-ship port, as, being much nearer open water than Buenos Aires, it had an anchorage which windjammers could reach unaided, or with small expense for towage. A line of Portuguese sailing vessels, well built and equipped, and manned by excellent seamen, traded to Monte-video from Lisbon, and from ports in France, Spain and Italy, bringing out general merchandise and coal, and lifting cargoes of hides, tallow and wool. They traded also to ports in Brazil, despite the competition of steamers. The Portuguese, who were the first mariners to find a way to India around the Cape of Good Hope, have a wonderful tradition of seamanship in sail, maintained for 600 years, which lingered even until the middle of the twentieth century, when there were still some oceangoing sailing vessels under the Portuguese flag.

From Montevideo we put out to sea and coasted northwards for 1,020 miles to Rio de Janeiro in Brazil, taking four days on the passage. When we entered the superb and famous harbour of Rio, I began to feel that I was on a luxury sightseeing cruise. Never before—or since, except at Rio itself—have I seen such a glorious natural haven of ships. Sydney Harbour, in Australia, almost equals it, but lacks the surrounding mountain peaks which make Rio scenically wonderful.

Rio de Janeiro is the capital of Brazil, which was a Portuguese colony, until it became a republic in 1889, but the language, customs and sentiment of this huge and fertile country remain Portuguese. We picked up a pilot, and, after an easy approach, berthed at a quay alongside a beautiful square at the foot of the main street. Nothing could be handier!

For several days, we were loading coffee and rubber, with agreeable evenings ashore, handicapped only by the chronic complaint of junior ships' officers—shortage of cash—but, as the pleasures of Rio were plentiful and cheap, the Second Mate and I managed to enjoy ourselves without being ruined, financially or otherwise.

Apart from the financial, and possibly the moral, considerations, I felt it would be distinctly imprudent to make the pace *too* hot in these delightful South American ports, as the Captain's eagle eye would detect any signs of undue lassitude next morning, when there was work to be done. I couldn't afford to risk a reprimand, or an adverse report from him at the end of the voyage, which might put me "on the beach".

So I was careful to return on board about midnight, as respectably as possible in the circumstances. We finished loading, and embarked some passengers, then cleared out, bound northwards along the coast of Brazil to Bahia (also known as San

Salvador) on the Bay of All Saints. This was a run of 737 miles from port to port, which took three days.

We were now in the Tropics, as Bahia is 12 deg. S. of the Equator. This is one of the oldest Portuguese settlements in Brazil, picturesque with its white houses, bright flowers and vivid green trees. It was a substantial city of some 200,000 inhabitants, many of whom were Negroes, the descendants of slaves brought from Africa in the bad old days, to work in the sugar plantations and cottonfields.

We lay there three days, loading bales of cotton, mahogany logs, sugar and tobacco. I was now quite convinced that the life of a steamship officer was giving me opportunities of "seeing the world" with very little effort required on my part; and I was being paid as well!

A few more passengers came aboard here, and we had almost a full cargo, but we were scheduled to make one more call on the homeward run—at Las Palmas, in the Canary Islands, to load wine and bananas.

The passage from Bahia to Las Palmas, 2,600 miles north-easterly across the Atlantic, took ten days. We were in tropical waters for most of the passage, and saw several windjammers flat becalmed, or struggling to make headway in the fitful light airs of the "doldrums". Our route led us within sight of St Paul's Rocks, one degree north of the Equator, a barren uninhabited group of islets, which is the only landmark in this tract of the ocean, and usually given a wide berth by sailing vessels, as it is unlit; but to us it was a convenient fix, as we passed it in day-time.

Our next sight of land was the Cape Verde Islands, in 17 deg. N., a Portuguese possession off the coast of Senegal, West Africa. On voyages in sailing vessels, outward bound from England, I had spent some anxious hours, as an apprentice and Second Mate, looking out for these islands, which are a hazard in hours of darkness if the ship's chronometer is not perfectly rated and the Master in consequence unsure of his position. This was usually the state of affairs (before the introduction of wireless time-signals) in ships which carried only one chronometer. An error of four seconds in the chronometer throws the calculation of longitude out one minute of arc (equal to one nautical mile on the Equator).

Sailing vessels usually took three weeks from England to the latitude of the Cape Verde Islands. In that period, no Captain could be certain if his chronometer had lost or gained, and to what extent. A fix on the coast of the Cape Verde Islands was desirable as a means of making a check on the rating of the chronometer. This was usually the only land likely to be sighted on voyages, outward bound from England to Australia, in cargo-carrying sailing vessels. The navigator's ideal was to sight the Cape Verde Islands from twenty miles or more to westward, in day-time; but if the Master was unsure of his position, and likely to be in the vicinity of the islands at night-time, he stood well to the westward, gave them a wide berth, and so lost his chance of getting a fix, rather than risk piling his ship up on the shore.

How different in steam! The S.S. *Rembrandt*, with her patent log and *three* chronometers, which could be compared one with the other, had every facility for exact calculation of our position at any hour of the day or night—provided that sun, moon or stars and a clear horizon were visible. She could hold a compass course in any weather, on the most direct track from port to port, without the interminable zigzag tracks of sailing vessels making tacks in winds of variable force and direction.

With three qualified navigating officers (in addition to the Captain) taking sights, and hourly readings of the patent log, we knew at any time with certainty exactly where we were, and when we would make a landfall. There was no need to give the Cape Verde Islands a wide berth. On the contrary, our route on this passage would take us between the islands of the archipelago. Confident of our position, we were able to navigate at full speed through the channels between the islands, and they were out of sight astern within a few hours.

Such efficiency and ease of handling the ship and its navigation, as compared with the caution and uncertainty of sail, made a deep impression on my mind. It was evident that steam was far superior to sail in every practical aspect, and the glory of sail would linger only as a romantic memory; yet, because the difficulties and dangers of handling sailing vessels were greater than those in steamers, the men who met those difficulties and dangers, and overcame them, required greater skill in seamanship, and greater physical endurance, than men who were machine propelled.

We arrived at Las Palmas, in the Canary Islands, on schedule and uneventfully. The port, on the shore of Gran Canaria Island, nestles at the foot of a volcanic cone 6,400 feet high, covered with bright-green forests and vineyards. The islands belong to Spain.

We remained only two days, taking in bunker-coal, and loading pipes of Canary wine and crates of bananas. Some Argentinian ladies among our passengers, who naturally could speak Spanish perfectly, were considerably amused—as we learnt later—by the appalling bad language used by the Spanish-speaking stevedores, of which we understood not one word.

Dozens of small boats lay alongside us, with hawkers offering fruit, flowers and singing canaries for sale. I was attracted by a canary which sang most beautifully in a cage. I bought it for a dollar and proudly installed it in my cabin, intending it as a present for my mother.

Alas, it never sang again. After some days, I realized that the wily vendor had substituted a dumb cluck when I wasn't looking.

We arrived at Liverpool, to berth in the Huskisson Dock, on 31st May, after a voyage which had lasted exactly twelve weeks.

I had eighteen pounds owing to me, and thought that it had been easily earned. The voyage had been practically a pleasure-cruise, in comparison with a voyage in sail, but in addition it had been an instructive experience for me. I had learnt how to work in a steamer, at sea and in port, and I was no longer "green" in steam. I was lucky, for many another young officer of that period made his maiden voyage in steam in much more difficult conditions than those I had encountered.

But there was a problem to worry me, as nothing is perfect. While serving as Third Mate, I was not "getting my time in" to sit for the Master Mariner's examination. The regulations of the Board of Trade required that, after passing the First Mate's examination, a candidate for a Master Mariner's certificate must have served for at least eighteen months at sea in a capacity not lower than Second Mate. From this point of view, my voyage in the S.S. *Rembrandt*, as Third Mate, would not count at all, and was therefore a waste of time.

I decided to leave her. Impatient as I was to get my Master's Certificate while I was still in the mood for studying, I signed off, drew my eighteen pounds, and went looking for a job as Second Mate. Once again, I was "on the beach", but at least I had now a satisfactory reference from Captain Royce that I served in a well-known steamer.

Eagerly I made the round of the shipping offices and employment agencies at Liverpool, only to find that vacancies were few and applicants many for work in steamers, in those times when hundreds of sailing-ship officers were striving to get into steam: men with much more seniority and experience than I. In these conditions, men who had steady work in steamers seldom left of their own free will, and the shipping companies could pick and choose to fill the few vacancies that occurred.

After a week of rebuffs, I began to rue my rashness in leaving the *Rembrandt* so impulsively; but the decision had been taken, and it was too late for regrets. Hope and ambition still buoyed me at the end of a second week of fruitless trudging the docks; but I was counting my pennies now, in anticipation of a long spell ashore.

At the end of the third week, I had almost made up my mind to apply for a job as First Mate or Second Mate in sail, to "get my time in" that way. There were several positions offering, for the usual long voyages, of a year or more, and the temptation was strong, for I still loved the real sailorizing ways of the windjammers. I tussled with myself, for this was a crisis in my career. If I had gone back to sail, I might never have got out of it again.

Fate took a hand in the game. I decided to make one more round of the steamship offices. The first office I entered was that of the Leyland Line, where the desk clerk now knew me well by sight, as I had pestered him a dozen times previously. He greeted me with some cordiality. "Our steamer *Texan,* trading to the West Indies," he said, "needs a Second Officer. See the Marine Superintendent without delay! You're the first in this morning!"

I hurried along. The M.S. was affable. I told him why I had left the *Rembrandt.* I needed to get my time in for Master. He was thoroughly sympathetic. "We can sign you on as Second Officer," he said.

My spirits fell as he explained further, "We sign on a Chief Officer, a First Officer and a Second Officer. We don't call them Mates on the articles. We call them Officers."

"Does that mean," I asked, "that the Second Officer is really the Third Mate?"

"You work three watches, four hours on and eight hours off. The Second Officer means Second Officer, doesn't it? If you serve eighteen months as Second Officer, that ought to satisfy the Board of Trade! If you don't want the job, plenty of others do!"

I concealed my doubts, and signed on. It would be a good experience, anyway. I had always wanted to see the West Indies.

CHAPTER FOUR

*A Voyage to the West Indies—The S.S.
"Texan"—A Silent Captain—Our Energetic
Chief Officer—Why a Ship is a "She"—The
Blue Caribbean—Jamaica Rum—The Port of
Colon in 1905—Beginning of the Panama
Canal—Yellow Fever and Mosquitoes—
Gigantic American Achievement—The Gulf
of Mexico—The Gulf Stream—The Port of
Tampico—The Mississippi Delta—Dropping
the Anchor—Quarantine at New Orleans—
Fever Raging—I Take a Chance—Key West—
Home Safe—"On the Beach" Again.*

THE S.S. *Texan*, 2,999 tons, Captain O. Lund, was an old-fashioned but well-found single-screw clipper-bow iron-hull steamer, 360 feet long and 41 feet beam, built by Harland & Wolff, and launched at Belfast in 1883. She had a "three island profile", with raised forecastle head, bridge and poopdeck, and welldecks before and abaft the bridge. She carried two old style iron anchors ("bowers"), like a sailing ship, and also had other features of sailing-ship design, such as teakwood companionways and rails, brass fittings, and planked decks. She had a speed of ten knots, and had been for many years in regular service on the run from Liverpool to the West Indies, with passengers, mails and general cargo.

The *Texan* had accommodation for thirty passengers. Their

cabins were ranged on the 'tween-deck, with long alleyways, and panelled dining-saloon, writing-room, smoking-room and lounge amidships under the bridge deckhouse. Some passengers were accommodated also in the steerage under the poop. This was the first vessel in which I had served in which the passengers were not merely extra cargo, but numerous enough to be as profitable to the owners as the more inert cargo in the holds.

Captain Lund was a Dane, who had served many years in English ships, in both sail and steam, and spoke English with only a slight trace of the Danish accent. This did not matter, as he was the most silent shipmaster I have ever known. He never spoke a word more than was absolutely necessary, and conveyed most of his commands with a swift glance and movement of his head or hands, by sign language, or by grunts of approval or disapproval. These were sufficient, as he was a very fine seaman, who quickly compelled respect. He was a short, stocky, broad shouldered, burly, powerfully built man, nearly as broad as he was long, with a red face, keen blue eyes and greying fair hair: a formidable personality.

The Chief Officer, James Thomas, was a keen man in his thirties, who had served his time in sail and held a Master's ticket. He was anxious to get on in the Leyland Line and obtain a command. He therefore took his duties very seriously, seldom smiled or joked, and felt it was his personal heavy responsibility to see that everything was shipshape and Bristol fashion.

The First Officer, John Kelly, was a bit of a rough diamond, and a few years older than I. He had served his time in sail, and gone into steam after passing his Second Mate's examination. He had passed for First Mate, and was getting in his time to sit for Master.

Soon after I joined the ship, I realized that my position as Second Officer was equivalent to that of Third Mate, and that my duties would be the same as those of Third Mate in the S.S. *Rembrandt,* standing watches at sea, in rotation with the Chief Officer and the First Officer, four hours on and eight hours off. I doubted whether this would be considered by the Board of Trade examiners as time served as Second Mate; but I decided to make one voyage to test the matter, and to gain experience.

The *Texan* carried a Chief Engineer, and Second and Third and Fourth Engineers, with six stokers and six trimmers. On deck we had eight A.B. seamen, a bosun, and a carpenter. The ship had also a Purser, who—thank goodness!—had most of the worries of looking after the passengers; and a chief steward, who controlled a staff of two cooks, three stewards and a stewardess.

As we were to call at several ports, the stowing of the cargo—2,000 tons of general merchandise, including chiefly textiles, hardware, fancy goods, groceries and other manufactured goods —in the four holds, required careful supervision so that it could be discharged partially at each port of call, in sequence, with a minimum of handling and without disturbing the trim.

The stowing of the cargo was the work of the experienced stevedores, but I was sent down below with a copy of the manifest to keep an eye on what was being done. The zealous Chief Officer plagued the foreman stevedore and the First Officer and myself with frequent inquiries and inspections of the progress of the work, until it was all stowed to his satisfaction.

The mails and passengers came aboard on sailing day, with several hours of excitement, as friends and relatives of the passengers came to see them off, obstructing the decks and alleyways. We were to "sail" at 3 p.m.

All persons going ashore were cleared off at 2 p.m., and the Chief Officer told me to make a search in any likely places for stowaways. This was new routine for me, and I felt at a disadvantage, with thirty passengers, all strangers to me, roaming around. The stewards were also told to keep an eye on bathrooms, toilets or other lurking places. In the bustle and excitement it would have been almost impossible to tell who was a passenger and who might be a stowaway. I scarcely knew even the crew members by sight. I looked into the lamp locker, rope locker, storerooms and a few other likely hiding-places, without result. If there were any stowaways, they would be detected in the usual way, when they gave themselves up through starvation or thirst, after the ship was at sea.

The tugs came alongside, we cast off our moorings, moved out into the Mersey, and my second voyage in steam had begun. After we had cleared the Bar and dropped the Pilot, the Chief Officer, First Officer and I began standing our watches in rotation on the bridge, as we headed southwards in the Irish Sea. Mine was the watch from 8 p.m. to midnight. Captain Lund came on to the bridge shortly after I took over, and stood there for two hours without speaking a word, until he was satisfied that I knew my work. Then he grunted, "Carry on!" and went below.

We rounded the Tuskar Rock lighthouse and the Saltees light-ship at the southeastern corner of Ireland, and stood away to the southwestward, getting our last sight of land at the Old Head of Kinsale, then set course across the Western Ocean for our first port of call, Kingston, Jamaica, a passage of 4,026 miles from Liverpool.

In this summer season, at the end of June, 1905, the weather in the Atlantic was mild, and the S.S. *Texan* churned along, doing all of ten knots, with no undue worries, as far as I was concerned. She was a comfortable old hooker, with good sea-going qualities in her class. She was one of the last of the old iron steamers, as steel had for many years replaced iron in hull plates in shipbuilding.

The Chief Officer was the only person who appeared to be worried by the weight of his responsibilities. After we were free of the main stream of traffic in the western approaches to the English Channel, he often joined the seamen on deck, during his watch—and even sometimes during his watches below —in scrubbing the decks and sand-and-canvassing the teakwood and polishing the brasswork. I must say he had everything spick and span, but his energetic example was not followed by the First Officer and myself, as we considered that an equally admir-able result could be achieved by giving whatever instructions were necessary to the efficient boatswain.

This was my first voyage across the Western Ocean to North America. We were seventeen days on the passage, and, being still very innocent in the ways of passenger-steamers, and of a sociable nature (as I hope I still am!) I enjoyed talking to the passengers—male and female, young and old—at meal times and in the mornings and evenings before I went on watch at 8 a.m. and 8 p.m.

Most of our passengers were British—owners or managers of sugar plantations or businesses in Jamaica, or government of-ficials, returning after a holiday. Like nearly all passengers, they were eager for information on the working of a ship and on the ways of the sea, and considered that a brassbound young officer was the very person to impart the knowledge they were so anxious to obtain. A sweet young planter's daughter on this voyage was the first passenger who ever asked me the question that nearly all sweet young passengers ask young officers: "Why is a ship called a 'she'?"

I answered the question to the best of my ability: "A ship is called a 'she' because she's sometimes difficult to handle—especially in confined spaces!" On further reflection, I added, "If she's a sailing ship, she's a thing of beauty. She has a waist and a figurehead, and ought to be well rigged, with graceful curves and lines. She has several companions, and is often attached to a b(u)oy! She has ribs and knees, earrings, eyes, stays, bonnets, thimbles and pins. She has a Mate to keep her in trim, but she needs a Master. Sailors love ships, and it's love that makes the world go round, so that's why a ship is called a 'she'!"

"How romantic!" the damsel sighed, as the moon rose over the Caribbean Sea; but, as I had to go on watch at 8 p.m., there was no time to impart further nautical instruction, even to such a keen student. She was the first of many passengers, eager for nautical knowledge, who brought me to realize that a ship's officer needs fenders if he wishes to avoid collisions—on deck.

Fifteen days out from Liverpool, we made our landfall at Turk's Island in the Bahamas, and steamed on through the Windward Passage (between Haiti and Cuba) to make port at Kingston, Jamaica, two days later, in that famous island of rum and pirates, the old "Port Royal" of the Spaniards. At this time, Kingston had an old-fashioned ramshackle appearance, two years before it was devastated by the terrible earthquake of 1907.

The island of Jamaica, 150 miles long and up to 50 miles wide, with mountain peaks rising to 7,000 feet, is in Lat. 18 deg. N., and has rich soil and a delightful climate, its shores washed by the Caribbean Sea. The island was discovered by Cristoforo Colon ("Columbus") in 1494, and annexed by him for Spain. His son was the first Spanish Governor of the island. The natives were at that time American Indians. The Spaniards established their capital, Port Royal, on the shore of the lagoon-like haven near the southeastern corner of the island.

The British took Jamaica from the Spaniards in 1655, and, after an earthquake destroyed Port Royal, built the town of Kingston in 1692. Large numbers of Negroes were brought from Africa to work as slaves in the sugar plantations, in accordance with the customs of that period, and the aboriginal American Indians were almost exterminated. The slave trade was stopped in 1807, and the slaves were freed in 1833, in response to the pressure of public opinion in Britain. Thereafter the Negroes, who had increased and multiplied, were employed for wages on

41

the sugar plantations, and in the rum distilling industry. Jamaica had then become, as it remains today, the principal supplier of sugar and rum to the British Isles.

We lay at the quay at Kingston for a week. All our passengers disembarked here, and all the cargo was discharged from the after hold, with Negro labour and our own steam-driven winches, derricks and running gear. In its place we took in the very cargo that would be expected at Jamaica—5,000 kegs of rum, which filled the hold to the deckhead. Some of this was for Liverpool, but most of it was to be delivered to the other ports we were bound for, on the Caribbean shore and the Gulf of Mexico. It was the best cure and preventive then known for yellow fever, malaria, cholera and other deadly diseases that raged in those parts of the world at that time.

Being busy on deck in the day-time, I had no chance to go ashore, except in the evenings, when a stroll through the colourful streets was more interesting than educative. We were warned to keep out of the lanes and alleyways, where many a sailor had been knifed when he was full of rum, and never seen or heard of again—murdered by robber gangs who took his clothes as well as any money or jewellery he carried, and dumped his body in the bay, weighted with iron or heavy stones.

The Negroes and Negresses were dressed in gaudy cotton prints, made in Manchester, and usually wore blue or red bandanas, spotted with white or yellow, knotted around their heads, in picturesque contrast with their shining ebony faces. The white residents strolled the streets wearing wide-brimmed Panama straw hats, with white linen suits, and usually smoking Havana cigars. The "tourist industry" at this stage had not been highly developed, and there were few attractions for the stranger ashore, in this city dedicated to the serious business of manufacturing and exporting rum.

When our valuable cargo was well stowed, we took in mails and some passengers for England and the intermediate ports we were bound for. The passengers included about thirty Jamaican Negroes who had been recruited to labour on the building of the Panama Canal. They were accommodated in the steerage.

Steaming southwards, 550 miles across the vivid blue Caribbean Sea, we arrived on the third day at the port of Colon, in Limon Bay, on the northern shore of the Isthmus of Panama.

Colon was named in honour of Columbus, who sailed into Limon Bay in 1502, but the town itself came into existence only in 1850, when it was selected as the seaport terminal of the Panama Railroad (completed in 1855).

The Isthmus of Panama, only 51 miles wide, connecting the continents of North and South America, was for centuries one of the worst obstacles to inter-ocean navigation in the world, equalled in that respect only by the Isthmus of Suez. The Isthmus lies in an east and west direction, washed by the Caribbean Sea on the northern side and the Pacific Ocean on the southern side, but the canal runs from N.W. to S.E.

The Spaniards made their settlement at Porto Bello, 20 miles to the east of present-day Colon. From there they made a track inland, and, on 25th September, 1513, Governor Balboa, standing "silent upon a peak in Darien", was the first European officially to discover the mighty Pacific Ocean.

Thereafter the Spaniards opened a road across the Isthmus, to the port of Panama, on the Pacific shore, and there built and equipped ships with which they explored the Pacific coasts of South and North America, and eventually far out into the Pacific to the Philippine Islands, New Guinea, Australia, Indonesia, and China.

The road from Porto Bello to Panama, crossing the Isthmus, was on the main route of trade from Spain to Peru, California, the Philippines, and China, but the expense of portage across the Isthmus was heavy, as horses, mules, and oxen could not live long in that pestilential torrid climate, where the fierce rays of the sun, only 9 degrees N. of the Equator, charged the air with humidity sucked from the sea and from the marshes filled with almost daily downpours of rain.

Human portage was used, of slaves and prisoners, but the loss of life was terrible, through ravages of yellow fever and malaria. It was not known then that these diseases were carried by the mosquitoes which bred in the swamps and foraged in clouds of millions to suck the blood of human beings or animals at nightfall.

The search for a sea route from the Atlantic to the Pacific, which would enable ships to sail from Europe or eastern America to China and India, led to the discovery of Magellan Strait in 1520, and the first passage of the Cape Horn route by the Dutch merchant adventurers, Schouten and Le Maire, in 1616.

For three centuries, Cape Horn sailors battled with the fierce westerly gales of the High South on the only open-water route from the Atlantic to the Pacific, to bypass the gigantic obstruction of America; yet that immense obstacle to navigation was only 51 miles wide at the Panama Isthmus, where a canal would save thousands of miles of sailing.

In 1850 the Panama Railway Company (a U.S. concern) obtained a concession to build a railroad across the Isthmus. The line was built in five years, not from Porto Bello, but from Colon, which came into existence expressly as the rail terminus port, to Panama. Thereafter, a steamship trade developed to and from the terminal ports, with rail transit across the Isthmus, but the cost of this rehandling remained heavy. An undersea electric telegraph cable was laid from Callao to Panama, connecting by a land line to Colon, and thence by undersea cable to Europe.

In 1879 a French company, headed by Ferdinand de Lesseps (engineer of the Suez Canal) obtained a concession to build a canal from Colon to Panama. Work went on for twenty years, with heavy loss of lives from "Yellow Jack", but made unsatisfactory progress, as the plan was for a canal at sea level, requiring very deep cuts through the spinal range of the Isthmus.

During the Spanish-American war of 1897, ships of the U.S.A. navy and seaborne supplies from the eastern States to the Pacific had to use the Cape Horn route or the Strait of Magellan, at a great strategical disadvantage. This caused the Government of the U.S.A. to intervene in the Panama Canal project. The Americans bought the concession from the French company, and negotiated a treaty of their own with the Republic of Panama in 1903. Work then began on the building of a high-level lock canal, to rise 85 feet above sea level at its highest point; but yellow fever, malaria and cholera again took heavy toll of lives.

In 1905, about the time the S.S. *Texan* arrived at Colon, the entire labour force had just been diverted from canal construction to the task of draining the swamps, and spraying the breeding places of mosquitoes with kerosene. This, and the installation of sewerage systems at Colon and Panama, enabled the mighty task of completing the canal to proceed, and the vitally significant waterway was opened in 1914. That event wrote "finis" to the sailing-ship route around Cape Horn, and for all practical purposes put an end to the great days of sail. The "short cut" through Panama, from New York to San Francisco, was 5,263 miles, as compared with 13,135 miles by the Strait of Magellan (for steamers), or about 14,000 miles via Cape Horn (for sailing vessels).

The Panama Canal route was commercially impracticable for sailing vessels, which would have to pay towage as well as canal dues to pass through; so sail inevitably went into the discard. Even though a few valorous old "windbags" lingered on, they were only the ghosts of the great tradition.

The S.S. *Texan* berthed at Colon. Our passengers disembarked, and our precious cargo of "medicine" was discharged as quickly as possible, so that we could clear out from this pestilential hole, where Yellow Jack was still taking toll of the heroes who were waging war on the mosquitoes. The town of Colon was a miserable looking place of wooden frame houses built on an island between Port Manzanillo and Limon Bay. It had a population of 3,000, mainly Jamaican Negroes and natives of mixed Spanish and Indian and Negro blood. A detachment of American marines and engineers were quartered there—heroes all, whose names are now almost unknown to fame, risking their lives to carry through one of the greatest feats of sanitation and engineering in human history. The bright green of the jungle came down to the shore in the precincts of the port, and we could only hope that our cargo of "jungle-juice" would help to allay the miseries of their existence.

At Colon we took on some passengers, then cleared out and headed northerly across the Caribbean Sea to Yucatan Strait (between Cuba and the main), then westerly across the Gulf of Mexico to Tampico, a run from port to port of some 1,500 miles, which took us a week. It was at this time that I made my first acquaintance with the Gulf Stream, that stupendous current which dominates navigation in the North Atlantic with its variations, and was to cause me to put on my thinking cap many a time in later years.

It is impossible to say just where the Gulf Stream originates. It is part of the great circulatory movement of the whole North Atlantic, due probably to the northeast trade winds and the rotation of the earth; but, as the stream circulates around the Gulf of Mexico (whence it takes its name) the water is warmed, and flows on northwards through the Florida Strait, running at an average velocity there of $3\frac{1}{2}$ knots; then flows northwards and northeastwards along the shore of the U.S.A., meeting the cold Labrador Current off the banks of Newfoundland, then passing eastwards with varying effects that reach as far as Greenland, Iceland, the British Isles and Norway. The Gulf Stream causes many things in the North Atlantic, including fogs and the melting of icebergs—a fickle jade that gives transatlantic navigators more worry than enough, as I shall have occasion to mention in later episodes of this narrative; but this was my introduction to it, at its nominal source.

Tampico, in Mexico, was an old Spanish—and, before that, Aztec—city. It is on the bank of the Panuco River, five miles upstream, and surrounded by lagoons and swamps. In Lat. 22 deg. N., Tampico is not as hot as Colon, but Yellow Jack had created ravages here also, as there were few sea-breezes to disperse the swarms of mosquitoes.

Our reason for calling at Tampico was to deliver 1,000 kegs of Nelson's Blood for the solace of the toilers on the oilfields, some 50 miles inland, and to load "case oil"—packed in four-gallon flat-sided tins, two to a deal case—brought to the port by rail from the oilfields. We were not allowed ashore, because of the danger of yellow fever, but swarms of mosquitoes acted as efficient carriers, from ship to shore, or from shore to ship. We took on a few passengers also, and, after four or five days, cleared out downriver and into the pure air and circulatory current of the Gulf.

Our next destination was New Orleans, on the banks of the Mississippi in Louisiana, U.S.A., a run from port to port of 710 miles. There we were to deliver 1,000 kegs of the Jamaica cure-all, and load baled cotton for the mills of Manchester.

Arrived off the mouths of the Mississippi, we dropped anchor at the South Pass, in water muddied far out to sea by a flood in the mighty river, to await a pilot.

The Chief Officer, in his immaculate "whites", went forward to the fo'c'sle head, to supervise letting go the anchor. I went with him, accompanied also by the carpenter and three seamen. The anchors had been unlashed on the previous day, and were now hanging overside at the bows, held in position by the friction brakes on the windlass, ready to let go.

The Captain was on the bridge, and rang the engines to SLOW and then STOP as we approached the anchorage. A seaman in "the chains", with the hand lead, kept singing out the depths in fathoms. By keeping the lead on the bottom, and noting the trend of the line, he could let the Captain know when the ship came to a dead stop, or began to drift astern: the critical moment for letting go the anchor.

It happened that one of the lady passengers from Jamaica had developed an admiration for the manly qualities of the Chief Officer. She took up a position immediately below the bridge, where she stood watching her hero with admiration as he prepared to "drop the killick". As the ship came to a standstill, the captain sang out, *"Let Go!"*

At this, the carpenter tried to unscrew the brake on the windlass, but it had become rusted, and would not budge. Despite strenuous efforts by the Chief Officer and the carpenter, the brake held fast.

After a few moments, Captain Lund became exasperated at the delay, and made one of the longest speeches of his nautical career. "What the hell's the matter forrard there?" he sang out, angrily, "LET GO THE ANCHOR!"

This rude remark to her hero was too much for the little lady. In a piping voice she sang out, "Don't you do it, Chief!"

The Captain shot a quick glance at the fair offender, swallowed hard, and controlled his feelings admirably. Luckily, at that moment, the brake yielded to persuasion, and the anchor went with a run, plunging to the bottom and dragging the cable over the windlass with a deafening rattle.

Soon a river pilot came out from Port Eads; and we proceeded slowly upriver for 110 miles to New Orleans, with the leadsmen chanting the marks most of the way. The pilot informed us that yellow fever was raging at New Orleans, and panic prevailed there, as people were dying at the rate of 200 a day. Among those who had died of the fever were the Archbishop and several other notabilities.

In these circumstances we had to proceed to the quarantine station. We dropped anchor there, and everyone on board was inoculated. Then we had to remain in quarantine for ten days, to see if anyone developed symptoms of the disease. This precaution was partly due to the fact that we had come from Colon and Tampico, notorious breeding places of yellow fever, and partly to protect us from infection at New Orleans.

Our anchorage was in the river, adjacent to miles of mud flats from which millions of mosquitoes flew on board every evening,

47

making the quarantine ineffectual, but probably the inoculation made us immune to their stings. The heat and humidity were very oppressive, and the inaction extremely tedious, but at last we were allowed to move to a berth at the quay, to discharge our cargo of the Jamaica Special, and to load bales of cotton to replace it.

All on board were warned not to go ashore; but, despite the risks, the Third Engineer and I—being young and foolish, and unwilling to leave the far-famed port of New Orleans without seeing something of its notorious gay life—decided to take the chance.

We went ashore one evening, and visited the "Old City"— founded by the French in 1718—a most picturesque place, with its narrow streets, buildings with beautiful iron-trellised balconies, and lively cabarets and "dives". New Orleans was ceded to the U.S.A. in 1803 by the "Louisiana Purchase"; but its population remained one of the most polyglot of the world, with a preponderance of French and Italians, and many Negroes and mixed breeds. We found that the "gay life" was raging even more furiously than usual, as the citizens had evidently decided to have a last fling before the Yellow Jack laid them low.

After a jolly good spree, we returned on board, and awaited with some trepidation to see if symptoms of the fever developed; but presumably our inoculation was effective, or luck was on our side, as we remained in normal health. We were exposed to as much danger from mosquitoes on board the ship lying at the wharf as we were when promenading the streets nearby.

After a week, we cast off the moorings and proceeded downriver with a pilot, homeward bound.

Steaming southeastwards for three days across the Gulf of Mexico, we rounded Key West at the end of the Florida Reefs, and passed through the Florida Strait to head for home, a run of some 5,000 miles from port to port.

I felt that I had gained a great deal of practical knowledge in the navigation of this colourful and historic part of the world, which was all new to me. Many years would go by before I again saw the Caribbean Sea and Key West, during the 1939-45 War, in circumstances which would give me a weighty responsibility; but as Second Officer of the S.S. *Texan*, away back in 1905, I was carefree, or nearly so.

We arrived back at Liverpool on 28th August, 1905 after a

voyage that had lasted a little over two months. My only worry then was whether I was getting my time in for Master. The Marine Superintendent of the Leyland Line assured me that it would be all right, and offered to sign me on for another voyage; but, on the principle of always going to the fountainhead of authority if possible, when in doubt, I sought and obtained an interview with the Examiner of Masters and Mates at the Board of Trade Office in Liverpool.

I explained the case to him. He advised me bluntly to leave the *Texan* and get a *real* Second Mate's job. "You're only wasting your time," he said.

That settled it. I went down to the dock and told the Marine Superintendent that I had decided to leave the *Texan*, and why. He was irate. "You've gone and spilled the beans to the Board of Trade!" he roared.

"Well, sir," I said. "The beans were spilled long ago. The B.O.T. knows very well that a Second Officer is not a Second Mate, but only a Third Mate, in reality. I can't afford to waste my time."

So ended my career with the Leyland Line, and I was "on the beach" again—unemployed and hoping for the best.

CHAPTER FIVE

In the Doldrums of Unemployment—I Decide to go Back to Sail—The Barque "Santa"—A Narrow Escape—I Join the S.S. "Jura"—My Third Voyage in Steam—The Captain's Daughter—Cape Flyaway—Buenos Aires—Magellan Strait—Tuning Vera's Piano—The Nitrate Ports of the West Coast—Antofagasta —Iquique—Pisagua—With Saltpetre to Hamburg—Aground in a Fog—Cardiff and Home —My Friend, Jim Watt—A Step Up the Ladder.

FOR three weeks I trudged the docks and pestered the clerks at the shipping offices—in vain! Nobody who owned a steamer wanted a young First Mate or Second Mate, when they could get older, more experienced men by merely beckoning. The iron entered into my soul, and I began to feel that my choice of a career as a mercantile marine officer had been a big mistake, as evidently I had entered an overcrowded profession.

If anyone had offered me a shore job at the equivalent of six pounds a month and keep, I would have "chucked" the sea forever—or was this only a passing mood? At the mature age of twenty-two, I almost agreed that my father had been right when he had warned me, seven years previously, that there was no security in the seafaring life.

This, too, was only a passing mood. On considering the matter further, I decided that the only way to get my time in as First Mate or Second Mate would be to go back to sail. After three weeks of hope dampened by despair, I now had a hankering for sails over my head and another voyage around Cape Horn. I made inquiries, and soon heard that J. J. Rae & Son, shipowners, needed a First Mate for their barque *Santa,* lying in the Wapping Dock, loading general merchandise for Valparaiso.

That would mean a westward passage, beating to windward, around Cape Horn, and all the hard work and discomforts of that life, which I could envisage only too well; but, between the devil and the deep blue sea, I preferred the sea. I therefore called on Mr Rae and offered my services. He offered me a job as First Mate at six pounds ten shillings a month, and my fate was sealed.

But not entirely! Like all owners of sailing vessels, Mr Rae had to be frugal to make ends meet. Instead of signing me on, there and then, he decided to defer that formality until the barque was ready to sail, which would be in three weeks. In the meantime he suggested that I should go on board daily, to supervise receiving the cargo, as Acting Mate, at thirty shillings a week.

The economy he would effect by this ruse, in the accounts of the voyage, would amount to only a few shillings; but every shilling counted, as all wise shipowners knew. I resented this meanness, as it appeared to me, but in the end his failure to sign me on prematurely—from his point of view—proved to be another of those turns of the wheel of fate which determine a young's man's destiny; for, if I had gone to sea again, in sail, as a First Mate, on a voyage of up to two years, I might never have returned to steam.

But who can anticipate the chances, big or little, which make or mar us? Certainly not a sailor "on the beach", with the soles of his boots wearing thin! He must take what offers, or starve. I therefore went down to the Wapping Dock, at 7 a.m. on a Monday in mid-September (1905) to begin work.

The *Santa* was a trim barque of 800 tons, but in a very grimy condition. All hands, including the Captain, had been paid off at the end of the previous voyage, and only a watchman was living on board. Her yards were bare, her paintwork and decks covered in city soot, her sides mottled with rust, and she looked altogether forsaken and forlorn.

At a glance I saw that plenty of elbow grease would be required to get her ready for sea, and that a First Mate's talents would need to be exercised to the utmost to work her to windward round the Horn; but I was in the mood for work.

Mr Rae arrived on his bicycle soon after 7 a.m., and explained the situation to me. "It's hard nowadays," he complained, "to pick up a general cargo here for Valpo! The steamers are taking away our trade to the West Coast, going through Magellan Strait. Why couldn't they leave the West Coast alone? There's plenty of other places they can go to. I've been trying for weeks to get a full cargo for this barque, but I've got to cut freights to compete with those dirty, smoking steamers. I wish I'd sent her to Cardiff to load coal, but nowadays the steamers are even carrying coal to the West Coast."

"Mark my words," he continued, grumpily, "in a few years there won't be a stitch of sail left under the British flag, and Old England will be beggared. All our wealth came from sail, didn't it? Yes, and yet they throw it away. Well, young man, this is what I want you to do. Stand by and receive the cargo I've managed to obtain, which the merchants will be delivering this week and next week. It will come in lorry loads, from a dozen different consignors. All you have to do is take delivery of it, check the packages and sign for them, and direct the carriers to stow it in the dockside warehouse, ready for loading. When we have enough for a full cargo, I'll get stevedores to load her, and riggers to bend the sails, and then I'll sign you on as First Mate for the voyage, after I've engaged a Master and made all the other arrangements."

He rode away on his bicycle, and I was left alone with my thoughts for an hour or two, until the first lorry load of cargo arrived. This was duly stowed in the warehouse, safe from weather and theft. Then I had to wait another hour or so, with nothing to do but sit and think, until another lorry arrived. So it continued for a fortnight, with nobody in a hurry, as the cargo steadily accumulated. In this situation I was neither a sailor nor a landlubber. My work was no more than that of a tally clerk.

On Saturday morning, Mr Rae paid me my thirty shillings; but, on the second Saturday, he expressed the opinion that he hoped it would be possible to load the barque and clear her out in the following week.

That evening, while sampling some of Cain's brew in a pub frequented by shipping men, I happened to hear that a Second

Mate was wanted in a steamer owned by Japp & Kirby, of Chapel Street. She was the S.S. *Jura,* a cargo-vessel trading to South America.

Throughout Sunday I tussled with my conscience, wondering if I was morally, though not legally, bound to give Mr Rae notice before applying to Japp & Kirby for the job in the *Jura.*

I put the point to my father, who expressed the opinion that it would serve Mr Rae right if I left him without notice, since he had engaged me only on a casual basis, instead of signing me on in proper form. That settled the moral and legal point, but there was still a practical point.

If I went looking for the job in the *Jura* on Monday morning, and failed to get it, Mr Rae might also sack me from the *Santa* for failing to turn up for work at the dock at 7 o'clock that morning. I would therefore be "on the beach" again, but this was a risk I decided to take. It was a crucial decision for me.

Before Japp & Kirby's office opened at 9 a.m., I was standing at the door, in company with an older man, obviously a seafarer, who arrived at the same time as I.

My heart sank when I saw him, as I supposed he was my rival for the Second Mate's job, and would probably be given the preference, because of his greater experience and poise. He chatted with me affably, without disclosing his identity, and then asked me if I was intending to apply for the position of Second Mate in the *Jura.*

"Yes," I said. "Are you applying for it too?"

He threw back his head and laughed. "Do I look like a Second Mate?" he asked. "As a matter of fact, I'm the Master of the *Jura!*"

At this moment, a clerk unbolted the door, and said to him, "Good morning, Captain!"

I stood aside as the Captain entered. He beckoned to me, and we sat on a bench in the waiting room, while he asked me my qualifications. He was Captain Raymond Parker, a Nova Scotian and an old sailing-ship man.

After a few questions, he said, "You'll do. You can start straight away, at seven pounds a month, and supply your own mattress and bedding. We're sailing today at 3 p.m., bound for Greenock to load whisky, then to Newport for coal, for Buenos Aires. Be on board at eleven o'clock!"

Having barely two hours to get ready, I hurried home, arriving there at 10 a.m., to find that Mr Rae had just been on his bicycle, looking for me, and wanting to know why I hadn't turned up for work. My mother, in her candid way, had told him that I had gone looking for a better job. At this he rode away in a huff.

As there was no time for me to see Mr Rae and explain matters to him, I wrote and posted a letter to him, apologizing for any inconvenience I may have caused him. I then, with my fond mother's help, hurriedly packed my sea-chest and sea-bag, rolled up a mattress, pillow, blankets and sheets, and, engaging a growler cab, arrived on board the *Jura* in good time.

So began my third voyage in steam. At last I had what I needed, a chance to get my time in for the Master Mariner's Examination, by oceangoing service as a bona fide Second Mate in a steamer; but, though I felt some twinges of conscience at chucking the *Santa,* I knew that Mr Rae would soon fill the vacancy, from the many well qualified sailing-ship officers "on the beach" in Liverpool at that time. As far as I was concerned, that sudden change of course in my career was decisive. I had finally, and perhaps providentially, escaped from the hardships and the allure of life under sail. . . .

The S.S. *Jura* was a new vessel, launched in 1904 (one year before I joined her), from the shipyards of W. Pickersgill & Sons, Sunderland. She was a steel-hulled, joggle-plated, single-screw, cargo-carrying steamer of 3,492 tons gross; 361 feet long, 46 feet beam, 17½ feet depth, with the "three island" profile of raised forecastle head, midship-house and poop, and two welldecks, each with two hatchways.

She was a well-found vessel of her class, with a triple-expansion engine developing 343 nautical horse-power, and a speed of ten knots. She did not carry passengers, and was in service as a collier and general cargo carrier to South American ports. The accommodation for her complement under the fo'c'sle-head and the poop and in the midship-house was ample but skimpy in its furnishings. The bridge deck was 198 feet long, the poop 31 feet and the fo'c'sle 38 feet. She could carry 4,000 tons of cargo.

Everything was shipshape and Bristol fashion, and she had steam up and was almost ready to clear out when I went on board at 11 a.m. on 3rd October, 1905. The Mate was James Watt, a young and keen man with exceptional personal contacts

54

in the nautical world. His uncle was Marine Superintendent of Japp & Kirby. He told me this, and added that his father was Commodore of the Cunard Line and Captain of the crack transatlantic twin-screw liner, R.M.S. *Campania!*

With such examples to inspire and guide him, Jim Watt had excellent prospects of advancement in the nautical world of keen competition; but he was also a fine seaman, and an efficient officer and jolly companion.

I was duly signed on as Second Mate. The Third Mate was Nils Askeland, a blond Norwegian, aged thirty, who had served his time in sail, and held a Norwegian Mate's ticket. He was a seaman as good as they're made, who had looked for a job in a British ship to improve his knowledge of the English language. The Engineers—Chief, Second, Third and Fourth—were Scots, as usual, and all pleasant fellows. We looked forward to an agreeable voyage in this new and well-found ship, with no passengers to bother us.

Some general cargo had been loaded at Liverpool, but, though lightly loaded, we did not need ballasting for the short coastal run of some 200 miles northwards, in narrow waters and fine weather, to Greenock, at the mouth of the Clyde. There we loaded 1,000 cases of whisky and some heavy cases of agricultural machinery for Buenos Aires. This cargo was stowed in the two holds evenly, but might need some restowing at our next port, Newport in Monmouthshire, South Wales, where we were to proceed to load coal.

Handling cargo was almost a pleasure with our steam winches and derricks. After a stay of two days at Greenock, we cleared out, and in two days more arrived at Newport, in the busy Bristol Channel—my first visit to that historic waterway, which in earlier days was Britain's main gate to the Western Ocean.

Here we loaded 3,000 tons of best quality South Wales coal for the Argentinian railways—a valuable cargo indeed of "black diamonds", even if everything was smothered in black dust while we loaded it; but that scarcely mattered, as there were no passengers.

Then came a surprise, as one day a lorry arrived alongside, with a small upright piano on it, and Captain Parker personally superintended hoisting it inboard, and stowing it, lashed to the bulkhead, in the dining-saloon.

Watt, Askeland and I were puzzled, wondering what was the purpose of a piano in a collier, but I was secretly pleased, as among my underdeveloped talents was the ability to play a piano—a very little, "by ear", mainly. I thought I might be able to have a go at it sometimes, to relieve the tedium of the voyage.

Then Captain Parker explained: "This is for my daughter, Vera, to practise on. She'll be coming with us as a passenger!"

That afternoon the Captain's daughter came on board with her luggage. She would be the only female in the ship. She was a delicate looking slip of a girl, eighteen years of age, but full of self-confidence, and well aware of her privileged position, which would compel the whole ship's company of twenty-five strong men to mind their language and behaviour generally in the presence of a lady. What a ruddy nuisance!

From Newport we had a short run along the coast, past Cardiff, to Barry Dock, where we took in 500 tons of anthracite for a special order in Buenos Aires, and filled our bunkers with steaming-coal and our tanks with fresh water for the voyage. The ship was now loaded to the Plimsoll mark and ready to clear out for foreign parts.

Wisps of fog obscured visibility in the Bristol Channel, a portent of the British winter from which we were escaping to the blue skies and bright sunshine of the Southern Hemisphere. Off Lundy Island, the pilot left us, and Captain Parker set course for Buenos Aires.

The three Mates stood watch four hours on and eight off. My watches were from 12 midnight to 4 a.m., and from 12 noon to 4 p.m. The Mate relieved me from 4 to 8, and the Third Mate followed him from 8 to 12.

The officers' cabins were under the bridge, next to the saloon. Before many days had gone by, all three of us were suffering from insomnia in our watches below, due to Vera's love of music, which led her to practise scales and exercises on the piano for hours on end, whenever she felt inclined. This often happened to be when one or another of the Mates below was dropping off to well earned and needed slumber.

Though she looked so delicate, Vera had the ability to thump the piano—and I mean thump—like a blacksmith wielding a hammer on an anvil, and to strike more wrong notes than right ones. The Captain was enchanted by his daughter's musical prowess, and one day he said proudly to the Mate, "What do you think of Vera's execution?"

"I would heartily approve of it," said the Mate.

Soon we were in the fine weather latitudes, and churning along beneath a sunny sky, far from land and from the busy lanes of shipping traffic, sighting only an occasional steamer or sailing vessel, with wide sea-room. In these conditions the officers of the watches, during daylight hours, could safely leave the bridge for awhile and potter around on deck, to vary the monotony with some sailorizing, such as splicing wires, sewing canvas, chipping iron rust, or freshening up paintwork, and going up to the bridge only occasionally. The man at the wheel would keep a lookout and blow a whistle if he sighted anything.

Captain Parker spent much of his time in daylight hours pacing to and fro on the bridge, checking the compass course and the ship's position by the readings of the patent log at hourly intervals. He was therefore pleased to see the Mates working with the seamen on deck, as long as the weather was clear.

Vera considered that she had a right to go up to the bridge whenever she felt inclined to talk to her Daddy. This was a serious breach of rules, but the Captain was indulgent, and gave her the run of the ship. She treated the Mates with disdain, considering that we were beneath the notice of such a privileged and important person as the Captain's daughter.

In the mornings, we took sights for longitude, and at noon for latitude, and handed our calculation of the noon position to the Captain each day when he pricked her off on the chart.

Being an old sailing-ship man, a Nova Scotian, and a Blue Nose, the Captain—who had obtained his Master's Certificate thirty years previously—had old-fashioned ideas. He mistrusted the rating of the chronometers, and told us bluntly that he had no objection to our taking sights but he had no faith in our calculations, as far as longitude was concerned. He said that latitude was his main stay, as nothing could go wrong with that; but for longitude he would stick to his own dead reckoning based on the compass course and the patent log.

We of the younger generation, while aware that our calculations depended on the accuracy of the chronometer, were convinced that our sights were reasonably good. The ship did not have wireless, and consequently we could not detect changes of rate by means of wireless time-signals; but she carried three chronometers, so that one could be checked against the others, and any change of rate detected. These instruments were always taken, in home ports, to the nautical opticians for checking and correction, and a daily rate of each supplied. Consequently, the

Mate and I smiled to ourselves when the Old Man told us that he thought our longitude was "all wrong".

One day at noon, when, according to our calculations, we were 300 miles from the entrance to the River Plate, the Captain commented, "You might be right, and you might be wrong, but keep a sharp lookout all the same!"

The Third Mate took over the watch on the bridge from eight to noon, while the Mate and I went below, but the Captain remained on the bridge.

Vera mercilessly thumped the piano—which had now become hopelessly out of tune through the slackening of its strings in the tropics—while the Mate and I tried to rest in our cabins.

As I was to go on watch at noon, I did not undress, but tried to study a little for my examination. Presently, thank heavens, Vera stopped strumming, and went up on the bridge with Daddy. Soon afterwards the Captain raised a great shout that sent me hurrying to the bridge. "There!" he sang out to me. "You put us 300 miles from land, but there's the land on the starboard bow, only twenty miles distant! A fine bunch of navigators you are!"

These remarks took me flat aback. I glanced at Askeland, who was standing silent and red-faced, but his left eyelid flickered in a wink which put me on guard. The helmsman stood like a graven image, staring impassively ahead. We all knew better than to contradict the Captain. The dark line on the horizon to the southwestward certainly looked like land, but I believed it to be a cloud-bank. To add to my confusion Vera excitedly squealed, "Oh, yes, Daddy, it's the land! I can see palm trees growing on it!"

I had a look through the telescope, and studied the cloud-bank—for such it was, I felt sure. A feeling of pity—the compassion of the young for the old—swept over me. I realized that the Captain, grand old seaman that he was, was afflicted with failing eyesight, and did not know it, or could not admit it.

I longed to say to Vera, "Those palm trees are growing on Cape Flyaway", but I curbed my tongue, and went below to arouse the Mate from his blissful slumbers. I explained the situation to him, as I understood it. He swore like a trooper, and hurriedly dressed; but, when he came on the bridge, Cape Flyaway was already dispersing, and the Captain and his daughter had gone below for tea.

Twenty-four hours later, we made a perfect landfall off the entrance to the River Plate, and the Captain made no further scathing comments on our navigation on that voyage.

We lay at Buenos Aires (or "B.A." as seamen called it) for a fortnight, discharging cargo. Vera went ashore to stay with the ship's agent and his wife and family, while the ship in her absence was covered in coal dust and profanity. We then took in ballast, as we had orders to proceed by the Strait of Magellan to the West Coast, to load nitrates.

Askeland and I went ashore together occasionally, to enjoy the night life of B.A., to the extent of our limited cash resources. When the time came to get up steam for our departure, three coal trimmers and two stokers—all Liverpool Irishmen—were missing. They had gone on the booze and had been shanghaied into other ships.

After a few hours delay, our agent completed negotiations with a crimp to deliver five substitutes on board, at twenty dollars a head—these being also Liverpool Irishmen who had been shanghaied from some other ship. So the old game was still going on. Our new men, after the booze had been sweated out of them in a few watches down below, were as handy at their work as those we had lost.

Steaming southwards along the coast of Argentina, we arrived in five days off Cape Virgins, the eastern entrance to Magellan Strait, 1,250 miles from B.A.

There were no pilots. We had to find our way through the Narrows to the port of Punta Arenas (Sandy Point), a Chilean town 100 miles inland from Cape Virgins. There we dropped anchor overnight, as we needed daylight to navigate the western part of the passage, another 200 miles from Punta Arenas to the Pacific Ocean.

This was all new ground to me. Magellan Strait is one of the most remarkable waterways in the world, its channel landlocked by mountains and cliffs of reddish rock, winding in and out like a fjord—at some places several miles wide and at others very narrow and dangerous. The Strait is entirely within the territory of Chile, even at its eastern entrance. It separates the large and almost uninhabited island of Tierra del Fuego from the main: and to the south of Tierra del Fuego is Cape Horn, on a small island.

Great was the courage of Magellan and his men, in 1520, when they sailed in their small ships into this fearsome defile, which must have seemed to them like the Mouth of Hell, leading to the unknown; and great too was their endurance, and the endurance of seamen for a century after them, who could work through the Strait only by scouting ahead with the ships' boats for 300 miles, sounding all the way, and dropping the anchor at nightfall among the cliffs and peaks probably inhabited by demons: yet this was the only seaway, known to the valiant Spaniards of that great period in Spanish history, leading to the golden land of the Incas, Peru, and beyond to the Philippines.

Even when the Cape Horn route was discovered by the Dutchmen, Schouten and Le Maire, in 1616, its howling westerly gales made the passage to the westward around the Horn hazardous and sometimes impossible, so that Magellan Strait continued to be used, at least by small sailing vessels, and then came increasingly into use again after the invention and development of steam propulsion.

Punta Arenas, on the northern side of the Strait, was a small Chilean town with some export trade in cattle and hides, but inhabited mainly by Indians. It was a "free port", with no customs dues or harbour dues.

Next day we reached Indian Inlet, and lay at anchor a cable's length from a cliff, on the face of which were painted in large letters the names of many ships which had passed through the Strait, some of the names in seemingly inaccessible places.

Not to be outdone, Nils Askeland got a pot of paint and a brush, and rowed in the ship's dinghy to the foot of the cliff. As he had been reared on the shore of a Norwegian fjord, he understood the art of rock climbing. He crawled up the cliff like a fly on a wall, painted the name *Jura* higher than any other —while we watched him with anxiety and admiration—then safely descended and rowed back to the ship, grinning with the modest pride of a hero.

On the third day we continued the westward passage, steaming at full speed, thanks to good Admiralty charts, and arrived at nightfall off Cape Pillar, at the western side of the Strait. From there we steamed full ahead into a howling westerly gale which whipped the waters of the misnamed Pacific Ocean into a furious contrast with the placid, glassy surface of the Strait through which we had threaded our way.

If ever I had doubted the superiority of steam over sail, those doubts were ended that night, as the *Jura* steamed into the eye of the gale, thrusting into the combers which broke and foamed

60

along her sides, flooding the forrard welldeck, and flinging icy spume and spray high over the bridge, as we clawed off the land in a manner which would have been utterly impossible under sail—that is, on a due westerly course in a westerly gale.

Yet the merits of our headway were not those of seamanship, but of engineering. The men who had built the ship and her engines, and the greasers, stokers and trimmers down below, sweating as they fed her furnaces with coal, provided the motive power, as the ship fought the gale and drew steadily away from the dreadful ironbound Patagonian coast of Chile which lay astern to our lee.

At dawn we were well to seaward, and hove-to for a few hours, with the screw turning slowly, until the gale blew itself out. Then we headed northwards, taking the rollers abeam, as the storm gradually abated.

We steamed full ahead, never more than from fifty to 100 miles offshore, into steadily moderating weather, and then into the fine weather, light airs, and quiet seas beneath the brilliant blue and cloudless skies northwards of Valparaiso. The steaming distance from Cape Pillar to our first port of destination, Antofagasta, was some 1,600 miles, which took us only six days.

As the weather cleared, Vera resumed her piano thumping, which now became intolerable, even to her father, as the piano was so painfully out of tune. He had disregarded the opportunity of having it tuned in B.A., and now, to my surprise, asked me if I knew anything about tuning pianos. I told him that I had seen it done, and understood the principles, or thought that I did, and that I would be willing to try to tune it.

"Ah, well," said the Captain, "you probably couldn't make it any worse than it is, so do your best!"

Vera hovered around anxiously as I began work, and frequently asked me if I was sure of what I was doing. I told her I was doing my best, as the Captain ordered, but, having no tuning fork, no tools except a shifting spanner borrowed from the Second Engineer, and no experience as a piano tuner, I succeeded only in making the instrument much worse than it had been before I touched it. This was taking a big chance, but even Vera knew it was so hopelessly out of tune as to be unplayable.

She valiantly tried a few times to play it, but the Captain then closed it, and locked it, and pocketed the key, saying to

me as he did so, "I've an idea that you ruined it on purpose!"
Perhaps he wasn't far wrong. . . .

After we had passed the latitude of Talcahuana, and then Valparaiso, we sighted almost every day one or more windjammers, sailing slowly northwards in the light airs and drifting with the current along the shore. We overtook them, and exchanged signals of identification. Some were arriving from Australia with coal, or in ballast, after running the easting down; others were from Europe with coal or general merchandise, into fine weather at last after taking a hammering for weeks beating to the westward around Cape Horn. These were nearly all bound for West Coast ports to pick up cargoes of nitrates. They included some stylish Germans of the famous "P" line. Several we saw were American "Down Easters", the flying Cape Horners, wooden built, with skysails above the royals, sailing from the Eastern States of the U.S.A. to San Francisco, Portland (Oregon), Seattle, or Hawaii, for cargoes of wheat, lumber or sugar.

The west coast of South America was the last great rendezvous of sail in those dying days of the windjammers. There they gracefully fluttered their white wings in their final, ineffectual defiance of tramp steamers—such as the *Jura*—which were now beginning to take even the coal trade and the nitrate trade away from them, to starve them to death.

I remembered the lamentations of Mr Rae, and wondered where his barque *Santa* might now be. Tossing about or hove-to off the Horn, I supposed, battling against the westerlies, with her decks flooded and her crew half starved, but undaunted. But for a chance remark heard in a pub, I would have been in the thick of her ordeals at that moment. My thoughts went out to her, and I felt like the humble person who said of the unredeemed sinner: "There, but for the Grace of God, go I. . . ."

A dozen sailing vessels were at anchor in the Bay of Antofagasta when we arrived. Some had been there for weeks, even months, waiting for cargoes of nitrate. We anchored half a mile offshore, and almost immediately our agent came on board. He had been informed by telegram from B.A. of the exact date of our expected arrival. Such a prediction was almost impossible for sailing vessels, which made port as and when they could.

The agent had succeeded in obtaining 1,000 tons of nitrate for us, from the mines in the interior. This was in transit and expected within a week. As this would not be a full cargo for us, he had telegraphed to other nitrate ports, and reserved 1,000 tons at Iquique, and 1,000 tons at Pisagua, to be held for our arrival on dates which could be exactly predicted.

What hope had the old windjammers against such competition? We were taking the bread out of their mouths, but there is no sentiment in business.

While we lay at anchor for a week, the crew were kept busy painting round the deck and topsides, in the perpetual war against rust. The bottoms of steamers were seldom fouled with seagrass and barnacles, as were the bottoms of sailing vessels. The vibration shook most of these growths off, and steamers seldom lay for lengthy periods at anchor, as the windjammers usually did, waiting for charters or cargoes. Too much capital was tied up in steamers to be left lying idle, and the steamship companies generally had better shore organizations for collecting and handling cargoes than the sailing-ship owners had.

Captain Parker invited several of the Masters of the windjammers on board the *Jura*—some of them old shipmates or cronies of his—and entertained them suitably. They came off in their gigs, rowed by their apprentices, in traditional style, and we did not forget the hungry days of our own apprenticeship. The other two Mates and I got some cakes, sweet biscuits, tinned fruit and other luxuries from the steward and handed them to the boys, who zestfully polished them off then and there.

Our cargo of bagged nitrates was brought out from the shore in lighters, and hoisted by the steam winches into the holds; but, in accordance with west-coast traditions, only one stevedore went down below into each hold to stow the bags. These men were of extra strong physique, and acknowledged experts at stowing nitrates, besides being apparently immune to the fumes of the nitrate which gave ordinary mortals a headache if breathed in for too long.

It was fascinating to see the stevedore shouldering a bag of nitrate from the sling, and dumping it exactly where it should lie, to make a stack which would be immovable in the heaviest weather. The weight of the nitrates was such that a full cargo occupied only part of the space in a vessel's hold, or holds; but it lay so inertly that no "shifting boards", or lashings, or tommings were necessary.

From Antofagasta we steamed northwards some 250 miles to Iquique, the principal nitrate port of the West Coast, where

63

we celebrated Christmas Day of 1905 and New Year's Day of 1906, in shimmering hot weather, and loaded some more nitrate. There were not less than twenty windjammers in this port, some of them having arrived months previously after a terrible hammering in the winter gales off Cape Horn, which in July, August and September of 1905 were the worst recorded in history. The town of Iquique had few attractions to offer, but the celebrations in the ships were lively, with singing of chanties, ringing of bells and firing of rockets to accompany the splicing of the main brace.

Our Captain had a coop of a dozen hens, which he had taken on board at Newport for the purpose chiefly of supplying himself and Vera with new-laid eggs. They had performed this duty fairly well throughout the voyage, being kept well fed with wheat. On fine days and in port they were allowed out for exercise on the after-deck for short periods, and had come to no harm; but it happened that a bag of nitrate burst when being handled inboard at Iquique, and some of the grains of saltpetre were spilled around the hatch. These lay disregarded until the hens discovered them, and began pecking at them eagerly, apparently considering them grit for their gizzards.

Next morning all the hens were dead. Poor Vera! Life at sea was one thing after another, for her.

From Iquique we steamed northwards forty miles to Pisagua, another nitrate port with an open bay, in which several windjammers were at anchor, in the deep water. We too anchored, and, after a week's delay began loading from the lighters, all the work being done by shore labour, with the aid of our steam winches.

When loading was completed, we hove up the anchor with the steam driven windlass, and steamed out of the bay. Just that! No rousing send-off; no trudging for hours around the capstan; no singing of the full-throated chanty chorus of "Rolling Home"; no running aloft to shake out sail; no pully-hauly to hoist the sails smartly. . . .

Just crisp orders from the bridge—"Heave away, Mister Mate . . .", and, later, *"Full ahead!"*

And we were homeward bound.

There was one problem in steamers which windjammers did not have to worry about—bunker-coal—and with this was an allied problem of carrying enough fresh water for the boilers

64

as well as for the needs of the ship's complement.

Our bunkers and tanks had been filled when we left Buenos Aires, but we had to take in both coal and water on the West Coast for the homeward run. This we did at Pisagua, the coal being obtained from a stack on shore brought from Australia in windjammers, which thus served a vital need of the steamers ousting them from the world's trade routes.

Bunker-coal was a high price on the West Coast, but, even with full bunkers and tanks, we did not have enough coal and fresh water to carry us from Pisagua, via Magellan Strait, to our destination port, Hamburg, a run of some 10,000 miles.

A windjammer could sail 20,000 miles, if necessary, without putting in to an intermediate port. She could keep the seas as long as she had food and drinking water—and lime-juice to prevent scurvy; but an average steamer's limit of range, without replenishments of bunker-coal and boiler water, was from 5,000 to 6,000 miles.

We took in coal and water on our homeward run at Punta Arenas, but even then we had to put in to Las Palmas, in the Canary Islands, for replenishments to carry us to Hamburg.

Windjammers were slower, but their working expenses per ton mile of cargo were very much lower than in steamers, and the capital investment in them much smaller than in steamers, in proportion to tonnage; but the twentieth century was the Age of Machinery, and of Speed at Any Price. Those factors wrote *Finis* to the Days of Sail. . . .

We arrived at Hamburg in mid-March, 1906, and began to discharge immediately. The Captain's wife was on the quay to greet him and her long-lost daughter, who had benefited greatly in health by her prolonged pleasure cruise in summer climes.

Mrs Parker and Vera went home by train and channel steamer. We didn't miss Vera! She had a refining influence on our rough manners throughout the voyage, but we didn't go to sea to be refined.

Our orders at Hamburg were to proceed from there in ballast to Cardiff to load coal. When we cleared the mouth of the Elbe, the sea was dead calm, and a thick fog was closing in. "A nice kettle of fish!" the Captain growled. We got a bearing on Scharhorn, then proceeded on our compass course, going slow, with extra lookouts and our steam whistle continually blaring its warning message, and visibility at less than fifty yards.

It was an eerie and unnerving experience—my first time on the bridge of a steamer in a peasoup fog, and that in the North Sea, where hundreds of other vessels, great and small, in steam and in sail, were crawling and feeling their way, wailing like lost souls. We thought, or hoped, that the fog would soon lift; but, instead, it thickened.

The Captain now developed superhuman powers of endurance, as he remained on the bridge almost continuously and did not take off his clothes and boots, or lie down, for two days of intense alertness and anxiety. The Mates continued to work three watches, but we never undressed, and lay on our bunks in our watches below for only fitful snatches of sleep.

On the second night out, as we were now working two watches, I finished my watch on the bridge at 8 p.m. and went below, relieved by the Mate. I was feeling very uneasy, as I knew that the Captain and Mate were doubtful of our position. Just as I was dozing off, the ship struck something with a dull thud, then dragged heavily over it in a series of bumps. I jumped out at once and sprang up to the bridge. The engines were already stopped.

"Get a hand-line and sound all round!" the Captain sang out to me. We could hear the deep-toned fog signal of a lightship, seemingly far off. Soundings showed that the *Jura* was in seven fathoms all round. I reported the soundings as I made them. We had come to a standstill.

"Let go the anchor!" the Captain sang out. I ran forrard with Askeland and two seamen, and we dropped the killick. I then hurried to the bridge with Askeland for further orders. The Chief Engineer was already conferring with the Captain and the Mate. "I think she scraped over a sandbank and has freed herself," said the Captain. "Tell Chips to take soundings in the bilges, and see if she's sprung a leak."

The carpenter attended to this. "By all that's holy," the Captain vowed, "I won't move her from here till this blasted fog lifts, if we have to stay here till doomsday. If we haven't scraped a hole in her bottom, the Saints are on our side."

Presently the carpenter reported that there were no signs of a leak. "Good!" said the captain. "But here we are and here we'll stay!"

Everyone agreed heartily. At 7 a.m., getting daylight, the fog cleared a little, and we saw several fishing smacks anchored half a mile away. I went over to them in the dinghy. They were French, with not a word of English among them. They appeared suspicious of me, thinking that I might have something to do with the Government or the Fisheries Department. I knew no French worth mentioning, but I waved to them in friendly greeting and sang out "Bonjour!" which was almost the only French word I could think of.

I ranged alongside the nearest smack, made the dinghy fast, and clambered aboard. Putting on a look of the utmost bewilderment, I pointed to the *Jura*, shook my head in a puzzled fashion, shrugged my shoulders, pointed in the direction of the distant fog signal, looked up to heaven, shrugged my shoulders again, and kept on saying "Where? Where?"

This mime proved effective, as the skipper produced a chart of that region of the North Sea. It was the dirtiest chart I have ever seen, creased, smudged and almost illegible. With a horny thumb he pointed to a spot on the chart, which, with some peering, I was able to identify as the West Hinder Light Vessel. Then with much volubility in French and pointing to the chart, he conveyed to me the exact position of our ship, and the direction in which we should steer to be clear of any more shoals.

I thanked him, by saying many times, "Merci, beaucoup!" which I suddenly remembered.

Then I pulled back to the *Jura* in the dinghy, but by the time I got back on board, a bleary sun was beginning to peer through the thinning fog, and, half an hour later, we got under way in full visibility, and reached Cardiff without further incident.

We berthed at Cardiff on 2nd April, 1906, after a voyage that had lasted six months since our departure from Liverpool. A diver went down to examine the bottom, rudder and propeller, but he found no damage.

On this voyage I had become very friendly with the First Mate, Jim Watt. When the *Jura* berthed at Cardiff we were given home leave, and travelled up together by train to Liverpool. On the way there, Jim surprised me a little by saying that he would speak to his uncle, the Marine Superintendent of Japp & Kirby, to see if he could get a job for me as First Mate.

Not being fully aware of the importance of "knowing somebody who knows somebody", I thanked him, but did not seriously expect anything to come of his offer.

A few days after I arrived home, I received a letter from Japp

& Kirby, informing me that I had been promoted to First Mate in the Company's service, at eight pounds ten shillings a month, and ordering me to proceed without delay to Sunderland to join a new ship ready for her trials there, the S.S. *Shira*, Captain J. Cann.

First Mate of a steamer on her maiden voyage! Well, that was a step up the ladder; but whether my promotion was due to my merits, or to the magical power of influence, or to sheer luck, I had no means of knowing.

CHAPTER SIX

First Mate of the S.S. "Shira"—A Maiden Voyage—A Crabby Captain—Ham, Turkey and Champagne—Bugs in the Fo'c'sle—Loading Coal at Barry Dock—Bound for the Mysterious East—Gibraltar and the Mediterranean—Port Said—The Suez Canal—The Red Sea—We Arrive at Bombay—Coolies and Chloride of Lime—A Fakir's Trick—I Go Down with Dengue Fever—Cargo at Karachi —Home Again.

ARRIVED by train at Sunderland, I put up at the Royal Hotel overnight. Next morning, after breakfast, I went in a horse-drawn cab with my dunnage to Pickersgill's shipyard, where the S.S. *Shira*, having been launched a few months previously, was in the final stages of being fitted out for her trials and her maiden voyage. In her size and design she was a sister ship of the *Jura*. I joined her on 9th April, 1906.

Leaving my sea-chest, canvas bag and bedding at the foot of the gangway, I went on board. A large number of men were busy, putting the finishing touches to the fittings, and splashing paint on, here and there. She certainly didn't look as though she'd be ready for her trials in two days time, as scheduled.

I noticed a stocky, pugnacious looking man in a tight fitting grey suit. He was standing on deck watching the men at work Going up to him, I asked, "Are you a dockyard manager?"

He glared at me, and snapped, "No. I'm the Master of this vessel. Who are you?"

"My name is Bisset," I told him. "I've been sent from Liverpool by Japp & Kirby to join the *Shira* as First Mate."

"Is that so?" he commented, looking me up and down with obvious dislike. "Then what d'ye mean by strolling on board at nine o'clock in the morning? Don't you know work begins at seven o'clock? I've been here for two hours waiting for you!"

Somewhat taken aback at being addressed in this brusque manner, I controlled my feelings, and said quietly, "My instructions are to join the ship today, and here I am. What do you want me to do?"

Captain Cann had been informed, in a letter from the Marine Superintendent of Japp & Kirby, Captain Watt, of my appointment, and knew that I had been Second Mate in the *Jura*. "I suppose you're a special friend of the M.S., eh?" he sneered.

"Not specially," I said, curtly. I did not like the suggestion that I had gained promotion by favouritism, but I had no desire to be at loggerheads with the Captain, and I was puzzled at his hostility.

It did not occur to me until later in the voyage that he suspected I might "tell tales" on him—that is, report to the Marine Superintendent any irregularities I might notice in his dealings with stevedores, ship chandlers and others in foreign ports, who sometimes gave secret commissions (known as "New Hats") to the masters of cargo-vessels in connection with purchases of ship's suppplies and the like. Such matters were at that time quite beyond my experience, and I had certainly no instructions or any desire to "tell tales" on Captain Cann. He was probably annoyed at having such a young First Mate—I had not yet turned twenty-three—who was too green to be taken into his confidence in the matter of New Hats.

"Well," he said, gruffly, "you and the Second and Third Mates will sign articles at 11 a.m. today. In the meantime, you'll be able to find your own way around. See the dockyard foreman, and check over with him the list of stores on board."

The accommodation for the officers in the *Shira* was the same as in the *Jura*—skimpily furnished. The First Mate's cabin had a bunk with no bedding, a washbasin without running water, and little more. I dumped my baggage in it, and began work. The task of checking the stores turned out to be a lengthy one, at this first fitting-out of the ship. Practically everything in her, including the fittings and fixtures, as well as her gear and provisions, was listed on the specification. She was to be handed over to the owners, ready to put to sea immediately.

The Chief Engineer had been for several days inspecting and testing the engines and other machinery. It took me the best part of two days to go over her from stem to stern, and from truck to keelson, examining everything in detail, including all cordage, lamps, the anchors and cables, flags and all gear above and below deck, and the equipment on the bridge—everything being brand new—as well as the usual ship's stores required on a voyage.

In the meantime the shipyard workers had cleared up the chaos on deck, and got her into seagoing trim in a lively and efficient manner. Stone ballast was taken in, as we were to proceed in ballast to Barry Dock in South Wales, to load coal for Bombay. The crew were duly signed on. The full complement consisted of the Master, Mate, Second Mate, Third Mate, Boatswain, six Able Seamen, Chief Engineer, Second, Third and Fourth Engineers, donkey-man, six firemen, four trimmers, cook, carpenter and steward—29 men all told.

There is a distinct feeling of a special occasion when a ship moves from the builders' yards, to make her first voyage. Even if she is only a tramp, as the *Shira* was, this is her first and perhaps her only day of festive glory, when all who have had a hand in fashioning her take pride in seeing their work well finished and put to the test.

At the appointed time—10 a.m. on 11th April, 1906—the Engineers had steam up and everything was in readiness. A party of officials came on board. They included directors of the shipbuilding firm, W. Pickersgill & Sons, with the heads of their departments, architects and engineers; and representatives of the owners, Japp & Kirby, including the Marine Superintendent, Captain Watt, who had come from Liverpool; besides officials of the Board of Trade, Lloyds Insurance, the Port Authority, a Marine Surveyor and Compass Adjuster, and representatives of the local Press and shipping newspapers.

To entertain this party, and suitably celebrate the occasion, Pickersgills had sent on board a large hamper containing a ham, a roast turkey and all the trimmings, together with a supply of champagne, whisky and beer: all this in charge of an elderly butler garbed in "tails", who with our steward set the tables for the repast in the saloon.

71

With a pilot on board, we towed out into the stream, and cast off the tug on reaching open water, at noon, in a light fog. Then the *Shira's* trials began, as we ran a measured distance—from lightship to lightship—at full speed for about twenty minutes offshore, logging ten knots, while the experts prowled around, scrutinizing everything. Then tests were made of the steering, and of running at half speed, and slow, and going astern. Then the anchors were let go, to test them and the cables and the windlass. Next, all steam cargo winches and the steering engine were left running for ten minutes.

The Marine Superintendent, the Captain and the Chief Engineer being satisfied, and no one else raising any objection, the documents were signed, transferring the S.S. *Shira* from the builders to the owners. All the "heads" then repaired to the saloon, and made short work of polishing off the victuals and grog, with speeches of mutual congratulation, and toasts wishing her a long and prosperous life.

The Compass Adjuster, slightly fuddled with seasickness or champagne, did his best or worst with the compass, and, at 2 p.m., the tug, which had been standing by, ranged alongside to take off the shore party.

All the officials, with jovial farewells, climbed unsteadily down the accommodation ladder, followed by the dignified butler—now also jovial and unsteady, as he, in company with our steward, had hastily finished off a bottle of champagne they had managed to keep aside.

The empty hamper was lowered to the deck of the tug, which shoved off, circled around us once, and gave three farewell blasts of her steam whistle, to which we replied, as she headed for the shore, and we were left alone with our ship.

"Heave away, Mister Mate!" the Captain ordered. I hove up the anchor, the engine telegraph clanged FULL AHEAD, and the S.S. *Shira's* seagoing career had begun.

So, too, began my responsibilities as Mate—second in command of a vessel of 3,495 tons—at the age of 22 years, 9 months, but I was then a seasoned salt with 7½ years of seagoing experience, and felt fairly confident that I would be able to do whatever could be reasonably required of me in that position, even though I was at first worried by Captain Cann's surly attitude to me.

He had been raised in a tough school, but so had I, as far as my experience went. He had ascertained that I was getting in my time to sit for the Master Mariner's examination. It would be within his power to give me a bad discharge at the end of the voyage, which would militate against my getting a Master's Certificate.

This put me at a disadvantage which he was quick to realize. I was compelled to humour him to a certain extent, and to put up with slights which otherwise would have been intolerable; yet, as I now view it, he was perhaps only trying, in his rough way, to keep me up to the mark, and to complete my nautical education, by finding fault, throughout the voyage, with almost everything I did, and never bestowing the slightest word of encouragement or approval, let alone praise; so that I soon became heartily tired of his snarling and grumbling, and carried on with my work to the best of my ability, not caring whether it pleased him or not.

Steaming along the east coast of England, we worked two watches—four hours on and four off—with the Second Mate, an older man than I, relieving me on the bridge. As soon as we got well under way in the North Sea, thick fog closed in, and the Captain came on to the bridge and remained there, alert for the dangers of collision or running aground.

He was a careful navigator, and we steered good courses from lightship to lightship. The fog remained thick for twelve hours, but, when I came on deck next day at 4 p.m., the weather had cleared, and we were doing full speed through the busy Straits of Dover.

On arrival at Barry, we had to moor between buoys in the centre of the dock for two days, to await a berth under the coal tips. During this time we got additional stores on board, including paint, rope and provisions. The forecastle hands formed a deputation to the Captain, to complain that there were bed-bugs in their quarters.

"Bed-bugs!" the Captain roared. "How can there be bed-bugs in a new ship?"

One of the firemen pulled up his shirt, exposing his hairy belly splotched with unmistakable bug bites. Another unrolled a piece of paper, in which he had the squashed bodies of three bugs. He showed these to the Captain. "Caught 'em last night, sir," he said.

"You must have brought 'em on board with you in your blankets from the Sunderland boarding house," the Captain said, probably making a correct surmise. Then he continued,

"Shake all your blankets, bedding and clothes over the rail, and drown the bloody bugs in the sea. That'll get rid of most of 'em. Then clear everything away from the bulkheads, deck and deckhead in your quarters, and the bo'sun will paint all the woodwork with carbolic acid disinfectant, to kill the rest of the bugs, and their eggs, before they breed some more. That'll do you now. Lay forrard."

The fo'c'sle hands turned to with a will to clear out their quarters, while the boatswain procured a tin of carbolic acid and a paint brush. Instead of breaking down the strong acid with water, he painted it into the cracks in concentrated form.

Next day the men complained that the stench of the carbolic gave them a headache, and they could not sleep. They said that the stink of the disinfectant was worse than the bugs.

"Let me hear no more o' this nonsense," said the Captain. "You can put up with the stink. It can't *bite* you!"

We moved under the tips for two days, to load 5,000 tons of best quality screened coal, to be delivered at Bombay for the Indian railways. No sooner were we made fast under the cranes than the Captain went ashore, to stay at a waterfront hotel, leaving me in charge of the dirty operations of loading. Wise man! He came on board occasionally, and usually made some sarcastic remarks to me, warning me that he depended on me to get a full cargo in, stowed so that it couldn't shift when we were at sea, and to keep the ship on an even keel.

I took little notice of his sarcasm. I knew by now that he was a nasty piece of work, and there was nothing I could do but put up with him. He had not a friend on board, except the steward, an oily creature who had served with him in several other ships.

For those two days and nights, life was a misery. We breathed and practically ate coal dust, which smothered every part of the ship. The coal came alongside in a long train of railway wagons, hauled by a shunting engine. As each wagon came under the crane, filled with ten tons of coal, it was hoisted bodily from its bogie and swung out over an iron chute leading to the hatchway. Then one end of the wagon was released, and the contents cascaded with a clatter and a cloud of black dust into the hold. This went on night and day. When one hatch was blocked with coal, we warped the ship along the wharf for 200 feet or so, to bring another hatch under the tip. In the meantime, trimmers went into the blocked hatch, to shovel the coal into the corners of the hold, and so to make room for the next loading, when we warped the ship back again to her former position.

Frequently I went down below into each of the four holds, to inspect the shifting-boards, ventilators, and hatch-beams, and satisfy myself that the coal was being levelled off properly into every corner. I felt it would be inadvisable to try to snatch a few minutes sleep in my bunk, as the Captain would be sure to stroll on board just at that moment, to accuse me of neglecting my duties. Therefore, blackened all over my body, and with my windpipe and gizzard choked with coal dust, I remained awake for 48 hours of horrible discomfort, until all the holds were filled with coal to the deckheads, and the ship was down to the Plimsoll mark, and on a perfectly even keel.

Then the Captain strolled on board, and, without a word of appreciation to the three sooty Mates, said, "She's in a filthy condition. Stand by to cast off moorings and take the towlines when the tug comes alongside, and get all hands to hose her down as soon as we're under way."

Such was life in a "dirty British freighter", in those grand days of the Empire's greatest prosperity, when millions were being made by shipowners and coalowners, sending British coal to the ends of the earth, while the officers and men of the mercantile marine, with small pay and little recognition of their merits, took the brunt of the hard and dirty work and never complained; for it was the tradition of our profession to deliver the goods, and to take the rough with the smooth.

We hauled out of Barry Dock, and it was good to feel the motion of the open sea and get the coal dust washed out of her and out of ourselves. First stop Port Said! I was thrilled at the prospect of seeing the "Mysterious East", of which I, like everyone else, had heard and read so much.

As we steered southwards across the Bay of Biscay, we had high westerly seas abeam, in which the *Shira* wallowed and rolled through an angle of thirty degrees, shipping green water into the welldecks at every roll, but without any rumblings of the coal down below, as I was pleased to remark to the Captain; for she was well stowed. He merely scowled and said, "If she takes a list, it will be your fault!"

Steaming at only 9 knots, deep laden as we were, we sighted Cape St Vincent on the fifth day out, and then headed eastwards, past Cape Trafalgar, through the Strait of Gibraltar, only nine miles wide at the narrowest point, between Cape Tarifa in Spain and the Moroccan shore.

When the rock fortress of Gibraltar came in sight—the British cork in the bottleneck of the Mediterranean Sea—I gazed at it with awe, for it was a symbol to the young Englishman of that day of all the courage and prestige of the British Empire: the controlling point of the sea route, via Suez, to India—"the Brightest Jewel in the Imperial Crown"—whither we were bound.

As we plugged along in the bright blue waters of the Mediterranean, beneath a sunny sky, I could see in imagination the maritime pageant of thousands of years in this great inland sea which was for so long the centre of the civilized world. There had sailed and fought the navies of the Ancient Egyptians, the Greeks, the Phoenicians, the Romans, the Carthaginians, the Turks, the Venetians, the Barbary pirates. . . . This almost tideless lake, 2,000 miles long and up to 400 miles wide, was indeed the cradle of the seagoing profession. It is, in a geographical sense, the vast estuary, or sunken valley, of the Nile, conjoined with the waters of the Don, the Danube, the Rhone and other rivers pouring down from the snow-clad roof of Europe—all these fresh waters filling the immense basin with such a pressure that the tides of the Atlantic Ocean can scarcely enter against them at the only ocean gate, the Strait of Gibraltar.

As I saw it first, in April, 1906, the Mediterranean had become, since Lord Nelson's day, and more particularly since the opening of the Suez Canal in 1869, a great highway of British seaborne trade to Egypt, India, China and Australia.

This was a steamer route, and not a sailing-ship route for our mercantile marine. The British naval bases at Gibraltar, Malta, Cyprus and Alexandria would dominate that route in time of war, and exercised a permanent influence on power politics in times of peace. Our naval and mercantile supremacy were unchallenged, and it seemed unthinkable that they could ever be challenged. We little realized what formidable struggles lay ahead of us.

Five days after passing Gibraltar, we steamed past Malta, and in another five days dropped anchor in the roadstead at Port Said, at the entrance to the Suez Canal, to wait for a Canal Pilot.

At last I was in the Mysterious East, as I quickly realized when we were surrounded by bumboats filled with gesticulating

Mate in a tramp (James Bisset in S.S. *Nether Holme*, 1906)

Liverpool Landing Stage, 1904, with S.S. *Umbria* alongside

(Nautical Photo Agency)

S.S. *Etruria*, built 1885

(Cunard Line photo)

A typical tramp steamer

(*Nautical Photo Agency*)

Western Ocean tramp in heavy weather

(*Acme photo*)

Cunard liner S.S. *Caronia*, built 1904

(Cunard Line photo)

Cunard liner S.S. *Carpathia*, built 1903

(Cunard Line photo)

and shouting Egyptians, wearing red fezzes, and clad in long blue or striped cotton caftan garments.

The Captain had given orders that everything portable on deck—such as loose ropes, paint pots and brushes and the like—should be stowed out of reach, and no bumboatmen allowed on board. It became then the duty of the Mates and the crew to line the bulwarks and take station on the poop and forecastle head, to thrust the more daring of these pirate-like pests overside when they attempted to clamber on board.

The ship was a pandemonium of profanity in English and Arabic, until the bumboatmen saw a police boat approaching, and contented themselves with trying to do business by standing in their own boats, holding up rugs, shawls, brassware, cigarettes and dirty postcards, loudly shouting out the prices.

Such was my introduction to the Mysterious East! Some of our crew bought the bargains offered, but the bumboatmen soon realized that we had no wealthy passengers on board, and rowed away to lie in wait for a more profitable ship. Presently a Canal Pilot came aboard, and we hove up the anchor and steered into the Canal entrance.

The passage through the Canal, 100 miles from Port Said to Suez, took us a day and a half, going at half speed, and anchoring for an hour at the Bitter Lake to allow a homeward bound P. & O. liner to pass. During the dark hours, we had a searchlight over the bows to illumine the buoys marking the centre of the Canal.

It was a strange sensation to be looking out from the bridge, to port or to starboard, over a sea of sand-hills, with only the narrow ribbon of the Canal ahead and astern. The ship seemed to have become landbound, the illusion heightened when Arabs riding on camels were sighted on the horizon. Ships of the desert! If they were strange to our vision, it must be equally strange to each Arab who beholds, for the first time, from camel back, afar, a steamer apparently making her way through the desert. . . .

The pilot left us at Suez, and we steamed for six days through the Red Sea, in dreadful heat which was almost unbearable, as we had no refrigeration, electric fans, or other comforts of passenger-liners. We rigged awnings, but they were skimpy things. The temperature hovered around 110 deg. F. in the shade, and the only breeze was a hot east wind off the desert of Arabia.

At last we passed through the narrow Strait of Bab el Mandeb and into the Indian Ocean, after having voyaged through land-locked seas for 3,316 miles since leaving the Atlantic Ocean at Gibraltar. In a geographical sense that entire distance, including the Suez Canal, is a gigantic strait—by far the longest strait in the world—and it was a distinct relief when we had Cape Gardafui abeam, and felt the ocean swell and the breeze from the wide open south with no smell of land in it.

In eight days steaming eastwards across the Arabian Sea we arrived at Bombay, after a passage of twenty-eight days from Barry Dock. We anchored in the Roads, two miles offshore. The bay is large, and a famous haven of ships, for this was "the Gateway of India" for thousands of years when the Phoenicians, and, later, the Arabs in their dhows, navigated the Arabian Sea; and later again a haven of the Portuguese, the first Europeans to find a seaway from Europe to India, around the Cape of Good Hope, in the 15th Century, A.D. The British East India Company took possession of Bombay in the seventeenth century; and all India was annexed to the British Crown by Queen Victoria in 1858, as a sequel to the "Indian Mutiny" of 1857.

Bombay City is on a peninsula eleven miles long, which forms a natural breakwater, enclosing the bay. There are many docks and wharves along the city waterfront; but, for some reason that I could not plumb, the agents or the consignees had decided to have our cargo discharged into lighters at the anchorage. This may have saved some docking expenses, but it involved a long stay in port, while our 5,000 tons of coal were discharged by manual labour.

Probably there was some "racket" in connection with the light-erage or stevedoring arrangements, and the employment of a big gang of coolies to handle the coal; for, though we had steam winches and derricks, these were not used to sling the cargo out of the holds into the lighters. Everything was done manually by the shore gang, as in sailing-ship days.

A gang of not less than 200 coolies came off, in the lighters, bringing with them about the same number of women and children. All swarmed aboard, and took possession of the welldecks and holds, to begin work, under control of their "serangs".

Their methods of working were primitive. They used shovels shaped like Dutch hoes, and dragged the coal with these into small flat baskets, each holding about forty pounds of coal. These baskets were handed up to the deck along a "human chain" and emptied down chutes into the lighters. As they worked deeper into the hold, the coolies rigged stages in a series of steps in the hatchways, and two persons on each stage lifted the baskets from one stage to the next.

Occasionally, when urged on by the serangs, they would break into a monotonous chanty, during which the baskets would fly up from hand to hand, without touching the stages; but after about ten minutes of this exhausting effort, the work would slow down, and be carried on to the accompaniment of much yelling and quarrelling.

For health reasons, the Port Authorities had insisted on latrines being built out over the ship's side for this mass of people, but very few of the coolies made use of them. The dark corners of the holds were good enough, and in consequence the holds were soon foul and stinking. To counteract the stench, we obtained several hundredweights of chloride of lime from on shore, and sprinkled it liberally in the holds every night. What with the broiling heat, the stench of excrement and the clouds of coal dust, life on board was a misery, alleviated only by the fact that the Captain spent most of his time ashore.

Discharging the cargo in this primitive manner took a fortnight. As we knew that we would be moving to the dock later, to load bagged rice and baled cotton for a French firm, most of the officers and crew did not go ashore in the evenings from our anchorage to see the sights of Bombay. After washing ourselves, and the decks, and disinfecting the ship, we settled down to reading or playing cards, and made the best of our uncomfortable situation.

The Mysterious East was sufficiently in evidence during the day-time, when, in addition to the horde of coolies, we had throngs of bumboatmen, including tailors, shoemakers, barbers and merchants offering all kinds of curios and junk. Among these were conjurors, snake charmers and fortune tellers.

One of our visitors was a mystic, who wore dark robes and a white turban. He was a well-built man, with a thick black beard. He usually came on board at lunch-time, and moved about the ship with great dignity, occasionally halting to stare into infinity, as though communing with the gods. He was a fortune teller, who carried on a sideline selling magic trinkets.

At first he got little business, but one day I noticed that his line of talk had attracted the attention of the Second Mate, the Engineers and several of the crew, who were listening intently as he explained, in good, measured English, his mysterious powers of seeing into the future, which he would be willing to exercise for one rupee per person.

The Second Mate said, sceptically, "Give us a proof of your magical powers!"

"Very well, sahib," said the mystic. "I will show you before all men. You bring me a sheet of newspaper, and I will spread it on the deck. We will both stand on the newspaper. You will hold a bamboo stick in your right hand, and you will not be able to hit me with it. Your arms will be perfectly free, and I will not move or jump off the paper, but you will be powerless to hit me with the stick!"

"Hypnotism?" asked the Second Mate.

"I make no explanations, sahib. I only say that you will be unable to hit me."

The Chief Engineer happened to have a newspaper in his pocket. "Try it, mon," he urged.

The mystic took the paper and examined it closely. The sheet when opened out was the standard newspaper size of 32 inches by 22 inches. "If you stand with me on that paper for half a minute," said the Second Mate, "and I have a stick in my hand, I'll give you a crack with it that you won't forget!"

"You like to bet me, sahib?" asked the mystic.

"All right, ten rupees!" The wager was laid, and the Chief Engineer acted as stakeholder and umpire.

"Now," said the mystic, "I will spread the newspaper on the deck." He walked to the break of the poop, a steel bulkhead, with a riveted door. There was a gap of about one-eighth of an inch between the bottom of the door and the deck.

The mystic pushed the newspaper halfway under the door, and said, "Now, sahib, I will go inside of the door, and you will stand on this side with the bamboo. We will both stand on the paper."

Before he could say any more, there was a loud guffaw from the assembled crew. The Second Mate looked dumbfounded. "You win, you bluidy old fraud!" he said.

The Chief Engineer enjoyed the joke as much as anyone. "You've been fair-r-rly caught, Mister!" he said. "Mon, who wad hae thocht o' such a thing!" He handed over the stakes to the mystic, who had not for one moment lost his dignity. The Chief took the Second Mate's arm. "Come awa' and hae a dram, laddie," he said, consolingly. "Yon fakir did ye doon, but it was a fair bet and ye maun be a spor-r-rt!"

So we learned something more of the inscrutable ways of the Mysterious East.

When all the coal was discharged, we hosed out the holds, then hove up the anchor, and took a tow from a tug to berth at the dock, in order to load a part-cargo, before proceeding to Karachi to complete loading.

It was imperative to keep the bagged rice and cotton dry, to prevent it from going mouldy, but this proved to be no easy matter. Showers of monsoonal rain fell at intervals throughout the day, with very little warning, between bursts of broiling sunshine. The squalls lasted only five minutes or so, but, when they came, the men working at the hatches had to stand by smartly to put tarpaulin covers over the hatchways, to prevent rain from going down into the hold.

In my eagerness to see this work properly done, I got wet through several times a day, and, instead of changing my clothing, I just dried out in the sun. Whether from this cause, or infection from the ordure of the coolies while we had been lying out in the bay, I developed dengue fever, with a high temperature and delirium, and one morning I was unable to rise from my bunk.

The Port Doctor came to see me. He was a chronic drunk. With a shaky hand he put some quinine powder into a cigarette-paper, poured it on the back of my tongue, and told me to wash it down with a pint of cold water. He came each morning with similar treatment.

For three days I lay in a fever, unable to take any food, and thinking that my end was near.

The Captain came to see me once a day. He said to me, "Dengue fever is nothing much! When I had it, I didn't lay up. No fear! The best cure is to get up and keep busy. I want you on the job looking after the stowage of the cargo, not lying in your bunk groaning like a stuck pig!"

The oily steward also looked in occasionally, and nursed me with very bad grace. On the fourth day, though still feeling very shaky, I got up and resumed duty. That day, the Second Mate went down with dengue, and I was left with only the Third Mate, a lazy shiftless fellow, to assist me.

Having taken in a half-cargo, we departed gladly for Karachi, 480 miles northwards along the coast, and arrived there in three days. The sea breezes cooled the ship off and blew the fever germs out of us.

At Karachi we completed loading, and then returned, by way of the Suez Canal, to the Mediterranean.

There, we proceeded to Oran, in French Algeria, for bunkers, and to discharge the bagged rice, and then on through the Strait of Gibraltar, and to Havre, to deliver the rest of our cargo.

We arrived at Havre early in August, 1906, and from there proceeded in ballast to Barry Dock, for another cargo of coal.

I had learnt something on that voyage, and now had a somewhat disillusioned view of the wonders of the Orient.

CHAPTER SEVEN

*Paid Off from the "Shira"—I Turn Down a
Chance of "New Hats"—"On the Beach"
Again—Chucking the "Orbo"—First Mate of
the "Nether Holme"—A Voyage from Mary-
port—Meet Percy Hefford—The Captain's
Rheumatics—Cleaning Up a Tramp—Naval
Coal at Barry Dock—Crew Desert—A Cold
Job—Pride and Luck—The Western Ocean.*

WHEN the S.S. *Shira* moored at Barry Dock, the Captain's wife
came on board. She was a bosomy blonde, with a cheery line of
chatter, and the Captain grew quite mellow in her company. She
had meals with us at the saloon table, and kept us all amused.

Another important visitor was Captain Watt, Marine Superintendent of Japp & Kirby, who came from Liverpool to inspect
the ship after her maiden voyage. In the presence of the Captain,
he congratulated me on her appearance and condition. He
told us that the *Shira* would be going on a two years time charter
between New York and Brazilian ports, and asked me if I would
sign on in her again for that period as First Mate.

This put me in a spot. I needed only another two months sea-
time before sitting for my Master's exam, and, if I went in the
Shira, goodness knows when I would be able to sit! I put this
point to Captain Watt, and he agreed that it would be advisable
in my own interests not to engage on such a lengthy voyage in

83

the circumstances. He said he would arrange for me to be paid off when the ship moved under the tips.

Out of Captain Watt's hearing, Captain Cann surprised me by saying affably, "You'd better come on this charter party, Bisset! Lots of 'New Hats', you know, in the South American ports!"— and he gave me a sly wink.

But I wasn't interested. My Master's Certificate was all that I wanted. Captain Cann gave me a good reference, and quite a cordial goodbye. "I'm sorry you're leaving," he said. "You've done your work very well!"

This change of tune, after all his grumbling and nagging throughout the voyage, left me flabbergasted, but came far too late to remove from my mind the memories of four months carping criticism that I had endured; so I left the *Shira* and Captain Cann without regrets.

I have sometimes thought, since then, that he did not really dislike me, but was only trying, in a misguided way, to keep a young officer up to the mark. There were, and perhaps still are, many in the nautical profession, as in other professions and businesses, who consider that the badge of authority is grumpiness; but an occasional word or smile of approval from a senior to a junior is more effective than perpetual scowling and growling; and though slackness should certainly be rebuked, severely if need be, a word of approval occasionally for good work is an encouragement, especially to younger men, to earn more of the same.

Paid off from the *Shira* on 13th August, 1906, I took train to Liverpool, and was "on the beach" again, looking for a short engagement, either as First or Second Mate. I was already a member of the Mercantile Marine Service Association, but now joined also the Merchant Service Guild and the Shipping Federation. These three bodies all had employment bureaus.

I found it harder than I thought it would be to find a vessel going to sea on a short voyage, in need of a Mate or Second Mate. Then, after a month of disappointments, I was told by the employment clerk at the Merchant Service Guild office that the S.S. *Orbo,* loading coal at Birkenhead for Huelva in southern Spain, wanted a Second Mate.

Taking the ferry across the Mersey to Birkenhead, I found the *Orbo* under the coal tip. My heart sank when I sighted her. She was a small, rusty and extremely dirty old tub, with not a remnant of the pride of the sea in her appearance; yet she was on a profitable run, carrying coal to Huelva and returning with iron ore, and making five or six voyages a year.

Going on board, I found the Mate, a man with a grey beard, who appeared to be at least seventy years of age. Everything was covered in dirt and disorder. The Mate showed me my cabin. It was half full of coal that had found its way in through an opening in the bunker hatch. I climbed over it, to look at the accommodation. There was a narrow bunk and a settee, and a porthole five inches in diameter, partly obscured by paint on the outside. I lifted up the horsehair cushion on the settee and it fell to pieces in my hand. There were cockroaches and filth everywhere.

I said to the venerable Mate, "This ship's in a dirty condition!" and he answered, "She's all right when she gets to sea!"

"Maybe," I said, "but I doubt it. I'm going ashore to look for another ship."

"But you can't do that!" he remonstrated. "We've nearly finished loading, and we're due to clear out tonight. We can't go without a Second Mate, and you've taken the job."

"I haven't signed on yet!"

"Well, why won't you sign on?"

"The accommodation's not fit for a dog!"

The Mate looked at me scornfully. "Some o' you young fellers are too damn' particular," he growled.

I returned on the ferry to Liverpool and told the official in charge of the Merchant Service Guild employment bureau why I had "chucked" the *Orbo*. Later that day, the owners of the *Orbo* formally reported me to the Guild for leaving them in the lurch. The Guild told them to improve their accommodation!

I was "on the beach" again.

Three weeks went by, and I was beginning to feel seriously worried. Then I got another call from the Merchant Service Guild, this time to join the S.S. *Nether Holme,* owned by Hine Brothers, of Maryport in Cumberland, as First Mate, at eight pounds a month. She was bound for Swansea, to load coal for Bermuda, and from there to eastern Canada, to load lumber for Glasgow. She was scheduled to take two months on the voyage —just what I wanted!

Maryport is 120 miles northward of Liverpool, by rail. I saw the owners' Liverpool agents in the forenoon of 1st October.

They engaged me and told me that I would be required to be on board the *Nether Holme* at Maryport that same evening, as she was to sail next day.

I rushed home to get my seagoing outfit ready, and within two hours I was trundling down to Exchange Station in an old four-wheeled growler, with my dunnage stowed on top. The train journey from Liverpool to Maryport took eight hours, with long stops at local stations, and three changes.

Winter had set in. When I arrived at Maryport, at 11 p.m., icy rain was falling and a northwesterly gale was raging. The gloomy, gaslit station was deserted, except for a solitary porter. In a mournful voice, he informed me that there were no cabs available at that time of night to take me to the docks, a mile away. "You'll have to foot it," he said.

"What about my baggage?" I asked.

"Mebbe old Charlie is outside wi' his barrow."

I found old Charlie, sleeping underneath his barrow, in the drenching rain, keeping himself dry and warm under a covering of gunny-sacks. "It's nobbut a mile from 'ere," he growled. "I'll take ye there for two bob."

We hoisted my sea-bag, sea-chest, and roll of bedding on to his barrow, covered them with the sacks, and trudged through the deserted streets of the town in the driving, dismal rain.

Maryport was a town of 10,000 population, with a reputation among sailors because of its local industry of sailcloth making. Its docks, fronting the Solway Firth, were used chiefly by fishing trawlers and coasters. When we arrived alongside the S.S. *Nether Holme,* she was in darkness, except for the dim light of a hurricane lantern in the caboose, where the night watchman was dozing by the galley stove.

The lights at the dockside showed me her outlines, and my worst fears were realized. The S.S. *Nether Holme* was a rusty, slab-sided tramp of antiquated design. She was a single-screw steamship of only 1,492 tons gross, built in 1888 by Thompsons of Sunderland. She was 277 feet long, 37 feet beam and $19\frac{1}{2}$ feet deep, with a "three island" profile, and a speed of 8 knots.

Going on board, I rooted out the elderly night watchman, and between us we got my gear down to my cabin, which was under the poop, and in total darkness, as the ship did not have electric light. I struck a match and lit the oil-lamp on the bulkhead.

The cabin was very small, with a bunk, a settee, a chest of

drawers and a cracked washbasin. Everything was in disrepair and covered in dirt. Evidently my predecessor as First Mate of this old hooker was not ship-proud, to put it mildly. If the whole ship was like the Mate's cabin, I'd have some work ahead of me.

I had a mind to back out there and then, and return to Liverpool; but, being tired, cold, wet and hungry, I decided that at least I was out of the wet for the time being, and decided to stay where I was. So I got half undressed, rolled myself in my blankets, dowsed the glim, and fell asleep.

After what seemed like five minutes, I was awakened by a gruff voice announcing, "Six o'clock, Mister!" I sat up and saw a fat man with a walrus moustache, holding a hurricane lamp in one hand and a mug of steaming tea in the other. He put these on the chest of drawers, struck a match and lit the bulkhead lamp. "I'm Billy the steward," he announced. "I 'ope you'll like the old ship, Mister. I bin in 'er for nigh on twenny year, and she's a reg'lar 'ome from 'ome!"

As I was drinking the tea, there was a knock at the door. A cheerful-looking man of about my own age entered and introduced himself.

He was the Second Mate, Percy Hefford, and I took a liking to him straight away. He wore a working garb of black woollen trousers, sea boots, thick blue guernsey and muffler, and a badge cap askew in the right style of a Second Mate. "I've been in this ship for twelve months," he told me, "and I'm not dead yet. I'm getting in my time for First Mate, with only two months to go."

"I'm getting in time, too, and needing two months," I said, "but I nearly walked off her last night! I've been sent up here in a hurry. Are the Captain and the crew aboard?"

"Yes," said Hefford. "She's to sail at noon, in ballast, for Swansea, to load coal for Bermuda Naval Dockyard."

"Is there a Third Mate?"

"No," he told me. "We work two watches, and there's no bo'sun either! The Captain very seldom comes on to the bridge. We have only five A.Bs, and the Mates have to do some work on deck. She's in a mess because we have just been discharging iron ore from Spain. We took in ballast yesterday. The Mate got drunk, and the Old Man sacked him!"

"So that's why I was sent up in such a hell of a hurry," I commented. "I felt like backing out when I clapped eyes on this dog-box that I have to live in."

87

"She's just an old-fashioned tramp," said Hefford with a grin. "The Captain and the Mates and the steward live under the poop. The Chief and the two Engineers and the cook live over the engineroom, and the rest of the hands forrard. The Old Man suffers from rheumatism, and doesn't stay too long on the bridge. He's easy-going, and leaves the work and worry to the Mates, but he's a fine seaman of the old school. The old tub's a rattle-trap, but she's sound enough!"

With these few words, the Second Mate had told me most of the things I wanted to know. The more I saw of Percy Hefford, the more I liked him. We became and remained firm friends. I shall tell later what fate had in store for him.

As daylight came in, with rain still pouring down, I went out on deck to look at the ship and her gear and crew. All her ironwork was covered in rust, with no signs of recent chipping and painting. She had a short, deep welldeck forward and a long, shallow one aft. The decks and scuppers were covered in iron ore, and littered with neglected gear. Almost the first thing that took my eye was her old-fashioned steering gear. From the steering engine under the bridge, iron rods and chains were ranged on top of the bulwarks, leading to an uncovered rudder quadrant on the poop. I had thought that kind of steering went out of date when Noah piled the Ark on Mount Ararat. At least it was all open to inspection!

Hefford went forward, roused out the five A.Bs, and we put them to work clearing up. They were an elderly, scruffy lot, evidently not fond of work, and resentful at having a new young Mate who seemed too keen.

The Engineers were down below early, getting up steam—all Scots and men of few words. I made their acquaintance, and then went up to the bridge for a look around. It was as I expected, in the same neglected condition as the rest of the vessel—the brasswork on the compass, engine telegraph and wheel thick with verdigris, and the paint on the woodwork peeling.

The bridge itself was only a narrow gangway running athwartships, six feet above the deck. It was surrounded with match boarding, waist high, but was otherwise unprotected from the elements, except for a ragged canvas "dodger" amidships. The deck planking of the bridge looked as though it hadn't been scrubbed, or even swept, for months. It was gritty with coal dust and iron ore particles. I looked into the chartroom, which opened out of the steering engine house. It had a table, a settee, and chart lockers. The settee and books were soggy with damp from escaping steam. No wonder the Captain had rheumatism!

At 7.30, Billy the steward appeared on the poop, wearing an apron which had been white some years previously, and rang a hand bell for breakfast. The Deck Officers and the Engineers had their meals together, in a small messroom amidships, but the Captain took his meals alone in his saloon, under the poop.

He had not yet appeared on deck, but I decided that the time had come to make his acquaintance. I knocked at the door of his saloon, and, hearing a groaning sound within, opened it, and entered.

Captain James Roberts, Master of the S.S. *Nether Holme*, was a tall, ungainly-looking man, in his middle fifties, with grey hair and moustache, a red face, very keen blue eyes, and hands swollen with arthritis. He greeted me with a groan of pain, and winced when we shook hands. "Oogh!" he said. "So you're the new Mate. I'm glad you're here on time. Oogh! My rheumatics are giving me gyp this morning. It's this damned rain. Cumberland's the wettest hole in England. Glad we're clearing out of it today. Oogh! What experience have you had?"

I told him briefly, and he continued, "Oogh, you'll do. You can sign on at the company's office ashore this morning. In the meantime, get her ready to put to sea at noon. I hope you're not a drinker, like the Mate I've just sacked for drunkenness. If you're a sober man, we'll be friends. If not, out you go at the end of the voyage."

I assured him of my sober habits. As for getting out at the end of the voyage, I had already made up my mind on that point, so no comment was necessary.

During the morning, I went ashore and signed articles, and at noon a pilot came aboard, a tug took our tow rope, the Captain stood on the bridge, I went to the fo'c'sle head and Hefford to the poop.

The dock and harbour of Maryport were crowded with trawlers, coasters and other small vessels. "Stand by to cast off!" Captain Roberts sang out, through his megaphone.

This was the signal for pandemonium, as the Captain, the Pilot, the Tugmaster, the Dockmaster, and the boatmen running lines across the dock all began singing out at the top of their voices, as though we were engaged in the most intricate feat of seamanship ever known.

The S.S. *Nether Holme* was the pride of Maryport, her port of registry. A crowd of fisherfolk and townsfolk were at the dockside for the excitement of seeing her go out; for, though she was no leviathan, and certainly not in the pride of her youth, she was one of the biggest vessels frequenting that port, and she bore the name of Maryport, painted beneath her own name under the stern, to be displayed in far places where Maryport was never otherwise heard of.

Despite the driving rain and cross wind, we got her safely turned around, and headed out between the pierheads, and away to sea, doing a rollicking seven knots. She was very lightly ballasted, and high in the water, but she breasted the seas daintily enough.

As soon as the course was set, the Captain went into the chartroom, and stretched himself on his settee, groaning with rheumatics. I took first watch on the bridge, and, having three A.Bs in my watch, posted one at the wheel, one on lookout, and set one to sweep down and scrub the bridge deck, until he relieved the wheel after two hours.

Three days later we moored between buoys in Swansea, and by that time the decks were cleared of most of their surface grime, and some of the rust had been chipped away and the brasswork polished. Hefford and I had both turned to, during our watches, and for part of our watches below during daylight hours, to work with the A.Bs at cleaning ship and overhauling the deck gear.

On learning that we would not be going under the tips for three days, I ordered the five A.Bs overside in stages, to start chipping and painting—the proper work of seamen in port, which they thoroughly hated.

One of the seamen said to me in pretended seriousness, "Mister, if I tap her too hard with the chipping-hammer, I'm afeared it will make a hole in her side!"

"Carry on," I told him. "I've heard that excuse many a time, but I've never yet seen a hull plate holed with a hammer."

The Captain was pleased, and Hefford amused, at my efforts to make this rusty old collier look presentable; but it was soon borne in on me that the A.Bs were disgusted at my zeal, and disliked having a leisurely pleasure-cruise spoilt by a young Mate with fancy sailing-ship ideas of furbishing ship.

Evidently they thought that they were going to be hounded throughout the voyage. As soon as we moved to the dockside, the whole five of them cleared out, bag and baggage.

I was not sorry to see them go, as, without refusing orders, they were a surly, resentful crowd who had been allowed by my boozy predecessor to do as they pleased. The Captain fully supported my efforts to get his ship into seagoing trim and smarten her up.

"Good riddance to bad rubbish," he remarked, when I told him that all the A.Bs had deserted. "We'll get a new crew with no trouble makers. It's best to make a clean sweep!"

We now needed five new men quickly, but these were not easy to get in Swansea. The Captain went ashore, and, with the aid of a friendly Board of Trade official, signed on five new seamen, who came aboard just before midnight.

Only one of these, an elderly man named Perkins, had served in a steamer. The other four were young Welsh fishermen, experienced only in sailing coasters and trawlers, but keen and willing to work.

We warped under the tips, and, in twenty-four hours of horrible discomfort, hard work, worry, crashing noise and clouds of black dust, we had our holds filled to the deckheads with 3,000 tons of naval coal, and the bunkers also filled with the utmost quantity that could be stowed—in fact, with forty tons more than could properly be stowed.

The extra loading was dumped on top of the hatch. A few hatch-boards had been left off underneath the heap, the idea being that the heap would gradually subside as coal was used from the bottom of the bunkers. This was against regulations, but a common practice, as bunker-coal was cheap at Barry but dear at Bermuda, and difficult to obtain at the lumber port in eastern Canada where we were bound.

It was on the Captain's orders that we took on the extra bunker-coal. He was a wise old bird. The ship was now down to the Plimsoll, in fact nearly down to the gunwales, but overloading was sometimes winked at in those days of get and grab in the coal trade.

A young naval officer came aboard, as we now had the status of a naval collier. His duty was to see that we were properly loaded and in seaworthy condition, but he missed the very point that he was supposed to detect—the gap in the hatch-boards under the dump of bunker-coal on deck.

After asking a few formal questions about our draught and tonnage, he signed our clearance papers and went ashore without causing us any trouble.

At 8 p.m., the seamen, firemen and trimmers were mustered at the break of the poop, to make sure that none had deserted at the last moment. All being present and everything else in order, we warped out into the centre of the dock, to be ready to go through the lock at high tide, 9.30 p.m.

While we were doing this, one of the stern mooring lines—a thick but rotten old Manila hawser—carried away, and got foul of the propeller. We hove in the fag-end, but it was impossible to tell in the darkness how much of the hawser was still wrapped around the screw—which, in our deep-laden condition, was a good six feet below the surface.

As Hefford was in charge on the poop when the hawser had carried away, the Captain called him a this, a that and the other. "We'll miss the tide," he lamented. "We'll have to warp back to the dockside, and get a diver to go down tomorrow morning to free the screw. That'll be another day's demurrage!"

Then, fixing me with a baleful stare, he said, "There must be a Jonah on board!"

In the meantime I had been examining the broken hawser by the light of a hurricane lamp, and, finding it to be rotten, decided that a few fathoms of it round the propeller would have no more effect than a bundle of straw. It would be gone in less than five minutes after we got under way.

When the Captain had calmed down a bit, I suggested that the Engineers should turn the propeller with the hand gear slowly in the opposite direction to that in which it had been revolving when the rope was caught.

"But how will we know if it's free?" the Captain said, looking worried.

On an impulse I said, "I'll dive down myself then, to feel if it's cleared!"

"What! Can you swim and dive?"

"I could go down all right with a guide line!" I said.

"All right, Mister, carry on!" The Old Man was all smiles. He knew as well as anyone that the rotten rope was probably not dangerous, but he had to do something to "clear his yardarm" in case of accident.

There was no time to waste if we were to get away on the tide, so the Engineers turned the propeller in reverse half a dozen times. Then we dropped the weighted bight of a handline over the stern, drew it up tight under the keel in the vicinity of the propeller, and made it fast to the rail on each side. This would be the guide line for me to go down on.

I was now beginning to regret my rash offer. The night was pitch dark and bitterly cold, with a strong northwesterly wind and squalls of sleet driving across the dock. As I peeled off my oilskins, sea boots, cap, jacket, guernsey, trousers and socks, and stood in my thick woollen underwear, the wind cut into me like a knife, and I realized that I had a cold job on hand.

But it was out of the question to back out now. All hands and the cook were standing by, as interested spectators of something unusual. The dinghy was lowered, and made fast to the guide line. Two hurricane lanterns were hung out over the side and stern. In my underwear, which I hoped might keep me warm, I slid down the rope into the dinghy, followed by the Second Mate.

Hefford bent a lifeline around my waist. "I'll pull you up with this if you stay down too long," he said, encouragingly.

There was no time to lose, so I plopped over the gunwales into the water, and held on for a moment, to get my breath. It was all that I could do to suppress a yell, as the water was far colder than I had thought it would be. My teeth were chattering, but when I glanced up and saw the faces of the Captain and all the crew watching me over the taffrail, I knew that I would have to go on with my rash proposition.

Taking a deep breath, and grabbing the guide line as low as possible, I ducked my head under the water and pulled myself down, hand-over-hand, until I touched the tip of one of the propeller blades. I felt around for the hawser rope-end, without finding it, until my breath gave out, and I had to let go and return to the surface.

Hefford pulled me into the dinghy, and I heard the Captain singing out, "Is she free, Mister?"

"Not yet," I spluttered. My theory now was that I needed the impetus of a dive to get deep enough before losing my breath. I went to the bow of the dinghy, feeling that I was blue all over with cold. "Pay out plenty of slack," I muttered to Hefford.

Then I took a header into the depths, and, touching the screw with my outstretched hands and feeling around blindly, I made contact by sheer luck with the broken end of the hawser, which was draped loosely over the screw blade and riding free. With this I shot to the surface and broke water several feet away from the dinghy.

Hefford pushed out an oar and dragged me alongside, hanging over it like a wet rag, but with the rope's-end still in my hand. He hauled me and the rope's-end into the dinghy, singing out to the men above to send down a line. This he bent to the old hawser and told them to haul away.

I crouched in the bottom of the dinghy, shivering, as Hefford sculled it along the side to the short Jacob's ladder amidships. When we reached this, I had recovered sufficiently to climb to the deck and rush down to my cabin, where Billy the steward met me with a steaming glass of grog. He also had a footbath ready and a can of hot water, this being the only bathing-facility the *Nether Holme* had to offer.

While I was thawing out and dressing, the engineers down below were turning the propeller slowly with the hand gear, and the men on the poop were hauling in the hawser as it was freed.

Presently the Captain poked his head into my cabin doorway and sang out, "Good work, Mister. She's all clear now. You did a man's job all right, and thank you very much."

Hefford came down and joined me in another glass of grog. Just as we drained our glasses, the Pier Master sang out through his megaphone, "Come ahead with the *Nether Holme!*"

Throwing on our greacoats, we dashed on deck. An hour later we were standing down the Bristol Channel into a strong headwind and a choppy sea—bound for Bermuda and a warm and sunny clime.

Freeing that hawser had been a cold job—and a lucky one, as I well knew, for I had made contact with the rope's-end by a mere fluke in the utter darkness of the water. I had volunteered to do it on an impulse, and had carried on through pride and perhaps vanity. I might easily have caught my death of cold. It was one of those silly things that a young chap offers to do when he's impatient of delays.

Lundy Island was abeam, and we were headed westwards across the Western Ocean, into the teeth of a gale, plunging bows under, deep laden as we were, submerged like a half-tide rock, and shipping seas fore and aft. My only consolation was that this weather was washing the coal dust out of her.

She was wallowing along, doing all of five knots, just a rusty, dirty old tramp; but, now that she was in her element, she had her own pride, as every ship has when she gets well under way, free of the shore·

CHAPTER EIGHT

Excitement in a Collier—The S.S. "Nether Holme" Bound for Bermuda—The Captain's Retiring Habits—Dirty Weather and Flooded Decks—Securing a Hatch—An A.B's Broken Thigh—First Aid in the Fo'c'sle—Paddy the Fireman Runs Amok—Blood in the Stoke-hold—The Captain's Pistol—Securing the Prisoner—We Arrive at the Bermudas—Why Men Go to Sea.

WHEN Captain Roberts set course from Lundy Island for Bermuda, distant some 2,800 miles southwesterly, he retired to the steam-filled chartroom, remarking, "Call me when you sight the land."

I thought this was intended to be a joke, but, as the voyage proceeded, the Captain remained in the chartroom or in his quarters under the poop, and never went on to the bridge while we were in wide waters. He left everything to the Mates, but, as a matter of routine, we reported to him our noon observations and anything unusual. From his prone position on the chartroom settee, he was sufficiently aware of what was happening, and content to remain in the background there or under the poop, alone with his thoughts, his rheumatic pains and a bottle of rum.

On my first watch, I discovered that only one of our five A.Bs was able to steer. He was Perkins, a reliable old salt. The four young Welsh fishermen had no idea of handling a wheel, as they were used to steering only with a tiller. Apart from that, they were handy seamen, and keen to learn. I had to stand by and instruct the two in my watch, while Hefford did the same with the two in his watch. Old Perkins also constituted himself an acting bosun, and spent hours patiently teaching the green hands to "box the compass", by reciting from memory its thirty-two points in correct sequence around the full circle.

When we were three days out of port, the heap of loose coal stacked on the after end of Number Two hatch had almost subsided through the opening we had left in the hatch covers, leading down into the coal bunkers.

I was anxious to have this hatch secured as quickly as possible. At the 8 a.m. change of the watch, the glass was still falling, and the wind shifted and began to heap up a nasty cross-sea. Leaving Hefford at the wheel, I went with the five A.Bs and the carpenter along to the hatch to secure it while Hefford brought her head to, with the engines at "slow".

Expecting that she would ship water at any moment, I put two of the men to shovelling as much of the loose coal as possible into the hatch opening, while with the others I rigged lifelines and got the hatches ready to put in position. No sooner were the lifelines rigged than she shipped a heavy sea, which swept across the deck, taking us off our feet. We narrowly escaped being washed overboard, and the hatches along with us.

Water poured into the bunker, and loose coal washed around on the deck. It was all that we could do to hang on to anything handy, until she steadied a little.

Then we got the hatches into position, and battened them down, with two tarpaulins and stout wedges. As a further precaution, we lashed a breakwater of planks across the coamings. In the meantime, the engineers down below had set the bilge pump going to clear the water shipped into the bunker.

Having finished that job, I decided to have a look at Number One hatch. I went there with the men, but in the next minute a heavy sea crashed on board, filling the welldeck to the top of the bulwarks. We hung on as best we could, but our only qualified A.B., old Perkins, was caught off balance and swept off his feet.

I made a grab at him, but missed, and thought the poor old chap had been washed overboard. Then, as the ship freed herself

somewhat, I saw that he was jammed under the steel ladder leading to the midship deck.

The carpenter and I reached him as the ship took another
heavy roll to leeward, again flooding the welldeck to our armpits. We clung to the ladder, and at the same time ducked under
the water and grabbed the unconscious seaman to prevent him
from being swept away. We got his head above water, and I
realized that he was stunned by a nasty gash in his scalp, where
he had made contact with the ladder.

The four Welshmen waded to help us. We were all soaking
wet, and looking like half-drowned rats, but we succeeded with
much difficulty in carrying the unconscious Perkins to his bunk,
through water that foamed to our waists as the ship continued to
plunge and roll like a mad thing.

Having made sure that everything about the deck was secure,
I returned to the bridge and joined Hefford. The wind by now
had settled down to a fresh N.W. gale, and I decided to keep her
hove-to until the weather improved.

In all this time, the Captain had not stirred from his settee in
the chartroom. He was supremely confident of the *Nether
Holme's* ability to ride through any trouble. I reported to him
that a man was lying injured in the fo'c'sle.

Pointing to the *Ship Captain's Medical Guide* in a bookcase
secured to the bulkhead, he said, "You and the Second Mate fix
him up if you can. Call me if you can't manage it. My rheumatics
are giving me gyp. Lash the old fellow in his bunk, so that
he can't roll out."

"I've already done that, sir," I told him.

"Good, carry on."

Taking the *Medical Guide*, which was soggy with steam—like
all the other books and papers in the chartroom—I went on to
the bridge and conferred with Hefford. The weather was now
showing signs of abating, so I posted the two most intelligent
of our four remaining seamen at the wheel, with instructions to
keep her head-on, and to call me if they sighted any vessel or
anything unusual. Then I provided myself with bandages, iodine
and the emergency bottle of brandy, and went accompanied by
Hefford to the forecastle.

Old Perkins had regained consciousness, and was groaning
with pain. "My leg's broke!" he said, pointing to his right
thigh. We bandaged his head, then examined the leg. One
glance was enough to show that the main thighbone was broken,

about six inches above the knee. I gave him a stiff nip of brandy, and called the carpenter to make splints. Hefford studied the *Medical Guide,* while I hastened to the chartroom and reported the situation to the Captain.

"Ah," he said, "that's serious!" He sat up on the settee, and held his hands out in front of him. The knuckles were swollen with arthritis. He stood up, groaned, and sat down again. "Oogh, Mister, I think it will be better if you and the Second Mate can manage to set that leg without me. You have younger fingers than I have! Give him a double tot of grog, then fish and lash his thigh, the same as you would a sprung topmast or jibboom. Be sure you set it straight, Mister! Feel it with your fingers and lash the splints tight with plenty of bandages. And look lively before it starts to swell! Keep him lashed in his bunk so that he can't move, and tell Billy to give him three tots of grog a day to ease the pain. His shipmates will look after him. Report to me when it's done, and enter it in the log-book."

He sank back on his settee and closed his eyes. I got additional bandages, and sang out to Chips to look lively with the splints. When these were ready, Hefford and I set the broken thigh to the best of our ability. Perkins, his courage fortified by the internal anaesthetic, bore the pain stoically, but then suddenly went limp and mercifully became unconscious as we pushed and pulled the broken ends of the bone together, feeling them grate beneath the flesh. Having no real medical knowledge, we could use only our common sense, and trust to luck and to our experience in seamanship to make a good job of it.

When all the lashings on the patient were made fast, he recovered consciousness, and we left him as comfortable as possible. I reported to the Captain, and made the entry in the log-book as he had ordered.

Having now only four A.Bs—two in each watch, and one of them at the wheel—Hefford and I for the rest of the voyage did some work on deck in the day-time to make her presentable for arrival at Bermuda. The *Nether Holme* plugged along in finer weather, doing 160 miles a day.

Billy the steward, who was also the cook, served us a breakfast every morning of finnan haddock, which was slightly "off". One morning, when Hefford relieved me on the bridge, after having his breakfast, I went aft for mine, and found that Hefford had left a note on my place—"See *Hebrews XIII*, v.8."

99

Among the steam-dampened books in the chartroom was a tattered copy of the Bible. On looking up the text, I discovered that it read: ". . . the same yesterday, and today and for ever!"

A few days later, both Hefford and I came out in a white rash, which was very itchy. Consulting the *Ship Captain's Medical Guide,* we discovered that our symptoms corresponded with those of nettle-rash, which could have various causes, one of them being the eating of too much bad fish!

I showed this to the Captain, who grunted, "Well, throw the fish overboard!" This I did, much to Billy's disgust. We treated ourselves with lotions of Goulard's Extract, and doses of bismuth powder, and in a couple of days we were cured.

One morning, when we were fifteen days out, I heard a commotion forrard. One of the trimmers, Paddy O'Flaherty by name, a Liverpool Irishman, had refused duty and retired to the fo'c'sle. The Second Engineer, Don Cameron, a smallish man, but game for anything, had followed O'Flaherty—a gigantic fellow—and, with a mixture of threats and gentle persuasion, had induced him to return to the stokehold.

A few minutes later, when I happened to be on the bridge, I heard yells in the stokehold, and saw the engineroom crew scrambling in terror up the iron ladder through the fiddley to the deck. They were singing out, "Help!" and "Murder!"

The Chief Engineer and Third Engineer came out of their quarters on the run, and I sprang down from the bridge to join them. One of the firemen said excitedly, "Paddy O'Flaherty hit Mr Cameron on the head with a shovel, and he's done him in!"

We peered down into the stokehold, and saw Cameron lying near one of the furnace doors, with blood pouring from a gash in his head, while O'Flaherty was striding up and down, brandishing his shovel, and singing out, "I'll do the lot of you in!"

The Chief Engineer, though an elderly man, did not hesitate. "Come on, men," he said, "Follow me!"

He went down into the stokehold, followed by the Third Engineer and myself and two of the firemen. "Drop yon shovel, mon," said the Chief, firmly, to O'Flaherty. "Have ye gone daft?"

"I'll brain the lot o' ye!" bellowed O'Flaherty, swinging the shovel around his head, with a wild gleam in his eye. At this moment we received reinforcements, as Percy Hefford and two of the Welsh seamen, followed by some of the firemen and trimmers, swarmed down the ladder to join us.

"Take him, then," said the Chief. We surged forward. The wonder is that someone was not decapitated, but Paddy's rage suddenly evaporated, as he realized that he was outnumbered ten to one. He dropped the shovel and said, calmly, "I give in!"

With a little tactful persuasion, Paddy climbed to the deck, and went quietly forward to his quarters. In the meantime, the Second Engineer, who had been lying unconscious, came to. I got bandages and brandy, and dressed his wound. We helped him up the ladder and into his bunk.

During this period of excitement, Captain Roberts was in his saloon under the poop, taking a nap. He was apprised first by Billy the steward, then by the Chief Engineer and myself, what had occurred.

"Very well, then," he said. "I'll inquire into this. Bring O'Flaherty here."

We went out on deck, prepared to use force if necessary, and stood by, while a message was sent forrard to O'Flaherty that the Captain wanted him in the saloon.

He came aft almost at once, with a crazy grin on his face. The Chief Engineer and I were waiting for him at the break of the poop. We escorted him into the saloon. Hefford had gone to the bridge, to check the course, but, as it was a fine and clear morning, with nothing in sight, he left a seaman at the wheel, and presently joined us. The Third Engineer had gone down below into the stokehold.

As we entered the saloon, we saw that the Captain had put on his somewhat ill-fitting uniform jacket, with its four mildewed gold stripes on the sleeves. He was seated at the head of the saloon table, with the log-book and pen and ink in front of him. Alongside these was a huge, old-fashioned heavy revolver.

O'Flaherty swaggered into the saloon, and stood staring insolently at the Captain, grinning. "Take that grin off your face and that cap off your head when you come in here," said the Captain, picking up the revolver.

Paddy obeyed both orders promptly, and the Captain continued, "If you give any more trouble I'll drill a hole in you with this pistol. You've committed a very serious offence, attempted murder. What have you to say for yourself?"

"Upon my soul, I didn't mean to hurt him, sir!"

"You admit you struck the Second Engineer with the shovel?"

"Yes, sorr, but only on the spur of the moment!"

The Captain said to me, "Enter it in the log-book, Mister Mate. Charge of attempted murder. Prisoner admits he did it. Says he meant no harm."

I took the pen and wrote this at the Captain's dictation. We all signed it. Then the Captain said, "Put him in irons and lock him up until we reach port!"

He drew a pair of handcuffs from his pocket and passed them to Hefford. Meekly, the culprit held out his wrists; but years of shovelling coal had thickened the muscles of Paddy's naturally big arms to such an extent that the "bracelets" would not clasp.

"Never mind the irons, then," growled the Captain. "Lock him up and keep him on bread and water. If he gives any trouble, put a hole through him." He handed the revolver to me, saying, "Be careful with this gun, Mister. It has a hair-trigger and dum-dum bullets. If you have to shoot him, aim low. Now, take the scoundrel away out o' my sight!"

Hefford and the Chief Engineer took O'Flaherty by the arms and led him out, while I followed closely behind them, holding the pistol with extreme caution, pointed to the deck, for I had never handled firearms in my life, and I certainly didn't want to kill or injure anyone accidentally!

As I reached the door, the Captain whispered hoarsely to me, "The damn thing's not loaded. You'll have to bluff him, like I did!"

With this secret information, I felt greatly relieved. We marched the culprit along the deck, and halted at the door of the carpenter's shop. I kept Paddy covered while Hefford and the carpenter cleared everything out of the shop, which had iron bulkheads, deckhead and deck, and an iron door with a small glassed port in it.

This was to be Paddy's prison. Hefford put into it a straw bed, a covered wooden tub, a pail of fresh water, and a supply of ship's biscuits. On seeing these preparations, Paddy suddenly began to struggle violently. He yelled, with splendid defiance, "Shoot me! Go on, shoot me, you murderers! They'll hang me in Bermuda anyway!"

As he was wrenching himself free from the Chief Engineer and Hefford, I clubbed the pistol and tapped him smartly on the head with it. This dazed him for a moment, and we pushed him through the door, and locked it.

A few minutes later there was a crash, as Paddy broke the glass port with the heel of his hobnailed boot.

For several hours he howled insults and hurled biscuits through the porthole at anyone who passed, and kept this up at intervals during the day and night until we reached the Bermuda Islands two days later, after a passage of seventeen days from Barry Dock.

The Bermudas consist of one island and a cluster of islets, far out in the Atlantic, a thousand miles from the American shore, in the latitude of South Carolina, with a delightfully warm climate, tempered by the ocean breezes. We moored at the naval dockyard in the port of Hamilton, a British naval base.

The Captain went ashore to enter the ship and to make the arrangements to hand O'Flaherty over to the police. During the afternoon, two policemen arrived, in immaculate whites, and, being warned that the prisoner was violent and perhaps insane, called on the naval dockyard patrol of eight hefty bluejackets to assist them.

When the door of his cell was opened, Paddy threw himself to the deck, roaring, "If you're going to take me to jail, you'll have to carry me there."

This ultimatum presented no difficulties to the patrol. Obtaining a large capstan bar, they lashed him to it by his wrists and ankles. Then they shouldered the bar and marched him off to the calaboose.

He was tried a few days later by a civil court, and sentenced to three months' imprisonment, with hard labour, after which he was to be repatriated to Britain at the expense of the owners of the *Nether Holme*.

The Second Engineer made a good recovery from his scalp wound. Doctors examined the fractured thigh of Able Seaman Perkins, and said that we had made a fairly good job of setting it, but that he would have to lie up for some weeks in hospital before being fit to work again. He would probably walk with a limp for the rest of his life. He was therefore paid off, and arrangements made for his eventual return to his home port.

Such were the hazards of life in a tramp steamer, in those days when steam was finally ousting sail on the world's cargo routes, in the era of the twilight of sail. The little steamers were often rusty rattletraps, ugly and dirty in comparison with the glorious tall-sparred wind-driven flyers they were replacing on the world's waterways; yet they had a drab pride of their own, for the men who served in them had the zeal of all sailors to win through to whatever destination fate and the owners decreed for them, in voyages to ports near or remote, with the cargoes essential to their country's prosperity.

Though the events that happened in them were certainly not of world-shaking importance, and seldom reported in the newspapers, those events were lively enough for the men who were involved in them, since every ship's company is a little world in itself, within the circle of the sea and sky on the wide oceans. Those men carried on with their work, usually in discomfort, and often at peril of life and limb, not for honour and glory, and certainly not for high financial reward.

Most of them had first gone to sea impelled by a love of adventure, a desire to know what lay beyond the horizons and to be away from the cramped spaces and restricted movements of life on shore. They kept on going to sea partly from an ingrained sense of duty and discipline, but chiefly from the force of habit; for, as they grew older, their chosen profession was the only one they knew: yet, with all its disadvantages, poor rewards and risks, they would not have exchanged it for any other calling.

CHAPTER NINE

The Heyday of Coal-burning Steamers—The
Humble But Necessary Colliers—We Depart
from Bermuda in a Cranky Condition—Able
Seaman Stanley—My First Voyage in the
North Atlantic—We Sight the "Pretty Sisters"
—A Gale off Sable Island—Drifting to a Lee
Shore—The Gut of Canso—Icy Ordeal at Cape
Tormentine—A Cargo of Lumber—To Syd-
ney for Bunkers—The Cape Race Track—
Mid-Atlantic Hurricane—The Deck Cargo
Shifts—My Worst Voyage.

FOR ten days the *Nether Holme* lay at Hamilton, Bermuda,
in fine warm weather, discharging the cargo in leisurely fashion
with the labour of Negroes. The Captain made friends and spent
all his time ashore, keeping well out of the way of the black
dust that smothered the ship, and leaving everything to me and
to Hefford to attend to in his absence.

One of the Negroes said to me, with a grin from ear to ear,
"Massa, Ah doant like to carry dis coal. It makes dis nigger all
black!"

Hefford and I were as black as niggers ourselves, but we enjoyed a swim every evening in the harbour, and strolled ashore
for whatever recreations were available there—mainly drinking
in naval canteens and swapping yarns with junior naval officers.

At that time (1906) practically all steamers, including naval vessels, were coal-burners. There were few, if any, oil-burners. Naval and mercantile marine movement depended on the availability of bunker-coal brought in colliers, from coal-producing countries, to ports of call and strategic points where no coal was locally produced.

Britain had by far the biggest navy in the world—equal in tonnage to that of any other two powers combined—and by far the biggest mercantile marine. Her sea power was based to a large extent on the excellent quality of steaming-coal available for bunkering in her home ports, and transported in her colliers to coaling stations, along all the main sea routes. The colliers of that period, like the oil tankers of fifty years later, were as numerous as the vessels they served with the main requisite of mechanical propulsion.

The bunkers of steamers were insatiable maws; but "coaling ship"—that is, filling the bunkers—was a grimy operation, extremely inconvenient, especially in large passenger-vessels, as no method could be devised of keeping the clouds of fine black dust, rising from the hatches, from settling on the decks and penetrating to every nook and cranny in the ship.

The grime was at its worst in colliers, which carried coal not only in bunkers but also in their holds, and had to endure the grit and grime of both loading and discharging coal. Steamers of all kinds depended on the colliers, and on the man-killing labour of the firemen and trimmers sweating down below in their stokeholds—a work more appropriate for Satan's imps than for human beings—yet coal seemed to us to be the permanent requisite of steam propulsion at sea, and the smudgy symbol of the final triumph of machinery over the glory of sail.

We had no conception that the reign of the coal-burning steamers would be short in the perspective of history, and that they would soon be replaced by oil-burners, and the colliers by tankers, with a great gain in the ease of refuelling and in the saving of labour down below.

So the pattern of life changes at sea, as on land, and presumably ships powered by atomic energy will some day make the oil-burners obsolete; but, whatever the power of propulsion, ships must still be steered, and North, South, East and West will remain. . . .

When our cargo was almost discharged, the Captain came aboard, and I asked him if arrangements had been made for ballasting. "It won't be necessary," he said. "We haven't far to go to the next port, and she's ballasted anyway with her engines, bunkers, water tanks and bilgewater. She'll steer all right. Ballast is expensive here."

The *Nether Holme* was high in the water, her propeller and rudder partly exposed to view; but the Captain's faith in his ship was serene.

On 6th November, we cleared out from Bermuda in fine warm weather, and, after skirting the outlying reefs and shoals, set course for Cape Canso in Nova Scotia, en route to our next destination, Cape Tormentine, on the New Brunswick shore of Northumberland Strait, in Eastern Canada.

Cape Canso is approximately 820 miles almost due north of the Bermudas. We expected to make it comfortably in five days. This was all new ground to me, my very first voyage into the North Atlantic proper—offshore from New York, Boston and Halifax, cutting across the main routes of transatlantic shipping which in later years were to become very familiar to me.

I could scarcely have made my debut in these waters in less stylish circumstances than as Mate of the S.S. *Nether Holme* with her rusty slab sides and her screw and rudder half out of the water as she churned along, top-heavy and cranky in her steering, an ungainly old tramp, without a cargo, minding her own business, going somewhere from somewhere—nobody cared where, except those who were in her, and her owners in faraway Maryport, Cumberland.

At Bermuda we had taken on a Negro coal trimmer, to replace Paddy O'Flaherty, and a veteran A.B. to replace poor old Perkins. Our new hand on deck and on the bridge was Johnny Stanley, a naval pensioner, aged sixty-five, who was working his passage to England. He had served fifty years in the British Navy, some of his early years as seaman in "wooden walls" under sail.

Johnny had joined the Navy as a boy in 1855, during the Crimean War, and had served in famous old Ships of the Line, including H.M.S. *Duke of Wellington,* under Admiral Sir Charles Napier. What a link with history, and what a seaman he was, and what yarns he could tell! "I've seen men strung up to the yardarm," he said, "many a time, whipped up and away they go; and I've seen 'em keelhauled, too. Them were the days, sir. Eight hundred men on the gun decks, four to a gun, and give the henemy a broadside o' fifty guns, laying alongside 'im! I been in every port in the world, sir, damn near, and there's no place like 'ome!"

Johnny's contempt for steamers, and especially for the S.S. *Nether Holme*, was unlimited. He was in my watch, and I enjoyed yarning with him. "This old rattletrap," he said, "with her steering rods riding on the bulwarks and all, she'll finish up running aground, mark my words. She's top'eavy and she'll turn turtle if we run into a gale where we're going. Cape Canso we're bound for, ain't we, Mister? I know it, and the Gut o' Canso, too, in Northumberland Strait. I was there, forty years ago, come next Christmas, working out o' Halifax, Nova Scotia, in one of 'er Majesty's surveying vessels, making the Hadmiralty Charts, and I know all them parts, Mister, like the palm o' me 'and. Ever been there, Mister, at this time o' the year?"

"No," I said. "Not yet!"

"Well, Mister, we'll run into fogs, gales, ice and cold weather to freeze the ears off a brass monkey, before we sight Cape Canso at this time o' year, if we don't pile up on Sable Island meanwhiles. They say there's three places to keep away from— 'ell, 'ull and 'alifax—and I bin in two of 'em so far, by which I mean 'ull and 'alifax. This is my last v'yage before the mast, Mister, and I 'ope I don't finish up in 'ell, or in Davy Jones's Locker, which is the same place!"

Warned by Johnny's cheerful predictions of disaster, I went to the chartroom, got down the soggy charts of Nova Scotia and Northumberland Strait, and, spreading them on the table, studied our course. I asked the Captain, who was reclining as usual on his settee, if he had firsthand knowledge of our destination.

"Been there dozens of times," he said, nonchalantly, "in both sail and steam! I'm not green like you young fellers." Heaving himself off his couch with a groan, he pored over the chart with me, pointing out its features. "In a few days on this northerly course," he said, "we'll be out o' the fine weather and into the North Atlantic winter, which means gales or fogs, or one after the other and bitter cold. We'll be standing across the track of eastbound and westbound shipping coming out of New York, Boston and Halifax, or bound there from Europe, thick as bees at the door of a hive. Keep your eyes peeled in fog or dirty weather, give way to sail, including drifters of the fishing fleets, and to any steamer on your starboard bow. Go slow in fog and keep your steam whistle going. Take sights when you can, because you mightn't be able to get 'em after another day or two. Watch

Atlantic iceberg, with Ice Patrol aircraft

Atlantic iceberg, with Ice Patrol vessel alongside

S.S. *Mauretania* in the Tyne River, 1906

S.S. *Lusitania* passing the Old Head of Kinsale

H.M.S. *Hogue*, built 1902

(*Imperial War Museum photo*)

H.M.S. *Victory*, Nelson's flagship

(*Imperial War Museum photo*)

May, feeding a horse.

your dead reckoning and allow for the Gulf Stream, and give a wide berth to Sable Island, where many a fine ship has been piled up by lazy, incompetent or drunken Mates, while the Master happened to be below. If that's all clear, Mister, carry on, and call me when you sight Cape Canso!"

Having cleared his own yardarm with these comprehensive instructions, the Captain returned to his settee. Next day, the wind began to rise, and the glass to fall, and I discussed the situation a little anxiously with Percy Hefford. The *Nether Holme* was steering crankily, and shuddering at times alarmingly when her propeller was temporarily out of the water. We got a sight of the sun on the fourth day out from Bermuda, but then the sky clouded over.

During that day we sighted several vessels, eastbound and westbound athwart our course. In late afternoon, there was a sight I could never forget, as a large liner, westbound, appeared on our starboard bow, with long plumes of black smoke pouring from her two funnels. As she stood across our track, a mile ahead, doing all of eighteen knots, she became a blaze of light, on all her decks and in all her portholes, as the electric lights were switched on gradually throughout the ship, so that she seemed to us like a magical apparition.

Hefford and I stood together on our ramshackle bridge and easily identified her as the twin-screw Cunard liner *Caronia*, the pride of the Western Ocean, then in her second year of service. She was of nearly 20,000 tons gross, carrying 2,600 passengers and a crew of 700. Hefford and I looked at her with awe and longing. She seemed so far beyond our hopes and dreams.

At that moment we sighted another liner, coming up fast on our port bow, also a blaze of lights. She was the *Caronia's* sister ship, *Carmania*, eastward bound, out of New York for Liverpool. They were two of the most graceful passenger liners ever built, and were known as "the pretty sisters". I had seen them both at different times in port at Liverpool, but never expected to see them together in mid-ocean, meeting at dusk. We lit our oil navigation lights, and the *Carmania* passed astern of us, quite near.

Hefford remarked, "'Makes you envious, doesn't it? Wonder if we'll ever get into anything like that? Must be a wonderful life in them!" Then he continued, "The Germans have just taken the Blue Riband from the *Etruria* with the *Kaiser Wilhelm the*

Second, but Cunard will give 'em a shake-up soon, with the two new 30,000-tonners now being built."

"I've heard of them," I said. "One launched on the Clyde and one on the Tyne, sister ships."

"The one on the Clyde's nearly ready," said Hefford. "She was launched last June, and I've seen her in Brown's shipyards. She's gigantic! Four screws, four funnels, and they say she'll do twenty-five knots. Seems fantastic, doesn't it?"

"Yes," I said. "It does seem fantastic, in fact unbelievable. Did you hear what her name will be?"

"*Lusitania,*" Hefford sighed. "I'd give my soul-case to get a chance in a big modern ship like that!"

Next day, our old rattletrap ran into a howling nor'westerly gale. In her light condition she refused to steer, and fell off into the trough of the sea. The temperature dropped to several degrees below freezing-point. As we lay rolling and lurching, the icy spray froze on her upper works, adding top weight that seriously aggravated her cranky condition.

The gale increased, and we had neither headway nor steerage way. We estimated that our position was fifty miles nor'west of Sable Island. We were drifting on to a lee shore.

The Captain did not stir from his settee in the chartroom, but his anxiety was obvious. Both welldecks were frequently flooded with icy water. It was an ordeal to wade either to the poop or the fo'c'sle.

Hefford and I remained in the midships deckhouse, warming ourselves a little at the galley stove, when we were off watch. All the members of the crew, ill-clad for such weather, garbed themselves in improvised overcoats of gunny-sacks. The only warm place in the ship was in the stokehold, but how the men down below managed to keep the engines turning even at dead slow was a mystery. The rolling and lurching of the ship made it almost impossible for them to stand and shovel coal—yet somehow they did it.

For thirty-six hours the storm raged, and we now estimated that we were very near Sable Island. We had taken soundings, but they were next to useless for fixing our position, as the ocean floor, between Sable Island and Nova Scotia, is a fairly level bank.

At daylight on the second morning we sighted a long line of breakers, which we judged to be the outlying westerly shoals. She had drifted clear, but it had been a very close shave!

"I told you that she'd ride it out," commented the Captain. "She's a lucky old ship. Carry on, the glass is rising. When the weather eases, round the island to the eastward, and set course for the Gut o' Canso. Call me when you sight the land!"

Hefford and I, and most of the crew, were almost dropping with exhaustion, cold and lack of sleep, but we got bearings, as the weather moderated, and then stood up into the Gut of Canso, the very narrow strait between Nova Scotia and Cape Breton Island.

Arrived there, we let go the anchor in the lee of the land, in Chedabucto Bay. The Captain had decided that all hands, including himself, were in need of a good night's sleep.

Next morning the weather was clear, but the temperature had dropped to twenty degrees below freezing-point. The engineers had to thaw out the freshwater pump before we could have morning coffee.

Then we broke the ice out of the windlass, hove up the anchor, and proceeded on our way through the narrow Gut, and westerly along Northumberland Strait (between Prince Edward Island and Novia Scotia) to our destination, the harbour of Cape Tormentine, in New Brunswick.

In these narrow waters, the Captain came on the bridge, acting as his own pilot as we passed Pictou Island, and threaded our way slowly among the shoals. He was suffering intensely from his rheumatism, but there was no doubt of his nautical ability in this or any other difficult passage.

On 14th November, eight days out from Bermuda, we arrived at Cape Tormentine, and found that the harbour was nothing but a stone jetty projecting a mile into the sea, with a "J"-shaped wooden pier at the end.

A tall, gaunt man with a voice like a foghorn came off in a boat, and introduced himself as Mr Maude, pilot, harbour-master, magistrate, registrar of births, marriages and deaths, postmaster, mayor and general storekeeper of the township of Tormentine, which consisted of about 200 log cabins, a sawmill and a lobster-canning factory.

Everything on the shore was covered in deep snow. The Captain and Mr Maude swallowed two noggins of rum, and then proceeded to put the *Nether Holme* into harbour. Twice she jibbed, and we had to take a round turn out of her; but the third time, with the assistance of a little more rum and much strong language, she was bumped around the end of the pier and warped into a berth.

"Put all your moorings out, boys," shouted Maude. "It blows like hell around here." With that, he and the Captain staggered off towards the town in great good humour. Like everything else on board, our mooring lines were mostly shakings, so I had the anchor cable unshackled and put on shore as a safeguard.

Next morning, we began loading matchwood planks from railway wagons. Lumbermen did the stowage and our four Welsh A.Bs drove the winches. They were suffering from the intense cold, and awkward through inexperience, but with some instruction managed fairly well.

On the very first day, a derrick guy snapped, allowing a derrick to swing round with a crash and carry away the swifters of the foremast rigging. Luckily they went in the rusty splices, just above the rigging screws, within reach of the deck. They would have to be repaired before we put to sea again.

Our old naval pensioner volunteered to do the sailorizing, but, in the extreme cold, I considered it would be a cruelty to allow him to do it. Hefford and I therefore set to work. We turned the broken ends of wire up, and seized them; but, with the temperature touching zero, and our fingers frost-bitten, it was an agony, and the job took us several days and several bottles of rum to complete.

Bitterly cold nor'westerly gales, laden with sleet, frequently heaped the waters of Northumberland Strait into running seas, which swept over the pier and the ship, coating everything with ice. Then the hatch covers had to be put on, and work discontinued, until the squalls passed. We had also to put on the hatch covers when darkness fell and work ceased, about 4 p.m. The lumbermen showed wonderful skill and endurance in handling and stowing the ice-covered planks—allowing space, as they said, for the cargo to expand when it thawed in the Gulf Stream, so that it would not "bust our sides".

Through this precaution, or some miscalculation of the *Nether Holme's* capacity, the holds were all filled to the deckheads, while a considerable stack of the timber remained on the pier.

The Captain, who had obtained accommodation for himself on shore, strolled out to the pier and said to me, "Fill her up with deck cargo to the level of the bulwarks, Mister, and lash it all secure. We are allowed that amount of deck cargo at this time o' the year." He then strolled shorewards, smoking a cigar.

The lumbermen stowed the extra cargo on deck, and we lashed it down with wire falls stretched athwartships and fore and aft, and hove taut with the winches.

This was a complicated operation, as access had to be left to the doors at the break of the poop and the fo'c'sle, and lifelines rigged on top of the lumber for the crew's transit fore and aft. The task was made no easier when heavy snow fell, covering everything several inches deep.

When all was secure, there was still one wagon-load of frozen matchboards on the pier. "Dump it on top," said the agent. "Let it go over the side and collect insurance for heavy weather!"

"Not without Captain's orders," I told him. He fetched Captain Roberts, who came on board in a fuddled condition, and loftily said, "Take the lot, Mister. Lash it well!" Then he went to the chartroom and fell asleep.

I piled the extra lumber on the after-deck, and lashed it down with some old rope; but Hefford and I knew perfectly well that it could not be expected to hold if we shipped heavy seas abeam. I reported to the Captain when it was done, but asked him to inspect the work in the presence of the agent, as I felt I could not take the responsibility if the surplus loading shifted, or were lost.

He at once saw my point, and staggering out into the blizzard, inspected the lashings and said, "Very good, Mister Mate, if we lose it overboard in heavy weather, it won't be your fault."

An hour later, we cast off moorings, and, with the help of Mr Maude, got the ship out and headed eastwards down the Strait. Our destination was the port of Sydney, on Cape Breton Island, for bunkers, a run of some 300 miles, rounding Cape North, in Cabot Strait.

A few hours after we had left port, a blinding snowstorm developed. Our steam whistle and sounding machine were both frozen solid, so we anchored for twelve hours until the weather cleared. The snow now covered our deck-cargo twelve inches thick. Icicles hung in the rigging and coated the masts and derricks, the winches, the steering quadrant, the iron steering-rods, the taffrail, the bridge and everything else to which they could possibly cling.

It was as well that we anchored. When the weather cleared, we found ourselves within half a mile of the rocky shore, and ten miles north of our course-line! A nice miscalculation in narrow waters!

Investigation revealed that the spirit in the steering compass was clogged and almost frozen. We thawed it out in the galley, got some bearings, hove up the anchor, and carried on.

Presently we heard the Pictou fog-gun. A mist closed in, but we sighted the island, and got our bearings. The weather continued bitterly cold and foggy, but we felt our way along, and made Sydney without mishap two days later.

When we berthed under the coal tips, the Captain and Chief Engineer went ashore "to see about the coal". This involved considerable conviviality. They returned on board, decidedly unsteady on their pins, four hours after the *Nether Holme* was ready for sea.

We cast off and got away. The Captain's final instructions to me before he rolled into bed were, "Put her on the course for Fastnet, Mister, and lemme know 'ow she makes it!"

It was 2nd December when we cleared out of Sydney. The navigation from there to Fastnet Rock (off the S.W. corner of Ireland) is by way of the Cape Race route and the Newfoundland Banks, difficult enough in winter even for experienced navigators equipped with perfect instruments and all the mechanical and scientific aids of radio, radar and meteorological information; but we in the old *Nether Holme* had none of these aids.

Neither Hefford nor I had been on this route. The Captain appeared to be either indifferent to our worries, fatalistic, or unduly confident in our ability to avoid collisions, ice or grounding in the thick fog that blanketed us as soon as we reached the Newfoundland Banks. He retired to his cabin under the poop, suffering severely from rheumatism. I visited him there at the change of each watch, and reported our progress. His invariable comment was, "Carry on, Mister!"

Fortunately, westerly gales sprang up, and the fog cleared. In these gales the ship did some fancy rolling, but the high following seas helped her on. The snow melted, the icicles thawed, and visibility was fairly good; but seas broke over our deck-cargo abeam, and at such times the *Nether Holme* seemed rather like a submarine than a ship, as only her "three islands" were above water.

When we were in mid-Atlantic the gale reached hurricane force, and we took a purler over the stern. I decided to put her about and heave to, but, just at that moment, she took a terrific lurch to starboard, and the surplus cargo on the after-deck shifted and jammed against the steering rods on the starboard bulwarks.

Old Johnny Stanley, who was at the wheel, sang out, "The steering gear's jammed, sir!" In the next moment the *Nether Holme* was in the trough of the seas, wallowing helpless, as gigantic combers crashed on her from abeam.

I had no fear that she would founder, even if the hatches were stove in, for with her cargo of lumber she was unsinkable; but it was possible that she would capsize or that the deckhouses would be stove in or carried away.

Darkness was coming on. From the bridge I could see that the lashings of the surplus deck-cargo were holding, but the timber had piled itself underneath them on the starboard side, giving her a list as well as jamming the steering rods.

The carpenter and I, taking an axe each, and with lifelines knotted around our waists, crawled down onto the welldeck, and hacked away at the rope lashings until they parted. This released the load, which slid over the side and floated away as she righted herself; but she continued to lay beam on to the mountainous combers which crashed on her with terrifying force.

The steering gear was still jammed. The rods, badly bent between the fairleads, were immovable. In theory it might have been possible to bring her head to the seas by working the hand steering gear on the poop; but seas were crashing on to the poop, and in practice no man could have stood there unless he were very securely lashed.

I therefore decided to try to knock the pins out of the fairleads along the bulwarks, to let the rods ride loose.

Waiting for a relative smooth, I crawled over the deck-cargo to the lee side and, holding on to the cargo falls, knocked the pins out with a top-maul, and hastily retired before the next dollop crashed on board.

To my great relief, I saw that the rods were riding free, and, before I could reach the bridge, old Johnny Stanley was already bringing her head to the seas, and she rode out the gale without further damage.

Thirteen days after leaving Sydney, we made the Fastnet Light.

The Captain came often on to the bridge while we proceeded through Saint George's Channel and into the Irish Sea, in blusterous weather. One night, as I came off watch after four hours in driving sleet on the bridge, he said to me, "Go into my cabin, Mister, and you'll find I've left a pair of dry socks for you on the table, to warm your feet!"

Puzzled, I went to his cabin, and found that there was nothing on his table except a bottle of rum and a glass. This was the "pair of socks"—just his little joke.

A few days before Christmas of 1906, we docked at the timber wharf at Govan on the Clyde. So ended my first crossing of the North Atlantic, in the icy latitudes; and, although I have made many hundreds of voyages in those latitudes since then, that trip in the old tramp *Nether Holme* was one of the hardest of them all.

CHAPTER TEN

*The Pay-off from the "Nether Holme"—I
Need Two Days More Sea-time—Percy Hef-
ford's Generous Gesture—The Firemen and
Trimmers on a Spree—A Glasgow Music Hall
—Hullabaloo in the Fo'c'sle—A Policeman's
Caution—Launch of the "Lusitania" and
"Mauretania"—Able Seaman Stanley Signs
Off—Working My Passage to Swansea—My
Time In, to the Day—Time to Leave Her
—The Master Mariner's Examination—A
Tribute to Tramps.*

PERCY HEFFORD and I both intended to ask for our discharge
at Glasgow. We had had more than a bellyful of the old *Nether
Holme*. Hefford had got his full time in as Second Mate, with
a week or two over, and was now entitled to sit for his First
Mate's examination. But, on making a careful calculation, I
realized with dismay that I was two days short of my sea-time
required to entitle me to sit for the Master Mariner's examination.

The voyage having ended at Glasgow, everyone would be auto-
matically paid off, with the option of being signed on again at
the Captain's discretion. He suggested that both Hefford and I
should sign on again. He knew that he had two hardworking
young Mates who were sober and attentive to their duties, and
he did not want to lose us.

As soon as the ship berthed, I went ashore to the Board of Trade office to seek advice. I asked the B.O.T. official if there was any way by which I could get in my two days' needed sea-time without engaging for a voyage which might take many months.

"That's easy," he said. "The *Nether Holme* will be going from here to Swansea to load coal. She will be two or three days on the passage there. Stay in her, and take your discharge at Swansea instead of Glasgow! If the Captain will agree to that, you will have got your full sea-time in!"

Returning to the ship, I put this suggestion to Captain Roberts. He said, "All right, you can take your pay-off at Swansea, if Hefford will do the same!"

I conferred with Percy, who had already packed his gear and was ready to collect his pay and go ashore next day to catch the train to his home at Rugby. It was clear that the Captain wanted to retain our services in port at Glasgow, while the cargo was being discharged, and then for working the ship to Swansea, without the bother of finding two new officers.

Unselfishly, Hefford agreed to stay in the ship with me. That was the kind of man he was, a good friend. We told Captain Roberts of our decision to leave her at Swansea. He said, "Very well! I'll write to the owners to engage two new officers there, but I'll be sorry to lose you!"

We wondered a little at this cordiality. Then he added, "You'll be able to make yourself handy on the passage there." We couldn't guess what hidden meaning might be in this remark.

That afternoon all hands were paid off, except myself, Hefford, the Chief and Second Engineers, Billy the cook, and Able Seaman Stanley, who at his own request stayed in the ship as night watchman. It was obvious that he did not want to leave her. He was sixty-five years of age. After more than fifty years at sea, he had no home to go to, and no one on shore to care if he lived or died.

Johnny Stanley was a big man, weighing fourteen stone. He was in good condition, completely reliable and a very suitable man to be a watchman. He had his naval pension, but hoped that Captain Roberts might sign him on again, for one more last voyage, or at least as a "runner" to help work the ship to Swansea. He intensely disliked the idea that his seagoing career was finished.

After the men were paid off, they went ashore, and had a

few drinks at the nearest pub. Then the firemen and trimmers, who were all "Liverpool Irishmen", made inquiries about catching a train to Liverpool, and found that they had missed the train. They returned to the ship with their dunnage, and asked the Captain if they could stay on board that night, adding that they intended to catch the first train next morning.

This permission was granted, so they put their sea-bags into their bunks in the fo'c'sle, and went ashore for a few more drinks. The Captain said to John Stanley, "They'll all get boozed, so keep a good eye on them when they come on board after they are thrown out of the pubs."

"Aye, aye, sir," said Stanley.

In the evening, the Captain put on his blue shoregoing suit and billycock hat, and informed us that he was going to visit an old crony, and that he would probably stay ashore overnight and come back on board next morning, when shore gangs would begin unloading our cargo. It was a fair guess that he also intended to "get boozed". The Chief Engineer went with him, probably with a similar intention.

After tea, Billy the cook went ashore, and, soon afterwards, as the dock at Govan was a dreary place, Hefford and I put on our shore clothes and went to a music hall in Glasgow, where Harry Lauder was "bringing down the house" nightly with his latest hit, "Roamin' in the Gloamin'". In those days before moving pictures had caught on, the vaudeville theatres, which were known as "music halls", were almost as plentiful as cinemas are today. It cost us only a shilling each for a seat in the back stalls to hear Harry Lauder, and we could have stood in the promenade at the rear for sixpence.

Returning to the ship at 11.30 p.m., we heard a hell of a hullabaloo going on in the fo'c'sle. Johnny Stanley met us at the gangplank. "The firemen and trimmers have come on board drunk, sir," he said to me, "and they're fighting mad. It'll be a wonder if some of them don't get killed!"

I went forrard and had a look down the fo'c'sle hatch. A general brawl was in progress. As though sides had been picked, the ten men below were fighting in pairs, punching one another vigorously, swearing and yelling at the top of their voices. Blood was flowing from punched noses, and several of the combatants were rolling on the floor, while the panting, cursing and yelling made a perfect Kilkenny shindig.

A wharf policeman came on board to investigate. I took him

along to see for himself, and suggested that he should go down into the fo'c'sle to quieten them before murder was committed.

"I wouldna gae doon there for a thoosand poonds!" was his comment. "Let them be till the morning."

We stood by for a while, until the fighting gradually subsided, and the warriors went to sleep. Next morning, though most of them had cuts, bruises, and black eyes, they all went ashore together, apparently the best of friends, and that was the last we saw of them.

Our cargo was discharged by shore gangs. We spent a miserable Christmas on board, for Glasgow had few attractions to offer two young ship's officers who had not yet been paid off.

Talking to the stevedores and port officials, we heard of the launching of the giant new Cunard liner, *Lusitania,* from John Brown's shipyards on the Clyde six months previously, in June, 1906. She and her sister ship, *Mauretania,* built on the Tyne and launched in October, 1906, were the world's biggest ships, each of nearly 32,000 tons.

The *Lusitania* was the pride of the Clyde, as well she might be, for she was not only the biggest ship ever built, but, with her four propellers and turbine engines, which on her trials enabled her to attain a speed of 26 knots, she was the fastest merchant ship in the world, and the most luxuriously appointed. She and the *Mauretania* were designed and built for the Cunard service between Liverpool and New York, and had both now been delivered to the owners at Liverpool, for final fitting up before going into regular service in 1907.

Pictures of the *Lusitania* were on sale in Glasgow. Hefford and I each bought one. I intended to have mine framed, to present to my mother. The giant ship, with her four tall funnels belching black smoke as she tore through the water raising a curling bow wave and leaving a churned wake from her four propellers, was a vision to stir the imagination of two young officers in the old rattletrap collier *Nether Holme* lying at Govan on that dreary Christmas Day. She was something far beyond our utmost hopes, but there was no harm in looking at her picture wistfully . . . and wondering . . . if perhaps . . . some day, with luck. . . .

Most of our cargo had been discharged by Christmas Eve, and we were to clear out from the Clyde on 27th December, when the Captain would be able to pick up a crew to work the ship to Swansea. Hefford and I went ashore in the evening of Boxing

Day, and no one was left in the ship except Stanley the watchman, who was sitting by the galley fire, smoking his pipe.

When we returned on board at 11 p.m., there was no sign of Stanley. This was very strange, as he was certainly not a man who would walk off, or neglect his duty in any way. Except for a lantern and the fire in the galley stove, the ship was in darkness. I took the lantern, and we walked around the decks, calling out his name.

After a few minutes, we heard a weak moan, from overside. I peered into the blackness between the ship's side and the wharf, and again heard a faint groaning sound. Quickly I lowered the lantern on a lanyard, and there we saw Stanley up to his neck in the bitterly cold water, hanging on to a muddy, greasy stringer, joining the wharf-piles. He had fallen overboard when he was adjusting the plank gangway to the rising tide, and had injured himself, so that he was unable to pull himself up out of the water.

In a few seconds we had a Jacob's ladder over the side. Hefford went down and put a bowline around Stanley's shoulders. The two of us then tailed on and tried to hoist the heavy and now unconscious man up to the deck. Luckily at this moment the Second Engineer came on board. With his help we got Stanley up over the rail and onto the deck, and carried him into the galley.

Our shoregoing suits were plastered with stinking black Glasgow mud, but that was of little importance in the circumstances. Stanley was blue in the face and hands, and had cuts on his head. We thought that he was dead. The Second Engineer ran to get an ambulance, while Hefford and I stripped Stanley of his clothes, wrapped him in a blanket, and forced some whisky between his teeth. He began breathing heavily. How long he had been in the water we had no means of knowing, but only a man of iron constitution and will could have held on as he did until help came.

The ambulance men took him to the hospital. We never saw him again, but we heard later that he had recovered. It would have been a strange end to his long career at sea, mostly served in sailing ships, to be drowned in port, but he was one of those tough seamen who come through everything and never say die.

The *Nether Holme,* with a temporary crew, cleared out from the Clyde unballasted, except for bunker-coal, for our voyage to Swansea coasting in the narrow waters of the Irish Sea.

As soon as the Clyde pilot left us, Captain Roberts gave me the task of erecting a portable bulkhead of long and heavy planks at the after end of Number Two hold.

This, he explained, would be a temporary spare bunker for several hundred tons of coal, to avoid dumping the coal loose on deck, as we had done on the previous voyage. Building the bulkhead was work which should have been done by shore labour at Glasgow or Swansea, but to save money Captain Roberts had decided that we should do the work at sea.

"It's a simple job," he said nonchalantly. "I'll keep the bridge, and you and Hefford and two A.Bs can put it up in a few hours. I'll give you a quid each, if you make a good job of it," he added. "How's that?"

We knew better than to refuse, as we wanted good discharges, but the "simple job" took us all the daylight hours of the two days on the passage to Swansea, and we had to stand watch on the bridge at night as well.

At Swansea we were paid off, and I was given the good discharge that I had thoroughly earned. I had got my time in, to the day, and I was very pleased to shake the coal dust of the *Nether Holme* off my feet.

She was the last of the small cargo-carrying steamers—contemptuously or humorously named "tramps"—in which I had the privilege of serving my time. I had now been in the merchant service for nine years. I had visited more than fifty ports, in all the continents of the globe; and I was twenty-three and a half years of age.

In two years since I had obtained my First Mate's certificate, I had made five voyages, in five different steamers, and I had managed to get my time in, to sit for the Master Mariner's examination, at last.

I was very impatient. It had been impressed on me by wise advisers, especially by my father, that I should study for the Master Mariner's Certificate while I was still young enough to learn easily, before my brain had ossified. Many an officer had been satisfied to work for years as a Mate in sail or steam before attempting the examination for Master, but I was well advised to get it over and done with as soon as I had completed the minimum period of seagoing service.

Perhaps I am the only officer of the British mercantile marine who has ever had the hide to enter for the Master Mariner's examination with the exact minimum of service, to the very day, shown on discharge papers. There could not have been many others lucky enough to have put in the qualifying time without even one day over for good measure. My record in this respect could be equalled but not surpassed, but I was strictly within my rights.

I now realized that, during my two years in steamers (including the time in port and ashore), I had neglected my theoretical studies.

A hardworked Mate in a tramp steamer usually has little leisure or surplus energy, either at sea or in port, for mental concentration on theoretical problems. He has enough practical problems to solve from day to day and from hour to hour, and time never hangs heavily on his hands. He has not only to work, but also to keep other men working—and that is sometimes the hardest work of all.

Yet, as I had learnt more from practice than I could ever have learnt from books, I now had the "feel" of steamers. I knew what they could, and could not do, in fair weather and foul; and what the men in them could and would do.

But of the engines, and of the men who worked down below to make the engines work, I knew very little then, as now; for it is not the duty of a deck officer to make a steamer move, but only to control her movements and to signal to the men down below to make her move—or stop—but how the engineers do their work is their business, not his: and how the firemen and trimmers can work for hours in temperatures of 100 deg. F. or higher, day after day, without melting to a grease-spot, is their secret.

It was different in sail, where an officer, even more than an Able Seaman, had to be able to do everything in a ship, and to adjust her movements to the ever whimsical power of the winds, seas and currents, by brawn-power and brain-power, not by mechanical "horse-power".

Life in steamers was easier for the deck officers and deckhands than life in sail. I do not say that it was easier for the firemen and trimmers; but their work down below required more brawn and less brain than the work of seamen making or taking in sail.

Yes, I had got used to steamers, and I had nearly lost the desire to go back to sail. Occasionally, if I sighted a full-rigged ship with all sail set and everything drawing nicely, in a fair breeze in mid-ocean, I had a yearning to return to that life which had now become like a dream that fades.

I had become a "steamboat sailor" now; but what I had learned in tramps was this: that the men who serve in them do a valuable duty patiently and cheerfully, with no incentive of romantic glamour or glory, no publicity, much discomfort, and some hardships and risks, and very small reward. They move the world's cargoes, to feed the maws of trade and industry, but they get no thanks for it. Yet theirs is one of the most essential labours in the world, for without their steady endurance all seaborne trade and much of the world's industry would come to a standstill.

There they come and go, in and out of all the world's ports big and small, near and remote—the men in the little old slab-sided rusty tramps and coasters—their vessels unlovely and un-loved, the crews unrenowned—yet they "carry on" uncomplaining-ly, for they are the world's carriers on the oceans' ways, the drab and sometimes grimy heroes whose sagas remain unsung.

And whenever I see a tramp steamer, at sea, or entering or leaving port, or idle at anchor, or busy at a berth, I do not think with humility, "There, but for the grace of God, go I!"

Rather I think with pride: There go the ships, and there go the men in the ships, who keep the world's trade moving. They may be "unwept, unhonoured, and unsung", but I am grateful that it was granted to me to be one of them, if only for a while.

CHAPTER ELEVEN

*Master in Sail—The Square-Rigged Certificate
—Rusty on Theory—The Nautical College—
My Blue Paper—My Mother's Surprising
Suggestion—I Jack Her Offer Up—Studying
for Extra Master—An Anxious Fellow-student
—Liverpool Music Halls—I Pass the Extra
Exam—A Great Stroke of Luck—I Join the
Cunard Line—My First Cunarder, the
"Caronia"—One of the "Pretty Sisters"—The
Tussle for Atlantic Supremacy—Cunard's
Triumphs—I Am Welcomed by My Future
Shipmates—My Uniform Suit—Mother's
Wisdom—The Turning-point of My Career.*

HOME again in Liverpool, in January, 1907, I enrolled at
the Nautical College to take the examination for a Master's
Certificate. The Board of Trade issued two kinds of Master's
Certificate for "foreign-going" vessels—in sail or in steam. I
decided to take the examination for Master in Sail. This certificate, known as the "square-rigged" qualification, had one
obvious advantage. A Master in Sail was entitled to take command either of a sailing vessel, or of a steamer; but the holder of
a Steamship Master's Certificate was not thereby entitled to take
command of a sailing vessel!

At this time, when hundreds of oceangoing sailing vessels

were still in service under the British flag, the examination for Master in Sail remained as it had been for a long time previously. The handling of sail had not basically changed. Apart from this practical aspect, the examinations for Master in Sail and Master in Steam were the same in regard to the theory and practice of navigation, mathematics, flag-signalling, mercantile law, and so on. A Master in Steam was required to know the routines in steamers usually acquired from practical experience as a deck officer, but was not questioned by the examiners on the handling of sail.

The advantage of obtaining a Square-Rigged Certificate would be that it might come in handy if I found difficulty in getting a job in a steamer! I had every young officer's secret dread of being left "on the beach", and I still had some lingering ideas of going back to sail, especially if I could be offered command of a crack sailing vessel . . . for such are youth's dreams, the stuff of ambition. . . .

Seated in the classroom at the Nautical College, with a dozen other candidates for Master—some of them middle-aged men, with years of service as Mates in sail or steam—I realized how much I had neglected my opportunities for study since passing for First Mate nearly two years previously. But such opportunities while I was serving in the *Rembrandt,* the *Texan,* the *Jura,* the *Shira,* and the *Nether Holme* had been few! Now I was rusty on theoretical knowledge, and I didn't take kindly to the classroom. I longed for the open sea again.

But I stuck to it, and, after six weeks, felt ready to take the examination. The practice was that men who failed at a first attempt usually tried again, two or three weeks later, and sometimes had several failures before they got through. It all depended on the examiners' opinions, and there was no harm in trying. To my surprise, I passed the first time that I went up for the examination.

I hastened home full of joy, and showed my "Blue Paper" (the provisional certificate) to my parents. "Here you are," I shouted. "I've passed for Master, and I'm off to sea again, as soon as I can get a ship. No more exams for me!"

I was now stony broke, as I had found it easy to spend money ashore, even while enrolled as a student—far easier than to earn it at sea. I was determined to go down to the docks the very next day and look for a ship—any ship, whatever was offering.

But my dear mother said quietly, "Oh, yes, that's very good, and now you'll be able to sit for the exam for Extra Master!"

I was astonished, as I didn't know that she had ever heard of such a thing, and I replied, "Well, it's this way. Extra Master is a stiff exam. It's quite unnecessary. It's voluntary. It takes a long time, and, besides, I'm broke. I must get to sea again, to earn some money."

As had happened before, my mother's forethought proved on this occasion to be of crucial importance in my life. "You may be broke now," she said, "but an Extra Master's Certificate will stand you in good stead later on. If you'll go in for that exam, you can stay at home for nothing, and furthermore I'll let you have one pound a week for pocket money, for as long as it takes you to get through."

My father, a dour Scot, who, after many years of doubt, was beginning to believe that a sea-career could, in exceptional cases, become remunerative, was listening to this conversation. He broke in with, "Aye, lad, ye'll have to earn some money after all your idleness on shore, but I'd rather ye'd go in for the Extra examination, if ye can make sure that ye'll pass it, and study hard, and don't waste your time in music halls in the evenings, as ye've been doing—and don't forget to pay us the money back later!" he added, with a grin.

I considered this carefully. Then I jacked my mother's offer up to one pound ten shillings a week, and accepted it. Truly, mother love is the most unselfish love of all.

The money came in very handy. I studied all day at the College, and three evenings a week at home. On the other evenings I'd go out with friends, or sometimes alone, for a two-shilling seat at one of Liverpool's eight or ten "music halls", and try to forget about trigonometry, naval architecture, nautical law, and the many other worries of the Extra Master's examination.

The art of vaudeville at that time, before moving-picture entertainment had been substituted for the magic of living artistry, was at its peak of popularity. After my years of rough living at sea, I was enthralled by the dazzling personalities of the vaudeville stars, such as Dan Leno, Little Tich, Harry Lauder, Marie Lloyd, Fred Kitchen, George Robey, and others whose names were household words in Britain as they travelled on circuit, from city to city, drawing packed houses everywhere. Their polished performances were based chiefly on hearty humour, rocking the audiences with the belly-laughter that is good for the soul; but their great asset was their ability to "get across the footlights" and to arouse personal responses in the audience, in a way that photo-film art could never hope to do.

There were only two of us studying for the Extra Master's Certificate. We stuck close together, and helped one another to solve knotty problems. He was a Cunard officer, several years older than I, married, with two children. The Cunard Line had only recently made it a rule that promotion to senior rank in the company's service depended on the holding of an Extra Master's Certificate. This certificate was now required to be held by all junior officers before joining the Cunard service.

My fellow-student realized that younger men would be promoted over his head unless he made the effort to pass for Extra Master. He had obtained leave for three months—off pay—to sit for the exam, and he was anxious to pass as quickly as possible, while lamenting that his years of practical experience had caused him to forget much of his theoretical knowledge.

With these worries on his mind, he could not relax even for a minute. He wouldn't come out with me for a beer at lunch-time, and would never take an evening off from his studies to go with me to a music hall. As a result he became "bogged down". He even grew a beard because he was too busy to shave!

He knew more about practical seamanship than I, from sheer weight of experience, but I had the advantage of being young enough to be still free of care, so that I could learn without anxiety. I have a good memory for details, which is the main requisite in passing examinations in any field of learning.

After nine weeks, I went up for the examination, and was fortunate enough to pass. My worried friend with the beard took several weeks longer before he felt game to face the examiners. Then, in his over-anxiety, he failed. A few weeks after that, he tried again, and got through at this second attempt, by which time he was dithering about "like a paper man in a squall"—as the old salts used to say.

It was on 15th May, 1907, that I passed for Extra. The news was conveyed to me by the Board of Trade examiners, at the conclusion of the oral examination which followed the written tests. The examiners, a panel of three, were all elderly men, retired Captains of wide experience. The Senior Examiner broke the news to me with the words, "Congratulations, Bisset, you've got through all right! Now, what are you going to do?"

I hadn't any definite plan, but I said, with as much self-control as possible, subduing my elation, "I'll look for a ship!"

"How would you like to join the Cunard Line?" he asked.

"Nothing I would like better!" I replied, so surprised that you could have knocked me down with a crowbar.

"Well," he continued, "they take only officers with an Extra Master's certificate, and you're now qualified! Captain Lyon telephoned to me this morning to ask if I knew of a qualified man looking for a job. He's the assistant to Captain Dodd, Marine Superintendent of Cunard. I'll give you a note to him, now, and, if you take my advice, you'll go and see him immediately. Believe me, it's the chance of a life-time. Greatest steamship company in the world. If they want you to sail tomorrow, don't hesitate. Go!"

"Thank you very much, sir," I said, with mounting inner excitement.

The examiner wrote the note of introduction, signed it and my Extra Master's Blue Paper, and handed me these and the packet containing my references and discharges, which I had brought with me to the B.O.T. office for the scrutiny of the examiners. He shook my hand and said, "Best o' luck!"

I was out through the door like a shot from a gun, and hurried to the Cunard Company's office at the Huskisson Dock, with my thoughts on fire. I had never seriously contemplated such a step up in the nautical world as this. I had thought that one got such jobs only by having special qualifications, or at least previous experience in big passenger-liners.

But I had never served in a big passenger-liner. A quarter of an hour previously, I had not even known that I would pass for Extra Master. I began to wonder if all this was only a dream, and that presently I would wake up and have a nice morning cup of tea. But the busy Liverpool street-scene was too real to be a dream. I gained confidence as I neared my destination, and muttered to myself, "Why not, anyway . . . ?"

In a poky office, known as "the Hut", at the lock gates, I presented myself and my papers to Captain G. M. Dodd, and Captain Lyon. They scrutinized me—and my papers—carefully. Then they affably asked me questions about the ships I had voyaged in, and their Masters. They were sounding me out not only on seamanship but on my ability to give direct but tactful answers to questions, which is also a requisite of Cunard officers.

Then Captain Dodd suddenly said, "You'll do! We'll take you on, and see what you're made of. Join the *Caronia* as Fourth

Officer, at seven pounds a month. She's coaling, loading cargo, and provisioning now, and she'll sail for New York next Wednesday."

So that was that. . . .

The *Caronia!* I could scarcely believe my ears. One of the "pretty sisters", ocean greyhounds, the pride of the Western Ocean. . . .

Captain Lyon said to me, pointing out through the door of the hut to a big ship with two red-painted funnels topped with black, in the dock, "There she is! She's been having her first refit since she went into service three years ago, and she'll be back on the New York run, for the mid-week service, with the *Car-. mania,* next week. You join her on Monday morning. In the meantime, go to Raynors and get a uniform suit and overcoat and badge cap, and also a uniform frock coat. The outfit will cost you fourteen pounds," he added, with a grin, "—your first two months wages—but they'll open a credit account for you, as a Cunard officer, if you want to buy your uniform on tick!"

I was still feeling dazed by the suddenness of all this—passing for Extra Master and being engaged by Cunard, all within one hour—the most eventful hour I had ever known—but I managed to preserve what I hope was a calm demeanour appropriate to the occasion.

"Best o' luck!" The M.S. and his assistant shook hands with me, and Captain Lyon added, "You can go on board her and have a look around now, if you wish. Introduce yourself to Mr Gronow, the Second Officer, and tell him you've been taken on!"

I was walking on air as I went through the wharf-shed, and then stood looking up at the liner's immense bulk. The *Caronia,* 19,593 tons gross, was a twin-screw, steel-hulled steamer, launched at Brown's shipyard on the Clyde in 1904. She was 675 feet long overall (that is, including the forerake and stern overhang), 650 feet long in the keel ("between the perpendiculars"), and 72 feet beam. She therefore had approximately the proportions of length to beam (considered ideally as nine to one) defining an "Ocean Greyhound", despite her tonnage, which, when she was launched, was considered colossal.

To compare her with my previous ship, the rusty little old tramp *Nether Holme,* would be a comparison of the sublime with the ridiculous. She was nearly fourteen times bigger than the *Nether Holme,* but whereas the tramp carried a crew of twenty all told, this grand lady had a crew of 710, and carried 2,626 passengers as well!

She and her sister, the triple-screw *Carmania*—launched also at Brown's on the Clyde in 1904—were Atlantic Mail steamers. At their average speed of eighteen knots, they covered the distance between Liverpool and New York, 3,036 nautical miles, in almost exactly seven days. This meant that these two vessels, in themselves, could not maintain a schedule of regular weekly sailings from both terminals simultaneously, but they could do so easily with the alternation of older vessels, such as the *Umbria* and *Etruria*.

When they were launched in 1904, the *Caronia* and *Carmania* were by far the biggest Cunarders, and also the biggest ships in the world. The *Carmania* was the first Cunarder with triple screws and turbines, and she was slightly faster than the *Caronia*, which had reciprocating engines and twin screws. Yet these two "pretty sisters", though supreme in their beauty of line and luxurious appointments when they were launched, had not reigned long as Queens of the Western Ocean, and in fact failed to take the Blue Riband of the Atlantic from the crack German liners, *Kaiser Wilhelm der Grosse* and *Kaiser Wilhelm II*.

Speed was not the only requirement of the Atlantic mail-and-passenger service, but it was an important element in the intense competition between the British lines, and also between the British and foreign lines, for Atlantic supremacy. To meet that competition, the Cunard Line had now launched the incomparable sisters, *Lusitania* and *Mauretania*, which went into service early in 1907. They were not only the biggest vessels in the world (31,000 tons) but the fastest.

With an average speed of 23.10 knots, the *Lusitania* on her maiden voyage had wrested the Blue Riband from the Germans. A few months later, the *Mauretania* took the mythical trophy with a speed of 23.69 knots, and later attained average speeds of up to 26 knots and held the "record" for twenty-two years.

The *Lusitania* and *Mauretania* had therefore put the "pretty sisters", *Caronia* and *Carmania*, into a position of secondary magnificence.

Yet the *Caronia*, as I mounted her gangway, seemed to me a wonderful ship, of awe-inspiring dimensions, a scarcely dared dream or hope come true.

As I stepped onto her upper deck, I was amazed at the bustle and activity on board. There were stevedores, painters, plumbers, joiners and stewards everywhere. After wandering along what seemed to me miles of promenade-decks, alleyways, and companionways, I eventually found my way up to the bridge, and introduced myself to Second Officer Gronow.

And what a bridge! It stretched across the ship, above the boat-deck, and measured 86 feet from port to starboard. The centre part was enclosed in a teakwood house, with strong plate-glass "clear-view screens", and was known as the wheelhouse. The wings of the bridge were open to the sky, and extended a few feet overside, for convenience in docking and undocking.

Above the wheelhouse was a platform open to the sky, known as "Monkey Island". On it was a standard compass, used for taking bearings, as Monkey Island had all-round visibility. Below the bridge were the curved forrard extensions of the boat-deck and promenade-deck in the midship superstructure, on which passengers could stroll around without interruption. But they were not allowed on the bridge, except in the very rare cases when the Captain might allow that privilege to some person of great distinction, as a special favour or compliment.

I stared at the profusion of instruments and gear. Apart from the steering-wheel and compass, there were two engineroom telegraphs (port and starboard), anchoring and docking telegraphs, speaking-tubes, fire-alarm boxes, telephones, chart-tables, and all manner of gadgets and refinements that were new to me.

When I told Gronow that I was the new Fourth Officer, he welcomed me cordially, took me into the officers' quarters abaft the bridge, and introduced me to several others. They were a lively lot, and, when they found out that I was a sailing-ship man, they made me as welcome as the flowers in May. I was soon at ease. They invited me to have lunch on board, in the officers' messroom—a small compartment on one of the lower decks. Then Gronow took me on a tour of the ship, and showed and told me some of her characteristics and internal arrangement.

I went ashore, still walking on air, and hurried to Raynors, the naval tailors, to be measured for my uniform suit. As usual, they had a large stock of nautical uniforms, which with a few adjustments, could be delivered at short notice.

It was late in the afternoon when I arrived home. My mother greeted me with an anxious question, "How did you get on in your exam? Did you pass?"

I waved my Blue Paper at her, and said, teasingly, "Yes, I did, and I've got a ship, too."

"Quick work," she commented. "What ship?"

"The *Caronia,* mother. I'm a Cunard officer now."

It was her turn to be surprised. When she saw that I really meant it, her joy was unbounded. That was a very happy evening in our home.

CHAPTER TWELVE

*My First Voyage in a Cunarder—Getting the
"Caronia" Ready for Sea—Coaling, Watering,
and Provisioning—The Mails—The Captain
and Officers—Our Passengers Embark—3,336
Souls Afloat—The Exodus of Emigrants to
America—Officers' Stations on Leaving and
Entering Port—"Bon Voyage" at the Mersey
Bar—The Watches at Sea—The Officers'
Messroom—Welsh Sailors—"Full Ahead
Both" at Eighteen Knots—Our Pride and
Glory—Navigating from Shore to Shore—A
Call at Queenstown—The Last View of Erin
—Fastnet Abeam.*

WHEN I joined the *Caronia* on Monday morning, 19th May,
1907, she was coaling. She required 5,000 tons of coal for the
voyage from Liverpool to New York and return. She coaled at
both terminal ports. One of our problems was to keep the
passenger-compartments as free of coal dust as possible while
bunkering was in progress—no easy matter, as the passenger-
compartments occupied so much space in the ship!

The *Caronia* was a steel-hulled vessel, with a superstructure
of three decks occupying 500 feet of her overall length of 675
feet. The foredeck was 120 feet long, and the after-deck 50 feet,
including the stern overhang. There were two cargo hatches
forrard, and two aft. Most of the space around the enginerooms

and boiler rooms was occupied by the bunkers and freshwater tanks. The bunkers were filled through heavy steel ports in the ship's side, which were designed to be strongly secured from inside, to resist the pounding of the seas.

While the ship was being coaled, all the passenger-compartments were kept closed. The furniture in the saloons, smoking-rooms, and lounges was protected with linen covers. Despite these precautions, some coal dust penetrated to all parts of the ship. The stewards and cleaners had the task of removing this grime before the passengers came aboard. How they hated coaling! But it was a necessary ordeal in those days before oil-fuel had come into general use.

Watering a vessel of that size, for the requirements of the boilers and of 3,336 souls on a passage of seven days to New York, was a matter of nice calculation by the designers of the vessel. The intake was through hoses, from the dockside mains, to the cocks leading to the water-tanks—a responsibility of the carpenter, under the Chief Officer. The large quantity of water and of bunker-coal acted as ballast, and it had to be used progressively in such a way as not to disturb the trim and stability of the vessel at sea.

Food for 3,336 souls—that word "soul" is the old-fashioned but appropriate term for human beings of all sorts and ages in a ship—amounted to a considerable tonnage, and a big variety of hard liquor was included. Then, too, the *Caronia* was an Atlantic Mail steamer, and many tons of mail, in thousands of bags, were hoisted inboard to be stowed in the mail-rooms.

Every soul in the crew, including the stewards and stewardesses, had his or her own allotted task in the intense activity that was going on in all parts of the ship to get her ready. In addition to the crew of 710, a large number of shore officials, dockside workers, supply contractors, tradesmen, plumbers, carpenters, painters, clerks, and messengers were hurrying and scurrying and swarming all over the ship. I was bewildered at the amount of detail that needed somebody's supervision—but whose? Not the Fourth Officer's, I soon realized!

The commander of the *Caronia* was Captain John Pritchard, and the Chief Officer William Protheroe, both men trained in sail. They briefly but affably welcomed me, and I was ordered to attach myself as an assistant to Second Officer Gronow.

The navigating or "deck" officers were Chief Officer Protheroe, First Officer Barber, Second Officer Gronow, Senior Third Officer

McLellan, Junior Third Officer R. D. Jones, and myself—with the rank of Fourth Officer, but actually I was seventh and last in the galaxy of gold stripes on the bridge. Yet I felt as proud as Punch in my new uniform with its one gold stripe on the sleeve, which symbolized the bottom rung of the ladder of responsibility.

Sailing day arrived, and at high water the liner was moved from the dock upriver to the "Liverpool Landing Stage"—a pontoon, which, rising and falling with the tides, enabled the ship's gangways to be secured without the need of frequently adjusting them. Here our passengers came aboard.

The *Caronia* carried 300 first-class passengers, at a fare of twenty pounds and upwards; 326 second-class, at a fare of nine pounds; and 2,000 third-class, at five pounds a head. The accommodation and catering were compartmented according to these class distinctions, which depended only on each passenger's ablity or willingness to pay more or less for the various grades of comfort.

The first class had elegant cabins and recreation rooms on the two upper decks in the midship superstructure; the second class occupied the deck below them; and the third class were in three decks below the hull-line, with their promenade space on the forward deck.

Our third-class passengers streamed on board with much excitement and hullabaloo. A large proportion of them were emigrants from Ireland, and many were Jews and others from Eastern and Central Europe, all making for that land of great opportunities, America. This was the period of unrestricted immigration into the U.S.A., when almost any soul who could afford a steamer fare of five pounds could shake off the worries of Europe and begin life anew on the other side of the Western Ocean.

The Atlantic steamship companies competed keenly for this profitable trade in the migration of millions of Americans-to-be. The transportation of this great exodus from Europe to America was done chiefly in British and German ships, not in American ships.

The grand traditions of American seamanship in sail still continued, in the "Down Easters" rounding Cape Horn, on the long sea-passage between the east and west coasts of America, until the Panama Canal was opened in 1914. But on the transatlantic mail and passenger services, which catered for luxury travellers and also for the almost penurious emigrants from Europe, it was Britain and Germany chiefly that rose to the opportunity.

Liverpool, Hamburg, and Bremen were the main exit-ports of the emigrants from northern and central continental Europe and the British Isles. The Cunard Line had also several passenger-vessels transporting migrants westwards across the Atlantic from the Mediterranean ports of southern Europe.

Our third-class passengers were picturesque in their variety of garb and racial features, as they plodded up the gangway in seemingly endless procession, carrying bundles of luggage which perhaps contained all their possessions. Their accommodation down below, though certainly not luxurious, was fair enough at the price, with meals included. A week's discomfort was endurable for the benefit presently to be attained, of becoming Americans. Some would be millionaires there, and some hoboes, but the magic word "America" lured them all, and adventure was in their hearts.

At the advertised hour of sailing, 5 p.m., we cast off from the landing stage, assisted by two tugs.

On leaving port, the navigating officers were "on stations"—a routine until we reached the open sea (this routine applied also on entering port).

The Captain was on the bridge with the Pilot. He was assisted by the Second Officer, who in turn was assisted by the Fourth Officer (myself). My duty was to stand by the Second Officer, and to see that all orders from the Captain or the Pilot were promptly and efficiently carried out. I had to handle the engine-room telegraphs, and also to watch that the Boss Quartermaster (helmsman) and his assistant, the standby Quartermaster, obeyed helm orders instantly and correctly, and that the "Bridge Boy" (an Ordinary Seaman) kept the log of all engine movements, times of passing through locks and dock gates, and other manoeuvres. This log would be vital evidence in the event of collision or other mishap.

The Chief Officer and Senior Third Officer were stationed on the foredeck at the bows, attending to the mooring ropes, tug-boats' ropes, and the anchor if necessary. The First Officer and Junior Third Officer were stationed aft, tending ropes, to make sure that these did not foul the propellers. Seamen and boys were with these officers both forward and aft.

When the tugboat lines were made fast, the Pilot gave the signal to unmoor, and then said to me, in almost a conversational voice, *"Slow ahead both. . . ."*

I moved the handles of both the engineroom telegraphs, there was a double clang down below, and, with a gentle vibration, 20,000 tons of steamer, plus 10,000 tons of coal, water, provisions, cargo and mails, and 3,336 souls, were in motion, cast off from Europe and its ties.

After numerous orders for engine-movements, ahead and astern, port and starboard, we were turned and headed downstream. The Pilot calmly ordered, *"Half ahead both . . ."* and we gathered way and proceeded down the narrow and crooked channel of the Mersey.

In an hour we were abeam of the Mersey Bar Light Vessel, and pitching in a gentle swell and light breeze from ahead. The engines were now stopped as the pilot vessel approached. Her dinghy came alongside, and the Pilot, with a "bon voyage", left us.

Now the Captain gave the orders, *"Full speed ahead both. Off stations. Ring off the engines."* This last referred to the signal to the engineers that we had cleared the port, and that they, like the rest of the crew, were now on sea-routine, with regular alternation of watches.

When we were at sea, the seamen or deckhands and boys—and in some liners the officers also—worked in the old-fashioned alternation of watches—four hours on and four off, with dog-watches in the afternoon, as in sailing vessels. But in the Cunard Line the officers worked in three watches on the bridge—that is each officer had four hours on duty and eight off, at fixed times. There were two officers on the bridge in each watch, a senior and a junior. My watch was with Chief Officer Protheroe, from 4 a.m. to 8 a.m., and 4 p.m. to 8 p.m.

Two of the six quartermasters were always on the bridge when we were at sea—one at the wheel and one standing by. They were Able Seamen, selected for intelligence and general ability. Each took a spell of two hours at the wheel.

It was a duty of the helmsman to strike the ship's bell, with the appropriate number of strokes, at each half hour. This was an old routine, which incidentally helped to prevent him from dozing or day-dreaming, as he had to keep his eye on the clock as well as on the compass. But in big liners a bridge boy also stood by the Q.M. at the wheel, watching the compass with him, and so learning the trade.

Another Q.M. and boy were posted on the after-deck or poop—sometimes known as the "after-bridge" because there was an emergency wheelhouse there. Their duties were chiefly to tend the Patent Log, and to report its hourly readings to the bridge officer; and to dip the ensign at the gaff, as might be required to salute warships, or to return the signals of passing merchant vessels. They had also the duty of dropping a lifebuoy astern instantly in the event of the cry of "Man overboard!" or of a signal from the bridge.

In 1907, newfangled loudspeaking telephones, with brass fittings, had recently been installed in some liners, including the *Caronia*. These were connected from forward and aft to the bridge, and also from the engineroom to the bridge, as an addition to the old-fashioned speaking-tubes. But the telephones were far from perfect. Words came through them distorted to such an extent that they were often unintelligible, and sounded like a foreign lingo or the incoherent babblings of an idiot. At such times, especially when the ship was being docked or undocked, the average Captain would impatiently grab a megaphone and sing out his orders through it to the officers forward or aft—in a manner which was also sometimes unintelligible!

I was at first unable to make any sense of messages that came through the telephone, but, after some practice, I gained skill at interpreting its gabble.

In addition to the engineroom telegraph, there were on the bridge two "docking telegraphs", one connected to the forward end and one to the after end of the ship. These were in principle similar to the engineroom telegraph, but with appropriate markings, different for each end of the ship, for sending signals to and from the bridge.

The dial on the forward docking telegraph had markings such as STAND BY ANCHORS, LET GO ANCHOR *(Port or Starboard)*, SLOW AHEAD, and SLOW ASTERN—these two last-named being signals that would be sent from the officer at the bows to the bridge when the ship was being manoeuvred in the confined spaces of a dock.

On the after-telegraph, there were signals such as MAN OVERBOARD, LET GO LIFEBUOY, MAKE TUGS FAST, and CAST OFF MOORINGS.

All signals transmitted by these telegraphs were answered at the receiving end by moving the handle of the telegraph corres-pondingly, with the effect of acknowledging and repeating the order. At each move of the handle there was the clang of a bell in the instrument, to draw attention to the signal.

By using these telegraphs, we could dispense with oral orders by megaphone or telephone to the forward and after ends, or with the speaking-tube to the engineroom, except for detailed instructions. Nevertheless, when docking or undocking, there was always some singing out by shipmasters and officers, espe-cially if they had been trained in sail to exercise their vocal chords, or if they had orders to transmit to tugmasters and dock-men.

When we were on sea-routine, one lookout man was posted on the foredeck in the bows, and two in the crow's nest on the fore-mast. Their duty was to report to the bridge the position of vessels, lights, icebergs, derelicts, castaways, shoals, land, or any-thing else of an interesting or possibly dangerous nature ahead.

The crow's nest was fifty feet forward of, and ten feet higher than, the bridge. It had a range of visibility only slightly greater than that of the bridge. In fog or thick weather, two lookout men were posted on the bows, as visibility from that point (nearer to the surface of the water) was often better than from the crow's nest or the bridge.

The lookouts signalled to the bridge by striking a bell to at-tract attention, and then singing out their messages. The men in the crow's nest had the duty of correctly repeating the half-hourly bells sounded by the helmsman—proof that they too were awake and alert. At night-time, when repeating the bells, they looked at the navigation lights, and, if these were in order, sang out, "All's well and lights burning brightly."

At the order "Full speed ahead," the *Caronia* throbbed to life, leaving the Mersey Bar Light Vessel astern with the traditional Sailor's Farewell—three long blasts on the steam whistle. Our course was westerly to the Skerries Rock lighthouse, which we soon rounded, and then proceeded southerly through St George's Channel. Being on the 4 p.m. to 8 p.m. watch with the Chief Officer, I remained on the bridge. Soon we had the South Stack light on our port beam. The twilight spread over Caernarvon Bay and the mountains of North Wales, dim on our eastern horizon.

The Chief Officer went to the port wing of the bridge, then beckoned to me. Pointing to the shore, he said, sentimentally,

"My native land . . . and don't forget, Mr Bisset, that Wales was Wales before England was born!"

This was a slap at me for being English, but I kept a discreet silence. I already knew that he was Welsh, for I had served my time in Welsh sailing vessels, and, although I could not speak the Welsh language, I knew well enough the lilting accent of Welshmen speaking English.

It was a coincidence that, on my first voyage in a Cunarder, eight and a half years after my first voyage as an apprentice in the barque *County of Pembroke,* and on the same track at the outset of the voyage, I was again in the company of Welshmen. Captain Pritchard, Chief Officer Protheroe, Second Officer Gronow, and the Junior Third Officer, R. D. Jones, were all Welsh.

They had some advantage over the rest of us when they spoke together, as they occasionally did, in their melodious, antique lingo. The fact that four of the seven navigating officers in the *Caronia* were Welsh was exceptional, and I do not record it as typical of the British merchant service at that time or since; but I have known many Welshmen at sea, and my impression is that the men of that ancient race have contributed more to the traditions of British seamanship than is generally realized or acknowledged.

Now, as the *Caronia* surged along at eighteen knots in the fading light of evening, I was more acutely aware than before of her splendour and glory, and of my own so unexpected stroke of fortune in being on her bridge. Never had I been seaborne at such a speed, or in such a mighty vessel, or in the company of so many souls entrusted, however partially, to my care.

Most of those souls were promenading and milling about on the decks and in the alleyways, trying to get used to their unaccustomed surroundings. They were for the most part landsfolk, ignorant of our seamen's lore, and their ideas were of the destination rather than of the passage, but to navigators the allure of voyaging is not in the destination, but in the working of the ship along the route. To us, a voyage is from shore to shore, and what lies within the shores is of small significance.

The lights of the fishing fleets working out of Caernarvon Bay gradually became visible, and we altered course as necessary, to give them a wide berth. Ahead of us, tramp steamers and sailing vessels were outward or homeward bound in the narrow waters of the Irish Sea. We passed them, one after the other, in our arrogance and majestic pride, giving the men in them, no doubt, a vision of magnificence so far beyond their own scope as to seem unattainable. I remembered that, six months previously, on the bridge of the *Nether Holme* with Percy Hefford, I had sighted the *Caronia* and her pretty sister *Carmania* at sea in the western Atlantic, lighting up at dusk, and how envious we had been. . . .

And *now* . . . a dream had come true.

At the change of the watch, I went below for dinner. The navigating officers and the engineers had two separate messrooms on one of the lower decks, and ate all their meals there. The Captain, Chief Engineer, Doctor, and Purser had their meals in the first-class dining saloon with the passengers (it was not until some years later, about 1912, that the deck officers in Cunarders were put into the first-class dining saloon for their meals—and then at a table by themselves, so that they could come and go unobtrusively at the change of the watches, or in any emergency).

At 9 p.m. I turned into my bunk, weary from a long and exciting day. Many thoughts pounded in my head to the rhythmical accompaniment of the engines' pulsations. Then my ideas sorted themselves to a satisfactory formula. "This is the life!" I whispered to myself, and, with a contented sigh, turned my face to the bulkhead and fell asleep smiling.

When I went on watch again at 4 a.m., we had rounded the Tuskar Light, at the southeastern corner of Ireland, and were steaming at reduced speed in a W.S.W. direction along the Irish shore, breasting the light Atlantic swell in the dawn, making for our only port of call—Queenstown in Cork Harbour, on the south coast of Ireland, a run of 241 miles from Liverpool.

At 10 a.m. we embarked a Queenstown pilot off Daunt's Rock Light Vessel, and half an hour later we anchored at Queenstown (nowadays known as Cobh), within the well-sheltered lower bay of Cork. This port, with its easy entrance and good anchorage, was (like Falmouth Bay in Cornwall) much frequented by sailing vessels homeward bound with cargoes, as they could sail in without the aid of tugs, and lie at anchor to await orders by telegram from the owners, before proceeding to a port of discharge. I had been there twice under sail. But Queenstown was also a port of call for Cunard and for White Star liners on the Liverpool to New York run, both outward and homeward bound, to embark and disembark passengers and mails from and to Ireland.

We anchored half a mile offshore. A dozen or more sailing vessels were at anchor nearby, and those of us who had been in sail scanned them with a particular interest, knowing only too well the feelings of the men in them, now safe in this haven after months of buffeting and hard fare on the stormy Cape Horn route.

As we made the anchorage, several steam launches, known as tenders, came off from the shore, with passengers and mails, and soon were fast alongside. Our gangways were lowered, and our new passengers—chiefly Irish emigrants—came aboard with their baggage.

In the tenders were some privileged businessmen, who were vendors of Irish linen and lace, drapery, groceries, curios, and pictures and souvenirs of Ould Ireland. Some of these spread their wares on the decks of the tenders, and our passengers could go down the gangways to inspect and purchase the novelties displayed. A favoured few dealers were allowed on board the liner, to do business on our decks, by permission of the Chief Officer, to whom they paid privately a small commission for this privilege. This was a recognized perquisite of the Chief Officer in liners calling at Queenstown, but in sailing vessels the Master usually pocketed the commission.

Dozens of "bumboats" had come off from the shore, and were clustered around the stern of the liner. These were rowing-boats, laden with all kinds of Irish goods, including fresh provisions, for sale. Some were "manned" by women, who vied with the male bumboatmen in loudly crying their wares in a delightful Irish brogue. The bumboat merchants established a roaring trade with our third-class passengers and crew, with much noisy banter and chaffering, and the technique of line-and-basket delivery.

We lay at Queenstown for two hours. The Junior Third Officer and I were ordered aft to prevent bumboatmen from climbing aboard, as this would have broken the monopoly of the privileged few who had gained the Chief Officer's favour.

Half an hour before we raised the anchor, the dealers and other visitors from on shore were hustled into the tenders. Then the tenders were cast off, the gangways raised, the bumboatmen and bumboat women ordered to stand clear, and the order was given, *"Heave away the windlass"*, and the anchor was hove up.

We steamed slowly through the Heads, and dropped the pilot off Daunt's Rock at 1 p.m.

"Off stations! Full ahead both!" An hour later we were abeam

of the Old Head of Kinsale. The decks were thronged with promenading passengers, many of them dewy-eyed at what might be their last sight forever of Ould Ireland.

When I went on watch at 4 p.m., Fastnet Rock Lighthouse was abeam—our last sight of Europe—and I was sent up to Monkey Island to take the bearings of it.

Ahead of us, some 2,800 miles, on the other side of the Atlantic, was Sandy Hook, at the entrance to the port of New York, with no land intervening. This would be the first time that I would make that landfall, which, in many a voyage afterwards, would become so familiar to me but, as ever, the first voyage is the most memorable, for it has surprises in store, and experience to be gained.

When I went off watch at 8 p.m., we were fully clear of the land and its dangers. All was well and our lights burning brightly.

CHAPTER THIRTEEN

Officers and Passengers—Sobriety at Sea—The Thirst for Nautical Knowledge—Crossing "The Devil's Hole"—The Atlantic Deeps— A Strong Stomach—Our Track in the Iceberg Season—Navigational Equipment in 1907— The Wireless Operator—Radio at Sea in the Early Days—The Purser and His Duties— Captain's Inspection—The "Ship's People" —Detailed Organization of a Grand Lady— A Floating Beehive—Each to His Task.

THE Cunard Company's rules for the conduct of officers were based on the Company's experience of sixty-seven years in transporting passengers on the transatlantic route, since the first two Cunard steamers, *Britannia* and *Unicorn,* wooden-built paddle-wheelers with auxiliary sail, began the service in 1840. One of these rules, in 1907, was: "While at all times officers must be courteous and helpful to passengers, they must on no account invite them to their cabins, or vice versa."

That was a reasonable rule. Passengers at sea are on holiday, and not pursuing their ordinary avocations. They have nothing to do except to relax and enjoy themselves; but to a ship's officers and crew a voyage is work, and going ashore is the recreation. This is the basic difference between "the ship's people" and passengers, which some passengers fail to appreciate.

Another rule prohibited the navigating officers from drinking alcoholic liquor sociably with passengers. An officer might have a tot in the officers' messroom, or in his own cabin, on coming off watch, but never before going on watch. Most of the Captains and navigating officers were teetotallers when at sea. Too much was at stake. In the event of any mishap, if the Captain, for example, had been seen drinking even one glass of wine at dinner, some busybody would be sure to spread the false rumour, "The Captain was drunk!"

It was an advantage, for the Master of a vessel, or for an officer of the watch, to be able to swear at an inquiry into any mishap, great or small, that he was a teetotaller, or that he made a practice of never drinking when at sea. The rule was different in passenger-vessels from that in cargo-carrying tramps.

Passengers were living cargo. They could not be stowed in the holds under battened hatches, and forgotten. They were free to roam at random within their class accommodation. It was impossible for an officer to avoid them, the more so as the Company's rules, as well as ordinary courtesy, required officers to be polite and helpful in answering their questions. The thirst for nautical knowledge among passengers is insatiable. Officers are fair game in this hunt for knowledge.

Being off watch for a total of sixteen hours in each twenty-four, I could not spend all that time in my cabin or in the officers' messroom down below. Occasionally I wandered around on the promenade-decks, and took my share of the buffeting by the passengers. "What makes the sea blue?"; "Where do sea-gulls sleep?"; "What speed are we doing?"; "What causes fog?"; "Will we see any icebergs?"; "What causes the Gulf Stream?"; or, as the quizzer points to a wisp of smoke on the horizon, "What ship is that?"—these are only specimen openings in the game of "Ask the Officer" (he knows). As this game was almost a novelty to me at that time, I enjoyed it, and continued to enjoy it, to some extent, throughout all my years at sea.

When we were 300 miles to the southwestward of Ireland, we ran into a storm, and for a few hours the liner pitched and rolled. I overheard one of the lady passengers complainingly ask a deck-steward, "Why is the ship rolling so much? Is there anything wrong with her? And why is the sea so rough?"—as though he could help it.

Luckily she didn't ask me! The steward, an old hand, answered her reassuringly. "It's nothing much, ma'am. We're only crossing the Devil's Hole!"

146

"The Devil's Hole?" she gasped. "And what's that?"

"It's the deepest place in the ocean, ma'am!"

"Oh," she said, "is *that* all?"

The steward was exaggerating. This is one of the Atlantic deeps, a "hole" forty thousand square miles in extent, at the edge of the Continental Shelf of Europe. Soundings there have revealed depths of 2,520 fathoms (15,120 ft.), but several other Atlantic deeps are deeper than this, the deepest being the Virgin Trough, or "International Deep", off the Virgin Islands in the West Indies, 4,500 fathoms (27,000 feet) deep.

"The Devil's Hole" is not so named on official charts, and meteorologists scoff at the notion that it has any influence on the weather. Nevertheless, many experienced seamen agree that barometric disturbances are common in that region. This has nothing to do with the depth of the water, but is caused by the mingling here of air-currents from the Arctic region and the European land-mass. Yet the legend of "the Devil's Hole" has captured the imagination of many deck-stewards, who find it as good an answer as any, and its ominous sound calculated to relieve them and the ship's people of further responsibility.

On this occasion I heard a strange boast from a passenger. As the seas rose, and the *Caronia* began "shoving her nose into it", a few of the less hardy souls on the promenade-deck made for the lee rail and began quietly "feeding the fishes". Among them were a man and his wife. The husband was affected only slightly by Nautical Nausea, but his wife was suffering from intense equilibristic disturbances. He was standing by, holding her hand, and doing everything that he could to lessen her misery with comforting remarks.

Along came a fellow-passenger, one of those hearty characters who believe that ocean travel is at its best in rough seas. It was his boast that he always did forty times around the deck before breakfast, and ate four square meals a day in every kind of weather. He had a nodding acquaintance with the couple at the rail, and, sizing up the situation as one that required a little pep talk, he roared, "Good morning. Good morning. Lovely weather, isn't it? I'm sorry to see that your wife has such a weak stomach."

This was too much for the husband, who roared back indignantly and proudly, "She hasn't a weak stomach. She's throwing farther than anybody else!"

147

Soon the Devil's Hole and the storm were left astern, and the *Caronia* was thrusting along nicely at eighteen knots in fine weather. Our track at this season of the year (April, May, and June, when icebergs are adrift in the North Atlantic) skirted to the southward of the iceberg region. Our direction was south-westerly, on the Great Circle course, from Fastnet Island light-house to the meridian of Long. 47 deg. W. in Lat. 41 deg. 30 min. N.—known as "the Corner"—then westerly to the Sandy Hook Light Vessel at the approach to New York.

Though the *Caronia* was one of the largest and most up-to-date passenger-steamers in the world, her navigational equipment in 1907 was primitive in comparison with the array of uncanny "gadgets" to be developed during the years of sea service that then lay in wait for me. I can now look back on each of those developments as they mysteriously appeared at intervals on ships' bridges like magical objects conjured up by wizard technicians from the laboratories of science and the workshops of engineering research: the Gyro Compass; the Gyro Pilot or "Iron Mike"; the Fathometer or Echo Sounder; Radio Time Signals; Direction Finding instruments; Radio Telephones; and, above all, the marvel of Radar—these and many other scientific aids to the navigation and working of a ship were unknown and beyond our imagination in 1907.

The *Caronia* carried one wireless operator, who was a former Post Office landline telegraphist. He pottered about in the day-time and slept soundly throughout the night, and nobody paid much attention either to him or to his "fantastic instruments". The name "wireless telegraphy"—also known as "marconigram signalling"—indicated to our minds something newfangled and unreliable, and of not much practical use.

The Italian experimenter Marconi was not the "inventor" of radio, as is sometimes believed, and such a claim was never made by Marconi himself. The pioneering research into the pheno-mena of electro-magnetic pulsations or "waves" was done by scientists of many nations, including German, Italian, French, British, Russian, and American physicists; but Marconi had quite properly patented transmitting and receiving apparatus of his own design in 1896, and formed a company to sell the apparatus and the idea, at first specially for the transmission of messages over water—that is, principally for use in ships—in which, in the nature of things, wire-telegraphy was impossible.

It was for this reason that the name "wireless" came into use, as a dramatic description of a new kind of electric telegraph which could send signals by Morse code between ships out of sight of one another at sea, or between ships and the shore, far beyond visual or normally audible range. For centuries seamen had been accustomed to being isolated from the rest of the world when they were at sea, with no method of communicating with other vessels or with the shore except by flag signals or semaphore or signal lamps within a visual range of, say, five miles at most, or by siren blasts, megaphones, and leather-throated singing out within directly audible range.

The combat navies were quick to appreciate the tactical advantages of "wireless" telegraphy for transmitting orders and reports between units of a fleet on manoeuvres, or between ships and naval shore stations. The invention was given a practical test in 1898 when a Marconi apparatus was installed in the East Goodwin Light Vessel, in the English Channel, in communication with the shore signal station at South Foreland, seven miles away. The Light Vessel was rammed by a steamer in a fog on 3rd March, 1899, and the first wireless distress signal ever sent from a vessel at sea was instantly received on shore, and tugs were sent out to the rescue, to tow the damaged Light Vessel to safety.

After that convincing demonstration, the British and other navies began extensively installing wireless apparatus in ships and shore stations. The effective range of the early types of apparatus was little more than ten miles, but this range was quickly increased by experimentation. In this, as in so many other aspects of technical progress, the naval and military use led to developments which were later applied with great advantage to civilian purposes.

But, in its early stages, wireless seemed of little use in the mercantile marine, in the everyday working of ships at sea. It was envisaged as an emergency method of sending or receiving signals of distress, which happily are very rare. In other words, it was only "a gadget".

The first transatlantic liner to install wireless was the German S.S. *Kaiser Wilhelm der Grosse,* in 1900. The Cunarders followed almost immediately, beginning with the *Lucania.* The *Caronia* and *Carmania* were equipped with wireless at their launch in 1904, and all Cunard liners, like most other Atlantic liners, carried the equipment in 1907.

At this time there was no regular transmission of time signals or news broadcasts, and there were very few commercial "marconigrams" or wireless telegrams, and no music or voice broadcasts. The limit of range was between 150 and 300 miles, depending upon atmospheric conditions, which were little understood. There were no weather broadcasts, and the International Ice Patrol in the North Atlantic had not been organized. In these circumstances the wireless operators had little to do except to amuse themselves by calling up other ships, exchanging identifications in Morse code, which were of little practical use.

International Radio Telegraphic Conventions held at Berlin in 1903 and 1906 had not reached agreement on the control of the ether waves for commercial purposes, and had not even agreed on an international Distress Call signal. In British ships the Marconi Company in 1904 had authorized the use of the letters C Q D as a distress call. This was a development from postal and railway electric telegraphy in Britain in which C Q was the signal for all stations to stand by, and the letter D (for distress) was now added to it. It had been suggested at the Berlin Conference that S O S should be the Distress Call, chiefly because it was easy to send, and unmistakable: three dots, three dashes, three dots. But this suggestion had not yet been agreed on, and was not adopted until 1908.

Our navigational equipment in the *Caronia* included three chronometers; a Sir William Thomson standard compass on "Monkey Island"; two spirit compasses (one on the bridge and one in the after wheelhouse); a hand-worked Kelvin White sounding machine; and the Patent Log (towed astern). We had a Morse signalling lamp, and the usual International Code flags for exchanging signals with ships encountered within visual range. In common with large ships of other companies, we carried special "recognition signals" for use at night. These consisted of blue lights, flares and roman candles which emitted various combinations of red, green, blue, and white fire balls. Ships meeting in mid-Atlantic exchanged "ice information" (that is, the position of any icebergs sighted) by means of an "Ice Code" of special flags in day-time and Morse code-words at night-time, and by marconigram signals. I had no real difficulty in making myself familiar with the routine work, as I gave it my concentrated attention in my ambition to be acknowledged as competent. The principles of the navigation and seamanship required in handling the vessel were familiar enough to me; all that was strange to me was the magnitude of this floating palace and the details of her organization. I was too keenly interested in these details, whether I was on watch or off, to take much notice of the passengers. It was all fascinating to me.

I soon found that, contrary to rumours that I had believed when I was knocking about in tramps, the Cunard officers were neither supermen nor snobs, but just ordinary sociable coves like myself, though strict in attention to detail and self-discipline. They were helpful to me while I was green in the Company's service. Their front of decorum and brassbound glory in the presence of passengers was part of a necessary show to maintain the prestige of our service against the keen competition of the German and other transatlantic lines; but beneath those brass-bound tunics beat the hearts of gold of decent, hardworking, conscientious, and affable coves who had worked up from the bottom, as I had. They could mix with millionaires, if not with kings, without losing the common touch. This discovery was a comfort to me, and still is.

Our Purser, Joe Lancaster—who was known in nautical jargon as "Pay"—and his assistants, or "Dips" (who dipped pens into inkwells), had most of the worries of handling the passengers. The Purser was the nautical successor of the old-time "supercargo" who in merchant voyages was the representative of the owners, managing the ship's funds and the sale of the cargo.

In the earlier period of merchant adventurers, the owners themselves voyaged in their vessels to buy and sell merchandise in distant countries; but, as their fortunes and fleets increased, they stayed at home and appointed in each vessel a supercargo, who became rather oddly known as the "ship's husband". This term had nothing to do with marital status, but threw back to the original Anglo-Saxon meaning of the word "husband", as "householder" or master of the house, in the financial or economic sense of "husbanding" resources.

The Purser in a passenger-liner was the lineal descendant of the Ship's Husband, and therefore managed the accounts, but, in sailing vessels and small cargo vessels, these were usually managed by the Captain.

The word "Captain", though hallowed by usage, is a form of address rather than of descriptive function. His legal and actual status is that of Ship's Master, or "Shipmaster", and this term is generally used in official and formal documents to this day. It implies that his decision in regard to everything and everybody in the ship is final, and that his authority is absolute, even over that of the owner in person, or the owner's representative, while the ship is at sea.

Each morning at ten o'clock, the Captain began a tour of inspection of the ship, which took him an hour or more. He was accompanied on the lengthy walking tour by a Navigating Officer, an Engineer Officer, the Doctor, the Purser (or an Assistant Purser) and the Chief Steward. It was an impressive procedure, as so many eagle eyes roved for imperfections of any kind, and so many ears were cocked for complaints from crew or passengers. This was an arduous duty for the Captain, who had so many other duties. As passenger-liners were being built bigger and bigger, the companies eventually appointed a "Staff Captain" in each of the bigger ships, to relieve the Captain of this, and to assist him in other duties; but there was no Staff Captain in the *Caronia*.

Much of the Captain's work was clerical and administrative, in matters not directly concerned with navigating or working the ship, for his remained the final responsibility for everything, and he had innumerable forms to fill out or to scrutinize and sign. The administrative work on board was compartmented, with a devolution of responsibility in each department, but yet the Captain had to "know everything", and to be on duty or at call twenty-four hours in the day.

Of the "ship's people" (this term applies to all on the payroll, and does not include the passengers), the great majority were on the catering staff or cleaners of the passenger-compartments, under the control of the Chief Steward, who is under the Purser. These to a total of some 500 men and women, were concerned in no way with the navigation or working of the ship to her destination, and we on the bridge had no special interest in them, except that they kept us fed.

Similarly, we had no responsibility for what happened in the stokehold down below, where a dozen Engineer Officers controlled a staff of 100 firemen and trimmers, working in watches at their infernal task of shovelling 350 tons of coal a day into the glowing red maws of the twelve boiler-furnaces.

The number of Able Seamen or "deckhands" in the *Caronia* did not exceed thirty or forty. These included the six who were rated at Quartermasters and qualified to take the wheel. This number of seamen, when all were "on stations" with the six Deck Officers and the boys, on entering or leaving port, was fully sufficient for handling the liner to or from her berth.

In addition to the seamen or deck-crew proper, there were a number of tradesmen and specialists, such as carpenters and joiners, plumbers, fitters, the lamp trimmer, electricians, the wireless operator, the Master-at-Arms (ship's policeman)—and a band of twelve musicians! Ours was the first professional orchestra carried in a transatlantic liner.

Though I found these manifold activities of the ship's people intensely interesting, I soon realized that my duties and responsibilities were clearly defined and strictly limited, and not beyond my competence with due attention to the specialized tasks that were allotted to me.

After knocking about as First Mate in a rattletrap tramp with a Master who was chronically indisposed with rheumatics or otherwise, I was now the better able to appreciate the magnificient detailed organization of life and work in this stylish grand lady of the Western Ocean, surging on so serenely with 3,336 souls in her care; and each soul, including my own, as completely organized as a bee in a hive, as though by the embodiment of centuries of tradition at sea, plus modern progress.

CHAPTER FOURTEEN

*Divine Service—We Sight an Iceberg—The
Ice Season in the North Atlantic—The Be-
haviour of Bergs—Safety at Sea—Lifeboats—
Passengers' Questions—A Shipboard Concert
—A Moving Aria—Approaching the American
Shore—The Destination of Columbus—Nan-
tucket Shoals Light Vessel—"Down Easters"
—Sandy Hook Light Vessel—We Enter New
York Bay—That Great Port—The Narrows
—The Statue of Liberty—We Berth at Pier 54.*

ON Sunday morning, the Captain conducted Divine Service in
the main lounge on the first-class deck, in accordance with the
rites of the Church of England. This was a duty of all Masters
of passenger-vessels. Some liked to do it, and did it very well.
Others disliked the job, and would pass it on to anyone else, if
possible. The story is told of a rough old diamond of a captain
(not in the Cunard service!) who had little use for the letter H
in speaking, probably considering it a waste of breath; but he
was jovially pious, and loved to conduct Divine Service, always
with hymns of his own choice, which he announced by reading
the first two lines. His favourite was "Holy, Holy, Holy", which
came from him as " 'Oly, 'Oly, 'Oly".

But sincerity is the main thing, and many a rough shipmaster
of that breed has conducted not only routine Divine Services,
but also burials and christenings at sea, with the dignity that
comes from meeting any occasion with authority.

With other officers and ship's people, and a goodly number of passengers from all three classes, I attended the service, and felt the better for it. I have never since missed a Divine Service at sea if I could attend. Our vocation is one which gives many reminders of the workings of Providence, and most seafarers have a sense of reverence due to their constant observation of "the spacious firmament on high", and of the motions of the earth and its wide waters.

Even if there happened to be an Anglican or Protestant Episcopalian clergyman among the passengers, the Captain usually conducted the service, as the ship was *his* parish; but priests, ministers, or pastors of various sects were permitted to hold services for their own congregations at times and places in the ship announced on the notice boards.

Many people attended Divine Service at sea, who never went to church on shore. One man, filling in his entry form for the U.S. immigration authorities, put in the column for stating his religion—Cunarder!

On that fine and sunny Sunday afternoon on my first voyage in the *Caronia*, when I was strolling on the boat-deck at 3 p.m., putting in time chatting to passengers before I went on watch at 4 p.m., the lookout man struck his bell and sang out, "Iceberg fine on the starboard bow!"

The news quickly spread, and soon the rails of the decks on that side and forward were lined with passengers eager for a good view of the phenomenon, and even more eager to ask questions about it of anyone who might know the answers. I was in the firing line, and, even though this was the first iceberg that I had seen adrift in the North Atlantic, I had a fair amount of general knowledge on the subject, and had seen plenty of bergs to the south of Cape Horn.

I have seen more than enough of them since in the North Atlantic, and have answered many questions on them. I may therefore interpose some remarks here on their behaviour and characteristics.

The usual question asked by passengers is one expressing astonishment that the iceberg season in the North Atlantic is in the summer months, from April to September. The inquirers naturally associate ice with the winter.

The answer is simple enough! During winter the bergs are frozen in along the Labrador coast, and among the huge fields of pack ice offshore, quite immovable. They begin to drift only when they thaw, in the spring.

The source of these bergs is in the Greenland Ice Cap, which covers almost the whole of that large country, most of which lies to the north of the Arctic Circle, between the meridians of 20 and 60 W. Longitude—that is, centrally placed at the northern limit of the Atlantic Ocean. Borings and other methods of investigation have revealed that the Greenland Ice Cap is from 1,000 to 5,000 feet thick, covering mountains which give the icecap a summit elevation of over 9,000 feet.

The ice has been formed by the accumulation of snow throughout the ages, compacted by its own weight which in time welds the snow crystals into a solid mass of ice. The influence of gravity, and internal stresses within the vast sheet of ice, form glaciers, or solid rivers or arms of ice, which gradually grind their way down valleys and hill slopes to the sea. There the projections become waterborne, and huge masses break off, or are "calved", from the parent glacier. So icebergs are born, and some of them have been estimated to weigh over a million tons.

The movements of the bergs once they are adrift are controlled mainly by the set of the prevailing currents. The effect of wind upon their drift is negligible, because, although they attain lengths of 400 feet and heights of 200 feet above water, the great part of their mass is below water, and therefore subject to the influences of currents rather than of winds. But, indirectly, wind-directions and force may play a part in the migration of bergs by retarding or accelerating the currents.

The average berg floats with seven-eighths of its mass submerged but if it is made up of snow not completely compacted into ice, or if it is carrying a load of moraine or rock material, this figure may be slightly modified.

I was explaining this to the best of my ability to a charming lady passenger in the *Caronia* as we gazed at the still distant berg on our starboard bow, when, after apparently taking the information in and mulling over it for a few minutes, she said, "But what happens if the one-eighth above water melts away? You wouldn't be able to see the berg at all!"

I'm still searching for the answer to that one.

Fortunately, most of the thousands of bergs that become waterborne from Greenland are carried by the prevailing currents to run aground on the Labrador shore, or in the Strait of Belle Isle, or on the shore of Newfoundland, or on the Newfoundland

Banks. There they are frozen in, during the winter months, and may melt there in the spring, without going far adrift into the open ocean.

About one thousand bergs each year reach the Newfoundland Banks and ground there, but about three hundred drift southwards past the eastern edge of the Banks, and these become a menace to shipping until they disintegrate in the warm waters of the Gulf Stream. A large berg will dwindle away in two or three weeks. As it melts, pieces break off, and the berg rolls about in its new shape, adjusting itself to a new centre of gravity. When the berg calves, the pieces that break off are called "growlers".

In 1907 there was no International Ice Patrol to keep systematic watch on these beautiful but sinister things, and to warn shipping by radio of their exact position and southern limit, as there is today. Such information was passed from ship to ship whenever possible, but oceanographers had charted the approximate southern limits of the bergs in the northwestern Atlantic, in the vicinity of Lat. 40 deg. N., between the meridians of 40 and 70 deg. W. Longitude.

The bergs having reached the Gulf Stream to the south of the Newfoundland Banks are then carried by that current in a general N.E. direction, to melt and thus to be returned, as it were, to the Arctic. This leaves the N.E. region of the Atlantic, on the European side, free of bergs. But the "limit lines" drawn by hydrographers were not entirely reliable before the Ice Patrol was established. Freak bergs were occasionally reported south of those limits, and one berg actually reached the Azores before disintegrating. It was probably an exceptionally hard block, of some peculiar shape which caused it to drift rapidly; or it may have been caught in some eddy of the Gulf Stream.

The iceberg that we sighted in the *Caronia* was at first visible, at a distance of eighteen miles, as a bright flicker on the horizon, which became a white smudge as the liner forged ahead towards it, and then gradually revealed itself in all its sinister beauty of pinnacles and glistening prisms as we approached within five miles.

At this time I went on watch on the bridge, and had a good look at it through the telescope. Bergs are visible at great distances in clear weather in day-time, and even in moonlight they stand out clearly at several miles distance, for they refract light. On a dark clear night a berg can be seen from half a mile away.

In all these cases they are easily avoided. The danger is in fog or on dark overcast nights. In such conditions a shipmaster should reduce speed to slow, or should stop if he is within the iceberg region, in the season when they are adrift, or if he has been warned that they are in the vicinity, and he should remain hove-to until visibility improves sufficiently to enable him to proceed. He should do this irrespective of any desire to "break records" or make a passage. Such was the correct procedure before radar enabled icebergs or other solid objects to be "seen" in the dark or in fog.

Without radar, there was no reliable method of detecting bergs ahead in darkness or fog. Water temperature and air temperature are no guides. The presence of "growlers" (small lumps of ice grinding against the ship's hull plates) is a strong indication of a berg to windward, or in the line of drift; but these may be the fragments of a berg in the last stages of disintegration. They should be treated with extreme caution anyway.

In the clear sunlight we were in no danger of collision, and had to alter course only slightly to give the berg a sufficiently wide berth. We passed it at a distance of one mile, and it made an enthralling spectacle for the passengers, who gathered in groups excitedly discussing it. The ship's barber took photographs of it, which he had for sale next day, doing a roaring trade. My impression was that he had faked the prints with ingenious retouching, to make the berg appear much larger than it looked to the unprejudiced eye.

When we were abeam of the berg, it obliged us by calving and rolling over. It split with a series of reports like rifle shots, and its pinnacles fell with mighty splashes. A fresh breeze was blowing and moderate seas running, so that a surf was breaking around the base of the berg. This is one of the indications of a berg in these conditions, as the surf-line can be seen even at night-time; but in a calm sea at night-time, that indication would be lacking. . . .

Next afternoon at 3.30, when I was again strolling on the boat-deck before going on watch, the same charming lady who had interrogated me on the previous day now renewed the quiz. This time she had an equally charming friend with her, and their subject of discourse was the alarming one, "What would have happened if we had hit the berg?"

I had to explain that such a disaster had never happened to

any large transatlantic liner, and only once or twice in smaller steamers. It was unlikely to happen, because of the special precautions taken on lookout in liners in the ice region, during the iceberg season, and the easy manoeuvrability of steamers under way in the open ocean.

Collisions between sailing vessels and icebergs, I continued, had occurred many times to the southward of Cape Horn, when the vessels were driving on in a howling blizzard, running before the wind with visibility nil at night-time. In such a collision the vessel was invariably lost with all hands, since lifeboats could not live in the mountainous seas and howling gales which had caused the collisions to occur.

This explanation turned the subject naturally to our lifeboats, which were slung in davits, in a double tier, along each side of the *Caronia's* boat-deck, too conveniently near to where we stood to be avoided as a conversational topic. The liner carried forty boats, each capable of accommodating forty persons. That is, if the order were given to abandon ship for any reason, and to take to the boats, there would be accommodation in the boats for only half of the 3,336 souls aboard the liner.

This deficiency was in no sense unusual or contrary to prevailing practice. The ship and her lifeboats were inspected and approved by the Board of Trade and conformed in every way with laws, rules and regulations, and all other requirements of that period. The rules and regulations were a legacy of bygone years, when ships were much smaller and carried far fewer souls than the transatlantic Ocean Greyhounds. The lifeboat accommodation in Cunarders was similar to that in all other large liners, that is, capable of carrying one-half of the total ship's company.

It had not occurred to anyone in authority, either ashore or afloat, that this was a portentous lapse in logic, capable in the event of disaster, such as fire at sea, collision with an iceberg or a derelict, or the foundering of the vessel from any cause, of dooming one-half of the ship's company to a watery grave.

No one could be blamed for the apparent lack of forethought or imagination in this regard. Forty lifeboats slung in double tiers on the boat-deck and after-deck of the *Caronia* occupied the whole of the available space for boats under davits. The problem of providing sufficient lifeboat accommodation for the entire ship's company in a large liner, was a difficult one in marine architectural design. A very large number of cork lifebelts were provided in the *Caronia*, more than sufficient for the entire ship's company; and in the event of wreck there was much buoyant material handy from which rafts could be constructed if time permitted; but the dire fact remained that the lifeboats could not carry more than one-half of the total number of souls in the ship.

Nowadays, after the drastic experiences of two world wars and some few marine disasters in peace-time, passenger ships carry lifeboats for all, and also rafts with buoyancy tanks stowed on the upper decks, so that there is floatage for the entire ship's company.

Under peace-time conditions, and with modern navigational aids and safety precautions, sea-travel has become practically one hundred per cent safe. It is by far the safest method of travelling known on this planet. Excluding war-time hazards and disasters, the loss of life at sea in modern large mechanically propelled vessels in peace-time is virtually nil; and on any calculation sea-travellers take far less risks than travellers by railway, automobile, or aircraft transport, or than pedestrians crossing roads!

From this point of view it may fairly be claimed that human life nowadays is nowhere more safe (in peace-time) than in a passenger-liner at sea; but this safety was by no means as well established in 1907 as it is today. It had to be won, like many other advantages of modern life, at the price of bitter experience and the lessons to be derived therefrom.

Considering the millions of passengers who have been transported across the Atlantic in steamers in nearly 120 years of steam-driven traffic on that route, the losses of life at sea, even including those in war-time, are an infinitesimal proportion of the whole. The peace-time disasters have been relatively very few, and have "made news" because they are untypical.

The fact remained that any passenger embarking in a large liner in 1907, and in that period generally, had to take the risk of being among the one-half of the ship's company for whom lifeboat accommodation was *not* provided. The fair chance was that a disaster would not occur on a transatlantic crossing and that was rightly considered a more than 99.9 per cent certainty.

But my inquisitors demanded to be told everything. "How many people does a lifeboat hold? What provisions does it carry?"

Fortunately for me, Chief Officer Protheroe, who was also

going on watch at 4 p.m., happened along on his way to the bridge, and halted for a moment to pass the time of day with the fair charmers, who, seeing the three gold stripes on his sleeve and his maturity so obviously greater than mine, thrust this question at him: "What food would there be if we had to take to the lifeboats?"

"Well," said Protheroe, contemplatively, "there's fresh water, and—ah-h—biscuits. But," he added, a little apologetically, "there's no *menu*, you know!"

Then we excused ourselves and went on watch.

That evening at 8 p.m. there was a concert in the biggest lounge, with a collection in aid of seamen's charities. Among the passengers was a celebrated operatic soprano, who had kindly consented to sing at the concert. With such a star attraction, there would be no doubt of a "full house".

I was on watch on the bridge until 8 p.m. The weather was calm. With the usual lookouts set, we were belting along at full speed, and the liner was breasting the swells with scarcely any rolling or pitching. When I came off watch, I immediately made my way to the lounge, to enjoy my first shipboard concert, keenly looking forward to hearing the great soprano.

There was standing room only in the lounge, but I managed to squeeze in. On the dais was a grand piano, secured to the deck. Captain Pritchard was present, supporting the chairman of the Passengers' Committee which had organized the concert. Our orchestra was playing a lively overture.

Then followed several "items" of varying quality, including recitations, solos, duets, conjuring acts, and comic songs, all enthusiastically received. At last came the great moment, when the chairman had the very great pleasure and privilege of introducing the world-famous Madame Rosario, who would oblige with the tragic aria from the "mad scene" of *Lucia di Lammermoor*. . . .

The diva, who was of ample proportions, and gloriously gowned, bowed charmingly to acknowledge the rapturous applause that greeted her. Her accompanist took his seat at the piano, and soon her superb voice was soaring and trilling in the ecstasy of artistry, to bring tears to the eyes of all but the case-hardened or tone-deaf.

As she reached the *coda*, something happened up on the bridge. The lookout man, having sighted the dim sidelight of a full-rigged sailing vessel standing across our bows less than half a mile ahead, had instantly alerted the officer of the watch, who at once reacted by ordering, "Hard-a-starboard!"

The helmsman spun the wheel, and the liner instantly answered the helm. At her speed of eighteen knots, this sudden alteration of course caused her to list heavily to starboard.

In the main lounge, the effect of this manoeuvre was tremendous. Within a few seconds, the audience, the singer, the orchestra, about 200 chairs and tables, and innumerable glasses and coffee sets were precipitated in a struggling heap over to the starboard side of the lounge.

It looked like a panic, but the ship righted herself quickly. Realizing what had happened, Captain Pritchard picked up the capsized singer, whispered something reassuring to her, and persuaded her to return to the platform. There, though shaken, she too showed fine professional self-control, and smiled theatrically, but at the same time clung with a strong grip to the Captain's arm.

The Captain called for silence in a voice that had been well trained also—in Cape Horn gales. At this command, the shaken audience became silently attentive. "Ladies and gentlemen," the Captain announced, "there is positively no need for alarm. The concert will continue, and I should like to say that in the whole of my seagoing career I have never seen an audience moved as we have been moved by Madame's singing this evening!"

There was a burst of laughter and applause, and all traces of panic vanished. The stewards rushed in, and soon put things to rights. The concert continued, with an encore from the singer, who, like the ship, was on an even keel again.

On the sixth day out, as we began to approach the American shore, we sighted several sailing vessels ("skysail yarders") standing away to the southeastward, outward bound ("down East") on their long haul around Cape Horn, from the ports of Nova Scotia, the Bay of Fundy, Maine, New Hampshire, or Massachusetts, or homeward bound after voyages of three months or more from the Pacific—each voyage an epic of skill and endurance, if its story could be adequately chronicled.

Now, too, we sighted many steamers, converging to or diverging on various courses from those ports and from New York and the ports of the southern United States. The ocean was thronged here, and we were crossing the Gulf Stream.

A lady passenger remarked to one of our senior officers, "Isn't it wonderful how Columbus discovered America?"

To this the officer replied, as courteously as possible, "It would have been even more wonderful if he had missed it!"

During the night we passed the Nantucket Shoals Light Vessel, the first landmark of America, some 200 miles offshore. When I came on watch at dawn we were steaming westwards in sight of dozens of vessels of all kinds, including "Down Easters" out of New York, New Haven (Connecticut), and Newport (Rhode Island), and fishing trawlers, schooner-rigged, making for or returning from the Newfoundland Banks. At intervals we sighted other liners, and a great variety of tramps. There was no doubt of the nearness of land, as thousands of the smaller kinds of seabirds wheeled in the sky, ready to pounce for scraps in the wake of ships, or on unwary fish.

It was a fine sunny day. The engineers had been warned of our expected time of arrival, and at 9.30 a.m. we began to reduce speed. At 10 a.m. we stopped abeam of the Sandy Hook Light Vessel (9 miles offshore) which in those days was the recognized end of the Blue Riband run. Here we took on the New York harbour pilot, and went on stations. In another half hour we were rounding Sandy Hook to enter New York Lower Bay by the Main Channel.

America, here we come! The Main Channel trends sharply almost due North within the Lower Bay, and, in another hour, with tugs standing by, we were steering through the Narrows (one mile wide), between Staten Island and Long Island, to enter the Upper Bay.

Here we stopped and anchored at quarantine, while the medical and immigration authorities examined passengers and crew. Tenders also came alongside and took off our mail-bags. These procedures took several hours, and then we got under way, and proceeded to the pier.

New York has the biggest and best sheltered deepwater harbour accommodation of all the world's great seaports, and this is one of the prime facts which has made New York City what it is: the portal of America. The distance within the Upper Bay, from the Narrows to the southern tip of Manhattan Island, is seven miles N. by E., but the great port with its many bays has 520 miles of sheltered navigable waterways (measured along bulkheads and shorelines), and 200 deepwater piers.

The geographical layout of Manhattan Island, which is virtually a narrow peninsula of solid rock, between the Hudson River and the East River (a continuation of Long Island Sound), projecting sharply into the Upper Bay, enables vessels of the largest size to be berthed, as it were, in or at the city itself, in a fashion that is possible in few other great seaport cities.

This was the port that Henry Hudson, an Englishman in the service of the Dutch East India Company, discovered when he brought his little ship, *Half Moon,* into the Upper Bay in 1609. (The entrance to the Lower Bay was charted by the Spaniards a century previously, but it was Hudson who found the channel through the shoals off Sandy Hook.)

The Dutch settled here in 1614, and later named the place New Amsterdam. The English threw them out in 1664, altering the name to New York. Then the Americans threw the English out in 1776, but kept the English name.

The Statue of Liberty beckoned us in. It was erected on Bedloes Island in the Upper Bay in 1876, the gift of France to commemorate the first centenary of American Independence. May it be there, too, at the second centenary, and for many more centenaries beyond that! No one who first sights from seaward this colossal bronze image of the Goddess holding aloft her torch, with the skyscrapers of Manhattan beyond, Jersey City to port and Brooklyn to starboard, can fail to heed the message that is framed in her lips: *Welcome!*

I have seen her from that aspect many times in my forty years of service in Cunarders crossing the Atlantic, and always she is the symbol of everything that is best and biggest in America, the real America. . . .

And her eyelids are unwearied.

We berthed at Pier 54, in the Hudson River, at the foot of West Fourteenth Street. Down went the gangways and two thousand New Americans streamed ashore.

CHAPTER FIFTEEN

*New York in the Horse Days—Some Things
Have Changed—Cunard's Wednesday and
Friday Sailings—The Cunard Fleet in 1907—
Shipping Competition in the North Atlantic
—The White Star Line—Pierpont Morgan's
"Combine"—The American Line—Govern-
ment Subsidies to Cunard—The Twenty
Years' Agreement—The Hamburg-Amerika
Line—Norddeutscher Lloyd—The French
Line—Rivalry and Prestige—A Suicide at Sea
—The Lady Who Swooned—"Man Over-
board!"*

ANY young person who knows New York in the middle of the
twentieth century may find it difficult to imagine that busy city
as it was in the pre-automobile age.

That was how I first saw it in 1907. There were very few
automobiles, and those were "gas-buggies" of primitive design,
the playthings of the rich or of mechanical experimenters, who
were stared at, laughed at, and frequently sworn at, as they
spluttered along, frightening horses and pedestrians. The drivers,
perched on high seats, exposed to the elements, wore long "dust-
coats", goggles, and motoring-caps to protect themselves and
their clothes from oil, grease, and dust. But this was a rare sight,
as practically all the traffic in New York was horse-drawn.

There were no flashing stop-go signs. Hundreds of crossing-sweepers, with brooms, shovels, and handcarts, gathered horse manure in tons on Fifth Avenue. Fashionable ladies swept the dusty sidewalks with the hems of their ankle-length dresses; their waists were drawn in with corsets and belts, and their bosoms encased in tight-laced whalebone stays; their sleeves extended to the wrists; their necks were swathed in high collars; they wore big hats, usually adorned with ostrich plumes; and most women out of doors covered their faces in veils to protect their complexions from the city's dust. Horn-rimmed glasses were unknown, and would have been considered grotesque and horrible. Very few people wore glasses, except for reading.

Important men wore bell-topper hats and frock coats, with tight-fitting dark or striped trousers, ankle-boots, starched shirts and collars, cravats with jewel-pins—and almost invariably carried canes. Less important men wore bowler hats and sac suits, but in summer straw "boater" hat were numerous. The lower orders usually wore cloth caps. Boys and girls had button-up boots, and long stockings. Most boys wore knickerbockers, buttoned below the knees.

Many men wore beards, and waxed moustaches were extra smart. There were no cinema-palaces, soda-fountains, cafeterias, or supermarkets. At the piers downtown, dozens of Cape Horn sailing vessels were berthed, their tall top hamper an intricate and beautiful pattern against the sky.

It would seem that almost everything in New York has changed, except the Statue of Liberty and the cigar-store Indians.

Yet, the more New York changes, the more it is the same. Even in 1907 there were skyscrapers—though not piled in such profusion or height as the tremendous Towers of Babel there today. Wall Street was a canyon; Broadway at night-time a blaze of lights; the Bronx was both respectable and tough; and the Bowery as lively then as now, or livelier. The Elevated Railroad made the world's loudest clatter along Sixth Avenue; its passengers had interesting views into apartments along the route; and Times Square, where park bench philosophers meditated and fed the birds, was a green oasis, surrounded by the crags of Big Business.

The *Caronia* lay at Pier 54 for a week, and sailed for Liverpool on the following Wednesday, when the *Carmania* came in, and we met her in the Lower Bay. The midweek service was maintained by four Cunard liners, each taking seven days on the passage, eastbound or westbound, and remaining in port seven days at each end of the run. On this service there were, at any time, one vessel at sea eastbound, one at sea westbound, one in port at Liverpool, and one in port at New York. The *Caronia* and *Carmania* were supported in the "mid-week" service by two elderly but fast Cunarders, the *Umbria* and *Etruria,* single-screw steamers of 8,120 tons—famous sister ships, launched in 1884-85, which, despite their age, could maintain the average of 18 knots necessary to make the crossing in seven days and so meet the requirements of the mail contract.

The Friday sailings from New York and Liverpool were more stylish, as these were maintained by the *Lusitania* and the *Mauretania,* which, at normal service speeds of 23 knots, could make the crossing in five days. In theory, these two great sisters could have carried on the regular service by themselves, each with a stay of two days in port at each end, but in practice this was not enough time for discharging and loading cargo, handling mails, baggage, and passengers off and on, and coaling, watering, cleaning, and provisioning. Therefore, a third vessel alternated with them on the Friday sailings—either the *Campania* or *Lucania,* twin-screw steamers of 12,950 tons, sister ships which, launched in 1893, had service speeds of 22 knots, and could do the crossing in $5\frac{1}{2}$ days.

This arrangement meant that each of the vessels in this service, arriving on Wednesdays, lay nine days in port before her next Friday sailing-day came. This was a waste of time, but inevitable for smooth working of the regular passenger-and-mail service. It had already become obvious that the ideal of maintaining regular weekly sailings from both ends, with only two vessels, would require service speeds of 29 or 30 knots, enabling the crossing to be made in four days—an ideal that seemed a wild dream.

The Cunard Line therefore had seven or eight mail steamers operating between Liverpool and New York, to maintain a twice-weekly service from both ends, with sailings on Wednesdays and Fridays, and calling at Queenstown for Irish passengers and mails. In addition, two or three Cunard liners operated a service between Liverpool and Boston, sometimes calling at Halifax. These included the *Ivernia* and *Saxonia,* twin-screw steamers of approximately 14,000 tons, launched in 1900, but capable of service speeds of only 15 knots, and therefore requiring eight days for the crossing—too slow for the New York mail run.

Four or five Cunarders were engaged on the run from Mediterranean ports direct to New York, chiefly with emigrants and cargo. These included the *Ultonia, Carpathia, Pannonia,* and *Slavonia*—vessels of from 10,000 to 13,000 tons, with speeds of from 12 to 14 knots—comparative slowcoaches, and more serviceable than stylish.

Seven small vessels, averaging 3,000 tons, with speeds of only eight to ten knots, operated a cargo service between Liverpool and Mediterranean ports.

The Cunard Line thus had nineteen steamers in regular service, of which eleven or twelve called at New York. It was not uncommon to see three or more Cunarders lying at adjacent berths at the foot of West Fourteenth Street.

The paintwork of Cunard ships was (and is) of a striking combination of colours. The funnels are red, with a broad band of black at the top, and two or three thin black rings; the masts and derricks golden brown—which we called "Mast Colour"; the superstructure, boats, and ventilators white (with red inside the ventilator cowls); the hull black, with a white line between the topsides and a red boot-topping.

If further means of identification were necessary, the Cunard house-flag fluttered at the mainmast head—the golden lion rampant on a red ground, holding a golden globe in his paws —known to Liverpool wits as "the monkey with the nut".

On the staff at the stern was the "red duster"—the ensign of the British mercantile marine. In some of the ships, in which the Captain and a certain number of the officers and men belonged to the Royal Naval Reserve, the Blue Ensign could be worn, by permission of the Admiralty. When we were bound for New York, until we berthed, Old Glory was worn at our foremast head. Then it was lowered, and the Union Flag of Great Britain was hoisted there, indicating our next country of destination.

Between 21st May and 25th July, 1907, I made three voyages to New York as Fourth Officer in the *Caronia,* acquiring basic knowledge that eventually would become mere routine in the years ahead of me. In port I had opportunities of going aboard the *Mauretania* and the *Lusitania* and of seeing their splendours for the first time at close quarters. I went aboard other Cunarders, and also vessels of the White Star Line and of the German and French lines, which were in keen competition and rivalry with us, and I learnt something then, by first-hand observation, of the intensity of that competition which spurred the men in all Atlantic liners to their utmost efforts to be excellent.

The White Star Line was our chief competitor under the British flag, the more so as it was a Liverpool company, operating directly in competition with the Cunarders on the Liverpool to New York service. The name "White Star" referred to the house-flag—a large five-pointed white star on a red burgee (pennant), which had been first used by the Liverpool firm of Pilkington & Wilson in their fleet of fast sailing vessels carrying passengers, mails, and cargo to Australia during the gold rush of the 1850s.

In 1867, Thomas Henry Ismay had formed the Oceanic Steam Navigation Company, and bought the White Star Line and its flag. Most of the White Star steamers were built by Harland & Wolff at Belfast, and all had names ending in -ic. They had entered the transatlantic service in the 1870s with the *Oceanic*, and other fast, luxuriously appointed ships, which were built bigger and bigger as time went on. White Star steamers ran also to Australia, via South Africa. The second *Oceanic*, 17,274 tons, launched in 1899, was the biggest ship in the world at that time. She was still in service, on the Liverpool to New York run, in 1907, as also were the *Celtic* (20,904 tons), the *Cedric* (21,035 tons), the *Arabic* (15,801 tons), the *Republic* (15,378 tons), and the *Baltic* (23,876 tons). The latest addition to the fleet was the *Adriatic* (24,541 tons), launched in 1907.

These were big and comfortable vessels, with speeds of from fifteen to twenty knots. Though none of them had actually held the Blue Riband, they had provided, for many years, like the Cunarders, in regular rotation, twice-a-week sailings from Liverpool and New York, and had an excellent reputation. We had got ahead of them in size and speed with the *Mauretania* and *Lusitania*; but, in April, 1907, the White Star Line gained an advantage by re-routing from Southampton, via Cherbourg, to New York. This route provided quicker access for Americans to London and Paris than we provided with our terminal at Liverpool.

It was announced that the White Star Line intended to build two gigantic liners, each of over 45,000 tons, which would be by far the biggest and fastest ships in the world, and the most luxuriously fitted . . . the *Olympic* . . . and the *Titanic*. . . .

Behind the scenes in this intense competition were the efforts of the American financier, J. Pierpont Morgan, to form an international shipping combine. He and his associates, having already amalgamated many of the American railroad companies into a combine, attempted in 1902 and the ensuing years to merge the shipping companies of the North Atlantic into a similar cartel or group, which was named the International Mercantile Marine. They bought or gained majority share control of the White Star Line and of several other companies, including the Inman (an American company), the Red Star, Dominion, Atlantic Transport, and Leyland lines, and some other smaller companies, and made strenuous efforts to induce the Cunard Line, the two big German lines, and the French Line, to join the combine.

The immense and ambitious scheme would have obvious financial advantages to the shareholders of the merged companies —bigger dividends from monopoly or near-monopoly control, greater working efficiency and the elimination of cutthroat competition, plus probably the jacking-up of fares and freights if all or nearly all the big companies could be brought into the combine.

But the British, German, and French governments sensed the danger of allowing the biggest and best ships under their national flags to pass into foreign control. The International Mercantile Marine ("I.M.M.") was, in the final resort, American-owned, and was known as "the American Line". Yet, with shrewd diplomacy, the organizers of the combine allowed the ships of each of the companies in the merger to retain their previous national registrations, house flags, and identities, and to continue as before, to all external appearances. All that was altered was the financial control, which would gradually be made effective in practical control and reorganization of the services.

The implied threat to the companies which stayed outside the merger was that they would be squeezed out of the Atlantic trade by the financial weight of the combine. From the points of view of the British, German, and French governments, it was not only desirable, but essential that merchant ships under their flags should be available in time of war for use as troop transports, hospital ships, or as armed merchant cruisers. For this reason, the British Government offered the Cunard Line a substantial inducement to remain outside the I.M.M. combine.

As early as 1893, the *Lucania* and *Campania* had been built under Admiralty supervision, to serve as armed merchant cruisers if required, with a Government subsidy of £7,500 a year for each vessel. Several Cunard liners had been chartered as troop transports during the South African War of 1899-1901.

When the Pierpont Morgan group in 1902 attempted to bring the Cunard Line into the I.M.M. merger, the British Government countered with an offer to lend the Cunard Company two and a half million pounds (repayable over twenty years), to enable two new giant liners to be built, which would also be suitable for use as auxiliary cruisers in war-time· It was in this way that the *Mauretania* and *Lusitania* had been designed, built, and launched in 1906. Further, under a twenty years agreement, the Government paid the Cunard Company an annual subsidy of £150,000 for the maintenance of these two ships. In consideration of these benefits, plus the mail contracts, Cunard undertook to remain outside the I.M.M. combine, to retain its British ownership, and to put its fleet on charter at the disposal of the British Government in a national emergency.

The German and French governments also intervened, with subsidies or other inducements, to prevent the principal companies under their flags from joining the I.M.M. combine. These interventions prevented Pierpont Morgan's merger from attaining anything like monopoly control of shipping in the North Atlantic. The "American Line", including the White Star ships, became in effect only one of five big companies keenly competing on the transatlantic routes. The others were the Cunard Line, the Hamburg-Amerika Line, the Norddeutscher Lloyd, and the French Line (Compagnie Générale Transatlantique).

German seamanship has always been of high efficiency. In the late nineteenth and early twentieth century, the famous "P" line of sailing vessels on the Cape Horn route included the biggest and best appointed wind-driven craft ever launched. As early as 1847 (only seven years after the Cunard steamship service was inaugurated), the Hamburg-Amerika line had put its first steamers on the American run. This company in 1907 had ten beautiful liners maintaining a twice-weekly schedule between Hamburg and New York. These included five older vessels of 12,000 tons, and one, the *Deutschland*, of 16,000 tons, all very smartly appointed.

The four biggest and newest vessels in this fleet shone in any company, and were firm favourites among transatlantic travellers in both directions. One of them, the *Amerika* (22,225 tons), launched in 1905, was built by Harland & Wolff, at Belfast. The other three were built in Germany. They were the *Kaiserin Augusta* (24,581 tons, launched in 1906), and the *President Lincoln* and *President Grant,* each of 18,000 tons, launched in 1907. Though fast and very comfortable, none of these vessels ever held the Blue Riband.

The other big German company, Norddeutscher Lloyd, of Bremen, had begun steamship services to New York in 1857, and had a fine record of achievement. In 1907 there were four N.D.L. ships maintaining a once-a-week service between Bremen and New York, with calls at Southampton and Cherbourg.

The *Kaiser Wilhelm der Grosse* (14,349 tons) launched in 1897, took the Blue Riband of the Atlantic in that year with a speed of 21.91 knots. The *Kronprinz Wilhelm* (14,908 tons) was launched in 1902. The *Kaiser Wilhelm II* (19,361 tons) launched in 1903, took the Blue Riband in that year with a speed of 22.60 knots, which was also a "record" passage, and she surpassed this record in 1906, with a speed of 23.58 knots. This was almost equalled by the *Lusitania* on her maiden voyage in 1907, with a crossing at 23.10 knots, and narrowly beaten in that same year by the *Mauretania,* with a speed of 23.69 knots.

Such was the rivalry of the times. The fourth and newest Norddeutscher Lloyd liner was the *Kronprinzessin Cecilie* (19,400 tons), launched in 1907. She attained average service speeds of 22 knots, but never took the Blue Riband or set a record. Our *Mauretania* was the crack liner of them all, but the two German companies together, with fourteen liners in service, and sailings thrice a week, provided very serious competition that kept standards of service high and fares low. They were transporting hundreds of thousands of emigrants from Europe to America yearly, at cut rates, besides providing luxurious first-class and cabin accommodation.

The French Line at this time was providing a once-a-week service between Le Havre and New York, with three medium sized but stylish liners—*La Lorraine* (11,146 tons), *La Savoie* (11,168 tons), and *La Provence* (13,753 tons), the last named of these being quite new, launched in 1906. But the French were also planning big-ship construction, and had a vessel of 23,000 tons, *La France,* on the stocks.

In summary, there were thirty-seven smart and big liners on the North Atlantic run to New York, of which nineteen were British, fourteen German, and four French, in addition to a number of smaller passenger-steamers—Norwegian, Russian (Finnish), Italian, and others that I have not particularized.

Truly, New York attracted ships like a magnet, for it was the portal of Great America, the up-and-coming Land of Opportunity. There was intense but friendly rivalry and keen competition between the shipping lines, which continued until the outbreak of war in 1914. Each was striving to excel, but, in those days of unrestricted immigration to the U.S.A., there seemed to be scope for an ever increasing expansion, with no limit to the size and speed of ships that would be built in the contest for maritime supremacy, and for national prestige.

On one of my eastbound crossings as Fourth Officer in the *Caronia*, there was an extraordinary incident. At 7.30 p.m., an hour after we had passed the Sandy Hook Light Vessel, I was on watch on the bridge with the Chief Officer, when suddenly we heard a hoarse cry from the boat-deck on the starboard side, "Man overboard!"

Instantly the Chief Officer rang the engines to STOP, and then to FULL ASTERN PORT. With the helm hard-a-starboard, the ship was "swinging on her heel", and he steadied her on her opposite course, with both engines SLOW AHEAD. The Captain had come onto the bridge, and, at the same instant, an elderly steward scrambled up the companionway to the bridge, white-faced, gasping, "A man took his overcoat off and jumped overboard. . . . A lady saw him do it. . . ."

Losing no time, the Captain used the brassy, newfangled, loudspeaking telephone to the after-bridge, and said crisply to the quartermaster on duty there, "Man overboard! Drop a lifebuoy!"

"I dropped a buoy, sir, at the first cry," came the rumbling reply through the instrument.

"Is the man in sight anywhere?"

"No, sir, not in sight. I didn't see him fall. I was in the wheelhouse." (It was not a duty of the men on the after-bridge to keep a lookout at sea.)

"Drop another buoy, with a Holmes light on it," the Captain ordered. "Keep a sharp lookout."

Orders now flowed from the Captain in swift succession. To Chief Officer Protheroe he said, "Get all hands on stations again, Mister, to keep sharp lookout and search for the man gone overboard. Man the starboard sea-boat and swing her out ready to lower. Keep on this course, and we'll run slowly back, while I try to find out when he went over. Take bearings on the light of the lifebuoy." (This was now bobbing about in our wake, showing flame and smoke.)

It was nearly dark, but visibility was good, with a moderate N.W. breeze and choppy seas. Officers and men had gone off stations an hour previously, when we had passed the Light Vessel. They were snatching a meal before the change of the watch at 8 p.m., so that all were handy. In remarkably quick time, all the seamen were on deck, and placed where they could keep a good lookout.

The Captain now asked the steward, "What happened?"

Collecting his wits, the steward replied, "When everyone else went below to dinner, one lady stayed on deck, sitting in a deck-chair. She told me to fetch her coffee. When I came back with it in a few minutes, the lady was in a swoon."

"A *swoon?*"

"Yes, sir, a dead faint. I couldn't revive her. A man's overcoat and cap were in the deck-chair alongside her. They were not there before. The overcoat was neatly folded. I thought that he had put them there and gone to fetch the doctor. But when the doctor didn't come, I went to the saloon and fetched him. He worked on the lady, and brought her to. She stared wildly around, then she pointed to the man's coat and cap alongside her, and she said, 'That man jumped overboard!' She nearly fainted again at that, but I took no chances, sir. I threw a lifebuoy over and gave the alarm to the forebridge and the after-bridge."

"How long was she in a swoon?"

"Can't say for certain, sir. It might have been for a few minutes while I was away getting the coffee, then another ten minutes while I was fetching the doctor, and five minutes or so for him to bring her to."

"Hell!" said the Captain. "If that's right, the man who went overboard must have been miles astern when we stopped. Proceed at half speed now, Mr Protheroe, or we'll be too late to have any chance of saving him—that is, if he didn't break his neck when he fell, and didn't get caught in the propellers. You think then," he said to the steward, "that he jumped overboard twenty or twenty-five minutes ago?"

"That's about it, sir."

"I'll have to question that woman!"

At this moment the Doctor came up to the bridge, and said to the Captain, "No doubt a man *did* jump over. I've questioned the lady closely. She says that he came on deck, when dinner was about half way through. He was muttering to himself. He took off his overcoat and cap, and asked her permission to lay them on a vacant deck-chair at her side. She assented, and the next moment he climbed over the rail and plunged overboard. Then she swooned."

"Confound her!" roared the Captain. "She swooned at the wrong moment!"

"She couldn't help it," said the Doctor. "Tight stays and emotion too much for her."

"What was his name?"

"He was a stranger to her."

To the steward standing by, the Captain said, "Tell the Purser and the Chief Steward to find out from the cabin stewards and the dining-room stewards the name of the passenger who left the saloon early. Search his cabin and all passenger-compartments in case he's still on board. The lady may be suffering from delusions."

"She's quite lucid now," remarked the Doctor. "A man jumped overboard. No doubt about that."

We were running back at half speed on our course, with every available man keeping a sharp lookout. The Captain ordered me to Monkey Island to take bearings on the lifebuoy light that was now astern to eastwards. He pricked out our position on the chart, and calculated where the liner was went the man jumped overboard, as nearly as he could reckon from the evidence. This done, he ordered full speed ahead for a few minutes, until we neared the supposed site of the mishap.

Here the engines were stopped, and we scanned the surrounding seas in the dusk. The passengers were coming up from the dining-saloons, and beginning to stroll on deck, at first in ignorance of what had happened. But they soon heard the news, and excitedly lined the rails. In the meantime the Purser and Chief Steward had ascertained the man's identity, and found, on a search throughout the ship, that he was indeed missing.

Safety precautions in liners are such that it is practically impossible for a passenger to fall overboard accidentally. There was little doubt that the man had attempted suicide—and had succeeded. Yet the Captain had the duty to search for him, while any hope of life, or of recovering the body, remained.

The sea-boat on the lee side of the boat-deck was launched, manned by eight seamen and the Senior Third Officer. If this operation could serve no better purpose, it was good exercise. For an hour the boat circled the liner, without finding any trace of the man overboard. Then, as darkness had set in, with a fresh breeze and choppy sea rising, the Captain recalled the boat, put the ship about, and we proceeded on our former course.

Everything that could be done had been done. A report of the incident was wirelessed to the shore station. At the inquest, on evidence taken later in Liverpool and New York, it was established that the man who had jumped overboard had lost heavily in stock exchange speculations, financially ruining himself and many of his friends. Lacking the courage required to face this situation, he had taken a first-class steamer ticket to Eternity.

CHAPTER SIXTEEN

*Transferred to the "Ultonia"—The Mediter-
ranean Emigrant Service—Passengers, Mails,
and Cargo—The McKinley Tariffs and
American Oversea Trade—A Veteran Cap-
tain—Agreeable Shipmates—Austrians, Hun-
garians, and Italians—Confiscating "Colts"—
Meals in an Emigrant Ship—A Questionnaire
on Seagulls—Gibraltar—"See Naples and
Die!"—A Sailor's Roaming Life—Home at
Sea—Stromboli's Fiery Breath—Scylla and
Charybdis—Messina—The Adriatic—Trieste
—Emigrants and Trachoma—Fiume—Corfu
—Grapes at Almeria—A Cure for Seasickness
—Ellis Island.*

ARRIVING in New York on my third voyage in the *Caronia*,
on 25th July, 1907, I was transferred to the *Ultonia*, as Fourth
Officer, to relieve her Fourth Officer, who had been away from
his home in Liverpool for a year, on the Mediterranean to New
York run.

This was an Irishman's rise for me, as the *Ultonia* was an
"old tub", compared with the stylish *Caronia*, but my opinions
of my transfer were better left unexpressed, as I had no choice
in the matter. It would be a new experience, so I took the announcement cheerfully enough, moved my dunnage aboard the
Ultonia, and began my new duties.

Launched on the Tyne in 1898, the *Ultonia* was a twin-screw steamer of 10,402 tons, 513 feet long, 57 feet beam, with a speed of 12½ knots. She had one funnel, and carried a crew of 150, with accommodation for thirty or forty first-class passengers and 1,000 third class, and hold-capacity for 3,000 tons of cargo. For five years after her launching, she had been on the Liverpool to Boston run, and then was transferred in 1904 to the Mediterranean service, carrying chiefly Hungarian and Italian emigrants, general cargo, and mails. She was on this service when I joined her.

A voyage—from New York to Trieste, via several Mediterranean ports, and return to New York—occupied seven weeks. Four Cunard steamers maintained a schedule of fortnightly sailings on this route, the other three being the *Carpathia*, *Slavonia*, and *Pannonia*, occasionally relieved by the *Saxonia* when one of the vessels on the regular run required refit. The service had been inaugurated in 1904 under an agreement between the Cunard company and the Hungarian Government (one of the components of the Empire of Austria-Hungary) for transporting emigrants under official supervision. At this time the ports of Trieste and Fiume, at the head of the Adriatic Sea, were in the territory of Austria-Hungary.

During ten years, 1904-14, two million emigrants from Hungary and Austria were transported to the U.S.A., chiefly by the Cunard Adriatic service. In that period, also, two million emigrants from Italy crossed the Western Ocean to America, many of them in Cunarders. We carried also Greek emigrants from Corfu, and some Spaniards from Almeria. This vast movement of New Americans was supplementary to the exodus of emigrants from Russia, Germany, the Baltic countries, Britain, Ireland, and France, in vessels sailing from the ports of northwestern Europe.

Truly, America was "the melting pot", and the inscription on the base of the Statue of Liberty was apt:

> Give me your tired, your poor,
> Your huddled masses yearning to breathe free,
> The wretched refuse of your teeming shore;
> Send these, the tempest-tossed, to me:
> I lift my lamp beside the golden door.

The fare from Trieste or Fiume to New York was ten pounds

—modest enough, as it included board and lodging at sea for three and a half weeks on the westward passage—but in the aggregate of one thousand souls at ten pounds a soul, each voyage was a big financial operation, on the scale of monetary values at that time. The liners carried also mails and cargo both ways, and eastbound passengers who were chiefly former emigrants returning on visits to their old homelands.

When I joined the *Ultonia,* she was loading cargo. The chief exports from the U.S.A. to Mediterranean and other European countries were bagged wheat, baled cotton, tobacco, bagged ore, pig-iron, ingots of copper and other metals, and lumber. Very few manufactured articles were being sent from the U.S.A. to Europe, where almost every kind of factory-product was made locally at prices with which American exporters could not com-pete.

In the other direction, the importation of European manufac-tured goods to the U.S.A. was curbed by the policy of high pro-tection embodied in the McKinley tariffs of 1890. These tariffs heavily penalized the import of any manufactured goods which would compete with, or undersell, American-made goods.

In abandoning the policy of "Free Trade" (a tendency which had begun as early as 1861, at the end of the Civil War), the U.S.A. had struck a heavy blow at its own mercantile marine, which in earlier years had carried "Yankee notions" (hardware novelties) to all the world's ports. Under the policy of high pro-tection, return cargoes had become increasingly difficult to obtain, and the cargo-carrying trade under the American flag was restrict-ed almost to coastal traffic, and to the "Down Easters" voyaging between the east and west coasts of the U.S.A., via Cape Horn. Even this trade was threatened by interior coast-to-coast railroads.

It was only the massive movement of passengers, namely the emigrants from Europe, plus the tourist trade, and the mail-services, which enabled the transatlantic shipping services to flourish. The cargo was supplementary. It was profitable enough on the eastbound route, but harder to obtain on the westbound route.

From Mediterranean ports, we could carry only goods which would not be too heavily penalized by the U.S.A's high protec-tion policy. These included dried vine-fruits and figs, olives, olive oil, wines, sheet cork (from Spain), cases of oranges and tanger-ines, and casks of fresh grapes (also from Spain).

The Master of the *Ultonia,* Captain C. A. Smith, was a jovial old-style sailorman. His recollections went back to the iron-hulled clipper-bow single-screw Cunard liners which used auxiliary sails, and even to the last of the iron-hulled paddle-wheelers, the *Scotia,* which was in service until 1878. It was remarkable indeed to consider that the *Scotia* (3,871 tons), with her paddle-wheels and sails, took the Blue Riband in 1864 with a speed of 14.54 knots, and was faster than any of the screw steamers of her day and for twenty years afterwards. In fact, she was faster than the twin-screw *Ultonia* and many others of the Cunard fleet in service in 1907.

"Paddles grip the water better than screws. Wind in the sails is cheaper than burning coal," Captain Smith said to me, adding, "and the clipper bow cuts the seas."

That was an oldtime sailor's view of the modern progress that had discarded paddles, sails, and clipper bows in steamers. The main reason for the change in design was the ever-increasing size to which passenger-liners were being built. Paddles and sails on vessels of over 4,000 tons would need to be enlarged in proportion until they would become too bulky and unwieldy.

The use of steel plates (instead of the heavier iron plates), introduced in the 1880s, had enabled vessels to be built bigger without too much extra weight in the hull, and this enlargement in turn wrote "finis" to the paddle-and-sail design of the earlier years. A further disadvantage of paddle-steamers was that they could not lay flush alongside wharves, as screw steamers can do, for convenience in loading and unloading cargo (the paddle-boxes projected ten feet or more amidships).

Captain Smith had a large Roman nose, which had caused him to be given (behind his back) the nickname of "Sheeny" Smith, but in no sense disrespectfully, for he was a grand old shipmaster of the tough and jolly breed, who had been trained in a hard school, and could rise to any emergency with the instantly right reaction. It was a privilege to serve under his command.

The *Ultonia* carried a Chief Officer and four other deck officers. Chief Officer Simpson ("Simmy") was a rotund, rubicund, jovial man, with the twinkling brown eyes of a mischievous monkey—a fine seaman, but fond of pranks and funny stories. I was lucky to be in the four-to-eight watch on the bridge with him when we were on sea-routine, as he never allowed anything to put him out of his good temper.

The First Officer, Edgar Britten, then thirty-three years of age, was a keen man, who had been in sail for nine years before joining the Cunard service in 1901. He was well on his way up the ladder of promotion which would eventually bring him to the highest post of responsibility in the Cunard service, and a knighthood.

We were a cheerful crowd. The Second Officer was known as "Silent" Lewis—the most talkative man I have ever met. He was elderly, and had been passed over for promotion for many years, probably on account of his gift of the gab. He had never heeded the proverbs, "A still tongue maketh a wise head", or, " 'Tis better to remain silent and be thought a fool, than to open your mouth and leave no doubt of it." His talkativeness was in no sense malicious, but merely affable—and excessive.

The Third Officer, "Peddlar" Hughes, and I, as Fourth Officer, stood watch on the bridge as juniors or assistants, never in charge of a watch. All deck officers and deckhands were on stations when entering or leaving port, and on the same routine as that in the *Caronia* when the liner was at sea. Our boatswain was a Greek—a right seaman of the Cape Horn breed. We carried three doctors—one Scottish (Dr McIntyre), one Hungarian, and one Italian—and similarly the Masters-at-Arms, the purser's clerks, and the catering staffs and stewards included Hungarians and Italians, besides British.

In the earlier years of the Cunard Adriatic service, brawls had occurred on shipboard between emigrants of Italian nationality and those of Austrian-Hungarian nationality. These brawls were due to national tensions and enmity. To avoid them, the Company's agents at Trieste and Fiume would fill a ship, if possible, with Austrians and Hungarians, supplemented, if necessary for a full ship, with Serbians and Greeks, on the westbound passage; and reserve the bookings in other ships exclusively for Italians.

Sailing day came, and our eastbound passengers from New York streamed up the gangway. The third-class passengers were nearly all Italians, who had lived for some years in America, and were now returning to Italy to visit their parents or other relatives and friends. They were laden with gifts, and it was known that many of them carried revolvers. What better present to take to the old folks at home than an American Colt?

But, at the head of the gangway, the ship's police frisked every passenger and temporarily confiscated dozens of revolvers. There

181

were agonized protests, but it was explained that the weapons would be handed back to their owners when the passengers disembarked at Naples. A numbered check-ticket was given for each revolver seized, and the duplicate chits put under the trigger. This was done at the suggestion of the Italian Police in Naples, but the passengers were unaware of that. The Captain had the absolute right to refuse to admit armed persons on board. It was no use arguing, but very voluble arguments occurred before the weapons were handed over.

At last all were embarked, and we cast off moorings. Our first-class passengers included thirty or forty Americans, chiefly of non-Italian origin, who were going on tourist trips by this route direct to Spain or Italy. Our Mediterranean service was by no means as stylish as those from New York and Boston to Britain, France, and Germany· The American *Social Register,* and the gossip columns of the newspapers, seldom or never mentioned the names of passengers arriving or departing by the Adriatic migrant-ships; but they invariably published the first-class passenger-lists of the big liners on the other run.

After dropping the pilot at Sandy Hook Light Vessel, we went off stations and set course on the Great Circle route to Gibraltar, a passage of 3,194 miles, which at our average speed of $12\frac{1}{2}$ knots, would take fourteen days.

This track, for most of its distance along or near Lat. 40 deg. N., is in a warm-weather and usually fine-weather region of the ocean, especially in August. In mid-ocean, the track begins to trend southeasterly to Gibraltar (in Lat. 37 deg. 57 min. N.), and so passes on the northern side of the Azores Islands, though out of sight of the land there when the vessel is on her true course.

The food served to the third-class passengers consisted of their national dishes, prepared by Austrian-Hungarian or Italian cooks, with plenty of goulash for the Hungarians and spaghetti for the Italians, and cheap red wine at all meals. The service was rough and ready, but they seemed to enjoy it, and always asked for more. The foreign dishes were also on the first-class menu and served in the officers' and engineers' messrooms, varied occasionally by British or American style cooking.

There was no pampering of the passengers, as far as meals were concerned. Breakfast was served at 7.30, lunch at noon, and table d'hôte dinner at 6 p.m. An hour after those times, the tables were cleared, and any passenger who had overslept, or was seasick, had to be content with a hard biscuit until the next meal came around.

The dining-saloons were fitted with long, narrow tables, each accommodating fifteen or twenty people, who sat on hard swivel chairs, which were securely bolted to the deck. Around the edges of the tables, and down the centre, were strips of wood, three or four inches high, known as "fiddles". These were to prevent plates and dishes from sliding into the laps of diners. Above the tables in the first class were swinging trays, suspended by chains from the deckhead. These held glasses, bottles, and cruets. The sight of these contraptions, jerkily adjusting themselves to the motion of the vessel, did more to upset the equilibrium of the diners than the food itself. At dinner, each course was announced by the stroke of a gong. If a passenger arrived late, he began his meal with the course in progress, or, if a course appeared that he felt disinclined to tackle, he waited patiently until the next one was served. A light supper of savoury snacks was handed round at 9.30 p.m. This was the most sociable meal of the day, and was usually followed by singing and games until "Lights Out" at 11 p.m.

Being with Chief Officer "Simmy" Simpson in the four o'clock to eight o'clock watch, I was called each morning at 3.45 a.m., and went up on the bridge at 4 a.m., in pitch darkness. It is necessary for lookout purposes, in the safe navigation of ships, that there should be no lights shining on the bridge, or forrard of the bridge, so that a clear view may be obtained of anything ahead, including the navigation lights of other vessels. With the exception of a shrouded light that dimly illumines the compass for the helmsman, the bridge at night-time is in utter darkness. Officers and lookout men with long practice develop night-vision, like cats; but, in the 4 a.m. to 8 a.m. watch, daylight slowly comes in, with its gradually increasing visibility and widening horizons, to ease the tension of lookout.

Underfoot on the bridge deck were cross-slatted wooden gratings. Chief Officer Simpson would say, "Daylight's coming in. I can see the holes in the gratings." That was a valuable lesson in observation. I learnt many other things from him which young officers learn from seniors, but that remark remains in my memory as an example of the right seamanlike attention to detail that can come only from practical instruction.

In the creation of the Universe, the first words spoken were, "Let there be Light!"

In the seafaring profession, perhaps more than in any other, light and darkness, and the gradations between them, have vital meanings at every moment while the ship is in motion. The more light, the greater safety, when navigation depends so much on vision; but in the hours of darkness, the ship continues on her course; for no darkness beneath the sky can be absolute. Even at night-time, there is visibility on the waters, but vision is restricted, and each new day comes in with a sigh of relief that darkness has been left astern. The night lingers "in the holes of the gratings", reluctant to be dispelled, but day's victory then is near.

When we were twelve days out from New York, and nearing the Azores, gulls and other seabirds soared around the liner, as usual in the vicinity of land, to pounce on scraps thrown overboard, or on fish disturbed in our wake. Among our passengers was an intellectual young lady from an inland city in the U.S.A., who, chaperoned by her mother, was making her first pilgrimage to Europe, to visit the shrines of art and culture in Spain and Italy.

Keen to learn as much as she could about everything, she tackled me one afternoon with a series of questions about seagulls, giving me fortunately no chance to reply, as she answered each question herself as soon as she asked it. "Oh, officer," she said, "maybe *you* can tell me: where do seagulls sleep? Here we are in the middle of the ocean and no place for the poor things to go. Do they sleep on the wing, or do they just rest on the water? It seems to me that if they sleep on the wing they might run into the ship and get killed. Then, on the other hand, if they sleep on the water, the ship might run into them, or they might get toppled over by a wave. Maybe they go without sleep."

"Maybe," I agreed, wondering which part of her complicated question I should attempt to answer first. But she gave me no chance, as she continued her remarks at breathless speed. "My goodness, I'm glad I'm not a seagull! When I'm on the ocean I can just *sleep my head off*. Do you think they follow the ship the whole way over, or would they be different gulls every day? They all look the same to me, but I suppose officers with trained eyesight can tell the difference."

"Sometimes," I said, cautiously.

'But they certainly *are* beautiful, aren't they?" she rattled on. "Isn't it perfectly amazing the way they fly around without moving their wings? How do they do it? Is it true that they never follow Scotch ships? I don't believe that, do you? Scotchmen wouldn't be so *mean* as not to throw *any* scraps to the seagulls, would they? It's just a wicked English joke against the poor Scots, isn't it? Don't you *love* watching the seagulls? I could stand here all day and do nothing else. A lot of folks on board ship just sit around talking and eating and drinking and sleeping, and never see beautiful things like the gulls. Don't you think . . . My goodness, there's the dinner bugle! Wish I could stay and hear more about the gulls . . . perfectly fascinating . . . thanks a lot for such an interesting talk!"

This same charming lady, in her endless quest for information next day tackled the Captain, and said to him skittishly, "Is it true, Captain, that like all sailors, you have a wife in every port?"

Captain Smith smiled tolerantly. "No!" he said, firmly. "It is not true!" Then he paused, and added, "There are seven ports that I haven't been in yet."

On the fourteenth day out from New York, we steamed into the Strait of Gilbraltar—the "Pillars of Hercules" of the ancient legend—and dropped anchor a quarter of a mile offshore in the perfect haven sheltered by the gigantic natural rock-fortress that is the key of the Mediterranean. Though I had seen the "Rock" from a distance three years previously, when I was in the S.S. *Shira,* this was the first time that I had seen the naval base, the shore establishments of the navy and the military garrison, and the "Settlement" along its narrow shore: a sight to thrill a Briton then as now, for it was won by valour, and remained, as it does to this day, a fortress of freedom.

We stayed only two hours at "Gib." to disembark into tenders some of our passengers, who were going to Spain, and to deliver the mails, while bumboats surrounded the ship, doing a brisk trade, selling oranges and wine. Then we hove up the anchor, steamed out of the bay, and set course eastwards, rounding Europa Point, for Naples—a run of 976 miles, which took us three and a half days.

There we berthed at a wharf in the Mercantile Harbour, near the Customs House, on the northern side of the famous crescent-shaped Bay of Naples, with a smell of sulphur from Mount Vesuvius, emitting its plume of smoke ten miles away, on the eastern shore. This was my first visit to Italy. The Bay of Naples looked exactly like a coloured picture-postcard of itself—the sea and sky too brightly blue.

To the soul of the poet Naples is picturesque, but to the mariner the approach to the Mercantile Harbour, enclosed in an artificial breakwater, is merely a technical problem, and he has little time to view the scenery until the moorings are made fast. The tourist slogan of the times was, "See Naples and die!" Our Chief Officer, Simmy Simpson, commented, "What they mean is '*Smell* Naples and die. . . .'"

As we neared the wharf, our passengers were in a tremendous state of excitement. Nearly all of them were to disembark here. It was a return to the beloved native land that they had so often dreamed of in their years of exile. Their friends and relatives were massed on the wharf, behind barriers, kept back by operatic-looking police.

At last the gangways were down, and the returning venturers descended to set foot again on their native soil. At the head of the gangway, our ship's police stood on guard, with dozens of ticketed revolvers in a box on the deck. As each owner of a revolver presented his ticket, he was handed his weapon, pocketed it, and made his way down the gangway.

As soon as he set foot on his native soil—or, more precisely on the wharf stones—the Italian shore police, waiting there, frisked him and took his revolver away from him. The unlicensed importation of firearms into Italy was prohibited.

Loud were the lamentations. The confiscated Colts went into another box—on the wharf.

We lay three days at Naples, and discharged most of our cargo. This was the work of the stevedores, but the deck officers had to stand by, while the work was in progress, from 8 a.m. to 6 p.m., to exercise general supervision. In the evenings we strolled ashore, to enjoy the sights of Naples. There was a flower festival in progress, with dancing and singing in the streets and the little squares, and the carnival spirit in full swing. The Neapolitans certainly know how to enjoy life. I have never been in Naples when there was not a carnival in progress there; but though the sights of the city were lively, the smells were also lively, especially in some of the narrow streets and lanes, where public sanitation was not as well supervised as it is today.

It was being borne in on me that a sailor's life is a roaming, homeless, life; for he is never long enough in one place to be at home anywhere. His ship is his home, but, even there, he loses his friends almost as soon as he makes them—among the passengers, anyway, who are birds of passage, here today, gone tomorrow. His shipmates remain longer, but they, too, are likely to vanish from his ken, as he, or they, are transferred to other ships. Everything is in movement, the scene forever changing, from shore to sea, and from sea to another shore; or from winter and grey skies to summer and blue skies, in a matter of weeks, or even days, as his ship moves on through ever-changing degrees of climate and weather; and from country to country, where different lingoes, different garb, food, features and scenes forever greet him.

Yet, with all this restless movement, he is not discontented. There is a purpose in his life all the time; for, when one destination is attained and done with, he is bound for another, equally definite if only as a pinpoint on a chart, and, if he has not been there before, he can look forward to seeing something new: and, if it is a place that he already knows, he can look forward to knowing it better!

Every port is interesting to arrive at, but even more interesting to depart from; for then another port beckons. If he has any home, it is at sea. The famous line of Robert Louis Stevenson would make more sense to sailors if it were rewritten, "Home is the sailor, home at sea. . . ."

From Naples we proceeded southwards along the Italian shore, for one day's run, to the Strait of Messina, between Sicily and the Calabrian "toe" of Italy. I was on watch on the bridge from 4 a.m. to 8 a.m., when in the darkness before dawn we passed the active volcano of Stromboli, in the Lipari Islands. Only ten miles away on our starboard beam, it was breathing fire, not actively erupting, but the boiling lava inside its cone threw a baleful red glow into the sky, which increased and subsided alternately like the breath of a gigantic and hellish dragon.

No wonder the Italians have a "volcanic" temperament!

We steered into the narrow Strait of Messina, between Scylla and Charybdis, and anchored for a few hours in the harbour of Messina, to disembark our few remaining passengers and some parcels of cargo. Then we proceeded on our way, with a clear view of Mount Etna, mildly erupting, forty miles to the westward.

Our course now was past Cape Spartivento, and across the

mouth of the Gulf of Taranto, to round the "heel" of Italy at Otranto, and steam nor'westerly the entire length of the Adriatic Sea to the port of Trieste, at the extreme of that landlocked gulf, which is like an inland sea—but this is a great track of shipping in history, for opposite Trieste is Venice.

Our passage from Naples to Trieste, 800 miles, occupied three days. Now we were in a climate pleasantly cool in that midsummer season, for the Gulf of Trieste is surrounded by spurs of the Julian Alps. The city of Trieste, one of the chief seaports of Austria-Hungary, had shipbuilding yards, and was a base of the Austrian-Hungarian Navy. It was a bone of contention between the Austrians and the Italians, being very near the border between the two countries. About half the population of the city and province were of Italian descent.

Here, after discharging the mails and the last of our cargo, we coaled and watered ship, loaded some cargo, and got ready to take on our passengers. Eight hundred Hungarians—men, women, and children—had been assembled by the emigration authorities, in co-operation with the Cunard agent. We were to take on another 200 at Fiume, and some Greeks at Corfu.

Before embarkation, the emigrants were assembled in a compound near the wharf, to be medically examined by the ship's doctors. I was instructed to go with the doctors and interpreters and ship's police, and two or three of our uniformed deckhands, as a bodyguard or witness of events, in case of trouble of any kind. The intending passengers were formed into queues in the compound, leading into the doctors' hut, from which—if they passed—they filed out through a gate to the wharf and embarked.

I saw some pathetic sights there. The U.S. immigration authorities had a short list of diseases which debarred sufferers from admission to the States. One of these was trachoma, a disease of the eye marked by granular spots on the inner surface of the lids.

The doctors examined each intending emigrant carefully for trachoma, and apparently for nothing else! A pencil-like instrument was pressed against the upper eyelid, and then the doctor would grab the upper eyelash and turn the lid back on the pencil. If tell-tale white spots showed—trachoma—the sufferer was rejected then and there.

This was a terrible shock to people who had travelled perhaps hundreds of miles, after selling all their possessions, intending to go to America. Several times I saw whole families pass the doctor, except one young child, who had trachoma. There were

188

angry protests, and soothing explanations by police and emigration authorities, after which, with outbursts of grief, the whole family would tearfully give up the idea of making the voyage.

In hard cases such as this, there was sometimes an attempt at bribery and corruption, and large cash sums would be offered to the doctor to let the sufferer go on board. But, apart from his moral scruples, the doctor had to be hard, as immigrants were all examined again for trachoma at Ellis Island in New York, and any found suffering from that complaint had to be repatriated at the steamship company's expense.

There was a rare and expensive drug which, if applied properly for two or three days, had the effect of making a partial or temporary cure. Pedlars of this drug did a thriving trade at all Mediterranean ports from which emigrants were shipped. But it was sold illicitly, and many a distracted husband or father parted with hard earned cash for a phial of coloured water.

When all our passengers were embarked, we cleared out from Trieste, and steamed around the shore on a short passage of 110 miles to Fiume, a port deep in a landlocked bay behind the islands of the Illyrian Archipelago. Here we took in more cargo and mails, and more passengers, of the Southern Slav type. Life on the ship was now colourful and animated. Most of our passengers were from inland districts, and had never seen the sea before. They wore the national garb of their various districts, and were tremendously excited at the prospect of beginning life anew in America, a place of which they had little information, except that it was a land of golden opportunity.

From Fiume we proceeded southwards along the picturesque Dalmatian coast, in flat calm weather, while the emigrants adjusted themselves to shipboard life, and made the days and the evenings merry with music and song. The womenfolk and young children were quartered forward, and the men and boys aft—a rule strictly enforced after "Lights Out", but during the day all mingled freely on deck.

Two days after leaving Fiume, we put in to the Greek port of Corfu, and loaded a cargo of raisins, currants, and dried figs. We also embarked here some Greek emigrants, who could get along with the Austrians and Hungarians amicably.

Next we returned to Messina, and then to Palermo in western Sicily, to pick up mails and cargo at both places. Then we steamed on westwards across the Mediterranean to Almeria in southern

Spain, to fill the remaining space in our cargo holds with cases of oranges and tangerines, and casks of fresh grapes, packed in granulated cork.

So to Gibraltar for mails, and on through the Pillars of Hercules to the Western Ocean. It was then, as we breasted the ocean swell, that the fun really began, as the majority of our passengers saw the mighty ocean for the first time in their lives, and what they saw displeased them. Most of them became seasick, probably through excitement and a fear of the uncontrollable unknown, and the entirely unaccustomed experience. But they were brave, hardy, and sturdy people, and soon adjusted themselves.

When we were halfway across, one of our passengers, a Hungarian who had been studying English for some months previously, had a big idea. He discovered a cure for seasickness! The more he thought about it, the more sure he was that his idea was sound, and that it would solve the problem that had baffled mighty minds for centuries.

He explained the idea, in his self-taught English, to our Purser (Quayle), who advised him to put it in writing, in the form of a letter to the Captain. This the inventor proceeded to do:

Dear Sir Captain!

I have the problems of the sea been pondering. A remedy against sickness of the sea. Many things are recommend. Namely, eat nothing, drink nothing, eat lemons, lie down, gaze to the clouds, fill the mind with noble thoughts. All this is no use.

In a word, seasickness is loss of equilibrium. The problem is simple. To re-establish equilibrium!

The solution is namely simple. The passenger and the steamer form a block, a system. That is why he suffer. The solution is to separate the passenger from the ship.

How to do this? Easy. On the steamer must be established a large pond or basin full with water, and in it a floating cabin. Here can the sick person go. It is obvious that the surface water of the pond will be a calmness, and the cabin will float in a quiet lake. I leave all details regarding size and dimensions to you.

Your obedient servant,
H. LAKOSH
(Former schoolteacher)

There was no swimming pool in the *Ultonia,* or the ingenious inventor would have seen how water sloshes about in his "quiet lake" with even the slightest movement of the ship. But one part of his letter was correct. The cure for seasickness is to separate the passenger from the ship. This happens when he goes ashore.

Arrived at New York, we anchored in quarantine near the Narrows, within sight of the Statue of Liberty, and our passengers were all carefully examined again for trachoma.

After several hours of anxiety, all passed, except two. We proceeded to the pier, and all except these two were Americans-to-be. The unfortunates were taken in a government launch to Ellis Island, to await repatriation to the land of their birth. For a week, until our next sailing day, they could gaze at the Manhattan skyline, so near and yet so far, between their granulated eyelids.

CHAPTER SEVENTEEN

In Hospital for Refit—Kindness of Commodore Watt—I Join the R.M.S. "Umbria" —Famous Old Cunarder—Designed for Auxiliary Sail—Powerful Single-screw Steamer—"The Atlantic Submarines"— "Thrusting Into It"—How and When Sailors Sleep—Captain James Charles—Chief Officer Luke Ward—"Rigid Economy"—" 'Umbria' the Unready"—Her Open Bridge—We Arrive Late—A Burial at Sea—A Moving Experience —Captain Will Turner—Chief Officer Jock Anderson—The Steep Ladder of Promotion— I Leave the "Umbria" and Join the "Ivernia".

AFTER I had made four Mediterranean voyages in the *Ultonia*, she was taken temporarily off that run and went to Liverpool for refit. I left her there on 27th January, 1908, with sick leave—off pay—as I also needed a refit.

Four and a half years previously, when serving as Second Mate in the full-rigged ship *County of Cardigan*, I had injured myself at the port of Eten, in Peru, by jumping down into the hold on top of a heap of loose coal, which was our cargo. I had strained my innards and developed hernia, but, hoping that time would mend it, I had carried on. The doctors in the *Caronia* and *Ultonia* advised me to have an operation. Their advice was, "A stitch in time saves nine".

It was no use cracking hardy and pretending any longer to be a tough old salt. Doctor McIntyre (who later became Board of Trade Medical Officer at Southampton) insisted that I should have the operation, and the sooner the better, as otherwise my chances of advancement in the Cunard service might be affected by the physical disability. It was on his report to the Marine Superintendent that I was granted sick leave.

I entered the Stanley Hospital at Liverpool, with the usual suspicions of a person who doesn't like being cut up, and with the usual forebodings, as I had never been in a hospital as a patient. But all went well.

While I was in hospital, the Commodore of the Cunard Line, Captain Watt, and his wife, visited me, and invited me to stay with them for a week during my convalescence, at their home at Oxton, in Cheshire. This was a nice gesture from Captain Watt, as I was the most junior officer in the service. It taught me a lesson in *esprit de corps*. I felt then that I really "belonged".

Two years previously I had been shipmates with Captain Watt's son, Jim, in the S.S. *Jura*. Jim's sisters were lively girls, who helped to make my convalescence at Oxton more enjoyable. The matron of the hospital and Mrs Watt were sisters.

Five weeks later, I was fit for work again. I was appointed as Junior Third Officer in R.M.S. *Umbria*. I joined this famous old ship at Liverpool on 27th March, 1908. Her Master was Captain James C. W. Charles (who in later years rose to eminence in the Cunard service, and was knighted). He was a big and powerfully built man, trained in sail, who really loved the sea. He looked like a typical Englishman (if there is such a person), but, when chatting amiably to me, he took an early opportunity of putting over one of his favourite jokes. "Do ye know, Bisset, I'm neither English, Welsh, Scottish, nor Irish! Then what do you think I am?"

"A Manxman," I guessed.

"Wrong, I'm a Cornishman!"

There is a real point of pride in this, as anyone who knows Cornish people is aware. They consider, with good historical reason, that they are a race apart. In fact, there is a Cornish language, which has affinities with the Breton and Basque languages. "There were kings and castles in Cornwall," said Captain Charles, "when the English were only savages."

The S.S. *Umbria*, 8,128 tons, and her sister ship *Etruria*, launched at Elders' shipyards, Glasgow, in 1884 and 1885, were the oldest Cunarders still in service in 1908, but were now nearly at the end of their glorious careers (the *Umbria* was scrapped in 1910 and the *Etruria* in 1909). Both had held the Blue Riband. They had speeds of 18 or 19 knots, and were on the mid-week Atlantic Mail service between Liverpool and New York, alternating with the *Caronia* and *Carmania*.

I felt that it was a link with history to serve in the old *Umbria*, for she and her sister were the last of the Cunarders designed to carry auxiliary sail. She was a single-screw steel-hulled steamer, with two stumpy raking funnels, and three tall steel masts, on which yards for square sails had originally been crossed. Her square sails had been discarded early in her career, but she had carried fore-and-aft auxiliary sails for many years. These were no longer in use when I joined her. An indication of her sailing design was in her raised fo'c'sle-deck and poopdeck; but, instead of a raking or clipper bow, she had a straight (or "plumb" or "vertical") stem, which piled up a tremendous bow-wave when she was going at full speed.

When hard driven, as she usually was, she often shipped purlers over the bow. For this reason the *Umbria* and the *Etruria* were jokingly called "the Atlantic Submarines". The saying was that they went down at Fastnet and came up at Sandy Hook. In twenty-four years the *Umbria* had steamed 1½ million miles on the Atlantic Mail service, with an interlude as a troop transport during the South African war of 1899-1901.

She had been worn out through being driven too hard, by Captains imbued with the idea of "cracking on" and "making a passage" and "keeping her going"—a legacy of sailing-ship traditions. It was considered almost a disgrace to reduce speed, or to arrive an hour or two late, even after a heavy-weather crossing (nowadays, shipmasters reduce speed in heavy head-on weather, to avoid damage to the ship).

After so many years of hard treatment, the *Umbria* was showing the signs of wear and tear. Her decks were sprung and leaky, and much of her deck gear was not only old-fashioned, but worn. Her midship structure was not raised high, as in liners of later design. Her promenade-deck was below the level of the fo'c'sle-deck and poop. It resembled the "waist" of a sailing ship, and she could take seas over the rail onto this deck in heavy weather. Her boat-deck was almost flush with the fo'c'sle-deck and poop, and could also take seas and spray from forrard when she was "thrusting into it". In heavy weather, her passengers were sometimes confined below decks. Occasionally, seas were shipped down below to flood into the alleyways, over the deck sills of the companionways (but not into the sleeping cabins, dining-saloons, or lounges and smoke-rooms, which had sills in their doorways to the alleyways).

The *Umbria* carried 1,500 souls, of whom 1,200 were passengers. There were three classes—first, second, and third. The officers also lived in three classes. The Chief and First Officers had a cabin each on the upper deck. The Junior First Officer and the Second Officer lived on the second-class deck; and the Senior and Junior Third Officers shared a cabin on the third-class deck.

As Junior Third Officer I now had a rise of one pound a month in pay, and a stripe-and-a-half on my sleeve, but the accommodation down below made this another Irishman's rise for me, for the time being. My room-mate was Senior Third Officer Mott, a gigantic man who had the right to occupy the only bunk in the cabin, while I had to sleep on the settee. As we were in different watches, this sharing was not in itself a hardship, but the cabin was small and poorly ventilated, with a door and porthole opening onto the after welldeck. All day long, and for half the night, the third-class passengers (mostly emigrants from Ireland or continental European countries) were chattering, shouting, singing, and playing games near our cabin, and we could get little sleep. In port, with two steam cargo winches running day and night, outside our door, we also got little sleep.

I doubt if there is any calling in the world in which men work such "broken time", and have so little regular sleep, as men in the seafaring profession. This was certainly true under sail, when the entire crew kept "watch and watch"—four hours on and four hours off—every day and night for months on end, and learnt to sleep like cats, with one ear cocked for any alert of danger, and in bad weather had to work aloft through what should have been their watches below. That was at the all-too-frequent cry of "all hands on deck", especially in undermanned sailing vessels.

In steamers, the three-watch system of four hours on and eight off, with no sails to manhandle, is more humane, but this system has its snags, too. There can be no Sabbath Day of rest for the crew in a ship at sea. Every day is a working day, in a seven-day week. Even with three watches, officers work a 56-hour week, that is an eight-hour day, in two four-hour periods of duty daily in "broken time", which cannot be avoided.

I am not complaining, as a man goes to sea with his eyes open, knowing that it will be a hard life. The advantages of seafaring far outweigh the disadvantages, and "what can't be cured must be endured". The seamen and boys in steamers, under the two-watch system, worked twelve hours a day—that is, an 84-hour week, without any question of overtime payment. They never had more than $3\frac{1}{2}$ hours sleep at a stretch. On the other hand, their work in steamers at sea was much less arduous than that of seamen and boys under sail. The men with most responsibility—the two helmsmen in each watch—relieved one another in two-hourly spells, this being the longest period that any man could be expected to concentrate on watching a jiggling compass needle; but the others, chiefly on lookout, were not under great physical or mental strain.

An officer on watch has to be mentally alert for four hours, and this can be more tiring than mere physical work. He dares not relax, even for a minute, especially at night-time, as that minute could mean all the difference to the safety of the ship, in avoiding collision or any other hazard.

The first watch—8 to 12, morning and evening—was not so bad, as it enabled the officer to go to bed soon after midnight and get his natural sleep until 7.30 a.m., plus a couple of hours in the afternoon for good measure! But the middle watch—12 to 4, commonly known as the "graveyard watch"—kept the officer out of his bunk at the hours when slumber is sweetest. I was with the Chief Officer (Luke Ward) in the 4 to 8 watch, which meant getting up every morning at 3.45, just when the bed is pulling its hardest. It is during these hours of watch-keeping that the average officer vows that if he ever gets to be Captain "he'll sleep his head off".

But this is only wishful thinking. The Captain may spend hours reclining on his settee, but he never sleeps deeply, as he is on duty twenty-four hours a day, and the orders are that he is to be called if anything unusual occurs. He dozes fitfully, but part of his mind is alert all the time. He hears the bells sounded at every half-hour, and he is aware of the changes of the watch, and of changes of weather, and of any unusual sound or movement in the ship. Nearing port, or in fog, or the proximity of icebergs, or in heavy weather, he may get no sleep except catnaps for two or three days at a stretch.

Captain Charles was rare in my experience, as a shipmaster who slept heavily, during the night watches, after his vessel had cleared port. But he left orders that he was to be informed of the bearing of any lights sighted, or of any change of course, or indication of change of weather, or anything else unusual. It was my task to go to his cabin, on the instructions of the Chief Officer, to wake him, and this was no easy task. I would knock on his door, enter, put on the light, and call his name until he grunted something unintelligible, without opening his eyes. I would then make my report, and he would grunt again, still apparently deep in slumber. This was disconcerting, as it was my duty to make sure that my words had fully penetrated his consciousness. I hesitated to put a hand on him and shake him awake. I would stand there, repeating the report several times, until he would open his eyes, and say grumpily, "I heard you the first time!"

If the occasion warranted his getting up, he was grumpy in the extreme. Usually the reports that awakened him were merely routine. "All right," he would say, irritably. "Carry on!" Then he would add, "And put out my light, please!" or some similar term of anything but endearment, which filled me with forebodings of dire consequences--quite needlessly, for his grumpiness subsided into deep slumber again, as soon as I put out the light and softly closed the door.

Chief Officer Luke Ward (who, as Captain Ward, later became Marine Superintendent of the Cunard Line) was a fine seaman and a strict disciplinarian. His manner was more like that of a schoolmaster than a sailor. He kept me and everyone else on board bang up to the mark. He was a rigid economist in his supervision of ships' stores and gear. He was fond of using the words, "rigid economy", and Jim Watt once remarked to me, "The perfect example of rigid economy would be Luke Ward in a six-foot case!"

I may explain that the word "coffin" is never used by sailors. It is always "a six-foot case".

It worried Chief Officer Ward that the *Umbria's* gear was so antiquated, and hard to keep in working order. Soon after we had left Queenstown, an Irish passenger made a complaint to the Purser, who asked him to put it in writing. This the passenger did, as follows: "Sir, the hot water in the taps is cold, and furthermore there is none of it."

A state of disrepair prevailed throughout the *Umbria* during the six voyages to New York that I made in her. It was scarcely worth repairing her, as her days were numbered. The Chief Officer was only too well aware of her defects, which his best efforts could not overcome. On one occasion, when she arrived in New York, the immigration officials, coming out to board her at the Narrows, were kept waiting for several minutes because her accommodation ladder had become jammed, and could not be lowered. One of the officials sang out, "Come on, *Umbria* the Unready. . . ."

That really hurt the Chief Officer's pride.

The bridge in the *Umbria* was one of her most remarkable features, in comparison with the bridges of other liners on the Atlantic Mail run. It was the old-fashioned type of "open bridge" —that is, nothing more than a narrow platform athwartships, at the forward end of the boat-deck, entirely open to the sky, and without any enclosed or roofed wheelhouse in the centre. It had one brass handrail, waist-high, but no other protection. The idea was perhaps that officers and men on watch should not be pampered and made *too* comfortable, or they might fall asleep. Also, in the days when the *Umbria* carried sail, the open bridge had enabled the officer of the watch to keep an eye aloft on the set of the canvas at every minute, and to direct the handling of sail.

But when sail was discarded, the open bridge remained unaltered. After some years, it proved too rugged for steamboat sailors of the softer tradition, and canvas screens, known as "dodgers", were provided. These were secured with lashings to the handrail and rail stanchions, and had the effect of a waist-high weathercloth, which gave some protection to the lower limbs of the men on the bridge, but none to the upper parts of the body.

In bad weather, when she was "punching into it", and throwing seas and spray over the bridge, the weight of water sometimes bent the bridge-rails and stanchions flat. Thereafter, in heavy weather, the dodgers round the wings of the bridge were furled and only the small central part, where the wheel and compass stood, had this partial protection.

It happened that on my first westbound passage in her, the *Umbria* ran into a series of westerly gales, and lived up to her reputation as a "submarine". The Captain would not reduce speed. One blusterous night when I was standing with the Chief Officer and the helmsman at the wheel, she took a purler over the bow, which swept away the dodger protecting the wheel, knocked the three of us flat, and half drowned us.

Even then, Captain Charles would not give the order to reduce speed. He merely said, "Keep her going". He had unlimited faith in what the old lady could do, but, despite her best efforts, as the gales persisted, we took nine days for the crossing, and arrived two days late. This was serious on a mail run. Our wireless equipment had been installed six years previously, but was only of an experimental type, and, like everything else in the *Umbria*, was antiquated. Its effective range was only fifty miles. When we became overdue, its signals were not reaching the American shore stations. In view of the heavy weather prevailing, an alarming rumour was spread in New York that the famous old champion liner had foundered in mid-Atlantic and was lost with all hands.

We spoilt this story by arriving safe and sound, with an excuse as antiquated as the ship—"better late than never". But it was so exceptional for a Cunarder to be late that the New York newsmen were clamouring for the details of our supposedly dramatic mishaps.

Captain Charles, being a true seaman of the old school, had been on the bridge for long hours, by day and by night, during the gales, and for several days had missed his usual deep and healthy sleeps. As soon as the liner was docked the Captain retired to his cabin for a sleep. Then reporters swarmed on board, eager for "the story". The Chief Officer and other officers refused to be interviewed, or correctly ascribed the delay to the westerly gales. No lives had been lost, no one was injured, and no serious damage had been done to the ship; but some of the passengers, having been kept below decks with no impressions except of terrific pitching and rolling, hinted that something unprecedented must have occurred.

A bunch of the reporters, having found the Captain's cabin, gathered at his door, knocking and shouting for news. After awhile, the burly and very irate Charles emerged and drove them away with fierce and harsh words that he had learnt as a Mate in Cape Horners. Such words were quite unprintable in those days. The least offensive of his remarks was, "Get to hell out of this, you — — —!" (still unprintable, fifty years later).

As a result, they got even with him by publishing a sob-story that was utterly at variance with the Captain's rugged character. Under big headlines, they reported: "Captain Charles was so *unnerved* by his terrible passage that he was unable to speak to us."

There was nothing wrong with the *Umbria* except the increment of the years. She and the *Etruria* were the most powerful single-screw passenger-liners ever built. It was rare enough for a vessel of 8,000 tons to have only a single screw, but for a vessel of that size to be able to maintain a speed of eighteen knots for sixteen consecutive days (as the *Umbria* did on one passage with troops to South Africa) with only a single screw, was then, and would still be phenomenal. She was designed as an auxiliary cruiser, and, as half her crew belonged to the Royal Naval Reserve, she proudly flew the Blue Ensign on the staff at her stern, instead of the Red Ensign of the mercantile marine. Her passenger-accommodation, though so old-fashioned, was remarkably solid, with beautiful bird's-eye maple, teakwood and other panelling. She carried the first refrigerating machinery ever installed in a transatlantic liner (successor to the old-time "ice-rooms"), and, perhaps most remarkable, she had a pipe-organ in her music-room. In short, with all her faults, we loved her still.

On one of my westbound passages in the *Umbria*, I saw, for the first time, a burial at sea. A party of twelve Irish Roman Catholic priests had embarked at Queenstown for New York. One of them was taken ill, and, after we had passed Fastnet, he died, late in the afternoon, in the ship's hospital. This was not made known to the passengers generally, but the news soon spread among the crew.

After consultations with the other priests in the party, the Captain made arrangements for the body to be buried at sea at 4 a.m. next day—a time when few, if any, passengers would be on deck.

When I came off watch at 8 p.m., the Chief Officer instructed me to get the bo'sun and lamp trimmer along to the hospital, and told me to supervise the preparation of the body for burial. That meant, in nautical usage, to see that the body was weighted with two heavy iron furnace bars and neatly sewn up in canvas.

It is usually the Captain's duty to read the burial service at sea, but the priests had asked permission to conduct their own service for their colleague, and this was at once willingly agreed to by the Captain.

As dawn came in, at the 4 a.m. change of the watch, the engines were rung to STOP, the propeller ceased to turn, and the *Umbria* came slowly to rest. The sea was calm, and daylight was just breaking as the body was carried to the poopdeck, and placed on a plank beneath the taffrail, under the Blue Ensign.

The eleven priests had all donned their vestments, and the Captain and officers attended also, as a mark of respect, wearing full-dress uniform with frock coats. Most of the crew, including the firemen and trimmers—many of whom were Catholics—also assembled aft for a ceremony that, in the dawn hush, with the engines still, was intensely impressive.

The voices of the priests chanting their Latin prayers and responses in those surroundings of the wide waters, beneath the dawn tinged sky, rose as a cry from the grieving heart of man to the Great God above. It was a moment of sincerity and piety, profoundly moving.

Then came the words, spoken in English, "We now commit the body of our dear departed to the deep." Two uniformed quartermasters lifted the plank at one end, and the body slid over the side under the taffrail. The priests made the Sign of the Cross, the officers and uniformed men saluted, and a subdued moan of emotion rose from the crew.

The body sank quickly. The Captain, from long sea-habit, glanced appraisingly at the sky, and said crisply to the Chief Officer, "Carry on, Mister. Proceed on your course."

Soon the propeller set up its turmoil again, and we were off at full speed, and everything back to normal, with only the memory of a rare experience remaining.

Though many have been buried at sea, this burial, in regard to the number of clergy participating, was probably unprecedented. (Nowadays, when a death occurs in a large passenger-liner at sea, a report is sent by radio to the owners of the liner, who ascertain from the relatives if they desire the body to be buried at sea, or brought to port. If the latter, the ship's surgeon and hospital attendants embalm the body, and it is sealed in a leaden casket and enclosed in a "six-foot case" for transportation.)

After I had made three voyages in the *Umbria* with Captain Charles, he and Chief Officer Ward were transferred at Liverpool (in June, 1908) to other ships. This was a common practice in the Cunard service, sometimes for administrative convenience, to replace masters or officers going on leave or retiring, and sometimes by way of promoting a Captain or officer to a bigger or better vessel. The effect was that most Cunard officers saw service in many different liners, and became personally acquainted as shipmates with most of the other men in the service, at one time or another in their careers.

The new Captain of the *Umbria*, William Turner, fifty-three years of age, was a rugged "old salt" if ever there was one, for he had gone to sea as a boy of thirteen, and had served fourteen years in sail, rising to command of a full-rigger, before he had joined the Cunard service in 1883. Then, after twenty years as an officer in Cunarders, he had been appointed Captain in the Company's service in 1903, and had held command of the *Carpathia* and *Ivernia* before being transferred to the *Umbria*. He was a shortish, slim-built man, but with the broad shoulders and powerful arms that years of pully-hauly give to sailing-ship men. He was taciturn and austere, inclined to be shy of sociable contacts with passengers, but a very keen navigator and strict in his attention to detail. He usually had lunch in his cabin. I call him austere, because on several occasions when I had to make reports to him there at lunch-time, though he had the choice of the first-class menu, I noticed that his lunch consisted of a bowl of boiled rice, and nothing else!

Our new Chief Officer, J. C. ("Jock") Anderson, was also a man of sturdy character and fine knowledge of seamanship, learnt the hard way. I made three voyages to New York in the *Umbria* with Captain Turner and Chief Officer Anderson.

Seven years later, Will Turner was Captain, and Jock Anderson, Staff Captain, of the *Lusitania* on her fatal last voyage, in May, 1915. It was my fortune to have been associated with these two fine seamen as a junior officer, and to learn from them some of the many things that a young officer needs to learn when his feet are on the bottom rungs of that long ladder of the years of experience and increasing responsibility that is known as Promotion.

After eight months service in the *Umbria*, I left her in Liverpool in October, 1908, when I was transferred to a much bigger, more comfortable, more modern, but also slower ship, the *Ivernia*, on the run from Liverpool to Boston.

I cannot truthfully say that I was sorry to leave the *Umbria*, but she was a great ship in her day. She was built in the year that

I was born. She and I were both twenty-five years of age, but she was already antiquated, worn out in service, and at the end of her career, ready to be scrapped, whereas I was looking forward to the era of modern progress in which the *Umbria* would be merely a memory of a bygone generation's strivings to excel.

CHAPTER EIGHTEEN

WHEN I joined the S.S. *Ivernia,* at Liverpool, in November, 1908, as extra Third Officer, it was a rise. She and her sister, *Saxonia,* were two of the biggest and most comfortable vessels in the Cunard fleet. Launched on the Tyne in 1900, the *Ivernia* was a typical "Ocean Greyhound", a twin-screw steamer 600 feet long, sixty-feet beam, of 14,057 tons gross; but she had a speed of only fifteen knots.

When they were launched, the *Ivernia* and *Saxonia* rated for a few months as the biggest ships in the world, until the White Star *Oceanic* (17,000 tons) took that honour from them.

The "pretty sisters" *Caronia* and *Carmania* (20,000 tons) and the "magnificent sisters" *Lusitania* and *Mauretania* (32,000 tons), had put the two old "steady sisters" in the shade, and they had been relegated to the Liverpool to Boston run. Their

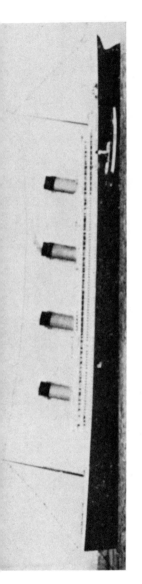

White Star liner S.S. *Olympic*, launched 1910

White Star liner S.S. *Titanic*, leaving Belfast on her trials, April Fools' Day, 1912
(*Topical Photo Agency*)

Officers in S.S. *Carpathia*, 1912

Back row: Italian doctor; Second Officer James Bisset; Roth, Hungarian supernumerary officer; Chief Engineer; First Officer Horace Dean; Assistant Purser; Purser E. F. G. Brown; Hungarian doctor. *Centre row:* Chief Officer Hankinson; Captain A. H. Rostron; Dr Frank McGhee.

Second Officer in S.S. *Carpathia*, 1912. Note my 3-inch starched choker collar

How *Titanic* struck the berg on her starboard bow
(*Artist's drawing from* Lloyd's Weekly News, 1912)

How *Titanic* sank
(*Artist's drawing from* Washington Post, 1912)

speed was not enough for the New York mail run, as they required eight days for the crossing; but as a consolation they were
famous as the "steadiest" ships on the North Atlantic. It was
claimed that they were designed for comfort rather than speed.
This quality made them favourites with passengers, especially
in the winter months, when gales must be expected.

The *Ivernia* (like the *Saxonia*) had a single funnel, extended
to a height of 106 feet above the water-level. This unusual
height was intended to give an extra forced draft to the coal-
burning furnaces, but the theory of one very tall funnel had
been discarded by designers of the bigger Cunarders, in favour
of two, and even four, shorter funnels.

Funnels were of greater importance in coal-burning steamers
than in the later developed oil-burning steamers. One advantage
of a tall funnel was that it carried the smoke and soot away
from the boat-decks—sometimes. To compare the silhouettes of
steamers as these have developed in a hundred years of steam
navigation is a fascinating study. The distant view of a steamer
in broadside is the first method of recognizing her, by the design
of her hull form, masts, funnels, kingposts and the profile of
her superstructure. It is amazing how many variations have been
introduced, and are still being introduced by designers. There
are funnels of many different shapes and rakes, some nowadays
placed aft on the poop.

In 1908, the engineroom, and consequently the funnel or
funnels, were amidships, immediately abaft the bridge. The
steamer with a single funnel placed centrally in the midships
superstructure appeared to be gracefully balanced. But in the
Ivernia and *Saxonia* the very tall single funnel detracted from
the graceful appearance of the vessel in silhouette. The funnel
was strongly stayed with steel cables, but looked precarious. The
modern principles of "streamlining" were scarcely understood,
or had not been scientifically studied. So these vessels, although
in their hull-form they were sleek ocean greyhounds, had what
looked like a factory chimney towering amidships, destroying the
symmetry of the design.

The freakishly tall funnel was an obstruction to airflow which
to some extent slowed the vessel's service speed. The *Ivernia*
had also four tall steel masts, 160 feet high. These masts were
vertical, like the funnel (not raked). Two extra masts had been
included by the designers in an attempt to balance the freakish
appearance of the tall funnel. Stump-masts and kingposts in the

modern style would have been more effective in use. The *Ivernia's* design was typical of shipbuilding ideas in 1900, which had already become out of date in 1908. I commend to anyone who has a "harbour view" in a busy port to take note of the variety in the broadside view of merchant ships, old and new. Experimentation is forever in progress.

The *Ivernia* had the tallest funnel ever fitted to a steamship, in her day or since. I cannot suppose that this had anything to do with her renowned steadiness at sea; yet that too was a fact. She was one of the steadiest vessels I have ever served in.

She carried 2,000 passengers, in three classes. A novel feature was the "Thermotank" ventilation system, which enabled passengers to control ventilation in their cabins—a forerunner of air-conditioning. In every other way the passenger-accommodation was comfortable rather than luxurious. This suited the Bostonians and other New Englanders who comprised most of our first- and second-class passengers: people of solid common sense and no swank. The third-class accommodation was occupied mainly by emigrants, on the westward run.

Not so comfortable were the officers' quarters, a group of cabins in the 'tween-decks around Number Three hatch. At sea they were good enough for their purpose, though isolated and poorly ventilated; but, when we were in port, it was almost impossible for the officers to get any sleep. The slings of cargo, up and down, and winches were rattling, day and night.

With a crew of 500, food for the "ship's people" was a big item in the company's working expenses. Food for the officers was good in the Cunard Line. I had no complaints to make on that score, after serving in sail and in tramps! I considered that I was in clover. But there were complaints, especially from the firemen and trimmers, that they were underfed. Their work was heavy, and it gave them big appetites. They lost so much weight by sweating that most of them had a perpetually lean and hungry look. In the long history of seafaring, no men have ever had such hard and brutalizing work as the firemen and trimmers in the big coal-burning steamers in the early years of the twentieth century.

As a deck officer I had practically no contacts with the firemen and trimmers, but many a time I felt pity for them as I saw them coming off watch and trudging wearily to their quarters, utterly done in, sweat squelching in their boots. Their faces, blackened with coal dust, and streaked with sweat, had a dulled animal-like look, and they seldom smiled. It was killing work.

In the smaller cargo-steamers of some British companies, the food provided for the crew was of poor quality—almost as bad as in "hungry ships" under sail. One of the smaller firms in Liverpool, Moss & Co., had the reputation, in common with other companies, of providing inadequate rations. One evening at the Seamen's Mission in Liverpool, I attended a lecture on First Aid that was being given by a local doctor. A good crowd was present, and the doctor began his lecture dramatically by uncovering a life-size model of a human skeleton. "Now, men," he said, "you all know what this is."

A voice from the back commented, "Yes, sir. It's one of Moss's trimmers!"

Captain Benison of the *Ivernia* was a grumpy and laconic shipmaster, with the reputation of being a hard driver. He had a fiery red face, from which he was given the nickname of "The Glowworm". He was not tactful, even with passengers. On one occasion, when the *Ivernia* was going dead slow in heavy fog, off the Newfoundland Banks, and many hours behind schedule, a Bostonian lady said to him, "Say, Captain, is it always foggy round here?"

The exasperated "Glowworm" glared at her, and growled, "How should I know, madam? I don't live here!"

Despite his gruffness, Captain Benison was a fine seaman, and a strict disciplinarian. The route to Boston in the winter months is occasionally beset by westerly Atlantic gales in mid-ocean, and by fog near the Newfoundland Banks and off the shores of Britain. Having joined the *Ivernia* in mid-November, I soon had an opportunity of seeing what made Captain Benison so short-tempered. He was under great strain, partly because he spent long sleepless hours on the bridge, in heavy weather or fog, as though he feared that the officers of the watch might lose his ship for him. This was zeal in the extreme. A Captain must sleep sometimes, but the "Glowworm" could never relax. That was his temperament, but he frayed his own nerves by overstrain, sometimes unnecessarily.

I was on watch with the Chief Officer, Sam Jones. We began our voyage with fog in the Irish Sea, proceeding at dead slow, with our steam whistle hooting mournfully at one-minute intervals. It was an ordeal to be on the bridge of a steamer in thick fog, in narrow waters, on a waterway busy with traffic, in the days before radar and direction-finding instruments were invented. The fog's fantastic curtain reduces visibility almost to nil. The ship can only grope forward, everyone on watch straining his eyes and his ears in readiness for instantaneous action to avert collision.

Other ships, though invisible, are heard hooting like lost souls, but it is difficult to judge their distance or course. The fog muffles and distorts sound. The fact that there is thick fog often implies that there is little or no wind. This means that sailing vessels are becalmed and have no steering-way. Their fog-horns are hand worked and emit only a feeble squeaky note.

A steamer must keep headway on, with steering-way, to avoid drifting. Very accurate navigation is essential, by dead reckoning, and soundings, since there is no sight of sun or stars, or of landmarks. In extreme cases she will anchor, but this is accepting defeat. A fog could last for days. It is better to try to grope a way out of it. A vessel at anchor could be rammed by another under way; but while she is in motion, with steering-way, evasive action of some kind is possible.

So she crawls on, waiting for the fog to lift, and hoping for the best. The officers of the watch are posted on the wings of the navigating bridge. It is a strict sea-rule—"No keeping a lookout behind glass"—meaning the plate-glass windows of the wheelhouse. Yet in the wheelhouse stands the helmsman with his eyes on the lubber-line of the compass, keeping the ship on her course, and ready at any instant to obey an order to "port the helm" or "starboard the helm" to avoid a collision. Extra lookouts are posted on the bow, since visibility is better in fog at a lower level than in the crow's nest or on the bridge. The concentration is intense (but what a miraculous invention was radar!).

The watches were relieved, as usual, every four hours, and the officers could go below for eight hours rest and relaxation, free of responsibility; but Captain Benison was on the bridge, or awake in his chartroom, in every watch, tireless. We compared notes afterwards and reckoned that he had gone without sleep for fifty hours, until at last we ran out of the fog, and were able to take bearings from Fastnet lighthouse, and he could set course on the Great Circle route southwesterly in open ocean, with rapidly improving visibility.

Then he retired to his cabin for a sleep, with the usual, "Call me if you sight anything unusual, Mister!"

Who'd be a Captain? I thought. No wonder he's cranky sometimes. . . . What a life!

On the second day after we had left Fastnet astern, I was on the bridge in the 4 a.m. to 8 a.m. watch, when the Chief Officer beckoned to me to join him on the starboard wing. "We're running into dirty weather," he remarked.

I looked into the blackness ahead and overhead, and saw that his prediction was correct. The ship had been forging ahead at her steady fifteen knots, in normal weather, but now a fresh southwesterly breeze had sprung up and raised a bit of a lop which had started her pitching a little, though she was riding it easily.

"The breeze is freshening," I commented.

"Too much," he grumbled. At that moment the crest of a sea slapped against the bows, and sent a shower of spray scudding across the forecastle head. It was 6 a.m. There was a hint of dawn in the sky. "Go and tell the Captain that we're running into heavy weather from ahead."

As I turned to obey this order, the Captain, wearing his greatcoat, stepped out on to the bridge. Dozing in the chartroom, he had become aware of the change without need of being told of it. That is what is meant by sea-sense. He had already studied the barometer, and set the pointer.

The bridge was in absolute darkness, except for the dim, shaded light on the compass, reflected on the intent face of the quartermaster at the wheel.

"There, Mr Jones?" the Captain called into the darkness, his eyes not yet accustomed to the murk.

"Aye, aye, sir. Out on the starboard wing. The breeze is freshening."

The Captain groped his way to the wing. "The glass is falling rapidly," he growled. "Looks like dirty weather! See that everything is secure round the decks."

As he spoke a heavy spray crashed over the bridge. We instinctively ducked under the canvas dodger for shelter. "You duck like a real seaman," said the Captain to me, shaking the spray off his own shoulders. "Been round the Horn?"

"Yes, sir, four times."

"Well, damn it, m'son, by the look of things we're in for a

worse dusting now than a Cape Horn snorter, or just as bad, anyhow!"

With that he returned to the chartroom to look at the barometer again. On the Chief Officer's instructions, I went with the boatswain and two seamen on a tour of the decks, to examine the lashings of all boats and gear from stem to stern. We found everything secure. A few early birds among the passengers were already astir. I warned the Chief Steward to see that all ports were closed and deadlights screwed down, and to inform the passengers, without alarming them, that we were running into heavy weather.

A few minutes before the change of the watch at 8 a.m., the sun appeared above a low, grey bank of cloud on the horizon. Yellow and brassy looking, it presaged wind and plenty of it. I do not understand why wind coming from the westward can affect the appearance of the rising sun shining through the atmosphere far to the eastward, but every sailor can "see" a wind coming from signs in the sky, and this is one of them. The Captain was on the bridge again, looking glumly at the brassy sun, as the two officers of the 8 to 12 watch arrived, clad in oilskins, sou'-westers, and sea-boots. The quartermaster who had called them had warned them what to expect.

"We'll be into the thick of it in an hour," said the Captain. "Are all ports, doors and lashings secured?"

"Aye, aye, sir," I reported.

To the incoming officers he said, "Call me at once if anything unusual occurs."

He retired to his chartroom, but not to rest. He wouldn't need much calling. He'd be there. The Chief Officer and I handed over the navigational details, such as the course, leeway, speed, engine revolutions, compass error, and barometer movements. Then we dived down to our quarters for a bath and breakfast.

I came up on deck again at 9 a.m. The wind had risen to a "fresh gale"—technically so defined when its velocity is between 37 and 44 knots. On our southwesterly course it was a wind from dead ahead. We were meeting the running seas head-on. These had now been whipped by the gale to an average height, from trough to crest, of twenty feet (seas between 12 and 20 feet high are technically described as "high").

The *Ivernia*, like all Cunarders built between 1875 and 1930, had a straight stem, and a counter or "cutaway" stern. The raking stem, which had proved so effective in clipper ships, was discarded in the design of the bigger steel-hull screw steamers for fifty-five years (it was restored in Cunard liners built from 1930 onwards, including the *Queen Mary* and all the later modern Cunarders still in service).

The straight stem was probably based on the idea of cutting through seas rather than riding over them; but if this was the idea it was theoretical thinking, as the modern reversion to raking stems indicates. The architects of the early screw steamers were obsessed with the novelty of mechanical thrust-propulsion from the stern, from which it appeared logical that the stem of a screw steamer should act like a knife, to cut through the seas, thereby reducing the pitching movement of a vessel which rides over the seas. The argument was valid when applied to smaller vessels, of up to 3,000 tons, travelling in slight or moderate seas of up to five feet in height. It remained a good argument when applied to larger screw steamers, in rough seas of up to twelve feet. In these cases the straight or vertical knife-edge stem did contribute something to the steadiness of a vessel of Ocean Greyhound proportions.

In normal weather, of smooth, slight, and moderate seas, a steamer with a straight stem travelling at full speed throws up a much larger bow-wave than one with a raking stem. This indicates the cut-and-thrust principle of the straight stem. But in "rough", "high", "very high", "precipitous", or "mountainous" seas, towering from twelve to sixty feet from trough to crest, the straight stem, when hard driven by the thrust from astern to encounter these seas running from dead ahead, tends to bury itself rather than to ride over the seas, and in consequence water is shipped over the bows.

This was happening when I went up to the boat-deck of the *Ivernia* at 9 a.m. during my watch below. I could not rest in my cabin. I was interested in the development of the gale, and in seeing how this renowned "steady" ship would weather it. I wondered too if Captain Benison would drive on, into the teeth of the gale, by hook or by crook, as Captain Charles used to do in the old *Umbria*. I felt that I would learn something. I had an instinct from my training in sail, when all hands were usually called out on deck in a gale to shorten sail or do whatever else was necessary. I felt that I ought to stand by.

The sky was overcast, with grey, murky clouds, and there was a rain-squall a few miles ahead. The wind-force was increasing, and the seas rapidly rising. All passengers had been advised, requested, persuaded, and—in a few stubborn cases—ordered to remain below decks. At every few minutes the ship put her bows under and scooped in the top of a sea that hurtled along the foredeck in a foaming cascade. Spray was flung high over the bridge. I saw the Captain join the officers of the watch on the starboard wing, and duck with them under the dodger at each burst of spray.

I went up to the bridge and stood by unobtrusively, out on the port wing, feeling that, as the most junior officer in the ship, I might be able to do something useful if required. I was there to be seen and not heard. We ran into a fierce rain-squall, with some sleet in it, screaming savagely over the ship, and visibility almost nil. The wind and seas continued to increase rapidly, to strong gale force (44 knots), and very high seas (up to thirty feet). Time after time the ship took heavy purlers over the bow.

At 10 a.m., the Captain was out on the starboard wing with the First Officer, while the Third Officer stood by the engine telegraph in the wheelhouse when three high seas in succession broke over the bow, flooding the foredecks and throwing heavy spray over the bridge. The Captain ducked under the dodger, then, shaking the salt water out of his eyes, made his way into the wheelhouse and sang out, "Half Speed!"

That was the end of driving on. The speed was reduced to eight knots, and the ship rode more easily, but now her bow lifted to each sea, and then dipped into the trough beyond, occasionally lifting her stern so that the propellers were out of the water and racing madly. This made her shudder from stem to stern.

The Captain beckoned to me. "Go down below, Mister," he said, "and take a walk quietly through the second- and third-class decks. Keep your eyes peeled and report to me how the passengers are behaving, and if there's any flooding down below."

I realized that the calm demeanour of even a junior officer strolling through would help to reassure passengers that there was no need for panic. The stewards and stewardesses were well trained in dealing with nervous passengers in heavy weather, but my little show of gold braid might be useful as a substitute for the Captain's normal morning inspection.

With the ship plunging and frequently shuddering, it was not so easy to take a calm stroll, but by keeping my feet well apart, and adjusting my gait to the ship's movements, I went un-hurriedly along the alleyways and through the public rooms, stopping occasionally to ask a steward or stewardess how things were. It was obvious that many of the passengers, especially the emigrants in the third class, were sick and some were frightened. Most had taken the advice of the stewards to retire to their bunks, accepting the time-worn explanation that we "were only crossing the Devil's Hole"—but the atmosphere down below was stuffy, and the smell of spew distinctly noticeable. At any inquiry from passengers, I put on what I hoped was a cheerful grin, and said, "Nothing to worry about! It's only a bit of rough weather, usual at this time o' year. We'll soon be through it."

I returned to the bridge, and reported to the Captain that everything down below was under control.

"Good," he grunted, but in an absent-minded way. His thoughts were now only on the weather and on his ship and her safe handling. At the change of the watch at noon, all the officers were on the bridge for observations. It was out of the question to take sights of the sun. The cloud ceiling was low and murky, and obscured the sky from horizon to horizon. Dead reckoning of our position by the readings of the Patent Log and of the compass course was not entirely reliable, as the estimation of drift was difficult. This was not in itself of great importance in mid-ocean, when there was no land hazard ahead of us for two thousand miles.

The barometer had dropped to a reading of 28.0, and was still falling. The noon entry in the log read: "Heavy gale with hurricane squalls. Mountainous seas. Ship pitching and labouring, and shipping large volumes of water fore and aft."

I went below for lunch, and then to my cabin, to lie in my bunk, fully clothed, for a few hours rest before going on watch again at 4 p.m. I knew then that a strenuous time was ahead. The weather was working up to a full-scale North Atlantic storm.

The North Atlantic in winter is no place for "flying-fish sailors"—so-called because flying fish are found mostly in the fair-weather subtropical latitudes, where sailing ships bowl along steadily for day after day, in the benevolent trade winds, with little work to be done except to "sweat up" the halyards at the change of the watch.

I have heard experienced seamen say that North Atlantic gales can be more severe than Cape Horn gales. This statement needs qualification. Much depends on the point of view of the observer —whether he is in a sailing vessel or a steamer, whether the steamer is small or big, and whether he is running before the gale or trying to make headway against it!

There can be no denying that Cape Horn gales—by which is meant in general all westerly gales of the high south latitudes on the fringe of the Antarctic ice—are of greater intensity and longer duration than North Atlantic gales. The reason for this is that the prevailing westerly gales in the southern Pacific, Atlantic, and Indian Oceans are almost continuously encircling the globe in the higher latitudes, to the south of Africa, Australia, and South America, with no land-mass there to impede their force. The result is that the seas are heaped up, by the almost continual whipping of the prevailing wind, to dimensions, in height and length, greater than those of seas anywhere else in the world.

It is there that the grandest, most awe-inspiring combers roll on in unending succession, attaining heights regularly of from fifty to sixty feet when the wind rises to gale force, and sometimes towering to eighty feet from trough to crest under hurricane conditions. These "greybeards" often extend 1,000 feet from crest to crest. To a seaman in a small vessel of, say 200 feet over-all length, and lowslung, with a freeboard of less than six feet between Plimsoll mark and bulwark rail, the gigantic seas appear as mountainous ridges of water, over which his vessel laboriously climbs, ascending and descending steep slopes of water, so that, when he is in the trough between two great combers, he has walls of water ahead and astern, blotting out the horizon. It appears then that he will be instantly engulfed, but, as though by magic, the ship rises to the crest ahead, and surmounts it, only to begin again a terrifying slither into the trough beyond—and so for day after day, perhaps week after week, poised on brinks and plunging into chasms.

North Atlantic gales are of shorter duration. At storm force the wind may attain sixty knots, with hurricane squalls of sixty-five knots for short periods. The seas may be heaped up to forty feet high, from trough to crest, in a storm, with exceptional—but rare—combers sixty feet high in a hurricane squall. The average length of the biggest combers in a North Atlantic gale is from 300 to 400 feet from crest to crest. These dimensions are formidable enough, but much less than those of the Cape Horn "greybeards". In a passenger-liner of 600 or 700 feet overall length, with her navigating bridge seventy feet above smooth-water level, seas forty feet and even sixty feet high do not appear insurmountable. The horizon is not lost sight of from the bridge, even when the vessel is in the deepest trough.

The comparatively smaller seas encountered in North Atlantic gales—smaller only in comparison with the supreme magnificence of the Cape Horn hurricane seas—are due to the fact that most of the storms in the North Atlantic are of a rotary character, and therefore the wind is not blowing for very long in a fixed direction. Before the seas are able to get into their stride, as it were, the veering wind sets up running seas across them. The result, known as "cross-seas", is a confused turmoil on the surface of the water. This occurs also occasionally in the high south latitudes, but is much less typical there than in North Atlantic storms.

The Atlantic being a "pond", though a big one, flanked by land-masses on its eastern and western sides, cannot readily develop westerly gales, sustained for weeks, as happens in the unimpeded waters of the high South. All westerly gales in the North Atlantic come offshore. Wind is the flow of air from a region of higher pressure to a region of lower pressure. Winds sweeping westerly from the Pacific across the North American continent have to surmount the impediment of the Rocky Mountains on the western side of a wide land-mass, which may deflect them or reduce their force. Their effect in whipping up waters in the Atlantic can begin only offshore. Seas cannot be fully developed to, say, forty feet high, within 600 or 700 miles offshore.

The landsman's word for seas, namely "waves", happens to be scientifically accurate. These heaped-up masses of water are undulations. The body of water is not carried along, as it appears to be, but is raised and lowered practically in the same place. The ocean is a filled bowl. The only progressive movement of its surface is in currents and tides, which circulate slowly around in the bowl. The "waves" or seas are formed on the surfaces of the currents and tides, but in themselves do not progress.

A spar of timber, floating awash, that is, almost submerged and not affected by wind, would make little forward progress in a storm. It would undulate up and down in the seas almost in the same place. Any forward movement would be due to the "scend" or heave of the ocean. That is a factor difficult to calculate. It is the impetus given to a floating object by the down-slope of a wave. That impetus, allied to a momentum of gravity, may carry the floating object at times through the trough between waves, and into the undulation of the neighbouring wave; but as a rule a spar awash would remain for a great number of undulations within the ambit or grip of one wave, before moving on to the next. An ocean current would move the spar from wave to wave, but that is not what is meant by the "scend" of the seas.

A vessel in motion, whether propelled by sails, screws—or oars—progresses over the undulations of the seas, affected only very slightly by the "scend". She is affected by currents, and tides, and also by winds, as are icebergs. A sailing vessel with no sails' set, or a steamer with her engines stopped, or a derelict vessel, would move over the undulating seas, slowly, by the impetus of currents and of wind-pressures on her hull and superstructure, slightly modified by the "scend". In a steamer under way by screw-propulsion, allowance has to be made by her navigators for these invisible factors, which are known as "leeway".

When Captain Benison reduced the *Ivernia's* speed to eight knots, his purpose was to enable her to ride the seas more easily, rather than to cut with her straight stem into their crests; and so to avoid shipping water over the bows which might cause damage on deck. But this is a problem for the master of any screw-propelled vessel driving into the teeth of a gale—a reduction to half speed does not eliminate the thrust of the bows into the seas. It lessens the impact, but half speed for one vessel may be equivalent to full speed for another. That depends on her engine-power.

Any thrust into head-on seas, even at a speed of two knots, uses the challenge of mechanical propulsion in defiance of the "natural" behaviour of an inert buoyant object floating on the surface of the water. The safest method of riding out a heavy gale, in a steamer as in a sailing vessel, is to "heave-to".

In a sailing vessel this means lying with the bow pointed as closely as possible into the wind. Only lower topsails and a stay-sail are set, braced sharp up, or in a hurricane only a goose-winged main lower topsail, to maintain steering-way. It is impossible in a sailing vessel to point dead into the eye of the wind, but she will ride out a gale hove-to with the wind and sea five or six points on the bow, and in this manner will ship very few seas.

In a steamer, to "heave-to" means to keep her head on to the seas, with the engine speed reduced to the minimum necessary to maintain steering-way—that is, to prevent her from falling off into the trough of the sea.

A vessel, either in sail or steam, which, through lack of steering-way, or faulty steering, "falls off" into the trough of precipitous seas, is in extreme danger, and is said to have "broached-to". This is a predicament difficult to get out of without damage. A vessel wallowing beam on in the trough may be rolled over on her beam ends and founder, or she may receive the full force of a crashing sea of thousands of tons which could wash away deck gear and superstructures and stave in the hatches.

The responsibility of the master of a steamer in a heavy gale with hurricane squalls requires him to decide the speed necessary to maintain steering-way, or, if he thinks it advisable, to thrust on and make headway. The foregoing remarks apply in general to gales encountered head-on. A gale may strike from any point of the compass. A vessel may run before a gale with the wind dead astern or on either quarter, but, if the wind reaches hurricane force and the seas are precipitous, it may be advisable to put her about and ride out the storm hove-to.

Shipmasters in 1908 did not have the advantage of the detailed weather reports and forecasts which are available by radio today. Most Atlantic gales are of short duration and the storm-centre is localized. The worst of them can be avoided by change of course on radio advice. Ship design has improved, speeds are far greater (enabling storms to be outrun or passed through quickly), and the bigger passenger-vessels, of 40,000 tons and upwards, are almost, if not quite, "stormproof" and immune to the uncomfortable effects of a "dusting".

The length of a ship in no way affects her ability to ride out precipitous seas. When the *Queen Mary* was launched, there were prophets of doom who declared that her length (1,019 feet overall) would cause her to "break her back" when she became "suspended" (as the prophets gloomily predicted), "with her bow on the crest of one wave and her stern on the crest of another!" This preposterous idea was based on ignorance of the nature of undulations and of the behaviour of buoyant objects in water. Seas have no rigid strength. They part, break and seethe along the sides of a ship riding over and through them. This is what happens when seas are shipped from forward—it is only the crest of a sea that occasionally slaps over the bow of a ship thrusting through it. A "wave" is nothing more than an undulation in water. Small vessels ride over it. Big vessels cut through it.

When I went on watch again at 4 p.m., the gale had reached its full fury. The wind was at storm velocity (60 knots), with frequent hurricane squalls (65 knots and over), and the seas averaged forty feet high, with occasional groups of three or four, rising to fifty and sixty feet, piled up by the squalls.

The Captain was on the bridge, his face tense and strained. "It should have blown itself out by now," he grumbled to the Chief Officer. "Twelve hours! But the glass is down to 27.60. It couldn't go much lower!"

The speed was now reduced to four knots. Like all shipmasters of his generation, Captain Benison hated reducing speed. It was a matter of pride with him to press on and to arrive on schedule. "Four knots!" he growled. "First the fog, now this. We'll make Boston a day late—two days—hell!"

The officers we were relieving handed over the details to us, and went below for a well-earned rest. But the Captain stayed with us, and, while he was on the bridge, the Chief Officer had to leave every decision to him. "Look at those seas!" said the Captain. "Getting higher and higher. Heaping up like mountains. Damn my luck!"

We went out to the port wing of the bridge. Darkness was already closing in, with an eerie geenish tinge in the sky below the heavy clouds. The curling crests of the combers stretched ahead of us, seeming to advance in endless succession, towering high above our bows, their steep black fronts streaked with lacy foam. There was a sinister phosphorescence in the crests of these seas, a gleaming that marked their lines in the darkness with a diffused radiance. The wind screamed. It whipped the crests off the seas into spindrift which flew through the air in flakes of foam. As our bow cut into the seas, one after the other, curtains of spray were flung high over the foredeck and the bridge, splattering against the glass windows of the wheelhouse and against the canvas dodgers on the wings.

The ship was not rolling, but she was pitching jerkily as she drove into the seas head-on. Suddenly we saw a group of three monster seas, which towered twenty feet higher than the others. They were sixty feet from trough to crest. In a minute we were thrusting into them. The first broke and foamed along our sides. The second and third crashed on the forecastle head, swept along the foredeck and pounded heavily against the lower bridge.

Sea and sky mingled in a grinding, crashing crescendo of tumult. There was a cracking sound, and, as the water poured away overside, we saw that three of the lifeboats, on the starboard side of the boat-deck, had been splintered to matchwood.

The Captain, shaking himself like a water-spaniel, sprang to the engineroom telegraph, and moved the handle to DEAD SLOW.

He had acknowledged defeat. We were compelled to heave-to. The propellers were turning over only enough to give us bare steering-way. To the helmsman the Captain said briskly, "Keep her head-on to the seas. Never mind the course or compass. Watch her bow. Watch the seas ahead. Be sure she doesn't fall off and broach to."

To me he said, "Stand by the helmsman, Mister, and see that he keeps her head-on."

"Aye, aye, sir!" I said, but I was thinking what a young officer has no right to think—why didn't he heave-to earlier and save damaging the boats?

The answer is—the Captain knows best. . . .

For the next three and a half hours of that watch, I stood by the helmsman, the Chief Officer stood by me, and the Captain stood by the Chief Officer—all in grim silence, intently peering ahead into the blackness at the flecked crests of the foaming mountainous seas, whipped by squall after squall.

Hove-to, the *Ivernia* was riding the seas as well as any ship of her size could be expected to ride them, but in the violent squalls she could not avoid pitching steeply as she plunged into the hollow of each sea and next minute rose giddily to its crest, shedding hundreds of tons of water from her bows as the spume and spray swirled over her.

At 6.30 p.m., the barometer had steadied. "Change coming!" the Captain announced. At that moment a terrific squall of wind and rain hit the ship like a final blast of hate. She staggered and shuddered, as though struck by a hammer-blow, then reeled, lurched like a drunken man, and listed over to port to an angle of twenty-five degrees. The bridge-boy, standing at my side, clutched at me for support, missed his grip, lost balance, fell to the deck, and slithered and rolled along to the port wing like a skittle in an alley. There he fetched up against the rail. We others were hanging on to anything handy. The air was filled with flying spray and everything was in confusion. The ship righted herself as she rose to the crest of a sea, put her nose into it, took a purler over the bow, and shook herself free like a living thing, then lurched to starboard as she slithered at an angle down the slope into the trough, her steering-way temporarily lost.

The quartermaster with quick presence of mind swung the wheel, and steadied her as she answered the rudder and rose to the next sea head-on. "Good work!" the Captain grunted.

We had avoided broaching-to. Then the air suddenly cleared of spindrift, and there was a queer silence. The whistling of the wind had ceased entirely. It was a lull. We were in the centre of the storm, its quiet heart around which all the furies raged.

"Watch for the change of the wind!" The Captain hurried to the starboard wing and peered into the black sky. In a few minutes a gust came—from the northwest. The gale had veered through a full quadrant from S.W. to N.W., and in another few minutes was blowing again from that quarter with rapidly increasing force.

"Half speed ahead!" was the order. The seas were still running from the S.W., under the impetus of hours of whipping by the wind from that direction, but now they would gradually subside to become a swell that would continue for hours. But, cutting directly across this swell, at right angles, were seas now being newly heaped-up by the N.W. gale.

The Captain returned into the wheelhouse. "Cross-seas, damn them!" he grumbled. Then he said to the Chief Officer, "Keep her head-on to the swell, Mister, until the cross-seas get up too high, then alter course gradually to West as you think fit."

With that he went into the chartroom. The surface of the ocean had now become wildly troubled and confused. The swell from the S.W. was still heaping up in seas twenty feet high, but cross-seas from the N.W. were running laterally into them, and increasing. The ship now began to do some "fancy rolling"—that is, to roll and pitch simultaneously, with a wild irregular movement, like that of a bucking broncho striving to buck off its rider and saddle.

The waters seethed, as though they were boiling weirdly without heat. Spray was whipped from the crests of the seas abeam, and, as the ship lurched, she took dollops of water from the weather side onto the after-deck. This was one difference between sail and steam. A sailing vessel, under press of sail with the wind abeam, heels over to leeward and ships water over the lee rail; but a steamer rolling in the trough of seas from abeam is more likely to ship water on the weather side, since she rolls as much to one side as to the other.

Eight bells struck for the change of the watch. The cry of the lookout men from the crow's nest, "All's well and lights burning brightly!" was not reassuring in the circumstances. Our relief came, and the Captain stepped out of the chartroom with a dark scowl on his red face—or so we could surmise, for we could not see him distinctly in the blackness on the bridge.

He conferred briefly with the Chief Officer and the relieving officer of the watch, but not to ask advice or even to give it—only to give orders, for, the instant that he stepped onto the bridge, his was the sole and full authority there. He went out to the starboard wing, eyed the seas ahead and abeam, then returned into the wheelhouse, glanced at the compass, and said, "Alter course to due West." Then he added, "Increase speed gradually as the seas abate."

His tactics were to run through the buffetings of the troubled seas on a middle course between the S.W. swell and the N.W. gale, to avoid a direct hammering from abeam on either side, by taking glancing blows from them on both sides, and at the same time to reduce the pitching movements of riding directly over the swells or the seas, head-on. It was a difficult decision, which only he could take, for in angry cross-seas any course that is steered must be uncomfortable. The ship is tossed like a cork in boiling water, and every decision as to course has its dangers.

Yet the decision must be taken, rightly or wrongly, and that is the shipmaster's responsibility in every crisis, big or small.

I went below, glad to be out of the wind, the wet, the cold, and the turmoil. After a meal I turned in to my bunk, but kept my clothes on, to be ready at short call if some emergency should arise. I put out the light, turned my face to the bulkhead, and, rocked in the cradle of the deep, fell instantly asleep without a worry in the world. The change of wind was a sure indication that we had passed through the centre of the storm, and that in a few hours we would be out of the worst of it.

At 3.45 a.m., I was called by the quartermaster, who brought in a steaming cup of tea, and at four o'clock I went up to the bridge. The Captain was still there, in his wet oilskins. He had not had a wink of sleep, and had not left the bridge and the chartroom for twenty-four hours.

But, during my eight hours below, the storm had abated. We had run through its outer rotating ambit on the westward side towards its verge. There was still a swell from the S.W., combined with high running seas, and a moderate gale from the N.W., creating cross-seas, but these were subsiding. The engines were now at full ahead, and we had returned to a southwesterly course.

After the change of the watch, and instructions to the Chief Officer, the jaded Captain, satisfied that all danger was past, handed his wet oilskin to a quartermaster, and went down to his cabin for a sleep. As he went, he said to the Chief Officer, "Call me if there is anything unusual, Mister. Clear up that boat wreckage when daylight comes in."

At dawn the skies had cleared, and the seas were subsiding. The Chief Officer rubbed his hands together gleefully, and commented, "That was a bit of a dusting, wasn't it?"

"She came through it all right," I said.

"She's a steady old tub."

At daylight, before the passengers were astir, I was sent with the carpenter, the boatswain, and some deckhands to clear up the wreckage of the three splintered lifeboats. It was remarkable that hammer blows of water had been able to splinter the yellow-pine planks of these clinker-built boats to matchwood, as though a giant had been at work with an axe. A weight of thousands of tons of water, from the crest of a curling comber, had stove in the canvas covers and then burst the planks apart, splintering them where they were fastened to the rock-elm timbers (ribs) by copper nails.

The boats, as usual, were secured to the radial steel davits by rope tackles connected to steel hooks in the bow and stern-sheets. These hooks were secured down through the keelson and keel timbers of American oak to steel keel-plates with strong bolts. The boats rested on wooden chocks on the boat-deck, secured with "gripes" lashed to deck bolts (a lifeboat must be secured in a manner which will allow it to be quickly cleared and launched).

The lashings of the boats, secured as they were to the hardwood frame timbers, had held, but the softwood clinker planks had been burst apart by the sudden heavy pressure and weight of water from the purler, which must have been colossal to shred the canvas covers and then to burst the planks from within.

Many of the splintered planks and most of the gear in the boats (including oars, mast, sails, buckets, bread-tanks, sea-anchor, rudder, ropes, lines, oil-bag, water breaker, spirit compass, and other items) had been washed overboard, but some had become tangled or jammed under deck-fixtures. We salvaged these.

The carpenter and boatswain freed the boat-timbers that remained secured to the falls by the steel hooks. The wreckage was cleared away, and stowed down below, before the first pale and shaken passengers came out on deck for a breath of fresh air and a pre-breakfast promenade after their ordeal.

Yes, it had been their ordeal. They now had the smiling faces of persons saved by the mercy of Providence from an awful and undeserved doom. It had been their ordeal because they had only their imaginations to rely on while the ship had writhed in the turmoil of the storm. Those with vivid imaginations or guilty consciences had suffered the most at the prospect of being plunged to a watery doom; but now all was well. The sun rose, like the passengers, with a sickly smile. The Atlantic Ocean had done its worst, and had failed to destroy us.

Four days later we ran into a fog to the southward of Sable Island. We had to reduce speed to half, and later to slow, as we groped our way towards Massachusetts Bay, hooting like a lost soul at every minute, and frequently sounding with the old-fashioned 28-pounds lead and pressure-gauge to check our position. (The Fathometer, or echo-sounding apparatus, had not then been invented, and we had no "direction-finding" radio instruments, or means of obtaining bearings in fog; and the "magic binoculars" of radar would have seemed to us a wild dream of something utterly impossible.)

Wraiths drifted by—fishing smacks and sometimes a square-rigged "Down Easter", or a steamer, big or small—all at risk of collision avoided only by keen lookout never relaxed. Occasionally, if we heard the steam whistle of another vessel ahead, we stopped. In these conditions, the Captain had no thought of leaving the bridge. He went for fifty hours without sleep before we reached the Boston Light Vessel and took the pilot on board. We were two days late.

"What happened?" asked the pilot.

Captain Benison smiled wanly. "Only fog at the start and finish, and a bit of a dusting in mid-ocean!"

"Some of your boats carried away!" said the pilot, observantly.

"Shipped a purler," was the laconic reply.

Understatement was meritorious. "The Glowworm", like

every other shipmaster in passenger-liners, was well aware that his living depended on the sale of steamer-tickets by the travel-agencies on shore. How could he admit that the North Atlantic could be uncomfortably stormy at times?

The pilot understood. "Got to expect it at this time of the year," he said with a grin.

The mist lifted as we steered through the channels among the shoals of Boston Bay, and into the calm and beautiful inner waters of Boston Harbour, to anchor at quarantine for two hours until "pratique" was granted. Then, with the aid of two tugs, we proceeded up to the dock and into berth.

The streets of the historic city of culture, churches, kindness, and decency were knee-deep in snow. There can be no more hospitable city than Boston. The Cunard mail-steamer service was inaugurated between Liverpool and Boston in July, 1840, in the little wooden-hull paddle-wheel steamer *Britannia* (1,154 tons). With auxiliary sail, she took twelve days for the crossing, and, when she paddled in past Fort Independence on her maiden voyage, all Boston went wild with excitement. The Captain received fourteen hundred written invitations to dinner!

The Cunard Line seemed to "belong" to Boston almost as much as to Liverpool. No people in the world surpass Bostonians in the understanding of seamanship; for here was the home of the Massachusetts whalers who roamed every ocean in their hey-day, in the eighteenth century, and as seamen and boatmen were unexcelled. They left a memory in sea history that can never fade, for they roamed afar, even into the uncharted waters of the great Pacific, to visit many islands and havens known then only to themselves; and Cape Horn was their regular and familiar homeward-bound landmark.

What these Nantucket men, and their neighbours of Maine and the "Blue Noses" of the Bay of Fundy, didn't know about build-ing and handling wooden ships under sail was scarcely worth knowing. They knew it from their British and Dutch an-cestors, with their own Yankee traditions added, and the result was a toughness and the sea-lore of the "iron men in wooden ships"—all the more remarkable because their era came to an end so suddenly when the ships, instead of the men, were built of iron.

Boston would be the last place in which to make a fuss about a storm in the Atlantic. When the *Invernia* berthed, the ship-news reporters came on board, and knocked at the weary Captain's door. "You're very late, Captain," they said. "You must have had a tough trip. What's the story?"

"The Glowworm" could scarcely keep his eyes open. He was too tired even to be tactless. "No story, boys," he said, quietly. "Nothing happened!"

"But, Cap'n—two days late! Why?"

"Fog!"

"Did you run into any storms?"

"Storms? Oh, yes, just a bit o' bad weather, y'know, and three lifeboats washed away by a heavy sea. Hardly worth mentioning. It's winter-time in the North Atlantic, y'know. Got to expect a bit of a dusting. The ship was very steady, y'know. Rode it like a duck."

And that was all.

I made two voyages with Captain Benison in the *Invernia*, with storms and fog on each of the four crossings, delaying our arrivals. On the homeward passage of the second voyage, we were due at Liverpool on Christmas Eve—but on that day we were fogbound off the southwest of Ireland, and anxiously groping our way towards a hoped-for landfall at Fastnet lighthouse.

After five days heavy weather in mid-ocean, with no sight of the sun or stars, we had entered the fog-blanket and reduced speed to slow, without any means of being sure of our position. The Captain had had very little, if any, sleep for days. He paced the bridge, anxious and irritable, frequently ordering the engines to be stopped, while we took soundings and listened intently for the Fastnet fog-signal, or for the much more dreaded sound of surf on the ironbound coast of West Cork or Kerry, where many a vessel under sail in bygone years had been driven to destruction by westerly gales.

At midnight the engines were stopped. Next morning, the fog was still thick, but it was Christmas morning. The Captain was on the bridge. He had not slept all night. Daylight came in, with light airs that swirled the veils of mist eerily, permitting occasional clear glimpses ahead and abeam. The ship was going slow ahead, her steam whistle hooting at one-minute intervals. The sea was smooth, and our decks were crowded with passengers, cheerily wishing each other a Merry Christmas.

To conform with custom, I went up to the Captain, and, with the proper mixture of cheerfulness and respect, said to him, "I wish you a Merry Christmas, sir!"

"The Glowworm" looked at me dolefully. "I don't want a Merry Christmas," he grumbled. "I only want to sight the Fastnet!"

Half an hour later he had his wish. The fog lifted and we sighted the lighthouse. Excellent navigation had keep us true on our course. The Captain went below, saying, "Full ahead, Mister", and had his first sleep for days.

Four hours later we had to call him at Daunt's Rock for the entrance to Queenstown.

Our Irish passengers were ashore in Ould Erin for Christmas Day, or part of it. They disembarked at 1 p.m. The weather was clear, and next morning we berthed in the Mersey, at the Liverpool Landing Stage.

The Marine Superintendent sent for me and informed me that he was transferring me from the North Atlantic to the Mediterranean service, and that I would be Third Officer in S.S. *Brescia* under Captain Arthur Rostron.

At that season of the year, the sunny Mediterranean appeared to me to be much more attractive than the foggy and stormy North Atlantic.

I have been in many fogs and storms in the Atlantic since that winter of 1908, and I now have a better understanding of Captain Benison's anxieties than I had then. I learnt many things from him, and one of them was that it's no use worrying. All proper precautions must be taken, but even the Captain must sleep—sometimes.

CHAPTER NINETEEN

Mediterranean Cargo-service—The S.S. "Brescia"—Captain Arthur Rostron—The Power of Prayer—Routine of Cargo-handling —Many Ports of Call—"Travel Broadens the Mind"—The Coal Wharf at Venice—Disputed Tallies—Greek and Turkish Ports—The Dardanelles—Constantinople—The Black Sea— Smyrna—Quails at Alexandria—Mediterranean Kaleidoscope—Glad to be Home—The Wreck of the S.S. "Republic"—Magic of Wireless—The Wreck of the S.S. "Slavonia"— Safety at Sea—My First Visit to London—A Commission in the R.N.R.—I Meet May.

WHEN I was posted to the S.S. *Brescia* in January, 1909, I had returned to cargo-carrying. Launched at Sunderland in 1903, she was the newest of a fleet of seven small steamers of the Cunard Line employed on a cargo-service between Liverpool and Mediterranean ports. The others on this service were the *Saragossa*, 2,166 tons (launched 1874) the *Cherbourg*, 1,614 tons (1875), the *Pavia, Tyria,* and *Cypria,* each of 3,000 tons (launched 1897-98), and the *Veria*, 3,228 tons (1899).

The two oldest vessels in this fleet, *Saragossa* and *Cherbourg,* were due for scrapping, and were scrapped in 1909, to be re-placed by the *Phrygia* and *Lycia,* which were purchased in that year from other owners, and renamed.

On an average, six vessels of the fleet were in service at any time, maintaining fortnightly sailings from Liverpool. They called at a great number of Mediterranean ports, and ranged also to the Aegean Sea and the Black Sea ports. A voyage occupied twelve weeks, including a week in the home port of Liverpool.

I remained for almost three years in this service, from January, 1909, to November, 1911. It was hard work! Despite the smart paint and the Cunard house-flag, these little steamers were only cargo-carriers. They took no passengers or mails, and had an average service speed of from eight to ten knots. They loaded general cargo from Liverpool, and coal, tinplate and sulphate of copper from Swansea, and picked up cargo of any and every kind, at ports of call along the Mediterranean, Aegean, and Black Sea shores, where the peoples of three continents—Europe, Asia, and Africa—have mingled, traded, and fought one another for thousands of years.

Cunard's Mediterranean cargo-service operated principally to collect and "feed" cargo to the Company's transatlantic services, including the Adriatic service from Naples, Palermo, Trieste and Fiume, and the regular passenger-and-mail runs from Liverpool. We were the humble handmaidens of the grand ladies of the Western Ocean. It was a comedown in the world to be working in a little cargo-steamer again, but practically all Cunard officers were posted to this service, in rotation, at various periods in their careers, as was only right, and to be expected. Life is a sequence of ups and downs for most people, and it is wise to take the rough with the smooth, without grumbling. Yet despite the comparative discomforts and constant hard work, this service had the compensation of never being monotonous. Calling at more than twenty ports on each voyage, we had a variety of quickly changing scenes, and a great deal of experience of docking and undocking, in ports of all sorts.

The climate along the Mediterranean shore is pleasant in almost every month of the year, and heavy weather is seldom met with "inside"—though we had to expect it sometimes in the Gulf of Lyons, and on our passages outward and homeward across the Bay of Biscay. The picturesque variety of the scenes and the peoples of so many different nationalities, encountered in quick succession, was as colourful as a kaleidoscope. Though we seldom lay more than a day or two at each port, there was usually some opportunity to go ashore.

A Mediterranean cruise is a luxury that many people are willing to pay for; but in this period of my young life I made a total of twelve voyages around the Mediterranean, not in luxury but in sufficient comfort—and not only did it cost me nothing in fares, but I was paid to do it.

The S.S. *Brescia*, 3,235 tons, was a steel-hulled single-screw steamer, 343 feet long and 45 feet beam. She had a "three island" profile—that is, a raised fo'c'sle head, midship-house and poop, with welldecks fore and aft, each with two hatchways opening to her four cargo-holds. She could carry 4,000 tons of cargo. She had a single stumpy funnel abaft the bridge, and two steel masts, sixty feet high, fitted with derricks. Her cabins amidships and the crew's quarters fore and aft were well found, with furniture, carpets, curtains, and other fittings of a quality seldom seen in cargo-steamers. They were secondhand from some of the Company's earlier-day passenger-liners which had been scrapped or refitted. Though worn and faded, they were luxurious enough to put the *Brescia* and the other Cunard cargo-steamers in a class by themselves.

The Master of the *Brescia* was Captain Arthur H. Rostron, who, at forty years of age, had now attained his first command in the Cunard service. Born in Bolton, Lancashire, in 1869, he had served his time in sailing ships around Cape Horn, and had been First Mate of a clipper ship, *Cedric the Saxon*. He had joined the Cunard service in the 1890s, making voyages as a junior officer in the *Umbria, Etruria,* and *Campania,* and then as Chief Officer in the *Pannonia* on her maiden voyage in 1903. He was appointed Chief Officer in the *Lusitania* on her trials in 1907, and did so well in that responsible position that he was promoted to Captain in the Company's service—and given command of the *Brescia!*

Arthur Rostron was a great seaman, who eventually (in 1928) became Commodore of the Cunard Line and was knighted. I had the privilege of serving under his command later in the *Carpathia* and the *Mauretania,* as well as in the *Brescia*; and at a later period again in the gigantic *Berengaria*. At all times I had the greatest respect for him as a seaman, a disciplinarian, and as a man who could make a decision quickly—and stick to it.

He was not the burly type of jolly old sea-dog. Far from it, he was of thin and wiry build, with sharp features, piercing blue eyes, and rapid, agile movements. His nickname in the Cunard service was "the Electric Spark"—which fairly described his dynamic quality. In his habits he was austere, with strong religious convictions. He did not drink, smoke, or use profanity, but his beliefs were his own, and he did not discuss them on board ship. He was a believer in the power of prayer. Very often, when he was on the bridge, and everything going smoothly, I have seen him stand a little to one side, close his eyes, and lift his uniform cap two or three inches above his head, while his lips moved in silent prayer. His faith was real, and we respected him for it. In addition to years of tough service in sail, he had qualified as an officer in the Royal Naval Reserve on a voyage in a British warship on the China station during the Spanish-American war. He had seen life in the rough and the raw, afloat and ashore, but his religious faith remained, as his source of inner strength.

He was not a typical shipmaster, either in appearance or in his inner piety; yet in any nautical crisis or routine work he was excellent in his profession: one of the greatest merchant sea-captains of his time.

The *Brescia* had a complement of thirty or forty men all told—no passengers, no elaborate catering arrangements and big catering staff, no swank, no fuss! We were working men, doing our share of the world's work, just that. She had three navigating officers—Chief, Second, and Third.

This meant that, when we were at sea, I as Third Officer had charge of a watch for the first time in my service with the Cunard Line; but on our route of many ports of call, we were so frequently "on stations", entering or leaving port, mooring and unmooring, that there was never a chance to settle down into a regular sea-routine of watch-keeping for more than a day or two between ports.

When we were in ports, all three officers were required to be on deck from 7 a.m. to 6 p.m. to supervise the loading and un-loading of cargo. We were on duty, in one way or another, on an average eighty hours a week, but we saw nothing to complain of in that. It was our professional task to work the ship on her scheduled routes, and we snatched rest or recreation as and when we could.

Before leaving Liverpool we would load a cargo of 3,000 tons of general merchandise, comprising almost everything of Britain's immense variety of industrial production, from salt and chemicals to textiles, pottery, machinery, iron and steel, fancy goods, whisky, salt fish, or re-exported goods such as baled cotton and wool, sugar, rum, metal ingots, ores, and everything else from the world's factories, mines, forests, fields, and fishing-banks that was handled in the many warehouses of that thriving emporium-city, Liverpool.

The stowing and tallying of crates, cases, bags, bundles, bales, packages of all shapes and sizes, for delivery in parcels to twenty or more ports along our route, was a matter of nice calculation by the stevedores; but the officers were required to tally the cargo, in accordance with the ship's manifest, and to see that it was stowed in a manner which would not affect the stability of the ship at sea.

The cargo had to be stowed so that it would be handy for un-loading at our many ports of call in their sequence. The parcels to be last unloaded, at the farthest ports, would be stowed in the bottom of the holds, and those to be first unloaded would be the last to be loaded, with the parcels for intermediate ports in sequence between. This was not easy, for example, if bags of salt or chemicals, or ores, which might burst, had to be stowed on top of foodstuffs, such as flour or sugar, which could be con-taminated, or on top of packages of textiles or other goods which could be damaged by contact with leaking chemicals or fluids.

Such problems are commonplace in all cargo-carrying vessels; but usually a cargo-steamer has only two or three ports of call, whereas we had twenty or thirty. To make loading more difficult, one hold had to be reserved for 1,000 tons of coal loaded at Swansea and delivered at Venice. This was a standing order that the Company had obtained for fortnightly deliveries of that quantity of anthracite to the Italian naval station at Venice. It conferred on the smart-looking Cunard cargo-carriers the status of colliers, in regard to one-quarter of our capacity on our out-ward-bound passages as far as Venice. Yet coal, like anything else, must be correctly stowed, and delivered according to the manifest.

With three holds loaded and one empty, we would clear out of Liverpool, and steam to Swansea in South Wales, a run of 236 miles, which, at our steady pace required forty hours in fine weather, from dock to dock, and three or four days in fog.

The coal would be loaded at Swansea in a few hours, and we would clear out on the tide, by night or by day, drop the Bristol Channel pilot at Lundy Island, and set course to get bearings from Bishop Rock lighthouse, the western outlier of the Scilly Isles. The course then was southwards across the mouth of the English Channel and the western side of the Bay of Biscay to

Cape Finisterre in Portugal, a run of approximately 500 miles from Swansea, taking from two and a half to three days, according to the weather. This was the roughest part of the voyage, as a rule, in seas or swell running from the starboard beam, which caused the ship to roll or wallow disturbingly in the troughs.

After sighting Cape Finisterre, we proceeded southwards along the coast of Portugal to Lisbon, getting bearings by landmarks. The run from Swansea to Lisbon, 830 miles, a passage of four days, was one of our longest spells of uninterrupted sea-routine in the entire voyage.

Thereafter it was a laborious sequence of entering ports, handling cargo, and clearing out of ports in rapid succession, for week after week, with short runs from port to port.

Despite long working hours, broken sleep, and the necessity for sustained vigilance on lookout and in navigation, as well as in handling cargo, I found the experience interesting and varied. It was usually possible to have a stroll on shore in strange surroundings, and to enjoy some of the advantages of travel, which supposedly "broadens the mind".

From Lisbon we proceeded to Gilbraltar, 302 miles, and from there had an uninterrupted run of 843 miles to Genoa, which took us from three and a half to four days.

At Genoa the complications began. There we would lie for two or three days, discharging cargo, and loading the produce of Northern Italy for consignment to America, via transhipment ports for the Adriatic emigrant service at Naples, Messina, or Palermo. Then, too, we were providing a coastal cargo service around the shores of Italy. There were very few Italian ports that we did not visit. We went on from Genoa to Spezia and Leghorn, then to Naples, where I was on familiar ground.

After two or three days juggling and tallying cargo in and out at Naples, we headed for Messina, and called there and at Catania in eastern Sicily. A little while previously there had been an earthquake, and the town of Messina was in ruins, with thousands homeless. The cargo we brought included relief supplies of food, urgently needed.

We then steamed on into the Adriatic, with calls at Brindisi, Bari, and Ancona—and so to Venice.

I had heard so much of the beauties and glories of Venice that it was a disappointment, after we had been piloted through the difficult approach of Port Lido, and the narrow channel, to find that we were berthed at a most desolate spot—the coal wharves of the Stazione Maritime, with nothing to see there except huge heaps of thousands of tons of coal, and the grime that goes with it. We began discharging our cargo in heat, dust, and general discomfort. The work was done by labourers from on shore, who shovelled the coal into skips holding half a ton. These were hoisted out by the derricks and tipped on to a heap on the wharf. It was an irritatingly slow procedure. Each skip had to be tallied by the Second Officer or myself against the tally of an Italian clerk. At the end of the day, the tally-chits were handed to the Chief Officer.

Tallying in Mediterranean ports was frequently "in dispute". The consignees' representatives either could not or would not count and add up correctly, or they had a different system from ours, which caused them to lose count—but always in the consignee's favour! For example, in a delivery of bagged salt, sugar, flour, or rice, the clerk would say, "I have received only 2,995 bags, instead of 3,000 bags shown in the manifest."

That meant that five bags were "in dispute". If there was no practicable way of recounting the bags in the wharf shed, the papers were signed accordingly—"Five bags in dispute"—and the consignee would claim a deduction.

This happened so often that junior officers, tallying on behalf of the shipowners, became exasperated. The story is told of a junior officer in this service who was sent aft by the Chief Officer, when the ship was at Alexandria, to receive on board, as deck-cargo, three elephants. Being tired of tallying, and irritable with the heat, dust, flies, and general discomfort, the junior officer supervised the loading, and then handed in a chit to the Chief Officer: "Received three elephants—one in dispute!"

A day's work tallying coal in the grime and desolation of the Stazione Maritime was scarcely a luxury-cruise tourist's introduction to the beauties of Venice; but in the cool of the evenings, we washed and brushed up, and boarded a ferry which ran the length of the Grand Canal, with several stops. So we became tourists and saw all the sights, from the Bridge of Sighs to the Doge's Palace and St Mark's Square, and at our leisure enjoyed a meal and drinks in the open-air cafes, and listened to the orchestras playing.

Venice had been the "Queen of the Seas" in the days when her merchant adventurers brought the produce of the Mediterranean here in small vessels; but their world was limited to that inland sea. They did not venture on the wide oceans, and their day of glory ended when the Spaniards, the Portuguese, the British, the Dutch, and the French, opened ocean routes to all the continents of the terrestrial globe. Now Venice lives on its reputation. It is stranded on the shores of time.

After our coal was discharged to the last lump, we hosed the black dust out of the hold, and steamed on to Trieste and Fiume. By this time most of our general cargo from Liverpool had been discharged, and a goodly portion of new cargo collected for transhipment to the Cunard Adriatic emigrant service, or to take home.

From Fiume we headed southwards in the Adriatic along the Dalmatian coast. Then, according to the seasons, and advices from the Company's agents, we called at Greek ports such as Patras, Zante, Katakolo, and Kalamata, for consignments chiefly of currants, raisins and figs; and then rounded Cerigo Island to thread our way among the many islands of the Greek Archipelago, going northwards into the Aegean Sea.

We usually called at Salonika, which in those days was a Turkish port. The Ottoman Empire still held a large part of the Central Balkans, including Macedonia and Albania, known as "Turkey in Europe". We discharged and took in cargo at Salonika, and then headed eastwards, past Lemnos Island, into the narrow Strait of the Dardanelles, bound for Constantinople. Little could I have imagined that, within six years, that "Strait Impregnable" would be the cause of the death of tens of thousands of gallant men.

The City of the Golden Horn—which the Ancient Romans called "Byzantium", the Greeks "Constantinople", and the Turks "Istanbul"—was in 1909 the Capital of the Ottoman Empire, which included Palestine, Syria, Iraq, Jordan, and Arabia, besides "Turkey in Asia" and the Balkan provinces of "Turkey in Europe". The city is on the European shore of the narrow Bosphorus Strait, which leads to the Black Sea. This is the cork in the bottleneck, capable of preventing the Russian Black Sea Navy from entering the Mediterranean.

Constantinople was the theme of an English song, popular in my youth:

> We don't want to fight,
> But, by Jingo, if we do. . . .
> The Russians shall not have
> C-O-N-S-T-A-N-T-I-N-O-P-L-E!

In 1909, when the Sultan still reigned, though with diminishing glory, Constantinople was a dramatically "Oriental" looking city. The Turks wore baggy trousers and fezzes, and their women-folk went heavily veiled in the streets. The glorious church of Saint Sophia was a Moslem mosque, and there were many other mosques and minarets and onion-shaped domes in the city's sky-line. The Grand Bazaar was a bedlam of clamour and a scene of vivid colour and movement—with coffee-shops plentiful in every street and alley.

The "Golden Horn" is the harbour, a fine natural anchorage, which could be considered horn-shaped. Here we discharged cargo from England and Italy, and took in Turkish goods for England and America, including bags of coffee beans, and bales of tobacco.

On some voyages, we then proceeded northwards through the Bosphorus Strait, and across the Black Sea, to the port of Kherson, in South Russia, to deliver English textiles or other manu-factured goods, and to load bagged wheat.

On leaving Kherson, we headed for home, calling on the way at Smyrna, Turkey's biggest port on the Asiatic side of the Aegean Sea, usually to load dried figs, and then went on to Alexandria, in Egypt, at the mouth of the Nile—the city of Alexander the Great, Julius Caesar, Napoleon Bonaparte—and Lord Nelson. There we loaded cotton, cotton-seed, onions, and occasionally live quails, in crates. The quails were kept supplied with feed and water, and delivered alive and prime at Liverpool for the English market.

Yes, there was plenty of variety—and hard work—on that cargo-run. . . .

After leaving Alexandria, we headed westwards along the shore of North Africa, with calls at Tunis, Algiers, and Oran—and so to Gibraltar and Lisbon, with a final port of call at Leixos (Oporto), in Portugal, to load casks of wine.

So home, and glad to be home—with a full cargo and many memories—to berth in Huskisson Dock in the Mersey, and never did grey, drab, stodgy old England seem a more decent, more sensible place than it seemed then to wanderers returned from a ten-weeks work-cruise among the vivid, polyglot, ex-citable and far too sophisticated people of dark-white and brown skins on the Mediterranean shores.

Returned to Liverpool in March, 1909, after my first voyage in the *Brescia,* I heard details of their experiences from survivors of a maritime disaster in the North Atlantic which was the big nautical news of that time, an incident of great historical interest in the development of sea-rescue work by the use of wireless. This was the loss of the Liverpool luxury liner, the White Star *Republic,* a vessel of 15,000 tons, which was rammed in a fog by the Italian S.S. *Florida* near Nantucket Light Vessel on 23rd January, 1909.

The *Republic,* with 460 American tourists as passengers, was eastward bound from New York to the Mediterranean. She collided at 5.40 a.m. with the *Florida,* which was westward bound from Italy to New York with 830 emigrants—mostly people evacuated from Messina after the earthquake—and both ships were seriously damaged, but remained afloat.

The wireless operator of the *Republic,* Jack Binns, sent out the C Q D distress call, which was the distress signal before S O S was adopted in 1912. The signal was picked up by the shore station at Siasconsett, Massachusetts, and relayed to all ships in the vicinity. One of these ships was the White Star *Baltic,* 24,000 tons, bound from Liverpool to New York. She was sixty-four miles from the scene of the collision. In the thick fog it took her thirteen hours to locate the two damaged vessels.

In the meantime, as the *Republic* was sinking slowly but surely, all her passengers and some of her crew were transferred by life-boat to the *Florida,* but her Captain, and a crew of forty-five, including Wireless Operator Binns, remained on board.

The *Florida* had no wireless, but Binns kept on sending messages from the *Republic* with his reserve storage batteries, long after the ship's electric power-system had failed.

When at last the *Baltic* hove into sight, her Captain saw that the *Florida* was badly stove in, and in danger of foundering. All passengers from both ships, and some of the crews, to a total of 1,650 souls, were transferred in lifeboats from the *Florida* to the *Baltic,* a remarkable midnight operation in the thick fog and bitter cold of January, with an ocean swell running.

As dawn came in, twenty-four hours after the collision, there was an inspiring sight. The fog lifted slightly, and it was seen that dozens of vessels of all kinds, big and small, were converging to the scene of the disaster, summoned by the magic call of wireless.

Nowadays, the nearest vessel to a sinking ship assumes respon-

"Women and children first!" Lowering *Titanic*'s lifeboats
(*Artist's drawing from* Lloyd's Weekly News, 1912)

Titanic's lifeboats lowered from S.S. *Carpathia* on our arrival in New York Harbour, off White Star Pier

(Brooklyn Daily Eagle *photo*, 1912)

S.S. *Carpathia*, with tugs, berthing at Cunard Pier, in New York City, with survivors of *Titanic* on board

(Brooklyn Daily Eagle *photo*. 1912)

Gold medal presented by *Titanic* survivors to officers of
S.S. *Carpathia*, 1912. The design shows *Carpathia* with lifeboats
approaching her amid icebergs. King Neptune above, anchor
and dolphins below

Inscription on obverse of *Titanic* medal

Titanic memorial service on U.S. International Ice Patrol vessel. This service is held each year on the anniversary of the disaster, at the spot where she sank

(*U.S. Coast Guard photo*)

sibility for rescue operations, and others proceed on their courses, unless specially requested to stand by. But in 1909 every ship within radio range—some of them 300 miles away—had altered course and groped through the fog to take part in the rescue. The *Republic* was taken in tow, but she sank, thirty-nine hours after the collision. Her Captain remained in her to the end, and was picked up from the water after she sank. The *Florida*, though her bows were stove in, remained afloat, and managed to make New York under her own power, escorted by naval and coastguard vessels.

Jack Binns, who became known as "C Q D" Binns, was hailed as a hero on both sides of the Atlantic. He was a modest chap, and insisted that he had only done his duty. What made this incident so remarkable was its demonstration of the value of wireless, which, until then, had been regarded as a fad or a useless gadget. The double transfer of so many passengers, first from the *Republic* to the *Florida,* and then of both these vessels from the *Florida* to the *Baltic,* without mishap, was a striking demonstration of lifeboat efficiency.

Responsibility for the collision was, as usual, a debatable point, but it was obvious that one or both of the liners had too much speed in the heavy fog in these busy waters offshore from New York. Many years would pass before radar and direction-finding gear would make navigation in fog safe. In the meantime this collision drew attention to the need for exact navigation on agreed tracks on the North Atlantic routes, and this led ultimately to the international agreements of 1913, which laid down the tracks for eastbound and westbound traffic on the various routes at different seasons of the year, especially during the iceberg season.

Though many Cunarders have been lost by enemy action in war-time, very few have been wrecked in peace-time.

In the earlier years of combined sail and steam, there were some wrecks, but these have no reference to present-day conditions. Since 1893, Cunard have had approximately one hundred steel-hulled screw steamers in service. Of these only two have been wrecked in peace-time—the *Carinthia* (first of that name, 5,500 tons) off Haiti in 1900, and the *Slavonia* (10,000 tons), on the Azores in 1909.

That is a remarkable record of safety, over sixty-five years, multiplied by the large number of voyages in a hundred vessels, giving the odds against wreck of perhaps 80,000 to one on any peace-time voyage. But, if the statistics are taken since the loss of the *Slavonia* in 1909, *not one Cunarder has been wrecked in peace-time in fifty years!* This increases the odds against wreck to mathematical infinity, in normal peace-time navigation—perhaps the proudest record that the Cunard Line holds, a result of the rigid training which impresses on all Cunard officers the priority that must be given to safety precautions.

All the more remarkable then, and almost inexplicable, was the loss of the *Slavonia* in the Azores in 1909. This occurred while I was in the *Brescia* on the Mediterranean run, and was of special interest to me, as I knew several of the officers in the wrecked ship.

The *Slavonia* was in the Cunard service carrying emigrants and cargo from the Adriatic ports and Italy to New York. She was a relatively new vessel, launched in 1903. The track between Gibraltar and New York passes twenty or more miles to the northward of the Azores. She was off her course to that extent, and, if her navigation or navigational instruments were not at fault, it is possible that the Captain or the officer of the watch intended to steer close inshore for a "fix" on landmarks. Whatever the reason, she suddenly ran aground, in a strange manner, being caught in a cleft between two submerged rocks—so that, although helplessly wrecked, she could not sink.

All her passengers and crew were saved, and much of her cargo and most of her fittings and gear were salvaged, but otherwise she was a loss. I do not remember the findings of the Board of Trade inquiry, but I do remember that the general opinion among officers of the Cunard Line at the time was one of bewilderment that such a thing could have happened to one of "our" ships.

Sea tragedies are so rare that they become big news—for land folk—when they do happen. But to the professional seafarer, these rare occurrences are only reminders of the need for more caution in daily routine. Whenever a wreck occurs, someone has been caught napping! That is the human factor, which operates in every human activity, and not only at sea. Normal happenings seldom "make news".

After I had made four voyages to the Mediterranean with Captain Arthur Rostron, he was transferred in December, 1909, to command of the *Veria*, another of the small Cunard cargo-carriers in the Mediterranean trade. I remained in the *Brescia*, but, as she was laid up at Liverpool over Christmas, I had three weeks leave.

I had made application, on Captain Rostron's recommendation, for training in the Royal Naval Reserve, and it was necessary for me to go to London for an interview at the Admiralty.

I took train from Liverpool, suddenly realizing that, though I had visited hundreds of ports in many countries, in all the continents, and I had attained the age of twenty-six, I had never visited London, the greatest of river-ports—and now I was bound there, not in a ship, but by the back-door entrance in a train!

Arriving in that manner, it is difficult at first to realize that London is a seaport. The imposing and serene West End is not obviously dominated by the shipping which gives the city its life. To find the ships in London you have to go looking for them in the drabber districts east of the City—in the lower reaches and the great extent of the docks below Tower Bridge, where many West-Enders never venture. In no other great seaport in the world is there such a line of demarcation, concealing the source of the city's wealth from many of those who benefit most from it.

West of Tower Bridge, London seems an inland city. East of that boundary, below the Pool of London, is the busy sea-gateway to the world.

Could Kipling have thought of that when he observed that "East is East, and West is West, and never the twain shall meet"?

My interview with the Admiralty was satisfactory, and I received a Commission as Probationary Sub-Lieutenant in the Royal Naval Reserve, dated 1st January, 1910. This meant that I would be called up for naval training at some convenient later date.

While in London I stayed with my young brother, Ormond Douglas Bisset, who was an apprentice clerk in the Moorgate office of the Royal Mail Steam Packet Company Limited, a big shipping company trading from Liverpool and London chiefly to South American and Central American ports, with important subsidiaries in mail services to Australia and cargo-service to the Mediterranean.

At my brother's suburban "diggings", I met some of his friends, including the girl who was to become my wife—May.

Perhaps May didn't realize it, or perhaps she did, but I knew that she was the girl for me. My leave ended all too soon, but I had made a little headway, and we agreed that we would write to one another.

I now had an incentive, and I felt that my visit to London had been well worth while.

CHAPTER TWENTY

Earning Promotion the Hard Way—Captain Melsom, the "Silver King"—Alik of Alexandria—The Adventures of a Stowaway—A Ride in the Black Maria—Justice and No Nonsense —The White Star Super-liners "Olympic" and "Titanic"—New Era of Giant Ships—Intense Atlantic Competition—The "Mauretania" and the Blue Riband—My Mediterranean Servitude—"Charlie" Morison—Cataract and Canaries—The S.S. "Phrygia"—Captain Capper's Indigestion—My Promotion to Second Officer—Called Up for Training in the Royal Naval Reserve—The Lure of London.

THROUGHOUT the year 1910, I made four cargo-voyages from Liverpool to Mediterranean ports in the S.S. *Brescia*, under command of Captain George W. Melsom. He joined the ship at Swansea, where we were loading coal. He had not served in a cargo-vessel since leaving sail many years previously. He came on board prepared for the worst, wearing a fisherman's rough woollen guernsey and sea-boots.

He was delighted to find that his new command was spick and span and spotless except for her temporary smother of coal dust —and that his officers were fully brassbound, in the best trans-atlantic liner fashion.

It did not take him long to change into his full rig, and thereafter he was every inch a Captain in appearance as well as authority. As soon as we cleared the loading-dock, the *Brescia's* decks, as usual, were hosed and the paintwork was scrubbed, and she was as smart a cargo-carrier as ever roamed the ocean highways.

To keep her furbished was Captain Melsom's pride and joy. Every Captain has his whims and fads. Melsom had been First Mate in a windjammer, and had not lost his keenness to make his ship a thing of beauty and a joy to behold. He was a pernickety man, who could never see an officer or a seaman doing a job of work around the decks without interfering to suggest a better method of doing it. He was within his rights, but a shipmaster's authority, being unquestioned, is better reserved for the more important matters requiring his attention than for supervising the details of a junior officer's or a boatswain's work.

The ship's stores included a pot of aluminium paint, used for touching up handrails on companionways and various pieces of decorative metalwork. Captain Melsom kept this pot of paint and a brush in his cabin. On fine days at sea he would walk around the ship, pot and brush in hand, delicately touching up the aluminium paintwork himself. It was his harmless hobby, but it earned him the nickname of the "Silver King". Despite this little oddity, he was a pleasant man, a good seaman, and a very conscientious servant of the Company.

On one of these voyages we had instructions to proceed from Fiume direct to Alexandria in Egypt, to load a full cargo of baled cotton, cotton-seed, and onions. This required a stay of ten days in that port. Egypt was at that time a British protectorate. Alexandria was a British naval base and coaling-station, and the site of the Khedive's Palace. It was a thriving city of half a million population, connected with Cairo by rail, and, being on the western side of the Nile Delta (100 miles to the westward of Port Said), with two thousand years of history as the main entry-port of Egypt, had a teeming life of its own—more so than it has nowadays, when Port Said has become the chief entry-port.

We berthed in the New Harbour, near the North Gate, site of the world's oldest lighthouse, the "Phare" or "Pharaoh", 400 feet high, built as a beacon by the orders of Alexander the Great in the year 331 B.C., when he founded a glorious Greek city and the world's first university and great library here.

Gone was the grandeur of ancient Alexandria, but the modern attractions—as they were in 1910—were lively and colourful. Shopkeepers, tourists, and entertainers of almost every nationality thronged the streets, and there were substantial British and French "colonies" of officials and merchants, besides the teeming Egyptian native population.

The *Brescia* had been at Alexandria many times before. As soon as we berthed, a crowd of Arab stevedores swarmed on board, accompanied by hawkers, fortune-tellers, conjurors, "guides" to the city's pleasures, and other nuisances, who greeted most of the crew as old friends.

Among these was "Alik", a remarkable man. The common herd wore long blue cotton gowns, and went barefoot. But Alik was a dandy. He wore baggy Turkish trousers, a well-cut coat of blue serge, a red fez with a tassel, highly polished elastic-sided boots, and carried a walking-stick. He was an Egyptian with delicate features, soft brown eyes, and a dignified bearing. He spoke English with an Egyptian and a Scottish accent, the latter acquired from long association with ships' engineers.

Alik was a self-appointed ship's messenger. He was ready at all times, for a small fee, to take clothes to the shore laundry, or to his home to be mended, to post letters, go shopping, deliver messages ashore or to other ships, or to do anything else consistent with his status as a gentleman of dignity who would not soil his hands with manual toil. As a messenger he was trustworthy.

The loading of the cargo proceeded with loud yelling in Arabic by the stevedores, which created a day-long pandemonium. At last, on a glorious golden evening, after filling our bunkers with coal, we cast off our moorings and slipped out past the Phare into the Mediterranean, homeward bound for England, on a non-stop run, our cargo-holds filled to the deckheads and all hatches battened down.

At 8 p.m., I took over the bridge to keep my usual watch till midnight. At 9.30 p.m., the Captain came on the bridge, and after cocking an eye on the weather, wrote out his night order book, and retired to bed, remarking, "I'm damned glad to be away from those howling dervishes"—his pet name for the Arab stevedores.

It was a soft and balmy night, with no moon, and innumerable stars powdering the cloudless sky from horizon to horizon over the "wine-dark sea"—as Homer described it. That description has puzzled scholars. Perhaps Homer, when he was going blind, or partly blind, saw both sea and wine as "dark"—or was he referring, not to the day-blue of the Aegean Sea, but to its night-purple tinge?

Being left to myself, I paced up and down the narrow bridge, glad to be at sea again, away from the sights, sounds, and smells of Alexandria, and pausing every now and then to peer into the compass to verify the course which the helmsman was steering.

At 11.30 p.m., when seven bells had just been struck, I had reached the port wing of the bridge and turned around, when in the velvety darkness I dimly saw a figure at the top of the bridge ladder. I took a couple of paces in that direction, and saw with astonishment that the figure had a fez on its head. The thought flashed into my mind, "Barbary pirates trying to capture the ship!"

I had been reading an adventure story on that theme. But the helmsman sang out, "Hey, Mister, 'ere's a Harab!" The shadowy figure was now slumped on the deck of the bridge in the darkness, wailing, "Please, Mister, this is Alik! I fall asleep in the coal bunker. I not wake up. You my good friend. Let me go on shore. My wife and children they die, if I no come home!"

"Stowaway, eh?" I growled, and dragged him none too gently into the wheelhouse to look at him by the light of the compass—the only light on the bridge. Sure enough it was Alik, but very dirty and bedraggled, snivelling and cringing, and entirely lacking in his usual dignity.

"Me no stow away," he wailed. "Me only sleep too long!"

The fact that he was dressed in old clothes proved that he was a liar. He was not the man ever to go near a coal bunker. He wanted a free passage to England. The ship's officers would be blamed by the owners for not having searched the ship thoroughly before leaving port. I was in no mood to give Alik any sympathy. I pushed him out to the port wing of the bridge. "Stay there," I said, "and keep your mouth shut, or I'll——"

I nearly said "—throw you overboard!" but curbed the words, and growled, "—knock your block off!"

Singing out for the spare hand of the watch, I sent him forrard to rouse out the boatswain, an old Cape Horn sailor, who came along five minutes later in no happy frame of mind at being rooted out of a sound sleep. "Here you are, boatswain," said I. "Here's an Arab stowaway for you. Lock him up until the morning, when the Captain will deal with him."

"Aye, aye, sir!" the boatswain growled, grabbing Alik by the scruff of the neck and bustling him roughly down the ladder.

"You know me. This is Alik. You my good friend," I heard Alik protesting loudly.

"You got me called out in the middle of the night, you heathen. Get in there!" roared the boatswain. After a very short scuffle, I heard the iron door of the carpenter's shop slammed to.

Next morning, Alik was brought before the Captain, who gave him a severe talking-to, and told him that he would have to be taken on to Liverpool, to be dealt with by the owners. A berth was allotted to him in the forecastle with the seamen, and he was given meals and clean clothes. Presently we discovered that his dandy clothes were tied up in a bundle hidden with his walking-stick in one of the lifeboats, ready to wear when he arrived in England—a full proof that his scheme to stow away had been carefully planned.

Alik quickly recovered his jaunty air. For the eleven days of our homeward passage, he was virtually a passenger. The Captain gave orders that he was not to be allowed to do any work. We had the idea that if a stowaway was compelled to work, he could not be prosecuted. That may have been true in those days, or at least a magistrate would take it into account in the stowaway's favour if he had worked his passage.

The Captain was determined to prosecute Alik, to make an example of him that would deter others. This was a matter of principle, but we began to feel sorry for Alik, who explained that his ambition was to get a job in a big London hotel, selling cigarettes. He thought that when we arrived in Liverpool he would be able to walk serenely ashore.

But the Captain thought otherwise. It was a cold, blustering night in March when we joined the stream of traffic in the Irish Sea, making for the Mersey. At midnight we were abeam of South Stack lighthouse, where there is also a Lloyd's Signal Station. Having no radio, we signalled with flags in the day-time and a Morse lamp at night. The Captain came onto the bridge and dictated a message to me which I transmitted with the Morse lamp: "S.S. *Brescia* bound for Liverpool. Please inform owners I have a stowaway on board."

This was duly acknowledged by the station. We rounded the Skerries into Lynus Bay and picked up the pilot. In the early hours of the morning we passed the Bar Light Vessel, and at 5.30 a.m. nosed up against the river wall and slid into the Canada Lock at the top of high water.

The growing daylight revealed Alik standing on deck all ready to go ashore. He had shaved, spruced himself up, and put on his number-one togs—baggy trousers, serge jacket, a brand-new fez, polished elastic-sided boots—and carried his walking-stick, just as we had known him in his old home town. But in the grey and cold dawn at Liverpool he looked sadly out of place.

As we put out our gangplank, two burly policemen walked on board. At a nod from the Chief Officer, they grabbed Alik, and said, "Come along with us!"

The police asked that an officer of the ship should go with them to the police station to lay the charge. I was told off for the job, and given the ship's log-book to produce as evidence. Standing near the wharf was a four-wheeled vehicle drawn by two sturdy horses—the "Black Maria", also known locally as the "Hurry-up Wagon". A third policeman was in the driver's seat. The wagon was only a strong wooden box on iron-shod wheels. Inside it had a wooden bench on each side, and there were two small windows with iron bars.

Alik with the two arresting constables and myself took our seats on the benches, and the back door of the box was closed. This was my first, and—as yet—my only ride in a Black Maria. We set off at a rattling pace over the cobbles, the driver apparently determined to beat his own record to the Dale Street Police Station, three miles away. The chief use of the Liverpool Black Maria was for transporting drunken rowdies to the lock-up. It smelt as if it had been frequently—and recently—used for that purpose. Alik was lamenting loudly, "Me no stow away! Me honest man!" then adding in his curious Scotch accent, "Oh, my poor wee wifie and bairns!"

The jolting of the wagon, and the stench, nearly made me landsick. When we arrived at the police station, the prisoner was in a state of collapse, his swarthy face blanched with fear and indignation, but he was hustled inside, where the officer on duty, after asking me some formal questions, entered the charge against him in the charge book.

Then Alik was taken below to the cells, and I was told that my evidence would be required at the police court at 11 a.m. This gave me time to go to my parents' home for breakfast, with a lively tale to tell of my latest adventures on land, in the Black Maria.

This being my first experience of a police court, I arrived early, and sat in the body of the court while several sordid cases were quickly dealt with. At eleven o'clock, the usher called out loudly, "Ali ben Mahomet!" and, from the cells below, Alik emerged,

246

full of self-assurance and now very smart with his vivid red fez making a splash of colour in the dingy court-room. He was brought in by two constables and placed in the dock.

According to Moslem etiquette, a fez is not removed in a court of law, or indoors in the presence of strangers.

"Take your hat off," said the Clerk of the Court.

Alik looked at him pityingly.

"Take your hat off!"

As Alik made no move to obey, a policeman's hand, the size of a shovel, swept off his fez with a mighty swipe, and it soared through the air to fall into the centre of the room.

At this indignity, Alik's hair bristled with rage, and be began to splutter strange words, until the two constables, one on each side of him, gripping his arms, succeeded in quietening him.

The charge was read, and I was asked to step into the witness-box. I took the oath by kissing a very grubby looking Bible. The ship's log-book was handed to me for identification, and I read aloud the extracts stating the date and time of sailing, and the circumstances in which the stowaway had given himself up. The police prosecutor and the magistrate asked me questions.

"How was the stowaway treated during the voyage?"

"He was berthed and fed the same as any member of the crew."

"Did you make him work?"

"No, he just strolled about like a passenger, and watched us work." (*Laughter in court.*) "Sometimes he was seasick." (*More laughter in court.*)

Then Alik was asked if he had anything to say. He had decided that eloquence was necessary. "I very good man," he began. "Very honest. Everybody knows me. I go on ship and fall asleep. I wake up in the night. I see only the sea. I think, my poor wifie and bairns will starve. I ask the Mister Officer, please put me ashore. The Mister he says, I will knock your bloody block off. I say, I dinna ken the ship will go to England. They lock me up. They treat me bad. The Captain he says, You Howling Dervish dog, I make you work. They give me no food. I canna live wi'oot food. They make me eat pork. I Moslem canna eat pig. I sick. I pray Allah let me go on shore. The ship she jump. I work all day and all night. The policeman hurt my arm. I very good man. Everybody knows Alik of Alexandria. I post letters."

247

"Were you ever in England before?" asked the magistrate.

"No, never!"

The Police Prosecutor now produced documentary evidence that the identical Ali ben Mahomet had been convicted as a stowaway in that same court at Liverpool five years previously, and had been sentenced to fourteen days imprisonment, and then deported.

"I forgot about that," said Alik. "That was a mistake. I no stow away. I work my passage."

"Have you anything more to say?" asked the magistrate.

"I good man—," Alik began.

But they had heard that already. "One month's hard labour," said the magistrate. "After that you will be deported."

Someone tossed the fez up to the dock, where it was deftly caught by one of the constables, who jammed it on Alik's head, slewed him around, and hustled him below, to be taken to Walton Jail. They have a quick way with stowaways at Liverpool, and no nonsense.

The *Brescia* cleared out again for the Mediterranean after a fortnight. Alik was repatriated in the next Cunard cargo-steamer, but was never again allowed on board Cunard ships. Six months later, when we were mooring at our usual berth at Alexandria, I saw the familiar figure coming along the quay—the same old immaculate Alik, jauntily swinging his walking-stick. He made no attempt to come on board, but, recognizing me, he cupped his hands and shouted, "Mister! Mister! Walton Jail a very good place!"

He continued his stroll along the quay, with the air of a man engrossed in affairs of importance, the perfect gentleman, who had mastered the art of living on his wits.

After I had made seven or eight Mediterranean cargo-cruises, each of three months duration, the novelty had worn off, and I was hoping that my turn would soon come to be rostered for duty again in one of the big passenger-liners; but promotion in the Cunard service never came quickly or easily. Every officer had to earn it the hard way, in the years of experience in the Company's small as well as big vessels, and patience was a necessity.

During the year 1910, when we returned to Liverpool after each voyage, the main topic of discussion among shipping people there was the building of the gigantic White Star liner, *Olympic*, then in progress at Harland & Wolff's shipyards in Belfast. She and her intended sister ship, *Titanic*, designed for the transatlantic mail-and-passenger service, each of 46,000 tons would be by far the biggest ships in the world, easily surpassing in size the two Cunard giants, *Mauretania* and *Lusitania*, which were of only 32,000 tons.

The two big Cunarders, launched in 1907, had ushered in the modern era of the gigantic "super-liners". When they were launched it was thought unlikely that any bigger vessels would ever be built; but their success was a challenge which was taken up almost immediately by the American-controlled combine, the International Mercantile Marine, which owned the White Star Line. The keel of the *Olympic* was laid in December, 1908. She was 882 feet in length overall (100 feet longer than the *Mauretania*) and 92 feet beam. Harland & Wolff's shipyard had to be enlarged to accommodate her. The biggest vessels built there previously had been the *Adriatic* (24,541 tons), launched in 1907, and the *Baltic* (23,876 tons) launched in 1904—these two having provided the challenge which Cunard had answered with the *Mauretania* and *Lusitania*.

Now the two new giant White Star liners would wrest supremacy in size from Cunard and all other competitors. The *Olympic* was launched at Belfast on 20th October, 1910, and lay there for eight months being fitted out. She had four funnels, and triple screws, a straight stem, raised forecastle and poop, and a very long midships superstructure. She was claimed to be unsinkable, as she had fifteen watertight bulkheads, the doors of which could be closed by electric control from the bridge. Her passenger-accommodation was luxurious on a scale never previously attempted. She was the first liner to have a swimming pool. Her dining-saloon, 114 feet long, could seat 532 persons.

As soon as the *Olympic* was launched, the keel of her sister ship *Titanic* was laid down. Work began on the second vessel immediately, from the same plans, with only minor modifications. A third giant sister was to follow (the *Britannic*).

In the meantime Cunard also had two new liners on the stocks, on the Tyne, but these were only of medium size, 18,000 tons—the *Franconia* and *Laconia* (the first ships bearing those names, which, after both these ships had been sunk by enemy action during the 1914-18 war, were applied in the 1920s to two new and slightly larger ships).

The White Star Line had also launched in 1909 two medium-sized ships, the *Laurentic* and *Megantic,* of 14,000 tons. The Hamburg-Amerika Line in that year had launched two fine steamers, the *Cleveland* and the *Cincinatti,* each of 16,000 tons. Norddeutscher Lloyd in 1908 had put into service the *Prinz Frederick Wilhelm* and the *Berlin,* each of 17,000 tons, and in 1909 the *George Washington,* 25,500 tons—the first of the "big" German liners.

The competition on the transatlantic route had therefore become keener than ever before, with no less than nine fine new ships brought into service in two years, and all the rival companies striving to be excellent. But imagination boggled at the magnitude and magnificence of the two new White Star super-liners of 46,000 tons. Wiseheads predicted difficulties in docking and undocking—"Too big to handle!"

Too big! What could be the limit of a ship's size? A dazzling new era was dawning. "Progress is inevitable. We must keep up with our competitors!"

The *Olympic* was fourteen times greater in tonnage than the *Brescia* in which I was plodding along: that is, she had a tonnage equal to a fleet of fourteen average cargo-steamers. She was a whole fleet in one hull. It seemed fantastic to me, as to many others who had begun our sea-careers in sailing-vessels of 1,000 tons. . . .

I heard two old salts arguing in a Liverpool pub:

"She'll be a floating palace."

"Floating boarding-house, you mean. Not like going to sea at all!"

"But think of all the work and wages—a thousand men working for two years building her."

"That's in Belfast, not here. A waste of money."

"And think of all the work for her people. She'll carry a crew of a thousand—seamen, firemen, trimmers, stewards."

"They'd be better on shore. She's so big, she'll bump into summat."

"She's unsinkable."

"My eye and Betty Martin! No ship's unsinkable."

"She's a credit to Old England."

"Ireland, you mean! And she's no damn good to Liverpool. She'll be sailing out o' Southampton."

So the arguments continued, but there was no doubt that

I.M.M. and White Star had struck a mighty blow for prestige and profits. Cunard and the Germans would need to look to their laurels. . . .

If a distinction is to be drawn between liners and mammoth liners, the launching of the *Olympic* in October, 1910, and her maiden voyage in June, 1911, were the crucial steps forward into the era of gigantic shipbuilding. But the *Mauretania* and *Lusitania* had inaugurated that era.

The *Olympic* did not succeed in taking the Blue Riband for speed from the *Mauretania*. On her maiden voyage she attained an average speed of 21.17 knots, but the *Mauretania* held the Blue Riband in 1909 with a speed of 25.89 knots, and in 1910 with 26.06 knots, setting a record which stood for twenty years thereafter.

That was the feather that remained in Cunard's cap.

In December, 1910, Captain Melsom was transferred from the *Brescia* and given command of a passenger-liner. His successor in command of the *Brescia* was Captain "Charlie" Morison, an elderly man who had missed high promotion in the Company's service, and was content to work out his time in cargo-vessels, in the few years before his retirement.

I made two voyages to the Mediterranean with Captain Morison. He was regarded with affection by all who served under him, for he was a fine old gentleman and a good shipmaster who neglected no detail of importance, but delegated responsibility to his officers, without carping criticism, in everything that came properly within their scope.

When he came onto the bridge, he was obliged to rely rather heavily on the officer of the watch for observations, as he suffered from cataract, and had almost lost the sight of one eye. A weakness of eyesight is a pathetic defect in a shipmaster, and was more so in those days than nowadays, when optical treatment and eye-glasses are of much higher quality than they were then. A Captain in those days, even if he were ageing and really needed glasses, would seldom, if ever, wear them on the bridge. Some shipmasters and officers, even today, feel that eye-glasses are not in keeping with the best nautical traditions, and will not wear them.

But eyesight is not everything, as Lord Nelson showed at the Battle of Copenhagen in 1801, when he put his telescope to his *blind* eye to read Admiral Parker's signal to cease action, remarking, "I'm damned if I see it!"

If Nelson, with only one eye, could win glorious battles, Cap'n "Charlie" Morison could certainly carry on without undue difficulty in command of the S.S. *Brescia*. He did this by leaving most of the routine work to his officers, and guiding us sufficiently with his authority, knowledge, experience, and sea-instinct, in anything that required his decision.

His harmless life-hobby was breeding canaries. In his cabin he had several cages of them, some of the larger cages being fitted out to hold a dozen or more birds, with proper facilities for nesting and breeding. In consequence his cabin was a twitter of singing and whistling from dawn till dusk. It was an aviary, and not only sounded, but smelt like one. Birdseed and bird-droppings were scattered on the deck; but "Charlie" was used to that, and, as he called each bird by a pet name, he was never lonely, and in consequence never grumpy or disagreeable.

I have never served under a more pleasant shipmaster than "Charlie" Morison. His cataracts and his canaries in no way impaired his efficiency in command. He exerted his authority quietly, effectively—and tolerantly.

In May, 1911, after having made ten voyages to the Mediterranean in the *Brescia* in twenty-nine months, I was transferred from her to the S.S. *Phrygia*, and promoted to Second Officer: a rise which I felt that I had worked to earn. This promotion, entitling me to two gold stripes on the sleeve and an extra pound a month in pay, came to me at the age of twenty-eight years, after thirteen years at sea, including four years in the Cunard service. I had gained experience, the hard way, but I did not feel that, as Second Officer in a cargo-steamer, I was soaring high in the nautical firmament. I had a long and stiff climb ahead, and I knew it. Cunard captains are not born with four stripes on their sleeve. They have to earn them.

The S.S. *Phrygia*, 3,352 tons, built at Middlesborough in 1900, and then named the *Oro*, had been purchased by Cunard in 1909 and renamed. She was a dull and slow ship, with a speed of only eight knots. She was in the same Mediterranean trade as the *Brescia*. She was in command of Captain R. Capper, an efficient shipmaster, who, being a martyr to indigestion, was inclined to be querulous and impatient.

In these circumstances, the two voyages that I made in her as Second Officer, from May to November, 1911, were anything but pleasant, the more so as, having then completed three years on the Mediterranean cargo-service, I was finding its scenes now too familiar and becoming monotonous.

Many years later (about 1921), I met Captain Capper again, and found him mellowed then by the years, affable, kindly—and cured of his indigestion!

How he was cured may contain a medical moral, if it were scientifically investigated. He told me the secret. During the 1914-18 war he was Master of a Cunard cargo-steamer that was torpedoed and sunk by an enemy submarine in mid-Atlantic. He was fourteen days afloat in an open lifeboat, with practically nothing to eat except meagre rations of biscuits, condensed milk, and water. He got his boat safely to land, and was decorated for his efforts. "But," he explained, "the enforced semi-starvation cured my indigestion. There's a saying that more graves are dug with teeth than with shovels—and there may be some truth in that!"

When the *Phrygia* returned to Liverpool, on 18th November, 1911, at the end of my twelfth Mediterranean cargo-voyage, I was overjoyed to be informed by the Marine Superintendent that I could leave her, as I was required by my Lords of the Admiralty to proceed to Chatham Naval Station, at the mouth of the Thames, to join H.M.S. *Hogue,* on 2nd December, as a Probationary Sub-Lieutenant, for one months training in the Royal Naval Reserve.

For this purpose the Cunard Company gave me seven weeks leave. The Company encouraged its officers to be in the R.N.R., and had to comply with Admiralty appointments. I had received my commission as Probationary Sub-Lieutenant, R.N.R., nearly two years previously, on 1st January, 1910.

Being green in the ways of the Navy, I was somewhat nervous of presenting myself for duty in a cruiser, but there were many Cunard officers who had been through the mill, and I was soon given the necessary advice. The first thing was to get rid of my dear old wooden sea-chest (with a picture of the *County of Pembroke* barque inside the lid), which had voyaged with me for thirteen years, and to invest in a regulation black tin uniform case, and a leather suitcase.

Into these went my uniforms, now fitted out with R.N.R. buttons, and one R.N.R. gold stripe, and an R.N.R. badge cap, plus the usual shirts, underwear, and accessories.

Thus provided, I wasted no further time, and took train to

London, to stay with my brother again for a week, before I was due to go downriver to Chatham.

I found my pal May as lively and lovely as before—more so, for absence had made our hearts grow a little fonder, and she didn't view a sailor's roving life with too much hostility. So, in the very little time then available, our friendship grew into a little more than friendship, and I began to have serious hopes.

Then the call of duty came, and it was time to leave her.

CHAPTER TWENTY-ONE

The Royal Naval Reserve—My Probationary Training—H.M.S. "Hogue"—Captain Keighley Peach, R.N.—Manners and Customs of the Navy—I Return to Liverpool—My Friend Percy Hefford—An Ill Omen—Atlantic Liners of 1912—The "Olympic" in Service—Launch of the "Titanic"—Building of the "Aquitania"—Bishop Chavasse Confirms Me—I Join the S.S. "Carpathia" as Second Officer—With Captain Rostron Again—A Pleasure Cruise—Passengers' Jokes—The Meaning of "Starboard" and "Port"—"Carpathia" Resumes Adriatic Emigrant Service to New York—The Black Hand—I See the "Olympic" in New York—The Maiden Voyage of the "Titanic"—The "Unsinkable" Ship.

BEING required to present myself on board His Majesty's Ship *Hogue* at 11 a.m. on 2nd December, 1911, I travelled from London to Chatham, a distance of some thirty miles, by train, via Woolwich, Dartford and Gravesend, skirting the right bank of the lower reaches of the Thames.

I was in a first-class compartment—on a Government pass—with one other man, who, like myself, was wearing civilian clothes. We got into conversation. He was a ship's officer of the

White Star Line, older than I. He explained that he had done several training courses in the Royal Naval Reserve, and was now a Lieutenant-Commander, R.N.R., called up to Chatham for a Senior Officers' technical training course. When we were nearing our destination he said, "Excuse me, I am going to change," and with that opened his suitcase and donned a uniform frock coat, buckled on his sword and belt, and, with his cap at a rakish angle, was transformed in a jiffy into a complete specimen of a smart R.N.R. officer.

I expressed alarm, thinking that I should have arranged to do the same, but my uniform was in its tin case in the luggage van at the rear of the train, "Don't worry," he assured me. "Only seasoned officers report on board in uniform! Probationary officers are not expected to be dressed. You'll be all right as you are."

When the train pulled in, an old porter, detecting that I was a greenhorn, asked me, "What ship are you joining, sir?"

"*Hogue*," I told him.

"Just in time to catch the picket-boat!" he said, and, grabbing my tin box and suitcase, trundled them down to the pier. Sure enough, there was the picket-boat, a steam pinnace which was casting off as I sprang aboard.

At first glance, I thought that the porter must have made a mistake. The pinnace, though flying the naval ensign and manned by naval ratings and a Petty Officer in uniform, was crowded with youngish men in tweeds, flannel trousers, and sweaters, some hatless, some with soft hats and caps, and all spattered in mud and earth. They looked ruddy, healthy, and self-assured, and presently I realized that they were junior officers of the Royal Navy who had been ashore for an early morning run with the beagles—a pack of small hounds used for hare hunting when the field follows on foot. I was glad not to be in uniform among such a scruffy lot.

Dozens of warships, big and small, lay at moorings in the harbour. The picket-boat made the round of the ships, discharging the muddy beaglers here and there, and eventually ranged alongside H.M.S. *Hogue*, moored off Sheerness. She was an old-fashioned cruiser, of 7,840 tons and a speed of nineteen or twenty knots, built by Vickers at Barrow-in-Furness, and completed in 1902. Her armament consisted of two 9.2-inch guns (one forrard and one aft), twelve 6-inch guns, twelve 12-pounders, three 3-pounders, and two submerged 18-inch torpedo tubes. She had a straight stem, four vertical funnels set close together amidships, and two tall steel masts. She was now almost obsolete, and was one of the reserve fleet.

I was the only one from the picket-boat for the *Hogue*. Getting on board, I was greeted by a pleasant young officer of the watch. This was the first time that I had ever been in a King's Ship. Everything looked bare and ugly. She had no midships super-structure, no wooden panels or rails or planked decking. She was grim, grey, and metallic. Her decks were almost deserted. Only half a dozen men were in sight. She did not have steam up. She was moored to a buoy, inert, but spotlessly shipshape.

The officer of the watch took me to the Commander's quarters. There, I met Captain C. W. Keighley Peach, R.N., who wel-comed me affably. He was a big, florid man, who looked more like a farmer than a sailor. He was nearing the retiring age, but despite his rustic appearance he was a good seaman, who had served his time in the old "wooden walls" under sail in the days before ironclads and "dreadnoughts" set the modern fashion of armoured naval might.

Having my papers, Captain Peach knew that I had been in sail. This was a prime qualification, in his opinion. He asked me detailed questions on my experiences in sailing vessels, and quickly put me at ease by his obvious pleasure at recollections of the bygone days. Then he said, with a sigh of regret, "Well, now it's all steel and machinery, more's the pity!"

To my disappointment he informed me that the *Hogue* would not be putting to sea. She had only a nucleus crew, and I would be the only probationary R.N.R. officer on board.

"You've joined at an awkward time," he said. "You will not get very much training. There will not be any regular course of instruction. If they had sent me a class of a dozen or more, it would have been worth while putting a Petty Officer in charge of you for gun drill and other training courses, but, as things are, all you can do is to get around, and keep your eyes peeled, and make yourself familiar with the routine of a warship, and you'll get through your probationary month without any trouble. To make matters worse," he added, "Christmas leave is starting soon, and out of your month on board you will have to take a weeks vacation on shore!"

With that he dismissed me, telling me to ask the officer of the watch to show me my quarters. I thought that life in the Navy promised to be pretty good. I had a small cabin to myself, like a steel box. I spent most of my time merely wandering around the ship, picking up what I could of the manners and customs of the Navy, drinking gins and bitters and swapping yarns at the proper times, and going ashore for a stroll in the afternoons or evenings. Then at Christmas time I had a weeks leave in London, which suited me very well, as May was there and we were young and free of care.

On 26th December, my leave expired, and I returned on board H.M.S. *Hogue*—in uniform this time. My month's probation ended on 2nd January, 1912. I was called to Captain Keighley Peach's quarters for an interview which quickly developed into an affable yarn about sailing ships. Then, as an afterthought, he said, "I'll declare you to be a fit and proper person to hold a Commission in the R.N.R."

So ended my probationary training. On leaving the *Hogue*, I spent a few more very happy days in London, and then returned to Liverpool and the Cunard service. My appointment as a Sub-Lieutenant in the R.N.R. was officially confirmed by a notice from the Admiralty on 25th January, 1912.

The Marine Superintendent informed me that I was posted for "general relieving duties" in the port of Liverpool for one month, while the S.S. *Carpathia* was being refitted, and that I would then join her early in February as Second Officer.

This was another lucky break. I could live at home with my parents, reporting daily to the Marine Superintendent for whatever handy work was required, relieving officers in Cunard ships in port while they went on shore with short leave.

At this time I renewed acquaintance with Percy Hefford, who had been shipmates with me in the old S.S. *Nether Holme* six years previously. He had passed for Master and Extra Master, and was now Third Officer in one of the Cunarders on the transatlantic run. When his ship was in port, he stayed at our home. His ambition, like mine, was to be appointed to the *Mauretania* or the *Lusitania*.

One evening when we were talking of this, the framed picture of the *Lusitania*, hanging on the wall of our sitting-room, where we were yarning and joking, suddenly fell to the floor with a crash of broken glass! It had been hanging there for five years, and the supporting wire had rusted through. We were both young enough to be a little shaken by the superstition that a falling picture presages death, but we passed it off with a jest, as there was no reason to suppose that the *Lusitania* was illfated.

At this time the Cunard Atlantic Mail services from Liverpool to New York were being maintained by the *Mauretania, Lusitania, Caronia, Carmania,* and *Campania,* together with the two new 18,000-ton liners, *Franconia* and *Laconia.*

To meet the challenge of the White Star super-liners, *Olympic, Titanic,* and *Britannic,* Cunard had placed an order with Brown's shipyards at Clydebank for a 45,000-ton liner, the *Aquitania,* the keel of which was laid in 1911. She was intended to work with the *Mauretania* and *Lusitania* to maintain the regular weekend departure schedules from both sides of the Atlantic. Liverpool was still the Cunard terminal port and home port, but the White Star services were now based on Southampton, and calling at Cherbourg.

The *Olympic* had been in service since June, 1911, and had proved a great attraction to passengers by her undisputed status as the biggest ship in the world. But she had a setback on 20th September, when, after being only three months in service, she collided with a British cruiser, H.M.S. *Hawke,* which tore a hole forty feet long in her side, above the waterline. This necessitated docking for repairs, and the incident gave some support to pessimists who insisted that she was "too big to handle".

The *Titanic* had been launched at Belfast on 31st May, 1911, and was being fitted out much more elaborately than the *Olympic.* She was described in newspaper reports as "the Wonder Ship", and "the Last Word in Luxury". Advance publicity acclaimed her as "the Unsinkable Ship" and as "the Biggest Ship in the World". In fact she was of the same design and dimensions as the *Olympic,* but in computations of gross tonnage the *Olympic* was 111 tons heavier: the *Olympic* 46,439 gross tons, the *Titanic* 46,328 gross tons.

Yet the *Titanic* was indeed a Titan—imaginatively named from that race of giants in Greek mythology, of planetary dimensions, the Sons of the Earth and the brothers of Time. The very name of this gigantic new ship had a fascination. It was a masterstroke of nomenclature and a challenge to fate. She was scheduled to go into service in April, 1912. No ship so stupendous in luxurious appointments had ever been built, or ever would be built. She would be the superb, the supreme liner. Her name, like that of H.M.S. *Dreadnought,* was an inspiration expressing the confidence of a seafaring folk at the zenith of power and glory.

I hoped that I would see her some day, in her pride, but I

had no premonition of what I was destined to see. . . .

During this period on shore, I realized that, at the age of twenty-nine, I had never been confirmed as a communicant of the Church of England. I had been duly baptized in my infancy, but, having gone to sea at the age of fifteen, I had missed the opportunity which comes to most youths to attend confirmation classes in order to qualify as a full member of the Church.

I discussed the problem with the Reverend E. V. Savage, Chaplain at the Mersey Seamen's Mission, in Hanover Street, Liverpool. He gave me the necessary instruction in the Shorter Catechism, and presented me on 7th February, 1912, as a candidate for confirmation by the Bishop of Liverpool, the Right Reverend Francis James Chavasse, a saintly and gentle man who was much beloved by the Merseysiders who were in his pastoral care. As I was due to go to sea again in a few days, the Bishop accepted me into his flock by confirming me in the chapel at his palace in Abercromby Square. He gave me my first communion and also a prayer-book, which remained with me throughout the years, at times when I needed it.

Three days later, on 10th February, 1912, I joined the S.S. *Carpathia* at Liverpool, as Second Officer. After being refitted, she was returning to her previous service transporting emigrants and cargo from the Adriatic and Italian ports to New York, making on an average seven voyages a year, in rotation with the *Pannonia, Ultonia, Slavonia,* and *Saxonia.*

Having been in this service as Fourth Officer in the *Ultonia* in 1908, I knew what to expect, as far as the routine work was concerned; but, fortunately perhaps, we never know with certainty what is ahead of us, as time unrolls to reveal the interruptions that, pleasantly or unpleasantly, may shatter all our humdrum anticipations.

My chief regret was that I would be away from England for a year. As a rule the ships in the Adriatic service were recalled to Liverpool, in rotation, after twelve months, for mechanical overhaul, stocktaking, and replacements and repairs of furniture and fittings, and annual holiday leave for the crews. This was the only Cunard service at that time not working directly from Liverpool on outward and homeward voyages from and returning to that home port at frequent intervals; but, from the administrative point of view, the Adriatic service was ultimately based on Liverpool, with year-long voyages, consisting of four-teen Atlantic crossings (seven round trips) between Trieste and New York to be accomplished before each ship returned to the home port at Liverpool to refit and pay off.

Though disappointed at the prospect of such a long absence from England, I was pleased at being again in a passenger-liner. The S.S. *Carpathia*, launched on the Tyne in 1903, was a twin-screw steamer of 13,603 tons, with a straight stem, a tall single funnel, and four steel masts. She had a speed of fourteen knots. She was specially designed for the Adriatic migrant service, and, with this in view, she originally had accommodation for 1,600 third-class passengers, 200 second-class; and no first-class.

In this way she was the forerunner of the modern "tourist-class" liners. She was in no sense a "luxury liner", but she was a comfortable and friendly ship. When I joined her, she was in the ninth year of her service, and well settled in to her steady work. She had a crew of approximately 300. Her Master was Captain Arthur Rostron—that highly efficient seaman, known in the Cunard service as "the Electric Spark"—under whom I had served for a year in the S.S. *Brescia* three years previously. He believed devoutly in the power of prayer.

The navigating officers were Chief Officer Hankinson; First Officer Dean; Second Officer (myself); Third Officer Rees; and Fourth Officer Barnish. Other officers included Chief Engineer Johnstone and six other Engineer Officers; Doctor Frank McGhee and two other doctors—one Hungarian, one Italian; the Purser, E. G. F. Brown; Chief Steward Harry Hughes; and the Wireless Operator, Harold Cottam.

Fifteen men of assorted abilities, associated as we were with one another and nearly 300 others of the ship's people in our various departments for working the ship, we had no inkling, at the outset of that voyage, that presently we were to be drawn into a maelstrom of tragedy and poignant emotion and disastrous mischance, unique in sea-history; and that the mind-numbing horror that lay in wait for us would remain vivid in the memory of each and every one of us to the end of our days.

The *Carpathia's* upper-deck passenger-accommodation had been refitted for a particular purpose on this voyage. In the ordinary course of events, after refitting, she would have pro-ceeded from Liverpool to Fiume with empty passenger-compart-ments, to resume the emigrant-carrying trade; but someone at the

Head Office of the Company had the bright idea of using her for a "Mediterranean cruise". She could take a limited number of cruise-passengers as far as Naples. There they would be transferred to the *Caronia,* to be brought back to Liverpool.

In 1912 the temporary use of passenger-liners as holiday-cruise vessels was a novelty. Perhaps that outward cruise in the *Carpathia* and return in the *Caronia* inaugurated the "cruise-craze" that later developed so extensively. The *Caronia* was taking cruise-passengers from New York to the Mediterranean, and would return to Liverpool for the transatlantic mail-run.

A great deal of planning was, and still is, required at Cunard headquarters to organize the movements of the many vessels in the Company's service, on the various routes, to allow for rotation in refitting the ships, transfer and promotion of officers, annual leave for the ships' people, and other routine or special requirements. The office work on shore in a big shipping company is a complicated game of chess, in which the ships are the pieces moved.

To make the *Carpathia's* accommodation pleasant for the cruise-passengers, her upper-deck cabins, which previously had the rating of second class, were furbished and fitted out as first class. The cruise was well advertised, and 200 pleasure-seekers embarked for a holiday-voyage to the "sunny Mediterranean". Among them were Captain Watt (then ex-Commodore of the Cunard Line) and his two daughters; Sir Robert MacConnel and his daughter, Muriel, and some well-known Belfast people, the Ross family and the McGuires, besides many others of wealth, culture, charm, and varied attainments—all in quest of relaxation, in holiday mood.

This was my first experience of a pleasure-cruise. I have had many since, but none more light-hearted. The officers, like the ship, had been furbished, and were expected to be fountains of information when not actually on watch on the bridge. Captain Rostron not only had no objection to our mixing with the passengers, but encouraged and urged us to be sociable. We joined in dancing, games, shipboard concerts, and shore excursions at Lisbon, Gibraltar, Algiers, Tunis, Bari, Venice, Fiume, Trieste, and other ports.

All kinds of jokes were bandied around, and seemed side-splitting at the time—mainly puns! The Doctor and the Purser were inclined to be unsociable. They walked up and down the deck together, in deep conversation on philosophical matters, presumably, as they didn't like to be interrupted. Miss McGuire nicknamed them "Brace and Bit".

"Why?" I asked her.

"They're a complete boring outfit!"

Miss MacConnel asked the Purser: "Don't you ever get homesick?"

"No," said the Purser. "I'm never home long enough!"

A steward said to one of the passengers, "Eight bells have gone, madam."

"I didn't take them!" she said, indignantly.

Catty jokes: "She's a decided blonde—she only decided recently. . . ." "She's a suicide blonde—dyed by her own hand."

Riddles: "What is pornography?"—"A book on chess!"

Nautical joke: The passenger in the Bay of Biscay who boasted that he had eight meals a day—"Four down and four up. . . ."

And so to Naples, and the end of an enjoyable cruise. One of our lady passengers, who had no sense of humour, was a highly educated person, who pestered all the officers for information on nautical matters. Doctor McGhee remarked to me one day when he saw her approaching us on the deck, "She's a good woman in the worst sense of that word!"

The studious lady asked me, "Why do you say 'port' for 'left' and 'starboard' for 'right'?"

"Is this a riddle?" I countered.

"No, I'm asking you for information on a serious matter!"

"Well," I murmured, "if you're looking forrard, the port side of the ship would be on your left, and the starboard on your right, certainly! But if you're looking aft, then the port side would be on your right and the starboard on your left! That's why, to avoid confusion, we don't use right and left. Those words depend on an individual point of view, whereas port and starboard define the ship's sides at all times."

"But if you're steering," she argued, "you must look ahead."

"Everyone in a ship isn't steering!"

"The bow is the sharp end, and the stern is the blunt end—is that correct?" she asked.

"You could call them that, but I've never heard those terms used by sailors," I said.

"Well, when you're looking towards the sharp end, starboard is on your right—why?"

"It's a nautical term!"

"But what does it mean?"

263

"It means what you've said. Starboard is the right-hand side of the ship when a person is looking forrard or ahead!"

"But what has it to do with a star or a board?"

"Nothing! It's just a nautical term."

"You don't know!" she said, triumphantly. "Well, I can tell you. I've just looked it up in my encyclopaedia."

"Good gracious," I gasped, "did you bring your encyclopaedia with you on a cruise?"

"It's very necessary, to improve the mind, but it's only a small encyclopaedia."

"Go on," I urged her. "Tell me what starboard means!"

"It means steering-board!"

"How?"

"In Viking ships they steered with a board overside, on the right-hand side as the steersman looked ahead, the way you can steer a canoe with a paddle. This was called the *steorbord* or steering-board. Hence the starboard side means the steering-board side!"

"But what about the port side?" I asked.

"It used to be called the larboard side."

"True enough, but why?"

"Larboard in Old English meant loading-board, or gangplank. That was on the opposite side of the steering-board, or starboard. So it was called larboard, but it sounded too much like starboard, so they changed it to 'port side', meaning the side of the ship nearest to the shore or wharf when loading," she explained, learnedly.

"You got all that from your little encyclopaedia?" I exclaimed, astounded.

"Yes, travel broadens the mind, doesn't it?" she said, earnestly.

In many years of being quizzed by passengers, I found that it helped them to remember the difference between port and starboard if I reminded them that P-O-R-T has the same number of letters as L-E-F-T. Similarly, the navigation light on a vessel's port side is the same colour as port wine.

Every profession and trade has its own technical terms, but seafaring men have to explain their mysteries to passengers—especially on pleasure-cruises—with as much patience as possible, and usually enjoy being quizzed.

After our cruise-passengers were disembarked at Naples, some minor alterations were made in the deck-cabins, which were divided into first-class and second-class, each with separate dining-rooms, so that the *Carpathia* now had accommodation for 150 first-class, 50 second-class, and 1,600 third-class passengers. The intention was to cater chiefly for American tourists in the first- and second-class, while continuing the emigrant-transportation trade in the extensive third-class accommodation on the lower decks.

We proceeded from Naples to Palermo in Sicily, for Italian and Sicilian emigrants, who had booked the entire third-class accommodation. These lively people were catered for by Italian cooks, stewards and stewardesses, and looked after by the Italian doctor, Italian purser's clerks, and Italian ship's police. The women's quarters were forrard and men's quarters aft, strictly segregated after "lights out" at 11 p.m. The living-quarters were multiple-berth compartments, with promenade space on the fore-deck and after-deck.

At our speed of fourteen knots, the passage from Palermo to New York required twelve days in fine weather. Soon after we left Palermo, the sinister "Black Hand" symbol of the Mafia secret society appeared in several places on the white paintwork throughout the third-class quarters.

The boatswain reported this with indignation to the Captain, who, equally indignant, told him to clean off the black hands with turpentine, and to renew the white paintwork. This was done, but next morning more black hands were found in new places on bulkheads and along alleyways. The symbols of intimidation had been put on with black paint.

Despite careful watch by the ship's police and crew, the culprits were never detected. As fast as the black hands were scrubbed out and painted over, new imprints were found elsewhere. This was extremely annoying. There was obviously a well-organized and determined gang of the Mafia on board, taking their gangster mentality with them to America. What their game was, we had no means of knowing. America would reform some of them and exterminate others, the incurables.

Early in April, we docked in New York, and lay ten days at Pier 54 discharging and loading cargo. While we were there, the gigantic liner *Olympic* arrived. It was the first time that I had seen her. She was berthed at the White Star Pier. I went on board her for a short visit of curiosity, and that was the first time that I ever trod the deck and bridge of a super-liner of over 40,000 tons

—a "leviathan liner", the first of her kind, in the long-ago of the spring of the year 1912, at the beginning of the modern age, with all its marvels and confusions.

Her promenade-deck was a quarter of a mile around. Her bridge was 100 feet from port wing to starboard wing. Her boat-deck was 75 feet above the waterline. Everything was colossal, awe-inspiring, and, as I thought, unwieldy. I was old-fashioned enough to think that she must be "too big to handle"—but that was only my innocence and perhaps envy. The young White Star officer who showed me her splendours explained that she was unsinkable. She had fifteen watertight bulkheads, the doors of which could be closed electrically by pressing a button on the bridge. She had a double bottom.

But very strangely she did not have a "double skin" in the sides of her hull, as the *Mauretania* and *Lusitania* had, for bunkers, and as the pioneer of all big ships, the *Great Eastern,* launched in 1858, had with her double hulls three feet apart. That expense had been saved, in the *Olympic,* as also in her sister, the *Titanic.* These new White Star mammoths were built with single hulls of riveted steel plates. The designers reckoned that a hole in the side, below water-level, would flood one watertight compartment below decks, and then the ship would remain afloat with the buoyancy of the other watertight compartments.

Unfortunately the watertight bulkheads had not been carried completely up to the deckheads. A leak too big for the pumps to subdue could cause water to overflow above the watertight bulkheads from one compartment to another. It was extraordinary that the designers had overlooked this possibility. The publicity that these big ships were "unsinkable" was tragic optimism.

The White Star people in New York were exultant at the news that the *Titanic* had completed her trials on 1st April— April Fools' Day!—with a speed of 22 knots, and that she had arrived at Southampton on 3rd April, in readiness for her maiden voyage, scheduled to begin from Southampton on Wednesday, 10th April, with calls at Cherbourg and Queenstown. If she maintained an average speed of 22 knots, she would arrive in New York on Tuesday, 16th April. The *Olympic* was due to leave New York on Sunday, and the *Titanic* would berth two days later at the vacated pier. The two gigantic ships would probably sight one another in mid-ocean. It would be a dramatic encounter, history-making.

News-cables reported that many prominent people had booked passages in the *Titanic* for her maiden voyage. Among them were the multimillionaires, John Jacob Astor, Benjamin Guggenheim, George D. Widener, Isidor Straus, Joseph Bruce Ismay (Managing Director of the White Star Line), Colonel Washington Roebling (builder of the Brooklyn Bridge), Charles Melville Hayes (President of the Grand Trunk Railway) and J. P. Thayer (President of the Pennsylvania Railroad)—some of the richest men in the world—and many others in the mere million-dollar class.

But wealth was not the only mark of world fame in the *Titanic's* dazzling first-voyage passenger-list, which included the names of William Thomas Stead, the greatest of living journalists, who was loved and hated by millions of people for his opposition to the Boer War, and for his views on "spiritualism"; Henry Harper, of the leading American publishing firm; Henry Burkhardt Harris, theatrical magnate and entrepreneur, one of the most prominent and admired men in New York's theatrical world; Major Archibald Butt, a personal assistant of President Taft of the U.S.A.; Frank D. Millet, one of the foremost American painters; Clarence Moore, one of the leading social lights of Washington, D.C. who was a famous horseman and sportsman. . . .

The lists went on and on. These famous people and their womenfolk were the *crème de la crème* of America's upper-class society. Their names were household words in that period when wealth, social distinction, or intellectual and artistic achievements occupied the newspaper space that nowadays is given to film-actors, sporting champions and criminals.

On Wednesday, 10th April, at midday, the *Titanic* left Southampton. She called at Cherbourg that evening to embark more passengers, and at Queenstown next day.

She left Queenstown at 2 p.m. on Thursday, 11th April, bound for New York, having on board 1,316 passengers and 891 crew—a total of 2,207 souls.

Of the passengers, 328 were travelling first class, 272 second class, and 716 third class.

She was not a "full ship". She was certified by the Board of Trade to carry 2,650 passengers and 897 crew—a total of 3,547 souls.

Cunard's *Mauretania* and *Lusitania* were each certified to carry 2,200 passengers and a crew of 900, total 3,100 souls. They were far better designed vessels in every way than the *Olympic* and *Titanic*.

On the day that the *Titanic* left Queenstown, westward bound for New York, the *Carpathia* left New York, eastward bound for Gibraltar and the Mediterranean. We had on board 120 first-class and 50 second-class passengers—chiefly Americans going as tourists to Europe—and 565 third-class passengers, who were chiefly Italians, Hungarians, Austrians, Serbians, and Greeks returning to their homelands on visits. In addition we had a crew of approximately 300, making a total of 1,035 souls in our care.

But the *Carpathia* was, fortunately, not a full ship on this eastbound passage. She was certified to carry 2,100 souls. Almost two-thirds of her accommodation below decks was vacant, and all too soon it would be needed.

CHAPTER TWENTY-TWO

The "Titanic" a "Hoodoo Ship"—Mishap at Undocking—Her Inadequate Lifeboat Accommodation—Premonitions of Disaster— Her Track Across the Atlantic—Publicity and Truth—Driving on to Arrive on Schedule— Shipmaster and Shipowner—The "Carpathia's" Eastbound Track—Ice Warnings— Our Wireless Operator—Primitive Radio Conditions—Visibility on the Fateful Night— The Aurora Borealis—The "Titanic's" Distress Signals—First S O S in History—"Carpathia" Rushes to Rescue—Captain Rostron's Preparations—Flogging the Old Lady Along—Sharp Lookout.

AT the outset of her maiden voyage, when the *Titanic* was leaving Southampton, at noon on Wednesday, 10th April, 1912, the problems of undocking a leviathan liner were graphically demonstrated. After her moorings had been cast off, and her propellers had begun to turn, her forward movement caused a sudden displacement of a vast volume of water inside the restricted space of the dock. This set up a suction which caused the American liner *New York*, berthed at an adjacent quay, to strain at her moorings.

The *New York* was a vessel of 10,500 tons. The sudden strain snapped her manila mooring lines. She swung away from the quay, drawn by the suction and by the pressure of a breeze, and bore down rapidly towards the port beam of the *Titanic* amidships. A collision appeared inevitable. The *New York* was entirely out of control, with her engines stopped and no officers on her bridge.

The Commander of the *Titanic,* Captain Edward J. Smith, was on his bridge with the Pilot, and all his officers were on stations. Captain Smith was one of the most experienced of the White Star shipmasters. He had commanded the *Adriatic* and the *Majestic,* and had made several crossings of the Western Ocean in command of the *Olympic* before being appointed to command the *Titanic* on her maiden voyage.

Instantly appraising the situation, he stopped the *Titanic's* engines. Though the giant ship continued under way, the surge of her propellers had ceased, and, as she glided ahead, the swinging stern of the *New York* cleared the port quarter of the *Titanic* with only inches to spare.

This narrow escape from a collision proved that the Master and the Pilot, and all others concerned in handling the big ship, had not yet acquired full experience of the theoretical and practical problems created by her massive bulk. The amount of water displaced by a vessel of 46,000 tons in motion is capable of mathematical calculation. As much as 60,000 tons may be pushed ahead of her and to the sides of the bow, creating an eddy or suction astern which is formidable in a narrow dock or embanked channel, its force depending on the speed at which the vessel is moving.

The *Titanic* had three screws, and it would have been advisable to use only one, at dead slow, to move her, with the aid of tugs, away from the wharf and out of the narrow mouth of the Itchen River and into Southampton Water; but even in that wider channel ships have to proceed slowly, to avoid damaging with their "wash" the embankments or other vessels at moorings.

Captain Smith or the Pilot, or both of them, had underestimated this effect. The development of leviathan liners had created new problems of many kinds, requiring a new kind of seamanship. Technical progress had been too rapid for mental adjustments to it to be fully made. This is typical of progress in all fields of human effort. Mistakes are made by pioneers for the benefit of those who come after.

The *Titanic* was a "hoodoo ship" from the beginning, but

only because she was a forerunner of the gigantic super-liners. Not one, but many errors brought her to disaster; but from each of those errors the necessary lesson would be learnt, to make her successors safe.

Typical of the way in which mental adjustments lagged behind technical progress were the regulations of the Board of Trade for lifeboats. The *Titanic* was certified to carry a total of 3,547 persons, passengers and crew. Yet the regulations for lifeboat accommodation were based on an old rule that was hopelessly out of date.

This rule, made in 1894, stipulated that "vessels over 10,000 tons" must carry sixteen lifeboats, with a total capacity of 5,500 cubic feet, plus rafts or floats with seventy-five per cent of the capacity of the lifeboats, that is, an additional 4,125 cubic feet.

As lifeboat accommodation is based on the calculation that one person requires ten cubic feet, the *Titanic* was therefore compelled by law to provide lifeboat and raft floatage for only 962 persons, while at the same time she was certified by the Board of Trade to carry 3,547 persons!

Apparently no one in authority had noticed this discrepancy. The *Titanic* had sixteen wooden-planked lifeboats and four "Englehardt" patent collapsible boats or rafts. The total cubic capacity of this floatage was sufficient for 1,178 persons, scarcely more than half of the 2,207 persons carried in the liner on her maiden voyage.

This was in excess of the Board of Trade requirements; but no one thought that lifeboats would be needed in an "unsinkable ship". No provision was made for boat-drill, or for lifeboat training of the crew. The regulations merely classified this huge vessel of 46,000 tons as "over 10,000 tons" and the tragic incompetence of that definition was not apparent, until too late.

The near mishap in the dock at the outset of the voyage was considered by some of the ship's people as an ill omen. This may have been superstition, or it may have been seamanlike judgment which took the form of a whisper that she was "unlucky".

The rumour had started several days before the *Titanic* left Southampton. Newspapers for months had been printing articles extolling her wonderful qualities, but, on the morning when she was due to leave Southampton, twenty-two men who had signed on in her crew were missing. At the last moment, thirteen others were signed on as substitutes. All members of the crew were British, and most of them had their homes in Southampton.

When she reached Queenstown, one man deserted. If he was affected by the fo'c'sle rumour that she was an unlucky ship, or if he had some premonition of his own, perhaps he was "fey".

Leaving Queenstown at 2 p.m. on Thursday 11th April, the *Titanic* steamed along the Irish coast in fine weather, and had Fastnet Rock abeam at 5 p.m. From there she steamed on the Great Circle course southwesterly for 1,634 miles, to the vicinity of the "Corner" or turning-point, in Long. 47 deg. W. Lat. 41 deg. 30 min. N., on the usual track of vessels westward bound for New York.

At this point ships veer almost due westerly, headed for Sandy Hook at the entrance to New York Lower Bay, 1,222 miles from the "Corner" (these distances are approximate, as the "Atlantic Tracks" were not defined in 1912, and shipmasters set courses at their own discretion).

At a speed of 22 knots, she would travel 528 miles per day of twenty-four hours of elapsed time, but, as she was making a westing through thirty-seven and a half degrees of longitude between Fastnet and the "Corner", the clock was retarded $2\frac{1}{2}$ hours in that transit, with a "gain" of time.

In three days travelling from Fastnet, that is, in $74\frac{1}{2}$ hours elapsed time, at 22 knots, she would cover 1,639 miles, and would arrive at the "Corner" at 5 p.m. on Sunday, 14th April.

To travel the distance of 1,222 miles from the Corner to Sandy Hook would require another 51 hours of elapsed time. Adding $2\frac{1}{2}$ hours for the further westing to New York, this gain would be occupied in the slow-speed passage of the harbour channels and quarantine delays. She would therefore berth at New York at the earliest at 5 p.m. on Tuesday, 16th April—an inconvenient time to arrive for publicity purposes. Moreover, a passage of six full days from Queenstown would evoke no paeans of praise for the "Wonder Ship" when the *Mauretania* was regularly making that passage in four and a half days.

Any reduction of the *Titanic's* speed below 22 knots, on the passage between the "Corner" and Sandy Hook, whether in the hours of darkness or daylight, would have meant either a night arrival in New York on Tuesday, or even a morning arrival on Wednesday, the seventh day out from Southampton—a slow passage in fine weather, with no excuses to be made for such an anticlimax to tremendous publicity.

In these circumstances, the requirements of publicity, or, as a later generation would term it, "ballyhoo", took precedence over sound and safe seamanlike judgment.

Captain Smith was at the disadvantage of having on board as a passenger the Managing Director of the White Star Line, Bruce Ismay. This may have influenced the Captain to maintain maximum speed, in order to keep to the expected time of arrival at New York.

The speed was increased to $22\frac{1}{2}$ knots during the hours of darkness on Sunday. This was the greatest speed of which the *Titanic* was capable. Her average speed on the preceding three days, from Fastnet to the "Corner", had been slightly less than 22 knots. As with all who recklessly press on to reach a destination, regardless of risks by the way, on land as on sea or in the air, the belief is that time gained is time saved—*but what do they do with the time they save?*

At sea, the shipmaster must be in sole command. He has the duty as well as the right to ignore any orders from the owner in matters concerning navigation. It has been denied that Bruce Ismay attempted to influence Captain Smith's decision as to the vessel's speed.

On Sunday morning, when the *Titanic* had not yet reached the "Corner", the *Carpathia* was plugging along at fourteen knots, eastward bound on the Great Circle course from Sandy Hook to Gibraltar. I was on the bridge in the 8 a.m. to 12 noon watch. On this third day out, covering 336 miles in a day of twenty-four hours, we were approximately 1,000 miles to the eastward of New York, but we were "losing time"—that is the ship's clock was being advanced one hour for each fifteen degrees of longitude in our easting (roughly 675 miles in that latitude).

Our course was easterly, a little to the north of the 40th parallel of N. Latitude. At 9 a.m., our wireless operator, Harold Cottam, handed up to the bridge a message he had picked up from the Cunarder *Caronia*, which was westward bound from Liverpool to New York. She reported sighting ice in Lat. 42 deg. N., extending from Long. 49 deg. W. to 51 deg. W.

This was nothing for us to worry about, as we were to the southward of it, but I informed the Captain, who remarked, "It seems to be a big field. Keep a sharp lookout. Carry on!"

The *Caronia's* message was picked up also by the *Titanic*. It was the first of several ice-warnings that she received during that day.

We had only one wireless operator in the *Carpathia*. He had a "shack" on deck abaft the bridge. His apparatus had a range of 150 miles. He could communicate with vessels beyond our visual range; but vessels that we could not see were of little interest and certainly no danger to us. From eye-level on the bridge, fifty feet above water-level, we had a view to the horizon eight miles away, and that was more than enough sea-room in which to avoid collisions with any other vessels, or with icebergs.

It was a clear, sunny day, with excellent visibility, but a sparkling frostiness in the air, caused by cold currents from the icefield to our north.

I went off duty at noon, loafed around, chatted with passengers, and had a nap during the afternoon. The eight to twelve watch was by far the best for getting in good sleeps at "natural" hours of rest.

When I came on duty again at 8 p.m., I noticed that two more ice-warnings had been picked up by Cottam. One was from the White Star *Baltic,* eastward bound, reporting ice sighted at 1.42 p.m. in Long. 49 deg. 52 min. W., Lat. 41 deg. 51 min. N. The other was from the Leyland Line cargo-steamer *Californian,* westward bound, reporting ice at 7.30 p.m. in Long. 49 deg. 9 min. W., Lat. 42 deg. 3 min. N.

Cottam mentioned also that the *Titanic* was now strongly within his radio range. She was sending a large number of commercial marconigrams to Cape Race in Newfoundland for transmission by cable from there to New York or to Europe. "Busy traffic," he commented. "Stock exchange quotations and that sort of thing for the multimillionaires!"

The icefield defined by the messages sent out by the *Caronia*, the *Baltic,* and the *Californian* was directly in the *Titanic's* track. She had received all these warnings.

As the *Carpathia* carried only one wireless operator, his instrument was left unattended while he took his meals, rest, and recreation. He sent and received messages only in Morse, with earphones clamped over his head. Being an enthusiast, he was to be seen crouched over his apparatus, sending or receiving messages, for many hours throughout the day, from 7 a.m. until 11 p.m. or even midnight.

Ships equipped with wireless usually carried only one operator. It had not occurred to shipowners that three operators are required to stand watches in rotation for an efficient twenty-four hours service per day. The main duty of the operators was to send and receive commercial marconigrams for passengers to and from shore stations, which relayed them as telegrams. Ships' messages were also transmitted as marconigrams. These included messages between ships, such as ice-warnings, or between ships and the shore, with expected times of arrivals or owners' instructions and suchlike.

When marconigram business was slack, the operators in ships "gossiped" unofficially with one another, often in a joking and sometimes profane and insulting manner. The operators nearly always knew what ships were within range, and exchanged at least identification signals and brief messages of greeting. There was no systematic organization of the use of "wave-lengths". The operators manipulated their crystal detectors, until they heard signals, and then joined in, listening for anything of interest, or sometimes "chipping in" with a comment or their own identification. Frequently an operator transmitting marconigrams would signal to another in his neighbourhood Q R L, meaning "Keep quiet, I'm busy", or G T H ("Get to hell!").

Nearing the shore, on both sides of the Atlantic, conditions in the ether were made chaotic by the activities of hundreds of amateurs, known as "tin-can operators", who cut in on ships' messages with their own comments, sometimes frivolous or sarcastic. These pests "faded" 150 miles from the shore, but, even in mid-ocean, there were usually half a dozen or more ships within range of one another at any time, and many of the operators, having met on shore or in training schools, were personally acquainted. They were a fraternity of pioneers, considered to be cranks, and had the curious habit of addressing one another as O M ("Old Man"). A common signal exchanged between them was G T H O M Q R L ("Get to hell, old man, shut up, I'm busy!"), or A S O M ("Wait a minute, old man!"). Acknowledgment of an identification was often T U O M G N ("Thank you, old man, goodnight").

At 9.40 p.m., Cottam handed up to the bridge a message he had just received from a westward-bound steamer, S.S. *Messaba*, reporting an extensive icefield sighted from Long. 49 deg. W. to 50 deg. 30 min. W., between Lat. 41 deg. 25 min. N. and Lat. 42 deg. N.

This was only a confirmation of the warnings we had received earlier in the day from the *Caronia*, the *Baltic*, and the *Californian*. On our course we had not sighted any ice. We were thirty miles to the southward of this field, which according to the various warnings received during the day appeared to be slowly drifting southwards from Lat. 42 deg. N., and now had its southern limit in Lat. 41 deg. 25 min.

Captain Rostron came on to the bridge, and I told him of the latest ice-warnings. He called the Wireless Operator and asked him what ships were within his range.

"The *Titanic*, sir," said Cottam, "coming in very strong. She seems to be only thirty or forty miles away, but may be more, as she has a powerful transmitter. She's sending marconigrams to Cape Race. Then there's the *Californian*. She's stopped her engines for the night because she's surrounded by ice."

"It must be thick, then," commented the Captain, quickly. "I suppose that the *Titanic* will have to slow down, or steer a more southerly course than the usual track. She'll be late in New York. It's hard luck on her maiden voyage! Any other ships near?"

Cottam told him that he had identified four others within his 150-mile range-radius of our position—the Norddeutscher Lloyd S.S. *Frankfort*; the Canadian Pacific S.S. *Mount Temple*; the Allan Liner S.S. *Virginian*; and a Russian cargo-steamer S.S. *Birma*. These were in addition to the *Messaba* and the White Star *Baltic* and the Cunarder *Caronia* identified earlier in the day. He had picked up faint signals also from the *Olympic,* now eastward bound out of New York, 500 or 600 miles to the westward of our position. She, like the *Titanic,* had a powerful transmitter, and carried two operators.

"Thank you," said the Captain. "I suppose you'll be turning in presently for the night?"

"Yes, sir," said Cottam. "I may listen in to Cape Race for awhile, in case there is any news of the coal strike in England."

I walked with the Captain in the darkness to the port wing of the bridge. The weather was calm, the sea smooth, with no wind. The sky was clear, and the stars were shining. There was no moon, but the Aurora Borealis glimmered like moonbeams shooting up from the northern horizon. The air was intensely cold.

Though visibility was good, the peculiar atmospheric conditions, caused partly by the melting of the large icefield to our northwards in the waters of the Gulf Stream, made the sea and sky seem to blend into one another, so that it was difficult to define the horizon.

Captain Rostron stood silently gazing ahead, and to the sky, and then turned to the north, watching the play of light from the Aurora Borealis. I knew better than to interrupt his meditations. Presently he raised his cap a few inches from his forehead, and uttered a silent prayer, moving his lips soundlessly.

After this he turned to me, and said, in a matter-of-fact voice, "You may sight the *Titanic* if she bears southward to avoid the ice. I don't suppose she'll try to run through it, when the growlers and bergs are so thick that the *Californian* has stopped for the night. Wonderful thing, wireless, isn't it? The ice has come south very early this year. There must have been an early thaw on the Labrador coast. We're in clear water here, but keep your eyes peeled, all the same!"

"We'll soon be into the warmer weather," I remarked.

"Who knows what's ahead?" he said, quietly, then added, "I'm sorry for Smith of the *Titanic*. After all the newspaper boasting, she's proved a slowcoach on her maiden voyage, and now this icefield will make him lose more time if he steers to the southward around it, as I suppose he will! She must be a wonderful ship, but all their newspaper bragging seems a kind of blasphemy, claiming that she's 'unsinkable' and all that kind of thing."

Aware of the Captain's piety, and respecting it, I murmured agreement. He changed the subject briskly. "The night's clear, and I'll turn in." Going into the chartroom, he wrote out his night orders, handed them to me, and, in his usual crisp manner, said "Goodnight!" and went to his cabin below the bridge.

The quartermaster at the wheel struck four bells for 10 p.m., repeated by the lookout man in the crow's nest on his bigger bell with the cry, "All's well and lights burning brightly."

The promenade decks of the *Carpathia* were deserted on this chilly night, and the ship gradually became silent as the passengers turned in to their bunks, free of care. At six bells (11 p.m.), all was quiet, except for the throbbing of the engines; and most of the lights on deck and in the passenger-compartments and saloons had been put out.

There was a light in the wireless shack. Cottam was listening to the stream of marconigrams sent out by Operator Jack Phillips of the *Titanic*. He heard Operator Cyril Evans of the *Californian*, trying to cut in with an ice-warning, "We are stopped, blocked by ice."

At that time (11 p.m.), the *Titanic* was not more than twenty miles from the *Californian*. The mammoth ship was driving on, at her utmost speed of 22½ knots, trying to make up time, and headed towards the icefield. Cottam smiled as he heard the curt reply from Phillips to Evans, "Shut up, old man, I'm busy!"

After that, Evans closed down for the night and went to bed. Cottam also hung up his earphones and got ready to retire. He had every right to do so, as Evans had. The *Titanic's* big-business marconigrams to Cape Race were not worth listening to.

At 11.40 p.m., the *Titanic* struck an iceberg, ten miles southwards from where the *Californian* lay at a standstill, and approximately fifty miles N.W. by N. of the *Carpathia's* position at that time. The collision had been a glancing blow on the starboard bow, and the big liner proceeded half a mile or more before she was stopped for investigation of the damage.

The wireless distress call was not sent out immediately. I had heard nothing new from Cottam at 12 midnight, when I was relieved on the bridge by First Officer Dean. I handed over the *Carpathia's* course and details to him, and went to my cabin below the bridge. Captain Rostron's cabin was in darkness. He had gone to bed two hours previously.

There was a light in the wireless shack. I saw Cottam unlacing his boots, getting ready to turn in. He had taken the headphones off his ears.

I undressed and got into bed. Not feeling very sleepy, I picked up a book and began reading. At 00.15 a.m., the *Titanic* sent out her first distress call: "C Q D C Q D C Q D (six times) M G Y (*Titanic's* call sign). Have struck an iceberg. We are badly damaged. Lat. 41. 46 N., Long. 50. 14 W."

Cottam was not listening at that moment. Ten minutes later, at 00.25 a.m., he idly picked up the headphones. At that time nothing was being transmitted. Instead of switching off and going to bed, he decided to call up Phillips of the *Titanic*. On getting the curt response—from Phillips—"K" ("Go ahead"), he began affably tapping out "G M O M (Good morning, old man). Do you know that there are despatches for you at Cape Cod?"

To his utter amazement Phillips broke in: "C Q D C Q D S O S S O S C Q D S O S. Come at once. We have struck a berg. C Q D O M. Position 41.46 N., 50.14 W. C Q D S O S."

This was the first time in history that the internationally agreed S O S signal of distress was sent out from a liner at sea.

Cottam, half-dressed, sprang up to the bridge, told Dean of the message, and then woke the Captain.

By this time it was 00.30 a.m., and I was dozing off to sleep. Suddenly I heard the Captain's voice, singing out orders up to the bridge. "Stop her. Send for the Chief Engineer. Send for the Chief Officer. Call all the Officers. Call all hands on deck and get ready to swing out the boats."

This last order particularly brought me out of my bunk on the jump. I flung on my clothes and overcoat, pulled on my boots and sprang up the bridge ladder to find out what was what. Dean tersely informed me in an excited voice, "The *Titanic* has struck a berg and has sent out the distress signal."

Already the *Carpathia* was being turned around. The Captain was in the chartroom, working out the course. He came out onto the bridge and said briskly to the helmsman, "North 52 West! Full ahead!"

"Aye aye, sir, North 52 West!"

The other officers, including the Chief Engineer, were now on the bridge. The Captain beckoned us into the chartroom, and said, "The *Titanic* has struck a berg and is in distress fifty-eight miles from here on the bearing N. 52 W. We will make our utmost speed in going to her rescue. Call out an extra watch in the engineroom and raise every ounce of steam possible. We may reach her in four hours. All seamen on deck for sharp lookout and to swing out the boats. We may have to pick up 2,000 or more people. All stewards on duty to prepare blankets, hot coffee, tea, and soup. The doctors to stand by in the dining-rooms. All gangway doors to be opened. Boatswain's chairs slung at each gangway. Pilot ladders overside. Forrard derricks to be rigged and steam on winches. Oil to be got ready to quiet the sea if needed. Rockets to be got ready. Everything must be done as quietly as possible so as not to alarm our own passengers."

All this, quickly spoken in Captain Rostron's clear and steady tones within less than a minute, roused men still drowsy to a pitch of intense alertness. The Chief Engineer hurried below. The Chief Officer attended to details on deck, telling us off for the various duties, while more and more orders flowed from the Captain.

Within a few minutes the engines increased the tempo of their thudding, and presently we were belting along at sixteen knots: the greatest speed that old lady had ever done in her life. The Captain called me to the starboard wing of the bridge. "Station yourself here, Mister, and keep a special lookout for lights or flares—*and for ice*! I will remain on the bridge. In this smooth sea it's no use looking for white surf around the base of the bergs, but you will look for the reflection of starshine in the ice pinnacles. We'll be into the icefield at 3 a.m., or perhaps earlier. Extra lookouts will be posted on the bows and in the crow's nest, and on the port wing of the bridge, but I count on you, with your good eyesight, and with God's help, to sight anything in time for use to clear it. Give that all your attention!"

"Aye aye, sir!"

As the *Carpathia* thrust on into the night, Captain Rostron stood silently beside me for a minute, his cap raised a little from his brow, and his lips moving in silent prayer.

Then, like an electric spark, he was hurtling around, galvanizing everybody to activity.

CHAPTER TWENTY-THREE

Hastening to the Rescue—Wireless Signals Cease—We Enter the Icefield—Navigating Among the Bergs—We Sight Flares—Grey Dawn and Choppy Seas—A Lifeboat in Sight— Picking Up the Survivors—We Realize the Appalling Reality—The Terrible Extent of the "Titanic" Disaster—"Women and Children First!"—The Living and the Dead—A Vortex of Calamity—A Watery Grave Indeed—Davy Jones's Locker Two Miles Deep—The Survivors in the "Carpathia"—Grief Beyond Words—Hoisting the Boats Up—The Tragic Scene at Sunrise.

ON the Captain's instructions, our wireless operator (Cottam) had signalled to the *Titanic* at 00.45 a.m.: "We are coming as quickly as possible and expect to be there within four hours." This was acknowledged by Phillips: "T U O M (Thank you, old man)."

After that Cottam did not send any more signals. He refrained from doing anything which would interfere with the transmission from the *Titanic*. He heard her signals answered by other ships—the *Frankfort*, the *Mount Temple*, and, at 1.25 a.m. —from a great distance (400 to 500 miles to the westward) by the *Olympic*. But there was no signal from the *Californian*, which lay only ten miles from the *Titanic's* position. Her wireless operator had shut down for the night and gone to bed before the first distress signal was sent out.

The land-station at Cape Race had heard the distress signal, and was relaying it to ships at sea, and to other stations on land. It was from this source that the news first reached New York, picked up by amateur wireless operators.

At 1.25 a.m., Cottam heard the *Titanic* signalling to the *Olympic*, "We are putting the women off in the boats." At 1.45, the *Titanic* called up the *Carpathia*: "Come as quickly as possible. Engineroom filling up to the boilers. T U O M G N."

When these two messages were handed to Captain Rostron, he envisaged for the first time the possibility that the *Titanic* might actually be foundering. Until then, he had assumed that she was seriously damaged—otherwise she would not have sent out a distress signal—but he expected that she would remain afloat, and that possibly the whole of her passengers, crew, and mails would have to be transferred to the *Carpathia*, or to other steamers which might hasten to the rescue.

It seemed incredible that the great "unsinkable ship" could actually sink. At 1.45 a.m., her wireless signals became faint. This indicated that the electric power-plant had failed, and that the reserve batteries were being used. At 2.05 a.m., her wireless signals ceased entirely. At this time the *Carpathia* had run twenty-four miles at the forced speed of sixteen knots. We were thirty-four miles from the *Titanic's* position.

At 2.40, when we had twenty-five miles to go, we sighted a green light on the horizon ahead. For a moment this was disconcerting. It looked like the starboard navigation light of a steamer, perhaps of the *Titanic* herself, unaccountably nearer than we had thought; but then the light vanished, and we knew that it had been a pyrotechnic rocket, flaring at 500 feet above sea-level to appear to us to be on the horizon from our distance of twenty-five miles away.

Though the night was cloudless, and stars were shining, the peculiar atmospheric conditions of visibility intensified as we approached the icefield with the greenish beams of the Aurora Borealis shimmering and confusing the horizon ahead of us to the northwards. My face was smarting in the frosty air as I stood on the wing of the bridge, keeping a lookout for icebergs.

When the green flare was sighted ahead, Captain Rostron ordered a rocket to be fired in reply, followed by the Cunard identification rockets of coloured balls of fireworks ("Roman candles"), and these were repeated every fifteen minutes, to let the *Titanic* people know our position. The sudden bursts of light from our rockets added to the difficulties of lookout, but they were an imperative procedure in the circumstances.

At 2.45 I sighted the glimmer of a starbeam in an iceberg three-quarters of a mile ahead of us on the port bow. I immediately reported it by singing out to the Captain, who was standing by the helmsman. He reacted promptly in a seamanlike manner, altering course to starboard and reducing to half speed.

Then he strode out to the port wing of the bridge to make his own observations, and, when he had sighted the berg and saw that we had avoided it with ample clearance, and that no other obstruction was in sight, he brought the ship back to her former course and moved the engine-telegraph handle again to FULL SPEED AHEAD.

I may remark now, in the retrospect of the years, that, in this incident, and what followed it, my own feelings and senses were concentrated to a rare pitch of intensity. I dare say that every man on the bridge and on lookout in the *Carpathia* felt likewise that his nerves were as taut as violin-strings, attuned by the hand of a master player.

Arthur Rostron, responsible for the safety of 1,035 souls in his own ship, but knowing that more than 2,000 people were in peril twenty miles way, and that every minute was precious, drove the *Carpathia* at forced full speed, in darkness, into the icefield in which the *Titanic* had met with disaster!

In taking this calculated risk, he relied on seamanship and sharp lookout, which had apparently been neglected in the *Titanic*. He knew—as every shipmaster of experience gained in the North Atlantic, and to the south of Cape Horn, knew—that icebergs are visible by starlight half a mile ahead in clear weather. That allows sufficient sea-room in which to avoid them.

In the *Carpathia* we had a dozen pairs of eyes on the lookout for bergs. It happened that I sighted the first one we met with, because I had been specially told off for that purpose, and I had keen eyesight, and I knew what to look for, and I was keyed up to abnormal alertness; but, if I had not sighted it, the men in the crow's nest, or on the bows, or on the other wing of the bridge, would assuredly have done so in time to sing out a warning to the men in the wheelhouse who were standing on the alert for that very warning.

The fact that the *Titanic* had struck a berg in calm weather on a clear night meant one of three things—insufficient lookout; responses too slow from her bridge; or that the big vessel at her full speed had not quickly enough answered her helm to avoid a collision.

Despite her extensive electrical installations, the *Titanic* either did not have a searchlight or did not use it. We in the *Carpathia* did not have a searchlight; but as our track was to the southward of the ice limits, we did not need one. In fact, very few merchant ships used searchlights, except in the passage of the Suez Canal.

The disaster of the *Titanic* was due to a combination of exceptional circumstances, and not to any one factor for which any individual could be blamed. The calm sea and the absence of wind to whip a surf around the base of the berg made sighting unusually difficult; the ice had come farther south than usual at that time of the year; finally, the berg was not isolated, but was part of an extensive field which greatly increased the mathematical chances of collision. Yet these were only some of the many exceptional elements that combined to produce the *Titanic* disaster. . . .

Within a few minutes we sighted another berg. We steered around it as before, and then sighted another, and another.

Captain Rostron later stated his earnest belief that the "hand of God was on the helm of the *Carpathia*" during that half-hour when, in eight more miles at forced full speed, we zigzagged among the bergs, clearing them with sufficient room as we sighted them one after the other.

At 3.15 we were within twelve miles of the *Titanic's* wirelessed position. At intervals we sighted green flares, and our course was steered now on bearings from these, but we could not sight the big liner's masthead lights, or any other lights of her superstructure or hull. At 3.30 there were numerous bergs surrounding us, and small growlers of ice grinding along our hull plates.

Captain Rostron reduced speed to half, and then to slow, as the *Carpathia* was steered cautiously towards a green flare sighted low in the water, at a distance difficult to judge in the continuing peculiar conditions of visibility. It appeared likely, but at first was not certain, that this flare was from a lifeboat.

We were longing for daylight. I glanced at the deck of the bridge, and to my joy could see the holes in the gratings. Daylight was coming in. The light of the green flare towards which we were steering had burnt out. Captain Rostron ordered the engines to be stopped. It was 4 a.m. We had arrived in three and a half hours.

Powerful is the force of routine. As eight bells sounded for the change of the watch, the lookout man in the crow's nest sang out the long-drawn wailing cry, "A-a-all's WELL and LIGHTS burning BRIGHTLY. . . ."

First Officer Dean was relieved on the bridge by Chief Officer Hankinson. At that moment, in the dim grey light of dawn, we sighted a lifeboat a quarter of a mile away. She was rising and falling in the ocean swell, and now, as so often happens at dawn, a breeze sprang up and whipped the surface of the water to choppy seas.

The boat was labouring towards us. In her sternsheets stood a man wearing officer's cap and uniform, steering with the tiller. Only four other men were in the boat, each of them with an oar, but rowing feebly, as though they were inexperienced, and also utterly exhausted. Huddled in the boat were twenty-five women and ten children.

With the breeze that had sprung up, the boat was on our windward side, and drifting towards us. It was not practicable to manoeuvre the *Carpathia* to windward of the boat, so that she could make fast on our lee side in the smoother water there, as correct seamanship required. A large iceberg was ahead of us, which would have made that manoeuvre difficult when time was the chief consideration. If the boat had been well manned, she could have passed under our stern to the leeward side; but, as she drifted down towards us, the officer sang out, "I can't handle her very well. We have women and children and only one seaman."

Captain Rostron gave me an order, "Go overside with two quartermasters, and board her as she comes alongside. Fend her off so that she doesn't bump, and be careful that she doesn't capsize."

I hurried with two seamen to the rail of the foredeck, where rope ladders were hung overside. As the boat came alongside, we climbed quickly down and sprang onto her thwarts, and, by dint of much balancing and fending off, succeeded in steadying the boat and dropping her astern to an open side door on "C" deck, where we made her fast with her painter to lines lowered by willing hands from the doorway.

Many of the women and children castaways were seasick from the sudden choppy motion of the boat caused by the dawn breeze.

All were numbed with cold, as most of them were lightly clad. Some were quietly weeping.

As they were in no fit condition to climb safely up the short Jacob's ladder to the side door, bosun's chairs were lowered, also canvas bags into which we placed the children, and, one at a time, they were all hauled to safety.

During this operation, we were occupied with allaying the fears of the women and children, and getting them safely out of the boat. They behaved well, waiting their turns to be hauled up to the door.

As we fastened one of the women into a bosun's chair, I noticed that she was wearing a nightdress and slippers, with a fur coat. Beneath the coat she was nursing what I supposed was a baby, but it was a small pet dog! "Be careful of my doggie," she pleaded, more worried about her pet's safety than her own.

When the women and children had been sent up, the four oarsmen and the officer climbed up the ladder—the officer being the last of the castaways to leave the boat. I followed him up, leaving our two seamen in charge of the boat, to hook her on to Number One derrick, ready to be hoisted to our foredeck.

The officer was a young man, Joseph Boxhall, Fourth Officer of the *Titanic*. I took him up to the bridge, to report to our Captain.

Without preliminaries, Rostron burst out, excitedly, "Where is the *Titanic*?"

"Gone!" said Boxhall. "She sank at 2.20 a.m."

In the moment of stunned silence that followed, every man on the bridge of the *Carpathia* could envisage the appalling reality, but not yet to its fullest extent. It was now 4.20 a.m.

Boxhall added, in a voice of desperation, "She was hoodoo'd from the beginning. . . ."

Captain Rostron took the young officer by the arm, and said quietly and kindly to him, "Never mind that, m'son. Tell me, were all her boats got away safely?"

"I believe so, sir. It was hard to see in the darkness. There were sixteen boats and four collapsibles. Women and children were ordered into the boats. She struck the berg at 11.40. The boats were launched from 12.45 onwards. My boat was cleared away at 1.45, one of the last to be lowered. Many of the boats were only half full. People wouldn't go into them. They didn't believe that she would sink. . . ."

"Were many people left on board when she sank?"

"Hundreds and hundreds! Perhaps a thousand! Perhaps more!" Boxhall's voice broke with emotion. "My God, sir, they've gone down with her. They couldn't live in this icy cold water. We had room for a dozen more people in my boat, but it was dark after the ship took the plunge. We didn't pick up any swimmers. I fired flares. . . . I think that the people were drawn down deep by the suction. The other boats are somewhere near. . . ."

"Thank you, Mister," said Rostron. "Go below and get some coffee, and try to get warm."

Our immediate task was only too clear—to search for the people in boats or rafts, and any other survivors. The increasing daylight revealed dozens of icebergs within our horizon. Among them were four or five big bergs, towering up to two hundred feet above water-level. One of these was the one that the *Titanic* had struck. Dozens of smaller "calves" or growlers drifted sluggishly on the choppy seas. To the northwards was a field of pack ice extending westwards for many miles.

On all sides we could see lifeboats making laboriously towards us, some dangerously overcrowded, some half empty. A mile away was a mass of wreckage, like an island, marking the spot where the *Titanic* had gone down. Captain Rostron decided that we must give priority to picking up the people in the boats. They were in danger of perishing from exposure to the cold, or perhaps of capsizing; and among them were a large number of women and children. They at least were living, and could be rescued; but it was unlikely that any swimmers could have survived in water that was almost at freezing-point, among those chunks of melting ice.

In four and a quarter hours, from 4.15 a.m. to 8.30 a.m., we picked up 703 survivors from the sixteen wooden lifeboats and four "Englehardt" collapsible boats. After 6 a.m., the *Carpathia's* deck-rails were lined with our own passengers, joined by increasing numbers of rescued people, anxiously watching each boat arrive. The rescue operations proceeded in a deathly silence. Except for an occasional working order, no one was capable of saying anything that would be adequate to the occasion.

The *Titanic* lay in Davy Jones's locker, two miles deep below us. With her plunge to those deeps, fifteen hundred people had been drawn down to death in the icy waters, to perish in a vortex hundreds of fathoms deep. Their bodies, with the added buoyancy of the cork lifebelts which most of them wore, would gradually rise again to the surface. If any strong swimmers had got clear of the down suction, or had clung to wreckage in the darkness, they would surely have perished of cold within two hours after being immersed. The surface temperature of the water, by thermometer readings, was 33 deg. F.—only one degree above freezing-point. This was due to the large quantity of ice floating in small pieces from the disintegrating bergs.

The dead bodies were *there*, totally or partially submerged, but, in the choppy seas, it was now almost impossible to sight them, as white lifejackets would have an appearance similar to that of the thousands of small pieces of floating ice or white-painted wreckage. A dead body floats almost submerged.

The water had a sinister greenish crystal tinge. People lining the decks of the *Carpathia* stared overside in shocked fascination and horror; for here, a thousand miles from land, the elemental ocean was, in truth, a watery grave, in which, as a quick count and calculation indicated, the lives of fifteen hundred human beings had been extinguished almost without warning—plunged from warmth, light, and gaiety to icy doom.

Captain Rostron ordered the *Carpathia's* ensign and house-flag to be lowered to half mast. The ship was in mourning.

At 8 a.m., when eight bells were struck, the lookout man's wailing cry of "A-a-all's WELL!" resounded like a ghostly sardonic lamentation, mocking the truth. But it had a meaning, beyond routine. In the midst of death we were in life.

Though so many had perished, many, too had been saved. For them, at least, all was as well as could now be expected.

I took over the watch on the bridge from Chief Officer Hankinson. It was of no importance that I had gone without sleep all night, and that I had already been on duty for twelve hours; for, like all the other officers and members of the crew, I was keyed up to the tenseness of action in which fatigue is unnoticed.

Now the morning sunlight rippled on the slight seas. The last of the *Titanic's* lifeboats was labouring towards the *Carpathia*. She was crowded with seventy-five survivors, and her gunwales were within three inches of the water; but a good seaman was at her tiller. He was Charles Lightoller, Second Officer of the *Titanic*. He had gone down with the ship, and had been picked up by Boat Number Twelve. He had taken command of her, and had picked up other survivors. We manoeuvred the *Car-*

pathia to windward, and drifted down to him, so that he was able to make fast alongside in our lee, and all the people in the boat were got safely on board.

Besides Lightoller and Boxhall, two other officers of the *Titanic* were saved. They were Third Officer Herbert Pitman and Fifth Officer Harold Lowe. All these officers had done grand work in launching the boats and handling them.

When Lightoller arrived with the last of the possible survivors, the best and worst was known. We had then received on board 493 passengers of the *Titanic*, comprising 315 women, 52 children, and 126 men. The rule when her lifeboats were lowered had been "women and children first".

We had also picked up 210 of the crew, comprising 189 men and 21 women. In all, we had 703 survivors on board, and the bodies of four men who had died of exposure in the lifeboats.

According to later published official estimates, a total of 1,503 persons had perished. These were 661 men, 101 women, and 53 children of the passengers, and 686 men and 2 women of the crew.

Of the women and children who had perished, some had timidly refused a chance to go into the lifeboats. Others in the confusion had been unable to reach the lifeboat stations from below decks.

The final roll-call of the dead and of the living, of both passengers and crew, revealed that 1,347 men, 103 women, and 53 children had perished; while 315 men, 336 women, and 52 children had been saved.

These figures indicated the supreme sacrifice made by the men who had stood aside on the *Titanic's* decks to allow women and children to enter the lifeboats.

There was no reflection of wrong conduct on the men who had survived in the boats. Some, including crew members, had been ordered to go to handle the boats. Others had been allowed to go or had jumped in when boats were being lowered only partly filled with women and children. Others had been picked up from the water.

Among the men who had perished were the Master of the *Titanic,* Captain Smith; her Chief Officer, H. F. Wilde—and First Officer Murdock, who had been on watch on the bridge when the collision occurred.

Her First Wireless Operator J. G. Phillips, had gone down, but the Junior Operator, Harold Bride, was saved.

The passengers who had perished included the millionaires

Jacob Astor, Benjamin Guggenheim, Martin Rothschild, Isidor Straus, Charles Hays, William Dulles, Frederick Hoyt, Clarence Moore, Emil Taussig, J. B. Thayer, Washington Roebling, and Harry Widener; the famous journalist, W. T. Stead; the theatrical manager, Henry Harris; President Taft's adviser, Major Archie Butt; the artist Frank Millet . . . and the many more. . . .

Among the survivors were Bruce Ismay, who, according to evidence, had jumped into a boat that was being lowered half empty; Henry Harper, the publisher; Sir Cosmo Duff Gordon; Baron von Drachstedt; Colonel Archibald Gracie; and others who had taken a proper opportunity to jump into boats, or had been picked up from the water.

The survivors were given immediate care and attention by our three doctors and by the stewards and passengers. Intense activity was going on, as the stewards found berths for the survivors.

Our first- and second-class passengers, and all the officers in the *Carpathia,* willingly gave up their cabins to women and children, and moved below to the third-class cabins.

In the meantime the *Titanic's* boats were being hauled up to the *Carpathia.* Our own boats, which were swung out on davits, had not been lowered. They were now returned to the chocks. Six of the *Titanic's* boats were hoisted up to the *Carpathia's* foredeck, and seven were carried slung overside in davits. This was all that we could conveniently hoist and stow. The others were set adrift.

When Lightoller's boat came alongside, the survivors previously taken on board knew finally the extent of their bereavements. If their loved ones were not in that boat, they had perished. At that moment seventy-five of the married women among the survivors, who had dared to cling to hope, had to face the fact that they were widowed, and that their children were orphaned. Others learned that a son or a father had gone. The extinction of hope came as a shock too terrible for the relief of weeping. The minds of the bereaved were numbed. There were no words that could comfort them. Anguish was silent. There was no hysteria. There was only a pall of unutterable grief, and a dazed staring from eyes of bewildered incredulity.

CHAPTER TWENTY-FOUR

The "Californian" Arrives Belatedly—Errors of Observation—Excuses for Apparent Neglect—Rockets and "Company Signals"— Wireless Operators Must Sleep—A Terrible Awakening—The Living and the Dead— Divine Service Held—The Bodies in Davy Jones's Locker—Ghosts of the Atlantic Tracks —"Carpathia" Heads for New York—Getting Free of the Icefield—Survivors' Narratives— Complicated Causes of the Disaster—How the Collision Occurred—A Split-second Calamity —The Web of Fate—Wisdom After the Event.

WHILE we had been picking up the survivors, in the slowly increasing daylight after 4.30 a.m., we had sighted the smoke of a steamer on the fringe of the pack ice, ten miles away from us to the northwards. She was making no signals, and we paid little attention to her, for we were preoccupied with more urgent matters; but at 6 a.m. we had noticed that she was under way and slowly coming towards us.

When I took over the watch on the bridge of the *Carpathia* at 8 a.m., the stranger was little more than a mile from us, and flying her signals of identification. She was the Leyland Line cargo-steamer *Californian*, which had been stopped overnight, blocked by ice.

Now she steamed up to within half a mile from the *Carpathia* and stopped. An officer, on the wing of her bridge, using hand-flags, signalled, "What's the matter?"

By Captain Rostron's order, I replied, with hand-flags, "*Titanic* hit berg and sank here with loss of fifteen hundred lives. Have picked up all her boats with seven hundred survivors. Please stay in vicinity to search for bodies."

This was the first exact information received by the *Californian* of the disaster that had occurred on her horizon, within an hour's steaming range if she had gone to the rescue.

Many excuses were subsequently put forward to explain why the Master and officers of this 6,000-ton steamer had so tragically failed to rise to the opportunity which had been theirs of saving the lives of perhaps every person in the *Titanic*.

There had been no wilful neglect on their part, but rather a deficiency of seamanlike reactions in extremely unusual circumstances. Her Captain had been careful for the safety of his own ship when he had stopped her for the night at the edge of the pack ice. He had done the right thing in ordering his wireless operator to send out ice-warnings, and a broadcast notification that he was stopped for the night.

The *Californian*, then, with her port and starboard lights, white masthead light, and stern light burning brightly, had been in no danger of collision or of being rammed as she lay at a standstill in mid-ocean, surrounded by pack ice, on a clear and frosty night, with no wind, and a smooth sea. She was snug, and there was no need to keep a sharp lookout. Her engines were stopped, and her fires banked, to keep a low head of steam up until the morning. Her Captain, officers, engineers, and crew could relax. Most of them had gone to bed early.

Watches had been kept on her bridge throughout the night, but they had been standby watches, with nothing much for the officers to do. At 11 p.m., the Wireless Operator (Evans) had gone to bed. He knew that the *Titanic* was near, though she was not then in sight. At this time also the Captain turned in. At 11.10, the Third Officer, who was on watch, saw the lights of a big liner, westward bound, on the southern horizon.

At 11.40, as the *Titanic* struck the berg, she had veered to port. This meant that her deck lights had suddenly become almost invisible to the Third Officer of the *Californian*. He surmised that the deck lights had been dimmed, to encourage the passengers to go to bed.

The Third Officer had been relieved at midnight by the

Second Officer and an apprentice. They noticed the masthead and side lights of the distant liner, which they assumed was heading southwestwards to get clear of the icefield.

At that moment, the *Titanic* was beginning to sink by the head. The watchers in the *Californian* thought that she was dipping below the horizon. Later, the Second Officer noticed that the disappearing liner was firing rockets at intervals. He went below, at 1.15 a.m., woke his Captain, and informed him of this. The Captain drowsily asked, "Are they Company signals?"

This was one of the most tragic moments of that fateful night. Rockets were the well-known signals of distress, but some of the big shipping companies were in the habit of using Roman candles—combinations of coloured fireworks, which resemble rockets—as signals of identification for their ships, especially when approaching Light Vessels or shore signal stations or the entrances to ports, but also at sea when passing other ships at night-time, at a distance beyond easy visual range for Morse-lamp signalling.

This was a practice which should never have been allowed, especially after all big ships were equipped with wireless. The use of fireworks should have been restricted to signals of distress. Confusion could arise, and, in fact did arise, tragically, when the *Titanic's* rocket signals of distress were mistakenly believed by the Captain and the Second Officer of the *Californian* to be "only Company signals".

That error of judgment was one of many such in the net of circumstances that dragged the *Titanic* to her doom.

On the Captain's drowsily murmured instructions, the Second Officer had tried to signal to the liner with a Morse lamp, but had failed to get a response. This was not surprising, as the officers of the *Titanic* were at that time occupied in lowering the lifeboats.

When the *Titanic* sank at 2.20 a.m., the Second Officer of the *Californian* thought that she had finally dipped below the horizon, going away to the southwestwards. If she had not veered to port after striking the berg, he would not have made this tragic error of observation. His view of the sinking ship had been stern on, at night-time, in the "graveyard watch", from ten miles away—and in those circumstances there was some excuse for his wrong thinking.

The Chief Officer of the *Californian* had relieved the Second

Officer at the 4 a.m. change of the watch. Informed that a big ship, which was now out of sight, had fired rockets two hours previously, he became concerned and puzzled. The Second Officer remarked that he had also sighted rockets or Company signals from a different vessel in the distance to the southeastward (these had been fired from the *Carpathia*).

At 5 a.m., the Chief Officer had awakened Wireless Operator Evans, who sleepily switched on his radio apparatus, and presently heard the startling news from the German steamer *Frankfort,* and later from the Canadian Pacific S.S. *Mount Temple,* that the *Titanic* was believed sunk.

At this time the *Carpathia* was picking up boats, but not transmitting wireless signals. Our operator was awaiting orders from Captain Rostron, who, like everybody else in the *Carpathia,* was preoccupied with the rescue work.

The Captain of the *Californian,* sighting the *Carpathia* stopped ten miles to his southward, had got under way at 6 a.m., headed towards us, and, in two hours of cautious navigation among the icefloes and bergs, came near enough to us for hand-flag signalling at 8 a.m.

So he learnt that, while he had slept snug, fifteen hundred people, whom he could have saved, had drowned. Yet, on analysis of the evidence given at the subsequent official inquiries, it became clear that heavy blame for their inertia could not be placed personally on the drowsy mariners of the *Californian.* There were excuses for their faulty reasoning at each stage. The blame lay on shipowners generally, for not having realized that one wireless operator in a steamer was not enough.

When the last castaways from the *Titanic* came on board the *Carpathia* at 8.30 a.m., Captain Rostron had a difficult decision to make. Should he remain to pick up dead bodies? Should he proceed, through ice, to the nearest port, Halifax? Should he continue his voyage, and land the survivors at the Azores or Gibraltar? Or should he return to New York, a run of four days, to land them at their originally intended destination, delaying the *Carpathia's* voyage-schedule by eight or nine days?

Or should he make a rendezvous by wireless with the *Titanic's* sister ship, *Olympic,* and transfer the survivors to her . . . at sea . . . with the lifeboats?

It did not take Captain Rostron very long to arrive at the correct decision—to return to New York!

The survivors had suffered more than enough. To remain there to pick up dead bodies from the sea would have added to the anguish of the widows and orphans and others bereaved. To search for, pick up, identify—and rebury in the sea—fifteen hundred corpses would be a lengthy, agonizing, and ultimately futile procedure.

Among the *Carpathia's* passengers was an American Episcopalian Minister. Captain Rostron asked him to conduct Divine Service in memory of the dead, and in thanksgiving for the rescue of the living. This service was held in the first-class lounge, while the *Carpathia* slowly made a circuit of the "island" of wreckage which marked the spot where the *Titanic* had gone down.

From the bridge, I sighted only one dead body. It was of a young man, semi-submerged, with his lifebelt on, seemingly asleep in the water, lying on his side. We did not stop to pick him up.

Most of the passengers and crew of the *Carpathia,* and some of the survivors of the *Titanic,* were crowding the deck-rails, to stare overside. Some stated later that they saw many bodies. They may have done so, or what they saw may have been floe-ice or wreckage. The Captain gave me an order, "Bear away from the wreckage southwesterly. . . ."

The *Californian* was standing by, and was now in wireless communication with us. Captain Rostron sent a wireless signal to her: "I am taking the survivors to New York. Please stay in the vicinity and pick up any bodies."

This was acknowledged by the *Californian.* At 9 a.m., in bright sunshine, we were steaming at full speed to the southwestward, away from that scene of death, with our load of sorrow—the bereaved, the shocked, the mind-numbed, humbly thankful to be alive.

An hour later, we received a wireless signal from the Master of the *Californian*: "I have not found any bodies, and I am resuming my voyage."

Being bound from London to Boston, he was evidently desirous of making as much progress as possible through the ice-field by daylight, and could scarcely be blamed for that decision.

If he had remained on the scene of the disaster and attempted to pick up the bodies from the water, no useful purpose would have been served. It would probably have taken him a fortnight to find them all. His ship would have become a floating morgue. He would have had no means of identifying the bodies. If he took them to Boston for inquests and earth burial, the identifications would still be difficult and perhaps impossible in most cases. All that he could have done in practice would have been to recommit the bodies to the deep. It was better, then, to leave them where they were, undisturbed.

Unweighted, and in most cases buoyed by lifejackets, the bodies of the *Titanic's* dead—the celebrities, the lesser-known, and the humble unknown to fame—were flotsam in the wide Atlantic for weeks, and some, it was believed, for months after the disaster.

A cable-laying ship, the S.S. *Mackay-Bennett*, went out from Halifax two weeks afterwards, and picked up 205 bodies, which were given religious burial; but this was the utmost that could be done for piety's sake. The mail steamers for many months gave the region of the floating dead a wide berth; the Atlantic tracks were haunted, and, even to this day shipmasters steer clear of the place where the *Titanic* sank.

As the *Carpathia* steamed to the southwestward with her load of sorrow, we passed dozens of icebergs in the first three hours, frequently changing course to avoid colliding with them, before we were able to set course for New York, in open water, after taking sights of the sun at noon, in Lat. 40 deg. 45 min. N.

I have never since seen, and never wished to see, so much ice as I had seen that day, so far south in the Atlantic. The early thaw, which had set this field of vast extent adrift, was one of the many unusual circumstances of the *Titanic* fatality. But, as a direct result of that disaster, the International Ice Patrol was established (in 1913) to survey and keep constant watch on all ice movements, and to warn shipping of them. Thereafter, the tracks of shipping in the North Atlantic were laid down by international agreement, to eliminate all risks of collisions with ice. Experience had been gained, but at a tragic price.

At the change of the watch at noon, when I handed over the course and details to First Officer Dean, I was dog-tired, after having been practically sixteen hours on duty throughout that night and morning of strenuous anxieties. All the ship's people in the *Carpathia* had been likewise under the stress and strain of exceptional duties and the poignant emotion that hung over the ship like a pall. I went below for a meal, and then to sleep in a bunk in a third-class cabin to which my dunnage had been transferred, when my cabin below the bridge had been willingly given up to one of the bereaved women survivors.

But restful sleep was impossible. I could only doze fitfully. At 4 p.m., I went up on deck, and talked to some of the survivors, including the three rescued officers, who were also finding sleep impossible. From them I learnt how and why the "unsinkable" ship had sunk. It had been a tragedy of errors, but those errors were a combination of fatal circumstances utterly unlikely ever to happen again. That was the crux of this disaster. It should not have happened . . . but it did happen!

According to what I was told that day, by the men who knew the facts, while their impressions and mine were only too vivid, it appeared that the odds against any repetition of such a calamity at sea were so great that we could only feel awed at the magnitude of the mischance.

The *Titanic* had been belting along at $22\frac{1}{2}$ knots when the lookout man in the crow's nest sighted the berg, dead ahead. He sounded his gong three times, and then telephoned his warning to the bridge.

First Officer Murdock received this warning, and gave the order to the helmsman, "Hard-a-starboard". This order was in accordance with the prevailing practice, a legacy of tradition— that is, from the days when helm orders referred to the *tiller*, as used in open boats and small ships, before steering wheels were introduced. In other words, the order "hard-a-starboard" meant, "Put your *tiller* over to the starboard side, hard, as far as it will go."

That was how this order was applied in British ships in 1912 (it continued to bear that meaning until a new practice was introduced on 1st January, 1933). Helmsmen understood that, on receiving the order, "Hard-a-starboard", they must put the *wheel* to port, thereby putting the *tiller* to starboard, and the *rudder* to port, causing the *ship's head* to go to port.

When Murdock gave the order, "Hard-a-starboard", the helmsman at the wheel of the *Titanic* reacted correctly, and the ship's head began to pay off to port.

The ship then had the iceberg on her starboard bow, but, as she passed close by it, the submerged part of the berg (comprising seven-eighths of the berg's bulk), protruding invisibly under water, scraped heavily along the *Titanic's* starboard side, opening up her hull plates on that side in a gash extending below her waterline for 300 feet from the forepeak, for approximately one-third of the ship's length.

Murdock immediately rang the engines to STOP and then FULL ASTERN, until the liner came to a standstill half a mile past the berg. He also pressed the control button that electrically closed the doors in the watertight bulkheads. The time was 11.40 p.m. Captain Smith came on to the bridge immediately, and ordered soundings to be taken in the holds forward as the ship began to settle down slowly by the head.

Inspection revealed that water was pouring into the six forward watertight compartments, gaining on the pumps which had been started without delay. There were sixteen watertight compartments in the ship, but the bulkheads had not been carried up to the deckheads. Consequently, as each compartment flooded, water poured over into the next compartment aft. Captain Smith then knew that his ship was doomed. He ordered the first wireless distress signal to be sent out at 00.15 a.m., the first rockets fired at 00.45 a.m., and at that time also gave the order to lower the lifeboats, with "women and children first".

The last boat was lowered at 2.05 a.m., and the ship sank at 2.20 a.m. She had remained afloat for two hours and forty minutes after striking the berg.

As the ship had collided with the berg not head-on, but had struck it a glancing blow with her starboard bow, it was evident that the disaster had been caused by a split-second mistiming in the alteration of her course. That is, if her head had paid off to port for another ten, or, at most, say twenty feet, she would have avoided striking the underwater base or "platform" of the berg.

A speed of $22\frac{1}{2}$ knots (say 25.9 statute miles per hour) is equivalent to approximately 2,280 feet per minute, or 38 feet per second. Assuming that the berg was sighted exactly half a mile dead ahead, there would be one minute and $9\frac{1}{2}$ seconds in which to avoid a head-on collision. In smaller steamers, which travelled at speeds of from 11 to 15 knots, the time margin between the first sighting of a berg and the alteration of course to avoid collision was correspondingly increased to as much as two minutes, which was ample for manoeuvring when a sharp lookout was kept and alert men were on the bridge.

It was therefore safe enough, in practice, to proceed at eleven knots, in an ice region, even in darkness, when night-visibility was good; but it was not safe for a vessel of the bulk of the *Titanic* to proceed at $22\frac{1}{2}$ knots among bergs, *when the sea was smooth and there was no surf breaking around the base of the bergs to assist the lookout man to sight them.*

A vessel of 46,000 tons, travelling at 22½ knots, develops a tremendous momentum through the water. The surge of her propellers, with violent disturbance of the water under her stern, causing the stern to press downwards, may interfere with her responses to movements of her rudder, making her slow in paying off when the helm is put hard-a-starboard or hard-a-port, unless her designers have allowed for this factor in the design and size of the rudder.

The Cunarder *Mauretania* was famous for her manoeuvrability at full speed. She answered her helm instantly in all conditions; but this quality was not built into the *Olympic* and *Titanic*. They were big and beautiful ships, but their triple screws may have affected their steering at full speed, to some extent. In seafaring, as in every other human activity, men may learn from experiences that are sometimes dire.

The immediate cause, or causes, of the *Titanic's* collision with the iceberg, then, *allowing that her speed of 22½ knots had to be maintained for publicity purposes on this maiden voyage,* could be analysed as an unforeseen delayed reaction, or delayed reactions that occurred in altering her course to port during the time margin of one minute and nine seconds that would normally have elapsed between the first sighting of the berg and her passing it abeam.

During that fateful sixty-nine seconds, the following sequence of events took place: (i) the lookout man sighted the berg; (ii) he struck his bell three times; (iii) he telephoned to the bridge; (iv) First Officer Murdock answered the telephone; (v) Murdock gave the order to the helmsman, "Hard-a-starboard"; (vi) the helmsman obeyed the order; (vii) the ship's tiller went to starboard, and her rudder to port; (viii) the ship's head paid off to port; (ix) the starboard bow struck the underwater ice and scraped along it for 300 feet of the ship's side, with sufficient force to open the hull plates, and then the ship veered off from the ice amidships.

Somewhere in this sequence of events there was a delay, or there were cumulative delays, amounting to a loss of a fractional period of time, *perhaps not more than one or two seconds,* which would have been sufficient, at the liner's speed of 38 feet per second, to enable her to clear the obstruction or to reduce its impact to a minor glancing blow.

That was the element of Fate in the *Titanic* disaster. Blind Fate had snipped the life-threads of all those people in one tick of the clock . . . like *that!*

But it would be grossly unfair to place the sole responsibility for this colossal tragedy on the lookout man, the officer of the watch, the helmsman, or even on the Captain—even though, in fact and in law, the Captain must bear the burden of blame when any mishap occurs in his ship which could have been avoided by timely precautions. . . .

As Captain Smith, and also First Officer Murdock, had gone down with the ship, they had atoned for any errors of judgment which might have been ascribed to them.

Their view of the sequence of events could never be ascertained; but this disaster was too tremendous to be explained away by finding one scapegoat, or two, or three, to bear the brunt of the blame. It could be explained, and was explained ultimately, as the fatal culmination of a long and complicated sequence of interrelated causes which lay deep in human nature itself—the errors of judgment made by many fallible men, in greater and lesser degrees of responsibility.

In the beginning was the brag. That was one of the prime causes of this fatality; for, if there had not been so much extravagant publicity, claiming that the *Titanic* was "the biggest ship in the world . . . the most luxurious ship ever built . . . the unsinkable ship . . ." and so on, then more attention might have been given to seamanlike considerations, of which safety at sea is by far the most important.

It would have been better for the *Titanic* to have arrived behind schedule in New York than never to have arrived at all; but her Captain took the responsibility of driving on at forced full speed into the icefield, to save a few hours of time on the passage, instead of reducing speed during the hours of darkness, or navigating on a longer course to skirt the icefield to the southwards.

Wisdom after the event is sad wisdom. The directors of the White Star Line had become bemused by their own propaganda. They believed that this ship was "unsinkable". A publicity catchword had warped their judgment of reality. This happens often in politics, with dire results, especially in international relations; but words are no substitute for facts.

If this giant ship had been built with a double hull, instead of a single hull, a glancing blow from an iceberg would not have sunk her. *If* she had four propellers instead of three, she could have developed sufficient speed to take the longer course, southward of the ice, without losing too much time.

Granting the decision to run through the icefield, *if* she had a powerful searchlight, the bergs could have been sighted more easily. Without a searchlight, *if* extra lookouts had been stationed on the wings of the bridge, to give oral warnings directly and not by telephone, the vital moments of time would have been gained. *If* her rudder had been designed to function more efficiently at full speed, she would have veered to port more sharply.

If her watertight bulkheads had been carried by her builders up to the deckheads, she would have remained afloat until rescue vessels had time to come up.

If, instead of relying only on distress signals by wireless and rockets, she had signalled persistently to the *Californian* with a Morse lamp, beginning a few minutes after the collision, such signals would most probably have been answered.

If the *Californian* had carried two wireless operators, instead of only one, the S O S would almost certainly have been heard in that ship only ten miles away.

When it came to launching the boats, *if* more boats and rafts had been provided, and *if* there had been boat drill, more lives would have been saved. . . .

These were contingencies which the foresight, not of any one man, but of the many concerned, could have met; but, because so much was neglected by so many, the tragedy of the *Titanic* had the inevitability of a decree of Fate. It was the first big shock in the modern era to remind us that nothing made and managed by human hands is perfect; that mechanical progress has limitations; and that the unforeseen is always likely to curb man's most grandiose strivings.

CHAPTER TWENTY-FIVE

Return of the "Carpathia" to New York—The
Survivors' Stories—Heroism of the Supreme
Sacrifice—The "Titanic's" Band—Lightoller's
Miraculous Escape from Drowning—Wire-
lessing the News—Radio Signals Jammed—
Anxiety in New York—We Arrive at Sandy
Hook—A Bedlam of Questions—The Man
Who Frothed at the Mouth—Pratique—Get-
ting Rid of the "Titanic's" Boats—The
Reporter Who Got on Board—"Gee, What a
Story!"—Survivors Disembark—The Yellow
Press—New York in Mourning—Senate Com-
mittee's Inquiry—Rewards and Medals—End
of This Volume.

AS the *Carpathia* steamed on westwards, making for New York,
she was a gloomy and silent ship. No one smiled. The usual
shipboard jollity was entirely extinguished. People walked
around or sat in silence, or conversed in subdued tones, almost
in whispers. Everyone was numbed by shock. The faces of widows,
tense and pale, their eyes staring in despair as they gazed to seaward, expressed grief inconsolable; but almost every one of the
survivors was bereaved, if not of relatives, then of friends. They
had been in the presence of a supreme sacrifice, and they knew
it; for now each person who had survived was acutely aware of

the splendid gallantry of those who had held back from the boats and gone down with the ship.

When the last of the lifeboats had been lowered, there had remained on board the sinking ship 1,390 men, 103 women, and 53 children.

Some of the women passengers had deliberately refused to go into the lifeboats. They chose to remain with their menfolk to the end. With them also stayed their children. It is possible that some of the women who made this choice did not believe that the ship would sink. Others, and some of the men, may have been "trapped" down below, on the lower decks, by the closing of the doors in the watertight bulkheads, and had been unable to find the escape ladders that led upwards from each compartment.

Of the women who perished, five were first-class passengers, fifteen second-class, eighty-one third-class; and two stewardesses. The first- and second-class passengers, being nearest to the boat-decks, had easy opportunities of entering the boats. All the children in the first and second class were saved. The fifty-three children who perished were all in the third class on the lower decks.

Of the men who perished, 115 were first-class passengers, 147 second-class, 399 third-class, and 686 of the crew.

These men (and another 43 who were later picked up in the water, making a total of 1,390 men) had all stood aside on the decks when the lifeboats were lowered, in obedience to the cry that was taken up and repeated from one end of the ship to the other: "Women and children first!"

In the final fifteen minutes before the ship sank, after the last of the boats had been lowered, these men thronged the upper decks, calmly and silently awaiting death. There they stood, millionaires and working-class men of many nationalities, sea-men, stewards, firemen and trimmers, shoulder to shoulder, in the equality, unity, and brotherhood of total unselfishness which each and every one of them deliberately accepted as necessary.

There was no panic. When the *Titanic* was in her death-throes, everything that is admirable and superb in human nature came to the fore. This was what made the survivors, and every-one else in the *Carpathia* when the facts were known, feel dazed, in silent, bewildered reverence and humility, with a feeling of pride, too, that so many men, of so many different kinds, had responded to death's imminent threat with courage and dignity.

Typical of this courage was the behaviour of the men of the *Titanic's* orchestra of eight musicians. They had been playing the usual shipboard light music earlier in the evening, finishing at 11 p.m.; but, when the ship struck, they assembled again in the first-class lounge, and began playing popular tunes, as though to assure the passengers that all was well.

Even while the boats were being lowered, the lively melodies of "Yip-I-Addy-I-Aye" and "Alexander's Ragtime Band" encouraged the people to remain cheerful. The bandmaster, Wallace Hartley, had previously been in the *Mauretania,* and had made hundreds of crossings of the Atlantic. Two others, Theodore Brailey, pianist, and Roger Bricoux, cellist (a Frenchman), had belonged to the small orchestra in the *Carpathia,* and had left her in Liverpool only two months previously. The first violin, Jock Hume, was a Scot from Dumfries; the bass viol, Fred Clarke, was a Liverpool man. George Krius and Percy Taylor were Londoners, and Jack Woodward was from Oxfordshire.

These eight musicians continued playing cheerful tunes, until the water flooded around their ankles. Then, as their final number, and adieu to life, they played the hymn, "Autumn", after the last boat had been lowered. Every man in that brave little band went down with the ship, and perished.

Captain Smith, with Chief Officer Wilde, First Officer Murdock, and Second Officer Lightoller, stood on the bridge as the ship went down. She was sinking by the head, at a steep slant, with the stern high in the air. Men on the decks moved aft as the waters engulfed her forward. Some jumped overboard and began to swim away. Others, perhaps unable to swim, were crowded on the poop as the weight of water flooding below decks overcame the ship's remaining buoyancy, and she glided at a steep angle, to founder head first, while a wall of water swept along the decks, washing hundreds of people overboard, at her stern. These were almost all drawn down by the suction which followed the ship to the deeps.

Second Officer Lightoller had survived by a miracle. He had stepped from the bridge into the water, and attempted to swim away, but was almost immediately dragged under by the suction of water cascading through the "fiddley" (gratings) of one of the enginerooms abaft the bridge. He was brought hard against the gratings of the fiddley, and held there under the weight of water pouring through, when suddenly, as the boiler-room filled, a great bubble of air and warm water, expelled by the dowsing of the furnaces, blurted through the fiddley from below, like a geyser. Its eruptive force carried Lightoller with it away from the side of the ship as she went down.

Being a strong swimmer, he struck out vigorously in the darkness, and by chance came upon one of the rafts ("collapsible boats") which had not been launched but had floated overboard. It was overturned, and men were scrambling onto its keel. In all, thirty swimmers succeeded in getting onto this raft.

It was a perilous safety, as the raft was awash, but one of the bigger lifeboats, which already held forty-five people, came over and took the thirty men from the raft. Lightoller then took command of this boat, and eventually brought it to the *Carpathia's* side.

These, and the many other stories which the survivors had to tell of their experiences, made the *Carpathia* a ship of sorrow and wonderment. We, who had merely hastened to the rescue, were now aware that chance had made us play our unrehearsed role in the final scenes of one of the greatest sea-tragedies of all time—great not only in the leviathan size of the ship that had gone down, and in the numbers who had perished, but also in its revelation of the workings of chance and mischance, and of the mysterious powers of Fate in human affairs.

This was a fatality unparalleled, illuminating the vanity of human wishes and the power of courage in extreme adversity. No wonder, then, that the people of two continents, and beyond throughout the world, informed only briefly of the fact that the *Titanic* had sunk, with heavy loss of life, were now eagerly awaiting the details of that tragedy, which only the survivors in the *Carpathia* could divulge.

The *Carpathia* was a crowded ship, with 1,740 souls on board. At 4 a.m. on Tuesday, when few people were on deck, Captain Rostron read the burial service over the four bodies we had picked up, and they were reconsigned to the deep.

The Purser and his assistants had by this time completed compiling and checking an exact list of the survivors that we had on board. The Captain instructed our wireless operator (Harold Cottam) to transmit this list as a marconigram, via Cape Race, to the office of the White Star Line in New York. The utmost accuracy was required, as the transmission of a list of survivors implied that those whose names were not included in that list had perished.

Unfortunately, our radio apparatus had a range of only 150 miles. Cottam could hear signals from Cape Race, but his messages were not getting through clearly. Hundreds of marconigrams were being sent out from Cape Race, and other shore stations, addressed to the Master of the *Carpathia*, from anxious relatives and friends of passengers in the *Titanic*, inquiring if this person or that had been rescued. Press telegrams in dozens were demanding details, and offering large sums in payment for exclusive news.

To make the situation more difficult, many of the survivors on board were asking Cottam to transmit marconigrams to their friends and relatives on shore, announcing that they were saved. Conditions in the radio shack became almost chaotic, as Cottam found it impossible to "clear the air" in the welter of signals that cluttered it from shore stations and other ships. But he worked on and on, to the limit of his endurance, with no sleep for two or three days and nights, sending and receiving, until the junior wireless operator of the *Titanic*, young Harold Bride —who, though rescued, was injured and suffering from shock and exposure—was able to give him standby help while he snatched an hour's sleep now and then.

The Captain had strictly ordered that no news-stories should be transmitted to the Press. He realized that there would be an official inquiry into the disaster, and that evidence would be taken on oath to ascertain the facts. The Press statements should come, not from him, but from the White Star office. Fortunately, Cottam was able to make fairly good radio contact with the White Star *Olympic*, as her course was converging to ours. Presently she was within 100 miles, or less, and the full list of survivors was transmitted to her and relayed to the White Star office in New York.

This discharged Captain Rostron's responsibilities in that aspect of the matter; but otherwise it became practically impossible for Cottam to cope with the deluge of signals or to answer the inquiries. Newspapermen in New York, unaware of his difficulties and of the weak range of his apparatus, became annoyed, and unfairly suggested that a "censorship" had been imposed on news, for some sinister purpose vaguely hinted at.

The White Star office released the news, received per the *Olympic*, in time for publication in the New York evening papers on Tuesday. It was to the effect that 1,800 persons had probably perished, and that 675 were saved, mostly women and children. We in the *Carpathia* had no means of knowing the intense excitement that this announcement would cause in New York and throughout America and the wider world.

The passenger-lists of the *Titanic* having already been cabled from Southampton, emphasizing the names of the multimillionaires and other celebrities on board, the first scrappy news received stunned New York with the prospect that so many people of national and international fame had perished.

As the truth of this surmise was gradually established by elimination of names such as those of Astor and Guggenheim from the published lists of the survivors, the excitement in New York mounted almost to a pitch of hysteria. Every newspaper printed full front-page stories and supplementary pages of news, descriptions of the *Titanic*, biographies of the presumed dead, and came out with black borders and pictures (drawn from imagination by staff artists), while declaring unreservedly that the wreck of the *Titanic* was "the world's greatest marine horror".

The arrival of the *Carpathia* in New York was awaited with tense anxiety and impatience. Then our passage was delayed as we ran into a thick fog near Nantucket Shoals, and had to grope our way for hours at dead slow with our steam whistle eerily blaring.

On Thursday afternoon, 18th April, the fog lifted, and at 6 p.m. we had Sandy Hook Light Vessel abeam, at the entrance to New York Harbour. Here for the first time we had an indication of the tremendous reception that awaited us. A fleet of more than fifty small craft, including tugs, ferry boats, steam launches, and yachts, crowded with newspaper reporters and photographers, relatives and friends of the dead and of the survivors, and adventurers who were merely urged by curiosity, converged towards the *Carpathia* as an unwanted escort for the pilot boat.

Captain Rostron gave the order, "Nobody to be allowed on board except the Pilot."

This was necessary to avoid confusion and delay at quarantine and the Customs, and also to protect the survivors of the *Titanic* from being harassed.

We were "on stations" for entering port. My station as Second Officer was on the bridge, while the Chief Officer was stationed at the bows, and the First Officer and Third Officer were at the stern.

The Third Officer (Rees) had the duty of receiving the Pilot on board. For this purpose the accommodation ladder had been rigged, and was lowered as the pilot boat came alongside.

When the *Carpathia* came to a standstill, the tugs, ferries, steam launches and yachts clustered around her, their occupants expecting that we would lower gangways to allow them on board. When they realized that this would not be allowed, pandemonium broke out. They came in close, singing out questions, some through megaphones, in a deafening clamour of confusion; some holding up wads of dollar bills in an attempt to bribe people lining the *Carpathia's* deck-rails to lower ladders or ropes overside, or to answer questions for publication, giving details of the *Titanic's* death-plunge and its causes and sequels. The officers stationed on deck, with our boatswains, seamen, and masters-at-arms, had a busy time fending these "pirates" off.

In the meantime, Third Officer Rees, at the accommodation ladder, was having a lively time. Five newspaper reporters had somehow managed to get into the pilot boat. Rees went down to the bottom of the ladder, and stood by as the boat came alongside. "Pilot only!" he warned.

The five newsmen attempted to get on to the ladder ahead of the pilot, but Rees, a strongly built man, fended them off, and, when they persisted, had to use force, giving one or two of them a sock on the jaw.

Then one of the reporters used a stratagem. He put soap or some similar substance into his mouth, and began frothing at the mouth, screaming hysterically, "Oh! My poor sister! My sister is on board! I *must* see her! Let me up, Mister, and I'll give you a hundred bucks."

"No," said Rees.

"Two hundred bucks!"

"No. Stand back. Captain's orders. Pilot only!"

Neither rush tactics, nor frothing at the mouth, nor bribes availed. Rees got the pilot onto the ladder, waited until he was on board, then followed him quickly up, as the ladder was hoisted, leaving the frustrated newshawks in the boat, putting on a remarkable exhibition of profanity.

As soon as the Pilot was on the bridge, our engines were rung to FULL AHEAD, and we steamed through the channels of the entrance shoals, and into the Lower Bay, followed and accompanied abeam by our escorting fleet, some of the small craft continuing to range alongside, as reporters continued their efforts to "get the story" in megaphone interviews.

At the Narrows we stopped in quarantine, and were boarded by the Immigration Department's officials and doctors. The inspection was a mere formality, as pratique was granted without medical examination of the survivors individually. This was a humane gesture in the circumstances. Darkness had now set in, with drizzling rain, as we proceeded into the Upper Bay.

Near the Statue of Liberty, a Cunard tug came out to assist us to our berth. The tugmaster had instructions from the Marine Superintendent that we should stop near the White Star Pier and lower the *Titanic's* lifeboats. We had six of these on our foredeck and seven slung overside in davits. These boats suspended overside may have interfered with our docking, and were therefore better got rid of. They were the only material salvage of the *Titanic*.

As we passed Battery Point, we saw a crowd of people congregated there in the rain. It was estimated in the newspapers next day that 10,000 people waited for hours at the Battery to see the *Carpathia* arrive. What they saw was "the impressive sight of the rescue ship steaming up the Harbour, brightly lit, with boats hanging overside, and sparks flying from her funnel", as one newspaper report described the scene.

We stopped near the White Star Pier and lowered the *Titanic's* boats—those off the foredeck by derrick, and the others with our davits. It was now 8.40 p.m., New York time. On the Captain's orders, I left the bridge to supervise the lowering of the boats. Men had come off from the White Star Pier in a launch, which took the boats in tow and brought them into the dock. Each boat had the name *Titanic* painted on it. They had reached their destination.

Small craft continued to throng around us. Photographers ignited magnesium flares as the boats were lowered.

When I returned to the bridge, after an absence of twenty minutes, as we got under way again, I saw a huge man, at least six feet four inches tall, and powerfully built in proportion. standing near the Captain.

"This man," said the Captain to me, "is on board without

my permission. See that he does not leave the bridge. When we get to the Pier, hand him over to the Marine Superintendent for necessary action."

With that, the Captain turned his back on the stranger, and busied himself with details of berthing.

"Who are you?" I asked the stranger.

"I'm a reporter from the *Globe*," he said, with a grin, "and boy, have I got the greatest story in the world? I've scooped them all. I've been interviewing the survivors and your crew. Oh, boy, what a story, *what a story*! But now the Captain won't talk! And who are you, Mister? What's your story? Is it true that the *Titanic's* officers shot the third-class women and children dead, so that millionaires could get into the boats? Is it true that you picked up people floating around on lumps of ice? Is it true that the band played 'Nearer, My God, to Thee'? Is it true that dogs were saved and children left to drown?"

"Don't ask me," I said, ruffled. "I'll tell you nothing. How did you get on board?"

"Never mind that! I'm only doing my job, that's all. I got on board. I made it. I was told to get the story, and I got it. You can do what you like with me."

I sized him up. He was twice as big as me, and I wondered what would happen if he decided to leave the bridge to get more stories.

"You heard the Captain's orders that you're to stay here until the ship berths?" I said.

"Sure, I heard them, and sure I'll stay here! *Globe Reporter on Bridge as 'Carpathia' Berths!*" he chuckled. "How's that for a scoop? Sure, I'll stay put. Gee, what a story, WHAT A STORY!"

It was 9.30 p.m. when we berthed at Pier 54, at the foot of West Fourteenth Street. Rain was still drizzling, but a crowd of 30,000 people had gathered to see the survivors of the *Titanic* disembark. The crowd was orderly, controlled by mounted police and foot police in glistening raincoats.

As the gangways were being lowered, I noticed that the Cunard Marine Superintendent, Captain Roberts, was waiting on the wharf, to be the first on board. "Will you come with me?" I said, firmly, to the big reporter of the *Globe*. "It's my duty to hand you over to the Marine Superintendent of the Cunard Line, to be dealt with for boarding this ship without the Captain's permission."

"Sure, I'll come with you! Lead on, I'll give no trouble," the big fellow chuckled.

I led him to the head of the gangway, and said to Captain Roberts, "Captain Rostron wants this reporter dealt with for getting on board without permission."

Before the words were out of my mouth, the *Globe* reporter had charged down the gangway like a bull moose and had disappeared into the crowd.

"Let him go," said Captain Roberts. "We've plenty of other worries on our minds. Good riddance to him!"

The surviving passengers of the *Titanic* began going ashore immediately, many of them wearing clothes given to them by the *Carpathia's* passengers and crew. Hundreds of flashlight photographs were being taken. Customs formalities were waived, and soon the survivors were being welcomed with tears of joy by relatives and friends, or taken care of by kindly persons and charitable organizations. Many of them were interviewed by reporters at the exit from the customs shed.

The *Carpathia's* passengers and crew, and the survivors of the *Titanic's* crew, with some few exceptions, remained on board overnight. It was desirable that the *Carpathia's* voyage to the Mediterranean should be resumed as quickly as possible, after port formalities were completed. The White Star company wished to keep the *Titanic's* surviving crew members under their supervision, pending the official inquiry, and to find new employment for them, or to pay them off.

But swarms of reporters and photographers now came on board, and remained until after midnight, getting stories from the survivors and from our passengers and crew.

Many of these stories, obtained from irresponsible or shocked persons, were highly coloured by imagination. Next day, and for several days, the "Yellow Press" published these stories with "sensational" headlines. There seemed no limit to the absurdities which could be printed. "The Captain was drunk . . . He committed suicide . . . First Officer Murdock shot himself as the ship went down . . . Third-Class Passengers were locked below deck and left to drown like rats . . ."

But the responsible editors of serious newspapers showed sound judgment and insight in sifting the facts from the mass of rumours and fables. They handled one of the greatest news-stories ever known (until that time) with dignity and eloquence. New York was in mourning. Flags flew at half mast throughout the city. Memorial services were held in churches of all denominations. The obituary notices of the famous people who had perished occupied many columns of type. Leader-writers rose to great heights, analysing the causes of the disaster and calling for preventive measures to make any further happening of this kind impossible.

Resolutions of sorrow were passed by innumerable organizations. Newspapers opened subscription funds for the relief of distressed survivors. The generous, emotional heart of America was touched, as seldom before or since. The *Brooklyn Daily Eagle* aptly summed up: "The heart of the nation throbs with grief for the bereft."

Britain, too, was in mourning. Flags flew at half mast in London, Southampton, Liverpool, and many other cities, and memorial services were held. There were tragic scenes at Southampton, where most of the widows, orphans, relatives and friends of the *Titanic's* crew lived.

To put a stop to the fantastic rumours that were flying around, the United States Senate appointed an Investigation Committee to take evidence on oath without delay. This inquiry opened at the Waldorf Astoria Hotel in New York on Friday morning, 19th April (the day after the *Carpathia* berthed).

The first witness examined was Bruce Ismay, who was in an invidious position, as already he had been bitterly attacked in the Yellow Press for having saved himself when so many others had perished. He was still suffering from shock, but told the Committee that when he stepped into a boat that was being lowered, only partly filled, there were no women, and in fact no passengers, on the deck nearby. He added that, in his opinion, the *Titanic* would not have sunk if she had struck the ice head on. He gave evidence of the ship's lifeboat capacity and other details.

Captain Rostron was the next witness examined. He was called at this early stage because the *Carpathia* was being got ready to clear out again from New York to resume her voyage. His evidence was seamanlike and forthright, as was only to be expected from him, and did much to refute senseless rumors.

Then the four surviving officers of the *Titanic* were examined.

Their evidence gave a clear picture of the facts. One of the Senators on the Committee, who was from an inland State, asked Fourth Officer Boxhall, "What is an iceberg made of?"

After a moment's consideration, Boxhall answered, with perfect seriousness and truth, "Ice!"

Next day, Saturday, 20th April, the *Carpathia* was cleared again out of New York, to resume her voyage, ten days behind schedule. The Cunard Company refused to accept any compensation from the White Star Line for this loss of schedule time and the expenses of the rescue.

At each port of call on our run to the Mediterranean and Adriatic, Captain Rostron was feted and hailed as the hero of the *Titanic* disaster. The facts had by that time become known authentically, and it was recognized that his fine seamanship had been responsible for saving many lives.

A vigorous controversy raged for many months on the causes of the disaster. Literary big guns entered the fray when George Bernard Shaw and Arthur Conan Doyle had an acrimonious dispute, in which both showed their command of words and their ignorance of seamanship.

When we returned to New York, early in June, after a voyage of seven weeks, with a full ship of immigrants, there were a dozen bags of mail, including thousands of letters, and hundreds of parcels, waiting for Captain Rostron, personally addressed to him.

The Captain gave me the task of opening these letters, and sorting out those for immediate notice from those that could wait. This task took me several days. Many of the letters were of heartfelt thanks from actual survivors or relatives and friends of survivors; others were from newspaper readers thoughout America and Britain, who had felt moved to write to express their admiration of a hero; some were from cranks; some from autograph hunters; and some were hard-luck tales from professional writers of begging letters who pester all celebrities; and some were offers of marriage (too late, the Captain was already married).

The parcels contained gifts of books, Bibles, jewellery, cigarette cases, pens, photographs, teapots, binoculars, and all kinds of things which the Captain already had, or did not need: but all the letters and gifts had to be answered in common courtesy—

a task which occupied the Captain's spare time (when he had any) for many weeks thereafter.

Then followed a round of public functions, at which Captain Rostron was presented with testimonials and illuminated addresses, and with cheques for substantial sums in dollars from funds raised by newspapers.

An artist was commissioned to make a plaque of his head, which was placed in the "Hall of Fame" in the New York City Hall—an honour, I believe, not previously accorded to any Britisher. Finally, he was summoned to Washington to receive from the hands of President Taft the Congressional Medal of Honor, the highest honour that the United States Government could bestow. He deserved all the rewards and honours that were showered upon him. As a shipmaster has to take the blame when things go wrong, it is also fair that he should be given credit when there is credit to be given.

The officers and crew of the *Carpathia* were not forgotten. A testimonial fund was distributed in the form of a bonus of two months extra pay, together with medals (gold for the officers and silver for the crew). I still have my gold medal. On one side it shows the *Carpathia* surrounded by bergs, with five lifeboats making for the ship. Above is King Neptune, with his beard flowing down on either side, and below dolphins and an anchor.

On the other side, the inscription on the medal is: "Presented to the Captain, Officers & Crew of R.M.S. 'Carpathia', in Recognition of Gallant & Heroic Services, From the Survivors of the S.S. 'Titanic', April 15th, 1912."

There were approximately 300 of the medals struck, of which fourteen were gold, and I sometimes wonder how many of those medals, and their recipients, are now extant, and where?

After this excitement, I made four more voyages in the *Carpathia* on the Adriatic service, and was paid off from her at Liverpool on 1st January, 1913.

I was then called up for twelve months' training in warships, to qualify as a Lieutenant in the Royal Naval Reserve. I was in my thirtieth year. May and I were married in London on 28th June, 1913, while I was on leave from naval training.

When I was paid off from the *Carpathia*, with the rank of Second Officer in the Cunard service, I had been at sea for fourteen years—approximately six years in sail and eight in steamers.

I have told of my experiences of those early years in sail and steam in detail not because they were unusual, but because my training as a seaman was similar to that of other young officers of that generation, at the beginning of the modern age.

With the outbreak of war in 1914, the old days and old ways, at sea as on land, came to an end. In a sequel volume to this, entitled *Commodore's Farewell*, my story will tell of bigger ships, bigger events, and bigger responsibilities that came my way; but, across the years, I look back on my service in sail, and in the little old tramps and fine ladies of the Western Ocean, with one regret: that those bygone days cannot be relived . . . except in memory. The real adventure of seafaring is not in wrecks or other disasters, which are rare. It is rather in the routines of working the ship safely, in wide and narrow waters, until she is berthed, and her moorings are made fast, and the telegraph points to FINISHED WITH ENGINES, and a voyage has ended.